To: Phil Adams Sr.
Box
Hill,

Given to Phillip while he was in the Hospital, having his Gallblater out. The Staff of the Hill Spring School bought this book.

Behind the Iron Curtain

BEHIND THE IRON CURTAIN:

RECOLLECTIONS OF LATTER-DAY SAINTS IN EAST GERMANY, 1945–1989

Collected and Translated

by

Garold N. Davis
Norma S. Davis

BYU Studies
Brigham Young University
Provo, Utah

BYU Studies Monographs

The Truth, The Way, The Life:
An Elementary Treatise on Theology

The Journals of William E. McLellin, 1831–1836

Hearts Turned to the Fathers:
A History of the Genealogical Society of Utah, 1894–1994

"We Rejoice in Christ": A Bibliography of
LDS Writings on Jesus Christ and the New Testament

Mormon Americana:
A Guide to Sources and Collections in the United States

Second Crop

© 1996 BYU Studies

All rights reserved. No part of this book may be reproduced in any form
or by any means without permission in writing from the publisher.
For information about subscribing to *BYU Studies,*
a quarterly multidisciplinary LDS journal, write to
403 CB, Brigham Young University, Provo, Utah 84602

Library of Congress Cataloging-in-Publication Data

Behind the Iron Curtain: Recollections of Latter-day Saints in East Germany.
   1945–1989 / collected and translated by Garold N. Davis, Norma S. Davis.
      p. cm. — (BYU Studies monographs)
   Includes index.
   ISBN 0-8425-2322-7
   1. Mormons—Germany (East)—Biography. 2. Church of Jesus Christ
of Latter-day Saints—Germany (East)—History—20th century—Sources.
3. Mormon Church—Germany (East)—History—20th century—Sources.
I. Davis, Garold N.   II. Davis, Norma S., 1935–   .   III. Series.
BX8693.B44 1996
289.3'431'0922—dc20   96-1118
[B]   CIP

Printed in the United States of America
10 9 8 7 6 5 4 3 2 1

*To the Faithful Saints
of East Germany*

"Lest We Forget"

Contents

Acknowledgments ... ix
Introduction ... xi

Part I: The Bombing of Dresden ... 1

  1 The Dead Need No Water
     Edith Schade Krause ... 3

  2 I Saw the Opera House Burning
     Erika Hermann ... 16

  3 Let's Follow Dad—He Holds the Priesthood
     Dorothea Speth Condie ... 32

  4 It Was the Hunger
     Wilfriede Kiessling ... 38

Part II: Rebuilding Zion ... 47

  5 If the Lord Needs Me, I'll Go
     Walter Krause ... 49

  6 The First Conference
     Walter Krause and Walter Kindt ... 55

  7 Odyssey to Find a Chapel
     Elli Polzin ... 63

  8 If God Is for Us, Who Can Be against Us?
     Elfriede Pawlowski ... 71

  9 The Story of My Patriarchal Blessing
     Elfriede Pawlowski ... 75

  10 They Shared the Last Crumb
     Eberhard Gäbler ... 79

  11 My Mission, 1953–1974
     Käthe Würscher ... 82

  12 A Second Mission
     Herbert Schreiter ... 96

  13 Twenty-five Years a Branch President in Neubrandenburg
     Otto Krakow ... 101

  14 A Dollhouse for a Chapel
     Renate Ritter ... 105

  15 All They Have Left Is an Organ and a Window Drape
     Paul Schmidt ... 110

Part III: Living with the Communists — 113

16 All the Promises Have Been Fulfilled
   Ilse Kaden and Herbert Kaden — 115

17 I Saw the Russian Tanks Coming
   Günter Schulze — 141

18 Book Burning
   Joachim Albrecht, Kurt Nikol, and Marianne Nikol — 150

19 The Border Guards Often Confiscated Them
   Erich Ortlieb and Marianne Zwirner Ortlieb — 174

20 Political Isolation
   Erich Ortlieb and Marianne Zwirner Ortlieb — 196

21 Church or School?
   Wolfgang Zwirner and Karin Zwirner — 207

22 Time to Put Out the Lights?
   Reiner Schlüter — 234

23 The Way Things Were
   Hans-Jürgen Schlüter and Ursula Höhle Schlüter — 243

24 Those Are Just Little Things
   Annelies Höhle and Ursula Höhle Schlüter — 263

25 Those Were Hard Times
   Käthe Wöhe — 276

26 The Gospel and the Government
   Erich Dzierzon, Gisela Dzierzon Heller,
   and Manfred Heller — 287

27 We Couldn't Have Church Literature
   Peter Menzel and Doris Menzel — 303

28 In the Valley of the Naive
   Manfred Schwabe and Elke Schwabe — 309

Part IV: A Brighter Day — 329

29 A Temple in Our Country
   Elke Schulze — 331

30 Conversion Stories — 336

31 We Hope They Call Us on a Mission
   Cornelia Ortlieb and Elke Schulze — 344

Index — 352

Acknowledgments

Many people have contributed to this project, the intention of which is to preserve some memory of the faithfulness of the members of the Church in the former German Democratic Republic (East Germany) who held the Church together under difficult circumstances during the forty years of communism. It is to these people themselves that we acknowledge our primary indebtedness. They lived the lives, they befriended us, they invited us into their homes, they told their stories. Thank you all!

We are deeply grateful to Manfred Schütze, former president of the Leipzig Stake and former president of the Berlin Mission. With the exception of chapter 6, "The First Conference" by Walter Krause and Walter Kindt (given us by Edith Krause), and chapter 11, "My Mission" by Käthe Würscher (given to us by John W. Welch), all the journals and historical information in part II, "Rebuilding Zion," were collected and edited by President Manfred Schütze and are translated and published here with his kind permission.

Our thanks to Sister Edith Krause who gave us a paper contained in chapter 1, part I, entitled "The Dead Need No Water." With the exception of that paper and "A Temple in Our Country?" written by Elke Schulze, all of the other materials were taken from taped interviews which we made ourselves in the homes of the members in the spring of 1990 and again in the spring of 1994.

For the difficult work of transcribing these tapes onto computer discs we are grateful to Maja Lund, Renate Reading, and Scott Sheffield, former graduate assistants in the Department of Germanic and Slavic Languages at BYU. We must take the responsibility for the translations ourselves.

Acknowledgments for the photographs are included in the caption for each.

We are especially grateful to Doris Dant, executive editor of BYU Studies, and to her staff for seeing the book through the press.

Finally, we offer our special thanks to Sister Elke Schulze of Dresden for assisting us "on site" in collecting and distributing materials, arranging hotel reservations, setting up appointments for interviews, and in general for being gracious and willing to assist with any request—reasonable or unreasonable. Thank you Elke!

Introduction

They had survived six years of war. Their cities had been bombed. On February 13 and 14, 1945, the city of Dresden was burnt to the ground by three heavy bombing raids. Those husbands and sons who had not fallen in the war were slowly straggling back from POW camps. They had very little to eat. A new geographical term now described the area: Soviet Zone of Occupation. The people were forced to clean up the rubble of their destroyed cities, to dismantle their own factories, and to send them off piece by piece to the Soviet Union. The new state, the German Democratic Republic (GDR—communist East Germany—founded in 1949), established a communist government that was officially atheistic and antagonistic to religion. In 1961 the government of the GDR built a solid wall—the Berlin Wall, officially called *antifaschistischer Schutzwall*, the Anti-Fascist Wall of Protection. A secret police system watched the people's every move.

Before the war, when Hitler's armies marched into Poland in 1939, the LDS missionaries had to leave Germany and eventually all continental Europe. But they left a strong and thriving Church in the eastern part of Germany. The major cities of this area—Berlin, Leipzig, Chemnitz, and Dresden—were among the few cities in Europe with multiple branches, many of which were old and well established. In Dresden, for example, the Church had been established longer than most wards in Utah; the Dresden Branch was organized in 1855 with a young convert, Karl G. Maeser, as its first branch president. Many of the people in these congregations were second-, third-, and fourth-generation members of the Church. The eastern area of Germany had been sending a continuous stream of converts to Utah for almost one hundred years, yet approximately ten thousand members were still in Germany when the missionaries were forced to leave. When Hitler's armies were defeated in 1945, the missionaries returned to Europe, but foreign missionaries were not permitted to enter the Soviet Zone of Occupation.

The Church in the GDR was battered and scattered. Most of the branch meetinghouses had been destroyed by bombings. Priesthood holders who had survived the war were taken to prisoner-of-war camps. Members from the eastern branches fled westward, and many ended up in refugee camps. Members had to be gathered. Meeting places had to be found. Missionary work had to go on. The Church had to be rebuilt.

The men who returned from the war were called to leave their families again, to go out as missionaries, but only within the borders of the GDR. In addition to proselyting, they were to find the scattered members and rebuild the Church. To hold church services, the members were shifted from back rooms in taverns to old theaters, to horse barns, and to bombed out casinos, which they had to rebuild themselves.

After the Berlin wall was built in 1961, members could no longer serve missions, even inside the country. They could have no teaching manuals, no Church magazines, no handbooks, no printed material, no temple. They could not attend the university except under exceptional circumstances, and then they were told that because of their religion they would neither be advanced nor permitted to hold administrative positions in their professions.

In the years following the war, the Church in the GDR was presided over by a sequence of mission presidents who resided for the most part in West Berlin. During this time, Berlin provided a door between East and West. The frequency with which mission presidents living outside the country were permitted to visit the leaders and the various branches of the Church inside the GDR varied over the years according to the attitude of the government officials and the political situation. On some occasions, General Authorities were given permission to enter the country. Mission presidents and General Authorities entered through this door; up until 1961 many members exited.

With the erection of the Wall, entrance into Germany became more difficult for mission presidents and General Authorities, and except for the elderly and retired, authorized exit was nearly impossible. In spite of their isolation, the members inside the Wall carried on the programs of the Church with even greater determination. Because of the severe restrictions against entering the country, however, the organization of the Church in the GDR was somewhat more complicated.

Johannes Henry Burkhardt was recognized by the government of the German Democratic Republic as the authorized spokesperson for the Church inside that country. Henry Burkhardt was born and grew up in Chemnitz (Karl-Marx Stadt), and his family had been members of the Church for three generations. From the Church's point of view, he was counselor to the mission president from 1950 to 1972. In 1972 the Dresden Mission was organized, and Henry Burkhardt was appointed mission president. For the first time, the presiding officer of the Church in the German Democratic Republic resided inside the country.

At first slowly, and then more and more rapidly, a brighter day began to dawn. On October 22–24, 1969, President Thomas S. Monson visited the GDR, and at a meeting in Görlitz, a city on the Polish border, he promised the members of the GDR that they would have all of the blessings other members of the Church enjoy (as reported in the Ensign, May 1989). On April 27, 1975, President Monson offered a dedicatory prayer for the country on a small hill near Dresden. In August 1977, President Kimball held a special conference in Dresden. In 1982 the Freiberg Stake was organized with Frank Apel as stake president, and in 1984 the Leipzig Stake was organized with Manfred Schütze as stake president. At that time, Henry Burkhardt was appointed president of the Freiberg Temple, which was under construction. In June 1985 came a day the Saints in the GDR never dreamed would come—the dedication of a temple in their own country. In April 1989, the first foreign missionaries in fifty years entered East Germany, and by the end of that year, the newly organized Germany Dresden Mission reported 669 convert baptisms. On the night of November 9, 1989, the Berlin Wall fell, and the long years of isolation were over.

These are the events that the Saints living inside the Iron Curtain experienced and told us. After telling us these stories, they invariably concluded with a statement such as "Oh, those were beautiful times; oh, those were wonderful days!" What irony! Or is it irony? In our materialistic, media-driven society of today, do we have the wrong idea about what makes us happy, what gives us joy, what makes life satisfying? In addition to its historical importance, the value of the material published here may be that it gives us answers to some questions about our own lives.

These are not our stories. They belong to those who experienced them and told them to us. We have collected, translated, and edited their stories because we believe them to be a valuable part of Church history that should not be lost. The stories do not present a complete or even detailed history. They are told by a relatively small number of the members of the Church who lived in the GDR in 1989–90, when we were serving as missionaries there.

The narrators do not always agree in detail or in their evaluation of the events they experienced. We have left the inconsistencies intact because these are their honest responses to the circumstances. By looking at the circumstances from various points of view, we sometimes come closer to the reality.

These stories tell little about the courage of the faithful members of the Church from East Germany who chose to leave their beloved homeland and flee to the West, always at great personal sacrifice. These Saints brought a fresh spirit of commitment into the wards and branches throughout Europe and the United States as they struggled to find a new home. Because they never forgot those they left behind, these members also provided a very necessary link between the Church members outside the Wall and those behind it. They sent packages of food and clothing, they wrote letters, sometimes they even gave financial support to those missionaries serving in the GDR. Without these members who fled the country, the stories in this book would certainly have had a different ending. We leave their part in history to be recorded by others.

Part I

The Bombing of Dresden

Dresden was the oldest area of The Church of Jesus Christ of Latter-day Saints in the eastern part of Germany. In 1939, at the beginning of the war, two branches thrived, one located in the older part of the city, the *Altstadt Gemeinde,* and the other located across the Elbe River in the "newer" part of the city, the *Neustadt Gemeinde.* In 1945, toward the end of the war, these two branches persisted in Dresden in spite of the loss of many men who were away serving in the German army.

The bombing of Dresden on February 13–14, 1945, was as unexpected as it was destructive. Because of its location far to the southeast (see map, next page), Dresden had been spared the bombings German cities further to the northwest had experienced. By 1945 the war was essentially over. The German armies were retreating rapidly. The German air defenses were gone. The Russian armies were closing in on Berlin and were at the outskirts of Dresden. But then the unexpected and unthinkable happened. The "Florence on the Elbe" was destroyed, and with it went one of the branches of the Church. The following eyewitness accounts of the bombing are in many ways representative of the experiences of Church members throughout Germany.

1
The Dead Need No Water

Edith Schade Krause

Edith Schade Krause lived in Dresden during the Second World War and is mentioned as Edith Schade in chapter 7. She lives in Prenzlau with her husband, Walter Krause (see chapters 5 and 6). In April 1991, Sister Krause was the keynote speaker at the Women's Conference held on the campus of Brigham Young University.

During the war, the large cities like Berlin and Hamburg had been suffering more and more bombing attacks, but up until 1945 things in Dresden were still very quiet. We had no heavy industry that supported the war effort and no military installations or similar targets for bombers. Nevertheless, the most horrible event of the war struck Dresden. On February 13, 1945, Dresden was bombed by the British and the Americans.

This Tuesday began like every other. After we closed the office, which was located next to the large city park, I took the streetcar to Seidnitz to help the Hubold family with some genealogical research. I visited one family or another nearly every Tuesday. So on this Tuesday, I was at their home, which was number 86 Winterberg Street, and they invited me to stay for dinner. After dinner and after completing our genealogy work, I was about to start for home. It was nearly 9:30. But we got to talking about this and that, and I was still there when the air raid sirens went off. They wouldn't let me leave. We expected to hear the all clear signal any minute, but like good German citizens, we packed a few things together and went into the air raid shelter in the basement of the apartment building. There were no public air raid bunkers in Dresden. While we were sitting there in the cellar, someone suggested that we go take a peek outside to see what was going on. We saw the Christmas trees in the sky [flares dropped from airplanes], and we knew that we were going to be bombed. Everyone was holding their breath. We had never experienced anything like this before. It wasn't long before we heard the droning of airplanes and then the explosion of falling bombs. We would hear this far-off rumble, and then the earth would shake like we were in an earthquake. After about half an hour, everything grew quiet, but it was very bright outside.

The all-clear signal sounded, and the air raid warden asked if anyone would go through the apartment building with him. I had been trained as an air raid warden and knew what had to be done, so I volunteered. I was the only one who didn't have an apartment in the building that needed looking into. When we came to the main floor, we found an incendiary bomb lying there that had not exploded—a dud. The man asked me what we should do, and I told him we should open the window and throw it out, which we did.

Scarcely had we finished making our rounds when we saw some new Christmas trees falling from the sky, and we knew that we were about to experience a second attack. Outside a fire storm was already raging, so we went into the cellar again. The second attack was much more furious than the first. In my mind, I was still carrying the picture of the bright red sky, the burning houses and trees, and now the bombs began falling much closer to our house. The noise was horrible. Judging from the sound of the planes, there must have been hundreds of them. The only thing that drowned out this roaring was the exploding bombs. I thought this inferno would never end, but gradually the roar of the planes became fainter and fainter. The air raid warden was the first one to leave the cellar, but he came rushing back to tell us that the apartment building was on fire. Everyone rushed upstairs to help.

On the second floor, an apartment door was open and heavy, black smoke was pouring out. The people who lived there were refugees from Romania, and they were screaming and running back and forth. An incendiary bomb had fallen directly onto a feather mattress, and that was what was causing all the smoke. I couldn't see any flames, and there was nothing else on fire. Since I was the only one who didn't live in the building, I was also the only one with a cool head, and it fell my lot to put out the fire. I called for the apartment fire watch—all women. As soon as the other people found that their own apartments were OK, they gave us a hand, and we formed a bucket brigade.

Fortunately there was still some water pressure in the basement, and we got the fire out, but not before one of the people helping me was overcome by the smoke. I knew something about smoke inhalation and told them to bring me a chair and some milk or black coffee. We put the man in the chair and then carried him outside into the fresh air and poured some coffee into him until he came to. We then helped him down into the cellar, and since he spent most of his time screaming that we should save his stamp collection, he remained conscious. His family stood around weeping and wailing, which I could understand, but I had to worry about the fire. The burned room looked terrible and the one next to it looked just as bad. Nothing much had burned, but there was black soot over everything. The fire warden thanked me, and we went outside.

There was a hurricane-force wind blowing, and we could hardly stand. We made our way around the house to see if there were any more fires. The place looked like a battle field. There were stone blocks lying everywhere, tiles from the roofs, and rubble from the buildings that had fallen down. Burning debris was flying through the air. We could not put out any of the ensuing fires because there was no more water, and more and more burning objects were flying through the air and landing everywhere. We tried to pull these away from the houses and the trees, all the time fighting against this howling wind. In the distance, we heard explosion after explosion from the enormous time bombs that had been dropped. The fire and the wind became so furious that there was nothing more to do but go back into the apartment building. I went with someone on an inspection tour of the building once more. After a while, the sounds of the explosions stopped, but the rain of fire grew stronger and stronger. Some of the people from the building came into Hubold's apartment to thank them and to thank me, but I was only worried now about the burning debris flying about.

About 3:00 A.M., we were all alone in the Hubold apartment, and we knelt in prayer. We had done what we could and had to leave everything else in the hands of the Lord. I was totally exhausted and had lain on the couch to pray in my sorrow when Sister Hubold came in and said it was raining. It was just a short shower, but it wet down the roof and the walls of the building and lessened the danger of more fire breaking out. We were very thankful and offered another prayer, and then I slept for a few hours.

Suddenly it was seven o'clock, and I decided to set out for home to see what had happened to my loved ones. Under normal circumstances that would have been a walk of two or three hours, but these were not normal circumstances. I said good-by to the members. What would I find at home? Would I even be able to get home? Would there be a reunion with my family? If so, when? I put my faith in the Lord and started out.

Rubble-filled street in Dresden. After the bombing of Dresden, Edith Krause had to pick her way through streets like this one to get home. Source: Richard Peter, *Eine Kamera klagt an* (Leipzig: Fotokinoverlag, 1982).

In this area, most of the houses were still standing, but the streets were cluttered with rubble. Still, it was possible to get through in spite of the bricks and blocks and tree branches. I was just twenty-five and very athletic, so it was not too difficult for me to climb and jump over the obstacles that lay in the street. The sky was dark and murky, but little by little it grew brighter. The streetcars were all damaged or burned out. The further I went, the worse it got. It looked terrible in the large park. The beautiful trees looked eerie with their bare branches. They were all split and broken and black with smoke, ashes, and soot. People were wandering around like they were in a daze. It had been the night of the *fasching* [carnival] parties, and in spite of the austerity caused by the war, the rich people in this area of Dresden had all been out celebrating. They came wandering by in their party costumes, their faces made up, smeared, and blackened, and in the big park this looked very grotesque. Many of the women had jackets or shawls or even fur coats over their shoulders, many of them with holes burned in them. It was eerie.

I looked at the dead bodies. The crying and the moaning of the wounded tore my heart. Again and again I head the cry, "Water, water." What could I do? I was not wounded, but I had no water, no medicine, no bandages, nothing, nothing. So I went on, hoping to make it as far as the office where I worked on Franz Liszt Street. The boss's villa was bombed and burned out. In the courtyard, some chickens were still alive, so I threw them a few handfuls of chicken feed and went on. I had no idea what had happened to the family.

Walking across the large park presented no problem, just a few detours. I could have walked down the broad Tiergarten Street, but the electric cables from the street cars were dangling down, and the street was blocked with burned out street cars. There was more destruction there, but because the street was so broad it seemed somehow softened. In the back of my mind, I heard the animals in the zoo screaming. I made it as far as Stübel Square, and then I came upon the first serious blockade. Bombed out houses were scattered across the streets. I began climbing over the rubble, and then I saw the first corpses that had been burned by the phosphorous bombs. The corpses were about a third as large as a living person, but their skin was tight, and they were brown like they had just returned from a vacation with a suntan. They had no clothes, but they all had hair on their heads. They were in all sorts of contorted positions, squatting, lying, and stretched out. I thought of a scripture from the Bible that describes people lying in the streets.

In the areas where the houses had a yard in front, it was easier to get through because fewer blocks had fallen into the street and I could walk around them. The night was over, but the day seemed like a night, murky and hopeless. I wasn't alone. There were individual people walking ahead of me and along side me, and we passed people going the other way, hurrying or walking in a daze. I couldn't think much about my home because I had to be very careful with every step. I asked people who were coming from the other direction if one could still cross the Albert bridge, but they just mumbled, "Maybe," or shrugged their shoulders. At Saxon Square, I made better progress because the square was so broad, and shortly before I reached the bridge, I asked some people if I would be able to get across. A man told me they had come from "over there." I assumed he meant the other side of the river, and I felt some relief.

When I was a little girl, I was always afraid to walk across a bridge because I thought the cobble stones would fall out from under me and I would fall into the water. This time my fears were justified, but I didn't have time to develop any unnecessary fears. I looked over the first section of the bridge and decided it would be best to stay to the right. I said a silent prayer and started across. I met another man and asked him how the bridge was at the other end. He encouraged me and told me that if I stayed on the right side I would get across safely, and I did.

But it was frightening to look down and see the broad, dark, and foaming Elbe, so I just looked straight ahead and tried to forget the threatening water below me. For years I had crossed this bridge every day to get to school and on Sundays to get to church, but the bridge I had crossed all those years no longer existed. Wherever I put my feet I felt danger, insecurity, and fear. When I finally had the bridge behind me, I looked down at the once beautiful grassy meadows that had formed the bank of the river. It was indescribable. Human bodies—or were they corpses?—lay everywhere. During the bombing, many people had run for the river—burning phosphorus torches—hoping to save themselves in the water, but fighter planes had repeatedly come low over the river and strafed these helpless people. This was repeated the next day, and there lay the bodies. Well, the dead need no water. I was glad I had not witnessed the strafing.

I had made it this far, and I was sure now that I could make it home. I had to do a lot of climbing over rubble until I got as far as Bautzner Street and from there on fewer of the houses appeared to be damaged. I was glad of that because I was getting very tired, although I wouldn't admit it to myself. My only concern was whether or not I would belong to that large group of people who had lost their home and their family. But I felt a sense of relief as I made my way through the familiar streets because, except for the dirt, soot, and rocks that were scattered everywhere, there seemed to have been little major damage done in this area.

I walked and walked until I came to the corner of Sebnitz Street where we lived. Our building was built back from the street, and after a few steps, I saw that it was still standing. I was so overcome and so thankful that I could not even cry. The door to the building was open. I climbed the stairs to the fourth floor, and there I found all of my loved ones safe and sound. Only then did my legs give out on me, and I had to sit down. I took off my coat and discovered that I was exhausted. It was noon. I had been walking and climbing over rubble for five hours, and the only thing I wanted to do now was lie down and sleep. We joined together in a prayer of gratitude that we had all been spared, and then sleep overcame me.

I don't think I had been sleeping for five minutes when I felt my mother waking me and saying in a very calm voice that we had to go to the cellar again because the planes were coming back. I told her I didn't care, I just wanted to sleep, but when she said that she needed my help, I got dressed. My sister Hella was standing in the kitchen and said, "Help me. I don't know what to do." I told her to get her rucksack with the emergency supplies and we would all meet in the cellar.

Our neighbors, the Lucas family, were in the cellar with us and asked us to say the Lord's prayer with them. They were good, pious people. The cellar was deep enough that we could not see out, and the sound of the exploding bombs sounded muffled and far away. I looked around to see if I could do anything, but there was nothing to be done. In my heart, I thanked my Heavenly Father that this time I was with my family.

The sirens were no longer functioning, so after the bombing had stopped, we decided to go back upstairs. We had no enthusiasm left as we dragged ourselves up the stairs, but we were happy to see that our apartment building was still standing. When we got to our apartment, we received a shock that brought us out of our weariness. All of the window panes were blown out, and millions of little glass splinters lay all over the apartment and over all the furniture. We shook everything we could off the balcony, and we swept, brushed, and cleaned up the little pieces of glass. It seemed like an eternity before we dared to sit down or to put anything on the table. Then we had to find cardboard or anything we could to cover the open windows. It was, after all, still February and very cold. What despair we would have been in at the time if we would have known that it would be three years before we could replace the glass in the windows. Fortunately there were three chimneys that went up through the walls of our apartment from the apartments below, and whether we were able to have a fire or not, we were never freezing.

There were no more raids, but the news we started getting about the destruction in the inner city was horrible. We spent the next few

Burning the bodies after the bombing. Source: Richard Peter, *Eine Kamera klagt an* (Leipzig: Fotokinoverlag, 1982).

days trying to take care of the members in our neighborhood and trying to find bread or something to eat. We had no electricity and no water. Over on Bautzen Street was a dairy that had a deep well, and we were permitted to fetch water from there. It was about one kilometer away from our house, but it was fresh, clean water. My brother Helmut and I were assigned to be the water carriers. We had to stand in a long line to get one bucket of water, but we didn't care about that. Everyone seemed to display a miraculous desire to live, and they were all very inventive when it came to getting water and food. We would fill a bucket and then put little boards over the top so that the water would not slop out on the way home. Every drop was precious.

The city of Dresden looked like a battlefield. The inner city was cordoned off because there was nothing there but ruins and corpses. In order to prevent the outbreak of disease, they laid railroad tracks down in the Altmarkt, piled them high with corpses, and then soldiers burned the corpses with flame throwers. Dresden had been filled with refugees fleeing from the east and with retreating troops.

Those were bad times, but they were also good times. As a family, we grew closer to one another and had to rely more on our Father in Heaven. Our prayers became more intense and our faith became unshakable. Of course the war was still going on, and everyone was preparing to flee to the West. Mother, Hella, my brother Harald, and I all had our rucksacks packed with the necessities for the journey, but we also had them ready in case we had to go into the cellar again. But when we saw the misery among the many refugees, we held a family council and decided that the Lord had not spared our home so that we could leave it. We decided that the Lord could protect us best right within our four walls. We knew, of course, that the Russians would come, and there were terrible stories going around about what danger we would be in, especially the women. But we were united in our faith that the Lord was stronger than the Russians. This strength that began to grow in us became unbreakable, and so we stayed. Earlier, Helmut had come home from the hospital and brought his bride, Lottel Schäfer, with him. They lived in Harald's room, and Harald moved over into our room.

From time to time during the first days, we heard the explosions of time-bomb capsules which caused more damage. Several brave people went through the rubble and disarmed the duds. Unfortunately, there were also plunderers active, but I could understand. The refugees and the wounded had to get clothing. It was, after all, winter.

At church on Sunday, we were able to determine that we had lost only one sister in the bombings and that the number of those who had been bombed out was limited. We young people of the branch organized an emergency service to get food and supplies to the older members. When the streets became passable again, the members from the Altstadt Branch came over to the [Church] services in the Neustadt Branch. Their branch house on Circus Street 33 had been bombed and was destroyed right down to the cellar. We also visited the members of the Altstadt Branch in their homes and held Bible studies and youth firesides. It was a time of great faith and inner harmony, but the marvelous old city of Dresden was no more and would never again regain its beauty.

It was a time of great testimony because the Lord helped us to help one another. Many refugees from the East were passing through Dresden, and we took up to as many as fifteen people into our small two-and-a-half-room apartment. Everything was shared; many things were sacrificed. Firm friendships were established which still exist today, beyond continents and oceans. We sat in the Church meetings and in the classrooms huddled in coats and blankets—very few brothers there—but we were thankful and full of hope because the Lord will not forsake his own, which includes all humanity.

We did much fasting and praying; we read the holy scriptures, and we sang the songs of Zion. Everyone had to work hard and put forth a lot of energy because the inner city no longer existed. It was often a long distance to the place of work, to the offices of the authorities, and to the stores. We had to go on foot, of course. But each little bit of progress was greeted with great joy. We had identification papers that showed we were employed and could not be taken into the military. That was also a blessing.

In early May, we held a district conference in Dresden. The branch house in the inner city had been bombed out, as I mentioned, and the rooms in the Neustadt branch were filled with refugees, so we held our conference in the rooms of the Evangelical Lutheran Church. As we sat together worshipping the Lord, we heard the droning of tanks. The Russians were approaching the city, but we went on with our conference.

On Monday, May 7, the Russians entered Dresden, and there was some street fighting. Helmut and Lottel went over to the Königsbrücker Street where there were some tank barriers and watched the fighting, but they soon came back. The city was given over to the Russians, but when the Russian tanks came into the city, some of the Hitler Youth set off some antitank bombs, and then there was more serious fighting. But by nightfall everything was quiet. The next day, the word went out that the war was over. There was no celebrating, no tolling of bells, no proud conquerors. Everything was quiet until the first Russian cars and trucks with Russian soldiers came into the city and put up posters everywhere saying that the war was over and that the civilian population should remain quiet.

The military arsenal on Königsbrücker Street was opened up to the public to get whatever food was left there. Helmut went over with a two-wheeled cart and came back after about two hours with a large sack of oatmeal. At the same time, a bombed-out cannery on our street was opened up, and we were told we could dig out the damaged cans of fruit. What a meal we had with canned peaches and vegetables poured over the oatmeal. As we were coming back home from the cannery, Harald wanted to plunder a shoe shop, but I couldn't permit it. There was no reason for us to give up our ideals now, when we needed God's blessing more than ever.

We continued going to church, and we went around helping the older people, and the Lord did not desert us. It is wonderful to feel the protection and blessings of the Lord the way we did in those days. It was indescribably beautiful.

The branch had to vacate the large meeting room to make room for the refugees, and so we had to meet in only two smaller rooms. We got going on our genealogical work again, as far as we were able, and in March 1946, two missionaries arrived in Dresden. These were priesthood holders who had been released from the German army and were willing to leave their families a second time, but this time to serve the Lord.

Each day there were streams of refugees passing through the city, and that meant many opportunities for us in Christian service. The missionaries put in a request to the Soviet commander for a new place to meet, and we were given the officers' club of a former army barrack. It had been hit by a bomb, and we had to rebuild it ourselves. The painters brought us ladders, paint, and brushes, but then they never came back. Two of the members, an artist and a poet, painted the first rooms for us so that we could hold sacrament meeting there after only one week. By the fourth of May, all of the rooms were completed, and we held a conference there.

We received many blessings during the remodeling. In spite of the fact that we had very little to eat, and we were mainly women, children, and older people—the young men were all in prison camps. We hauled heavy stones out of the building. Once a big block wall came crashing down. Fortunately, no one was injured, and we had the energy to drag the whole thing outside that same day. With eight women, two deacons, and two older brethren we were able to move a steel beam weighing several hundred pounds into the building and get it up onto the supporting pillars, about three or more meters high. The iron monger who directed the work could only say, "What amazing people you are. That went up there as if invisible spirits were helping." When one of the beams rolled over the hand of a young man, he was not injured. While taking a flag pole down from the roof, a missionary was saved from serious injury. Instead of falling, he was somehow able to jump from a beam. At night we were exhausted and hungry, but we collected around a little harmonium and sang hymns from the hymnbook with great enthusiasm. We called ourselves "The Builders' Choir." We built new benches for the classrooms. There was no way to buy curtains or drapes, so we took leftover rolls of newsprint which one of the sisters decorated with roses. She was a porcelain painter, and the paper drapes looked like they were made of silk. Our artist painted a red tapestry onto a wall as if it were hanging from the balcony. It was painted so realistically that everyone who saw it for the first time tried to straighten it a little and only then realized that it was painted. It was beautiful.

"Lace curtains" were sewn together from strips of gray material that was no longer needed for uniforms. We were very proud of them, even when visitors to a conference made fun of us because we had gray curtains instead of white. For us, they were the most beautiful curtains in the world. We cleaned up the surrounding park-like area, cleaned out the fish pond, and brought in fresh water. The entire piece of branch property was idyllic, and we used it for almost forty years. The city took over part of the property in later years, but we had many visits there from the General Authorities, and in 1977 it was visited by the Prophet Spencer W. Kimball.

The first help to arrive came from Elder Ezra Taft Benson, who visited Germany and directed the welfare relief supplies. We also received a great deal of help from our mission president, Walter Stover, a former German who was not afraid to work in this destroyed country. It is impossible to name all those who participated in this pioneer work. And so this tragic epoch was transformed into a blessed time where we all felt very

Edith Krause. Shown on the left some years after the events in this chapter, Sister Krause helped celebrate the ninetieth anniversary of the Primary. Courtesy Edith Krause.

near to the Lord because we recognized his hand in all things. The authorities supported us, the Church had not abandoned us, and we were able to help others by means of food and supplies from the Church welfare program. Later our brothers began returning home from the prison camps, but there was some mourning for those who did not return, who had fallen in the war.

2
I Saw the Opera House Burning
Erika Hermann

We interviewed Erika Hermann in her apartment near the tree-lined, fashionable shopping area renamed by the Russians the Strasse der Befreiung, *[Street of Liberation]. Her tiny apartment is filled with massive pieces of furniture—chests, end tables, a dining room set—all expertly designed and carved by her father (a master wood-carver) in deep-cut designs featuring hunters, shepherds, and animals.*

I was standing on the square in front of the post office at about 12:30 on a February day. There was a sharp wind, but it was bearable, and the sun was shining weakly through a sort of milky sky. It was beautiful. Suddenly the sirens gave the early warning signal—three toots for early warning. It was lunch time, and there were so many people coming and going—we still had the old streetcars then—I thought to myself, if anything were to happen here now with so many people moving about, stores open, shops full, it would be terrible. As these thoughts went through my mind, I never really imagined that it would come that very night.

Going home from work, I rode on the "perron," the open platform at the back end of the streetcar, and as I looked back I saw this marvelous picture: Saint Gregory's Gate, the Cathedral raising its filigreed towers up to the heavens, and the sun, so red, the red beams of light were somehow diffused through the white clouds and spread a reddish glow over everything. I saw the parliament house, then the terrace, the Church of our Lady *[Frauenkirche]*, and the Sekundogene Gate. Everything looked so beautiful. When we were almost across the Augustus Bridge—the one that is now called the Dimitrov Bridge—there to

Erika Hermann. Dresden, 1994. Courtesy Norma and Garold Davis.

the left was the Narrenhäusel with its wrought iron gate in front. And I saw it all so clearly just before the streetcar turned into the former Main Street *[Haupt Strasse]* (now called the Street of Liberation *[Befreiungs Strasse]*). And in the row of houses was the Thomas Fountains. In the middle were two streetlights, where a few of the old trees are still standing. Then the streetcar went through a little street (now called the Rosa-Luxemburg Street) with barely room for the streetcar and crossed over what was called the Kaiser-Wilhelm Square (now it's the Karl-Marx Square). We went by the Japanese Palace and then turned out toward the area where I lived.

I got home and lay down. Mother just said, "Are you feeling better?" I took a tablet called *koffetelin*—I remember that was the name—and in an hour my fever was gone. Then suddenly the doorbell rang, and there was my uncle standing at the door. He lived way out in Trachau on Gebler Street in the house my grandfather built. He had come all that way and said, "Guess what! Arno is home from Russia on furlough. He has frozen feet and has to go to an army hospital. He is not well. He has a fever. He is at home and wants you to come out to see him today. Couldn't you come out to see us this evening? He so wants to see you, and he has no idea where he will be next. He is supposed to go to Czechoslovakia." "Of course," said my mother. Arno was her brother. And the uncle—he was the husband of her sister—he lived in the house, too. There were four families living on the old family property.

And so we went. I wasn't feeling well, but the fever was gone, and we were glad to go. When we arrived, Arno said, "You look so pale and yet a little flushed at the same time."

"Yes," I said, "but my fever is gone. I have these wonderful tablets."

"Can you give me one of your tablets?" he said. "I have to leave before the day's over. I'm not supposed to be here. I've got to be at the Neustädter train station. I'm supposed to report in at an army hospital in Czechoslovakia."

I said, "Can't you go to the hospital here in Dresden?"

"No," he said. "I have my orders, and I have to report there. I have to leave this very evening. I have to be at the station by ten o'clock to catch the troop transport."

I said, "OK. Then I'll give you one of my tablets."

"Good," he said, and I gave him a tablet, and a short time later, when he took his temperature, the fever was gone. Then he said, "I wish you hadn't given me that tablet. If my fever is gone, they will ship me back to the front."

I said, "Oh Uncle, you know you have plenty of time for that."

The air raid report came over the radio hourly. At eight o'clock, they reported no air activity, but at nine we got the report again, and it said, "Heavy enemy aircraft approaching over northwest Germany. Further information will follow." My mother and I said, "We're heading for home." We had a very strange feeling.

Then my uncle Arno said, "You know what, I'll just come along with you."

And my other uncle, the one who had come to see us, said, "I'll go with you, Arno. I'll help you get to the Neustädter Station." So the four of us left and headed for the streetcar, which came right away, and then, just when we arrived at the stop where we had to get off, the early warning sirens sounded.

"Oh, we heard that once already today, at noon," I said. We said good-bye, and the two men went on.

"We'll just see how far we can get," they said.

I said, "Why don't you come to our place and get into the cellar with us!"

"No, we've got to get to the train station; it's already after nine." It was about twenty minutes past nine.

So we got home, and then it came. We hadn't heard anything, but suddenly the sky became pale and then bright. Those were the first flares; we called them the Christmas trees *[Christbäume]*. I had experienced that in Berlin. When you saw the Christmas trees, then you knew you were going to get it. I said, "Mother, we've got to get our emergency packs."

We always had an emergency backpack with extra clothes, shoes, and toilet paper. When I went to work, I always took my pack with me, over my shoulders or hanging on my bike. Then we had the streetcars, but after the bombing, I had to travel by bike, and I took my pack with me. I always had it stuffed full. You never knew when or if something was going to happen, and you had to have something with you. Of course, the most food you could carry would be a box of crackers or something like that, just for emergency. You couldn't carry a large supply of food. You were always hearing about those who had been bombed out and didn't have anything, who were just lucky to get out alive.

So the flares were out, and a moment later, we heard the sirens— full alarm. We headed for the cellar. We took an old lady with us who could hardly walk, and then it started. It was terrible. The window panes were bursting in everywhere, and soot came out of the furnaces. And the bombs that didn't hit—the ones that went over you—had this whistling sound. You could hear this shrill whistling and then it stopped, and then you heard the explosion. Finally, we were so happy to hear the all-clear sirens, and we went upstairs.

We swept up the broken glass. In the living room, a piece of the ceiling plaster had come down, and we cleaned that up. There was not much we could do about the windows at the time. We put up something—paper or cardboard. It wasn't long before the first dazed survivors started straggling out from the city. We had gone out into the street, and I even went down to the Elbe to have a look and saw this terrible ocean of fire. But the Church of Our Lady was still standing; I could see it in the light of the flames. And then I said—to show you how stupid we are—I said, "At least the opera house has been spared. Shouldn't we make some coffee?" I loved the opera.

Many who were coming out from the edge of the city were exhausted. We made malt coffee *[Malzkaffee]* and some tea and stood outside the front door (the windows in the door were all gone) and distributed warm drinks. But this was nothing compared to what was about to come. The night attack came, and it was much, much worse. We never thought we would survive it. But we did. Our Father in Heaven protected us. But the people who started coming out of the city then! So many fateful events!

Across from us lived an older couple; they had a daughter who had a crippled hand. But through the Association for the Disabled, she had been able to find a husband. The parents were so happy that their daughter was finally able to be married. After the first attack, they went into the city to check on the couple. They never came back. None of the family ever came back.

Another very nice family in our neighborhood had a daughter who had just gotten married; it was Mardi Gras *[Faschingsdienstag]*, February 13. They had had the wedding on the weekend. They lived on Röhrhof Street. The two younger daughters who were still at home said, "Oh, Papa and Mama, let us go over and celebrate with them. The wedding guests will still be there, and we can enjoy a little of the Mardi Gras." There was no celebrating on the streets then. No one was interested. So the parents let their two girls go, and in a little while, the entire wedding party was dead. Wiped out; nothing left of them. It was a terrible sight. Those were the kinds of things we experienced.

After things had quieted down a bit, another couple we knew came to see us. They were distant relatives, and they wanted to stay with us because all their family had died in the city. So we kept them with us until they were married—married and had a baby—and then they went away. Her husband had been on furlough.

A lot of people thought they would be safe in the big park *[Grosser Garten]*, and so many died there. That is the big park across from our church. Fighter planes strafed them down. So many were wounded and killed there in the big park that they set up a field hospital there. Those were bad times.

We were worried about the two uncles, Mama's brother-in-law, and her brother. Well, about four in the morning someone knocked, and there was the uncle. He said, "I just wanted to tell you—I came all the way from Trachau—that we are OK. I took Arno to the Neustädter Station in the city."

There was a bomb shelter in the cellar of the city hall. That's where my uncle took Arno. In the meantime, his fever had come back. "I wish Erika had given me another one of her tablets, but we're lucky to be alive," he told my uncle. Afterwards, my uncle had taken him over to the Neustädter Station. Fortunately, they had not been there during the bombing. So many people were killed there. Everyone was going somewhere, and there were refugees from Silesia. It was very bad.

The next day, February 14, I went down to the Elbe again. It was dark. The sun couldn't penetrate the smoke. You could not see very well; it was never really daylight—it was a true Ash Wednesday. There had been a storm during the night, a fire storm. The oxygen had just fanned the flames. I could smell the burning, and the people came wandering, wandering, wandering by.

There were some things one could do to help. We took in a woman the second night after the attack. She had been on night duty. She lived on Güterbahnhof Street. She said, "I couldn't get into my apartment. I have some things in the basement, but there was a dead woman lying across the stairs, and I had to turn around. Could I spend the night with you?"

"Yes, of course, you can stay here."

"Maybe I can try it again tomorrow?"

I said, "Yes, you can do that. You can leave your backpack here with us."

"Good," she said. "I probably won't be able to carry much. Then I'll be back." She tried, but she couldn't do it. The dead woman was still there, but someone had taken the ring off her finger. She was all burned, but the place where the ring had been was white. "It was horrible," she said. Then she said good-bye and thanked us. "There's no sense in my staying here in Dresden. I don't have anyone here anymore. I'm going somewhere else. I'll go to my relatives in the West."

"Yes, yes." And Mama and I just stood there with our tea. But there were many who were not so well off. Their hair was burned off; all their things were burned. They just wanted to get somewhere to relatives or friends, anywhere, just to save themselves.

After the second attack, the Church of Our Lady was still standing, but it collapsed on the afternoon of the fourteenth. The Nazis had set up a film archive in the catacombs, and the films had burned so violently that the building could not stand the heat, and the dome had collapsed. The next day I walked down to the river again, and I saw the opera house burning.

On May 6, 1945, as we were sitting at home eating lunch, we heard the frightful roar of cannons. What was that? We didn't know. Could that possibly be artillery? No, it couldn't be. It was like a drum

Twisted remains of the Opera House. The night Dresden was bombed, Erika Hermann believed the Opera House was safe from the widespread fires, but her relief turned to disbelief the next day when she noticed it, too, was burning. Source: Richard Peter, *Eine Kamera klagt an* (Leipzig: Fotokinoverlag, 1982).

roll of cannon fire, so powerful that the cupboard doors in the kitchen flew open; the dishes and the windows rattled. It lasted for about an hour; then everything was suddenly quiet. We couldn't explain it. The newspapers had said that our army would liberate Saxony, where we lived, from the advancing Russian army.

On the morning of May 7, I rode my bike to work as always, took the ferry across the Elbe, and rode on to the office. The bridges were still damaged, and I could get to work faster with the ferry. It was very quiet in the office, but suddenly our boss was called out. He had to go to the winery in Lockwitzgrund. It was a bombproof shelter, and there he was to receive instruction from the *Gauleiter* [Nazi term somewhat equivalent to mayor] Mutschmann. After about an hour, he returned and said, "Saxony has been liberated from the enemy. We can all relax." But Gauleiter Mutschmann had not been there, only his representative. We all went back to work. Saxony was safe. That was about noon. About one o'clock, a car came driving into the courtyard. It was the engineer who was responsible for electrical power. He had a red chevron on his white license plate. He came into the office and said to me, "You live in Neustadt?"

"Yes," I said.

"See that you get yourself across the Elbe as quickly as you can. The Russians are already in the forest behind Radebeul. Just drop everything and get home, right now." Our offices were in the Altstadt. I didn't say good-bye to anyone, just slipped out the back door of the office, got on my bike, and started home.

It was not easy. The SS [the elite Nazi officer staff] had taken over the Marien Bridge and wouldn't let anyone cross because they were about to blow it up. So I thought, the only way to get across is on one of the ferries, not the big one, but the little one; it was closer. When I got to the ferry, I could see that it was not going to be big enough. There were lots of people on the move. They had closed down the slaughter house, and the workers were trying to get across the river. The little ferry would hold only about thirty people at the most. On the other side of the Elbe was a group of German soldiers driving a herd of cattle. The soldiers demanded that the ferryman bring them over the Elbe to our side—to the Altstadt—immediately. The people weren't about to let him go off empty. They said, "You have to take us over. We want to get to our homes." We stormed the ferry—I with my bicycle—and when the ferry began listing badly, I thought we would all be dumped into the water. But the ferryman got us across, and we landed safely at the other shore. I got on my bike as quickly as possible, but it was pretty hard because we were pushing through soldiers and cows who were trying to get on the ferry, and no one was there to direct the loading and unloading.

I peddled down Leipzig Street, then turned into Rehefelder Street, and there I saw white flags flying from all the windows. I rushed into the house and locked the door because I could hear motors, heavy motors, like tanks. My mother was at home. Suddenly the power went out. We were in the dark. We had turned on the hall light because I had just come in and brought my bike in with me, which normally went down in the cellar. Then the power went out. We ran to the window and saw the first tanks coming from the direction of Radebeul, from the area Wilder Mann. The white flags were all out. We quickly closed the windows and pulled the curtains so that no one could look in. We didn't know what to expect. And the tanks stopped, some right in our area. And the women, several women with children went out and cheered the Soviet soldiers. The soldiers even handed out pieces of bread or things like that to the children. Bread was scarce at that time. I couldn't understand it; neither could my mother. But they were our occupation troops, the Soviets.

We couldn't sleep all night. We were especially afraid because we were on the ground floor. What's going to happen now? It was a wild night. Then they started coming, the stragglers, so to speak. They were partly Mongols and from other countries. Maybe Armenians, you couldn't tell exactly. Many of them had bicycles and wore large, white coats. You couldn't see what they had under their coats, and the bicycles were loaded down, too. This went on all night long and into the afternoon of the next day.

On the day after, that was then the ninth of May, we heard on the radio that we had capitulated and that Herr Dönitz—he had been put in as Hitler's successor—that Herr Dönitz would sign the capitulation papers. But we didn't know. We were afraid and kept the doors locked because we had heard a lot of things. And at night we didn't sleep downstairs but up on the third floor because several houses had been broken into on the first night. The next day we opened the door, and then some soldiers came.

One went from apartment to apartment and demanded, "Watch, watch!" I had my father's watch on my wrist because my golden watch had been at the jewelers on the thirteenth of February. The jeweler told me it had been burned up, but it was not burned up. They were able to save their safe which was in the basement. I learned about that years later. Everything in it became their beginning capital, including my watch. Naturally, they claimed I had never asked to have it back. "You've still got your apartment; be happy. We have to start all over again, outside Dresden, in Heidenau. Surely you can find yourself another watch." I wasn't so desperate to have it back, but I was curious to know what had happened to it. So, now my father's watch was gone. I gave it to the soldier, and then he saw another one. I told him, "That one is broken."

"No matter, broken. Watch, watch!" and he took that one. Oh well, he can get it repaired himself.

But then no one else came into our house because we had an old man in the apartment building who locked the door and put a piece of a tree trunk under the latch so that it wouldn't open. We had replaced the windows that had been blown out during the bombing—partly with glass and partly with boards. Mostly with boards until we could get real glass again. Yes, those were the first weeks.

But every night you heard things, and then the people began helping one another. Someone struck an air raid gong whenever any of the occupation troops were trying to get into our houses. And not far from our house was the commander's headquarters, so whenever anything was wrong someone came running fast. After that it was pretty quiet in our neighborhood.

After a while, we could go shopping again, but there was no meat. Bread, but no fat, not even sausage. So we helped one another again. If someone had some flour, we mixed it with cooking oil. It is good when you have a food supply. I think a lot about our instructions in the Church to have a year's supply of food. We had that idea also, but we couldn't store much variety. During the war, it was bad. We had a butter substitute we jokingly called *Affenfett* [ape's fat], a slang term, but that's about all we had. So we would mix flour with oil and cook it with some onions if we had them, and then we would spread it on our bread. After several weeks, we had the first "fat rations." And of course the first thing one wanted to do was take a slice of bread and smear it with this fat. But it didn't set well with all of us. We got diarrhea. Our bodies weren't used to it.

My relatives, the four families who lived out in Trachau in the house my grandfather built in 1898, had to go through a lot. There were disturbances every night. So my uncle got a big ladder long enough to reach the roof. It was then May, and it was a very warm springtime that year. He put the women and the two children to bed on the roof. There was a flat part of the roof—it was steep only on the sides—and that is where they spent the night. He always got them down again early in the morning. So at night the soldiers never found any women in the house.

One morning they waited for the uncle to come, and he didn't come, and he didn't come. They called down to the people on the street and asked them to see if the uncle was in the house. "And if he isn't in the house, come back out and put the ladder up. And if the door is locked, you will have to break in." They were afraid that the uncle might have been taken away, but they found him lying on the floor. He had been beaten and was only semiconscious. One of the men found the front door open, went upstairs, and opened a door to the roof. Then they could come down that way. The uncle had to be treated by a doctor, had to have his wounds bound, and had to have an injection. These things happened, at least until they were assigned to quarter troops in their house—a lieutenant and his men from the Red Army.

Some distant relatives of ours out in Radebeul had bad luck because they had to quarter ordinary soldiers. If there was anything in the house any of the soldiers wanted, my relatives had to carry it out to the truck, and it was taken away. The soldiers didn't take the big pieces of furniture like a walnut sideboard. They took other things they thought were more valuable. But the heavy furniture, they couldn't take that. But the family had some good luck later and got into a nice apartment and were able to buy some furniture. So the family had to start all over again. Yes, those were the first weeks.

And then we were, for all practical purposes, unemployed. I couldn't get to my office. The company had been taken over by the Red Army because it contained a production section including a meat market, a bakery, and a large motor pool—that is, what was left of the motor pool after the war. But the production section had been taken over, and we wanted to go back to work. We hadn't done anything to cross the authorities, even though our directors were not around anymore; at least they were not to be seen. And what was funny, a Red Army officer sat in my swivel chair in the closed section of the building and hosed us down because we wouldn't go away. He sprayed us with a fire hose and told us to go home: "This business is now occupied, and you don't work here anymore." They had let some of the people go back to work—transportation workers and those who were responsible for the supplies. But those of us who had worked in the office, nothing doing.

After half a year, I finally got a work permit, but everything had changed. In the meantime, I made a living as a "rubble woman." Since our business was closed, we had to report to a so-called employment office that was set up in front of the old city hall, right in the open. We had a work card; they stamped it, and we were put in different work details, like cleaning up rubble. On one occasion, we had to walk all the way across Dresden to the Altstadt, and on the way, we ran into a group of workers who were heading for Neustadt. Those things happened. But still, we were happy to be working. We thought we were going to be paid, but the first work details were *not* paid at all!

Street crew cleaning up the rubble left after the bombing of Dresden. Erika Hermann and Dorothea Condie's mother, Frida Speth, worked on rubble crews. Source: Richard Peter, *eine Kamera klagt an* (Leipzig: Fotokinoverlag, 1982).

Then one day we were standing around the employment office, a big truck rolled up, and we were all loaded in. "You're being taken out to the industrial area. You must disassemble a turbine factory which will be sent to the Soviet Union as reparation payment." So we had to climb into this big truck and were taken to the industrial area. When we got there—it was the former Brückner, Kadis, & Co.—they opened big iron gates, and there stood a Soviet major with his red stripes and some other big officials. We had a little orientation, and then we had to start removing fiberglass insulation from the pipes. It was very unpleasant work because the fiberglass got into your skin, and the first day I didn't even have a jacket. After that I took an old jacket and heavy work gloves with me, and it went better.

A Russian work party was also there, about nine men, who were forced laborers. One day we were sitting in the soup kitchen having our breakfast. We had a German boss who was in charge and told us what to do. Suddenly the door flew open, and one of these forced laborers looked in. He was a young man, but he looked much older than he was. He came in with an iron rod and told us to get out; we had to work; we couldn't sit around and eat breakfast all day. The old German boss said, "Now listen. None of that here. These women are not used to this heavy work, and they have to eat."

"I don't see why." I must say, he spoke very good German. Then suddenly he said, I can't repeat the exact words, but he made it clear that he hated us, because—he ripped off his shirt—because he had been tortured by the SS. They had burned a Star of David into his chest. We could also see that his ribs had been caved in and he had only a few teeth left in his mouth, in spite of his youth. It was terrible to look at. Then I could understand his hatred, even though we should not hate one another. But it says in the Bible, "An eye for an eye and a tooth for a tooth." Someone there recited that. It was terrible. We couldn't be angry with him when we saw that, and who knows what the others had gone through. That was one of the most lasting impressions I took with me from those days.

We worked. But I also got to know a very nice, young Russian. His parents were teachers; he was educated; he could even speak English. With my schooling, I could converse with him a little now and then, even though I didn't know Russian. He was very nice. His name was Ivan. He was our overseer and looked in on us because we were not working in the underground levels anymore. All of the basement rooms had been cleaned out; they were empty, and we were working above ground. We had to paint pipes and help label them with a number. This went on for a long time, and we were supposed to get some pay. But I didn't like it. I experienced so many things there that I never thought were possible for a woman to experience. I can't be more specific. But when you have children, you never know if you might not someday be put into a situation where you would have to behave that way just to get something to eat for the children. But I couldn't understand it. I had a different point of view.

Finally, I asked if I could quit. I had to go to the major's office—he had an interpreter—and I had to tell him why I wanted to quit. I said, "We are almost through, and I want to go back to work in my own profession."

"Yes, but try to understand. We need every able-bodied person. Come back tomorrow." And then the next day, "Are your reasons the same?" Of course, they were the same; what else could I say? Then he said, "OK, you can have your release papers." It may have been a few days later, but I got my release papers along with another woman who lived in my neighborhood. We were happy to get away from there. Even

Straightening track in Dresden after the bombing. Both women and men served on the crew. Source: Richard Peter, *Eine Kamera klagt an* (Leipzig: Fotokinoverlag, 1982).

though those are things you don't forget, you can't be angry. We had been protected and had survived it all. That was the main thing. We learned from the experience, but it was sad.

It was sad because I didn't even know whether my father was alive or dead. There was no mail in those days. There were many who didn't know. But I went on working as a "rubble woman" in various work details. Eventually, we started getting paid for our work on the disassembly details. It wasn't much, but at least we were getting paid. That had not been the case on the first details when we were doing nothing but removing rubble.

On one occasion, I had a detail on Arnold Street that lasted for several days. We had to tear up the street which was partly covered with asphalt and partly covered with large, heavy cobblestones. That was hard work for women, but there were also some men there, older men, who helped with the very heavy labor. We had to take up the large gas pipes because they were needed by the Russians—part of the reparations debt. It was so quiet there. There was not a house standing in which people could live, so this demolition was somewhat understandable. We worked under guard. Soldiers walked back and forth, and there was also a big boss who joined us on occasions for breakfast. He told us of atrocities that the SS had committed in his homeland. They had driven his family out of their home, wife and children, and his daughter who had a small baby. I don't know if I believe it or not, but he told us that the SS had thrown the little baby up in the air and caught it on a bayonet. That was incomprehensible to us, and he said, "You've got to believe me; I'm not lying. We want to make things better for you here." Well, we heard it, and whatever the others thought of it, they kept it to themselves. We weren't free to express our opinions, but we had to listen to everything.

Sometimes we had to unload coal cars with gigantic shovels. They were so big you could load a ton on them. That was men's work. But we had to unload them and then shovel the coal back into trucks. That was very, very hard. Everyone got back pains from doing this kind of labor, which we weren't used to. There was even a "rubble train" in the city for a while into which I helped shovel rubble. Oh, we learned such a variety of things. That was our difficult postwar period, but I was happy just to have survived.

In 1949, I was finally able to return to my profession, and I was happy to be doing real work once again. Of course, the rubble work had to be done, even in West Germany, but they finished it a lot sooner than we did. It was 1952 before we began the first reconstruction. One of the first projects was the Zwinger [a famous Baroque palace-art gallery].

There are a lot of people here who have experienced all of this who could tell you much, much more. There are just certain things that have stayed in my memory. I don't know if I did everything right in those days, the way I would now. But that is what our earthly existence is. We learn from all our experiences, and then we grow spiritually.

As I said, I never felt the stability in the Lutheran-Evangelical Church that I felt from the first time I was able to attend our Church on the Dr.-Kurt-Fischer Allee [*Allee* means boulevard, street]. Years before, I learned about the Church from relatives, but then I thought, no, I can't go up there on the Dr.-Kurt-Fischer Allee, that was a bad area. So many things had happened there in the past. The army was right next door. Once I was halfway there but then turned around. Then I asked Sister Heldmann to pick me up. That was on June 19, and I will never forget it. June 19, 1983. It was so wonderful; I could hardly believe it. I started going to church, and one day Sister Karin Zwirner said to me, "Why don't you come at 9:00?"

I said, "I thought it began at 10:50."

"No," she said, "at 9:00 we have our women's organization." I knew nothing about Relief Society until then. Later, when the missionaries visited me regularly, I began to learn. That was so lovely. I have never regretted it, quite the contrary. And even though I was somewhat older, I am so happy that I found my way to the Church. Just last Sunday, I was moved to tears when the two missionaries said good-bye. It was so sad; we had learned to love them so much. Nothing like that had happened to me before. I had never learned to love the people I became acquainted with from the first moment on. It is a strange experience for me.

Today the two young sister missionaries arrived. I have become acquainted with many people through my profession, but this is a wonderful atmosphere, and I don't want to miss any of it, even though my health prevents me from attending sometimes.

There are times when I am weak, when I can't concentrate, when I let my problems get the better of me, when I am inattentive. Then I lose a bit of the security I have from my faith. But somehow I am able to stay on the straight path and not be led astray. My faith has preserved me until now, and I have to work with myself; I have to overcome myself. Then here comes a feeling of guilt because I don't get to the temple often enough. But I can't risk going because I have these doctor's treatments every two days, and that requires a strictly regulated diet so that my digestive system will be in order to visit the doctor. If I would have to leave the session—that would be terrible; it would disturb everyone in the session, and I don't want that on my head.

I still have much to do for my other ancestors. Unfortunately, I don't have all the dates together, but I am working on it, and I hope very, very much that I can take care of it. I was baptized on February 2, 1984, and in 1985, I went to the temple for the first time. It was wonderful to be sealed to my parents, just wonderful. I had the feeling that my parents were in the room and that they accepted it. That was very strange. There were proxies there, a male and a female proxy, but that was such a wonderful feeling, as if they were right there in the room with me. I would never have thought it possible that someone could feel something like that. And I know for sure that if my parents had been alive they would have been baptized.

My father was a Christian, and he told me many things that I have since forgotten. But occasionally I find some passage in the Bible and say to myself, "My father told me about that." For example, Christ said, "What thou must do, go and do quickly"; my father was always saying that. He used so many expressions that came from the Bible, but I had forgotten them over the years. As I mentioned, I have had to relearn how to think, and now I remember so many things and say to myself, "My father knew that already."

My mother would have been baptized in any case. Probably the only thing that would have bothered her would have been going under the water at her age, but she would have done it. She would have loved to have been a member.

But my other relatives over in Leipzig have never understood, nor have those in Pinneberg. My cousin let me know she felt I had betrayed my religion when I was baptized. I did not betray my religion, quite the contrary. I deepened my religion. I know of nothing more wonderful; there could be nothing more wonderful than my religion. One has to treasure that, and one has to keep the commandments—that's the essential thing.

I pay a full tithing, and I am blessed for it again and again. Before, when someone would tell me that, I would think to myself that can't be true. But it is true. One receives so many blessings from tithing; it is wonderful. Many people won't believe you when you tell them that, but it is really wonderful.

There are so many things buried in my memory, some that are valuable to relate, some that are useless. But I am thankful that I am a member of the Church—very, very thankful.

3

Let's Follow Dad—
He Holds the Priesthood

Dorothea Speth Condie

After leaving Dresden for the West, Dorothea Speth Condie worked as a registered nurse. She served a mission in Stuttgart, where she met her husband, Elder Spencer J. Condie, now of the First Council of the Seventy. She has had many callings in the Church, including Relief Society president and wife of the mission president in the Austria Vienna Mission. She is currently a Gospel Doctrine teacher in Provo, Utah.

February 13, 1945, is an unforgettable day in the lives of thousands of people who were living in Dresden, Germany. World War II was in full fury, with armed forces on all sides pushing towards the German borders trying to end this terrible war.

We felt quite safe in our city of Dresden, the "Florence on the Elbe," with its many cultural, historic, and architectural treasures. Surely no one would try to destroy these. There was no heavy industry in the region, and this late in the war the population consisted primarily of women, children, and the elderly. However, burgeoning numbers of wounded and sick and thousands of refugees arrived daily from the German settlements beyond the Polish border. Even though all the other major cities of Germany had experienced numerous air raids, Dresden had been spared this terrible destruction.

It was 10:30 that February night when we first heard the dreadful sounds of the sirens and the roar of hundreds of planes and the explosions of the first bombs. When my father looked outside, he noticed strange-looking lights in the shape of Christmas trees lighting the dark sky and the darkened city. These were the flares used to guide the bombers.

We lived on the fourth floor of an apartment building and quickly realized that we needed to get downstairs, to the basement, which served as our bomb shelter. The first air raid lasted about forty-five minutes, and many homes in our neighborhood were set ablaze. But the area hardest hit was the inner city, where every building seemed to be engulfed in flames. For the time being, we seemed to be safe, but with the electricity, gas, and all communications cut off, we decided to remain in the basement for the rest of the night.

Around 1:30 A.M., we realized that the planes had returned and that bombs were exploding all around us. Would a bomb hit our house? Would only some or any of us still be alive in one minute or ten minutes or when this air raid ended? It was a terrifying experience! But when the silence finally returned, we were all still alive.

We were alive; however, we were trapped in the basement. One of the first bombs of the second air raid hit our corner house at an angle, setting the ground floor on fire so that the building started burning from the bottom upward. The stairway, our only exit, was already blocked by the fire. The only way out was a hole in our basement wall connecting the basement with the house next door. The hole had been made for this very purpose, but it was barely big enough to crawl through. We couldn't take anything with us. Our family and an older couple who lived on our floor managed to escape through this hole.

Most of the homes in our area of the city were now destroyed or burning, and the few that remained would soon be on fire. We all realized that we needed to get away from the burning houses immediately! Walking on the streets looked very dangerous because a firestorm with the force of a hurricane was raging, sending thousands of sparks and burning objects flying through the air, fueling and spreading the fires. In the streets, there were also many huge bomb craters adding to the danger.

Once outside, we gathered as a family and quickly held a council. My family consisted of my parents, my two older sisters, my twin sister, and myself. It was imperative that we not get separated as we set out to reach the Elbe River. The Elbe with its wide banks would be a perfect haven from the fire and the smoke that was starting to sting our eyes.

For the last time, we all looked at our house and all that we owned in this life, knowing that the flames would soon reach the upper level. We lived on a very nice wide street leading directly to the river, which was about four blocks from where we stood. For safety, we did not all walk together. My father took one of my older sisters and my twin sister

Dorothea Speth Condie as a teenager in Dresden. Courtesy Dorothea Condie.

and began to lead the way. My mother, my oldest sister, and I were to follow as closely as possible. As my father started walking, he headed towards a narrow side street instead of choosing the wide street which led directly to our goal, to the river. Mother stopped, not wanting to follow down the narrow, burning street and began calling Dad to try to persuade him to turn around and take the more direct route along our street, which seemed so much safer and quicker. But due to the firestorm, Dad could not hear her plea, and he continued walking along the narrow side street.

With each passing second, the distance between us increased, but Mom was still not willing to abandon her plan. Then I heard my older sister plead with her, "Mom, let's follow Dad; he holds the Priesthood!" With this reminder, we started to move quickly, trying to catch up with Dad, who led us safely in a roundabout way down to the river. We followed several other people into an old hospital building, where we could finally sit down, rest, wait out the night, and be protected from the firestorm and its terror.

After we had been there a short time, a neighbor lady entered the building. She and her elderly husband had lived on the top floor of our building for many years, and they had become our very good friends. But now she was alone, extremely upset and crying. As soon as she regained her composure, she told us that after she and her husband had left our burning building, they decided to walk straight down the wide street to the river. Her husband, tall and slender, walked very quickly leading the way, but she, somewhat short and heavy, could not follow so quickly, and lagged behind. Suddenly she saw her husband burnt alive in front of her eyes. Unknown to anyone, liquid phosphorous from one of the bombs had covered the street. It could not be seen but was immediately ignited whenever anyone stepped on it. There was nothing she could do to save her husband, she could only turn around and save herself.

We did what we could to comfort her and then said a silent prayer of thanksgiving that we had been spared. If we had not followed our father, we would have walked right into that liquid phosphorus. I learned that night how important it is that we follow the priesthood.

When daylight finally arrived, we started to walk along the river away from the death and destruction. We were part of a pilgrimage of thousands of people who were tired and homeless and in shock after what had happened. The injured remained behind, lining the path. These are images one can never forget! The smoke was so thick and stung our eyes so badly that we had to wet our handkerchiefs and put them to our eyes to relieve the burning sensation.

Thoughtful neighbors, whose homes had survived the destruction, offered us refugees warm drinks and sympathetic smiles. We really did not know where to go, but we decided to stop at the home of some Church members to let them know that we were alive. We arrived at their house in Leuben around 9:00 A.M., just at the end of another air raid. The Düennebeil family greeted us with tears of joy in their eyes to see us alive and took us into their apartment, where we enjoyed the luxury of a bath and a bed to sleep in and an opportunity for some much needed rest.

Sister Düennebeil, her son Dieter, and Grandpa Düennebeil, with their big hearts and love for the gospel and their fellowmen, had opened their home to several of us homeless families. Their three-bedroom apartment had welcomed the Deus family—a mother, grandmother, and four children—and Sister Sawatzki and her two young children—both refugee families from the East—and now our family of six. At night, to make things a little less crowded, my father slept on the couch at the home of an older couple, Brother and Sister Meyer, who lived close by. My mother and one of us children walked a few blocks to the home of an older sister who had an extra twin bed. Everyone else slept wall-to-wall on Düennebeil's living room floor, thanks to some more good neighbors who helped with the bedding.

How long could we live this way? This was a temporary, not a permanent, solution. Were there any vacant apartments in this destroyed city with tens of thousands of homeless people? Only a miracle could make this dream come true, but "with God nothing is impossible!"

After about two weeks, a knock came to the door. A good friend of ours asked us to follow him. Herr Hubold was not a member of the Church, but his wife and two children were baptized and were very active in our little branch. He also attended meetings quite often. He was on the board of directors of a private housing development which had survived the bombing. After that terrible night in Dresden, the housing board held a special meeting. Several families who had small children had temporarily left their apartments in order to seek safety in the country or with relatives in other parts of Germany. The question was raised, "Should not some homeless families, even if only temporarily, be invited to occupy these empty apartments?" But how does one select a handful of families out of tens of thousands in need? Herr Hubold asked for permission to invite his friends to move into these vacant dwellings. Permission was granted, and we and three other LDS families who had lost everything had a place to call home, fully furnished.

They were modest apartments with only one big bedroom, but we were deeply grateful and felt richly blessed. None of us had to leave the apartments at the end of the war, since none of the families wanted to return to Dresden and live in the Communist-occupied territory of East Germany.

When the Russians came in, they decided, for some reason, to set up their camp right there on the street where we lived. The Russian soldiers did not have a good reputation with young girls, and there were about four or five teenage girls in the LDS families living there, including my two older sisters. They all came to our house because my father was the only priesthood holder at the time and they didn't feel safe alone. It was about 10:00 at night, and everybody was afraid. When those Russian soldiers come and knock on your door, there is nothing you can do about it. You just have to let them in. At about 10:30, we noticed they were packing up. They were leaving. Near the apartment complex was a big racetrack. That was a good place to set up a camp, so at 10:30 at night they suddenly decided to move over there and set up. Afterward, we were told that one of the big communist leaders in Dresden, who had greeted the Russian army with a white flag, lived in that apartment complex, and he had a young teenage daughter. Even though he was a Communist, he was also a father and didn't like the soldiers camping right in our neighborhood. He used his influence and got them moved.

A few days later, the Russian soldiers received permission to go into any German home and take whatever they liked. They could plunder the homes and do whatever they wanted. I remember when they came into our house. You could hear them coming up the stairs in their big heavy boots. I think there were about three of them who came into our apartment. Of course, we didn't own much. I remember that after the bombing in which we lost everything, we received a second set of clothing and an extra pair of shoes, and that was about it.

We put anything that we didn't want them to take on the couch and put a blanket over it. Then my sister and I sat on the couch playing, trying to hide these things. The Russian soldiers looked through the apartment. One thing my mother had somehow saved from the bombing was an 8 x 10 picture of my brother, who had been killed during the war. It was the only picture we had of him, and he was in his uniform. The picture was hanging on the wall, and the Russian soldiers didn't like that—a soldier in a German uniform. They wanted to take the picture, and my mother really got upset. Somehow she got the message across to them that he was her only son who had been killed, so they didn't take the picture. They ended up taking one of Dad's suits and a pair of shoes, and then they left.

During World War II, we always had enough to eat, and we still had enough of a variety of things to eat. Things were rationed, but we still had enough sugar, we still could buy some chocolate, and we still had meat at least for Sundays or once during the week. We always had enough bread, and we always had enough potatoes. I never remember being hungry. But after the war, when the Communists, the Russians, came in, then we really went without. We ate bread with nothing on it and sometimes potatoes. There just wasn't enough to eat. I can remember going to bed hungry at night. When I got up from the table, I never really felt like I had had enough to eat.

After about 1948, when the food shipments came from the Church, then, at least, we had enough potatoes and bread again. Those food shipments were very much appreciated. They really saved our lives. That is one thing I will never forget.

Shortly after that, my father died and was buried in Dresden. After Dad died, my mother had to go to work to support the family. First she worked cleaning off old bricks so they could be used again. Of course, it took years to get rid of all that rubble. Then she went to work on a street crew. She helped pave the streets, and they didn't have the machines like they have today. They had to do a lot by hand, spread the tar, make it even. My mother worked mostly with women. There weren't many men left after World War II. They needed women to help in those kind of jobs, and my mother had been raised on a farm and thought she was strong enough. The funny thing is she enjoyed it. I think it was partly because she enjoyed the association with the other women. They really had a good time. My mother would come home from work and tell us how much fun they had. They worked hard, they really did, but she enjoyed it. Then the last few years, in the mid '50s or '60's—she was close to sixty then—she went to work in a factory.

Eventually my sisters and I, one by one, escaped to West Germany. Our mother lived in the same apartment until 1958, when she finally left Dresden and came west to live near her children. She is buried in Stuttgart.

4

It Was the Hunger

Wilfriede Kiessling

Wilfriede Kiessling lives near her daughter in the city of Freiberg. As we interviewed her in one of the classrooms of the Freiberg Chapel, we could look through the windows behind her at the colorful grounds and white facade of the Freiberg temple. It seemed a fitting framework for a life devoted to serving the Lord.

Although Sister Wilfriede Kiessling does not talk about the bombing of Dresden, her story is placed here because she served as the president of the Relief Society of the Dresden Ward in the years immediately following the bombing. Her brief story gives a graphic picture of what conditions were like in those years (1945–1948).

Wilfriede: My parents accepted the gospel when they were living in Schwarzenberg. My mother and I were baptized in 1925; my father and brother, in 1926. My other brother, who is two years younger, was baptized in 1927. And my younger sister was also baptized in 1927. We helped establish the branch in Schwarzenberg, before moving to Plauen. We were in the Church in Schwarzenberg for only about a year and a half.

There were six of us in the family. We moved around a lot because my father was working for the railroad and was frequently transferred; each transfer meant a promotion. So we moved from Plauen to Auerbach. In Auerbach, they were waiting for us to help establish a branch, which we did. We lived there about two years. Then my father was transferred again, and this time we moved to Freiberg. Oh, they were happy to get a family of six in the branch in Freiberg! So we went to work in the Church there and stayed

Wilfriede Kiessling. Freiberg, 1994. Courtesy Norma and Garold Davis.

another two years. Then my father was transferred to Penig in 1931. But there was no branch of the Church in Penig, so we had to travel about twenty kilometers to Chemnitz to attend church. That was rather difficult because there were no direct train connections between Penig and Chemnitz. We got bicycles for everyone and went to church by bike. But that wasn't so easy either—uphill, downhill, uphill, downhill. We soon had enough of that. And then there was the rain. It wasn't an ideal situation.

At that time, I was about eighteen. In Penig, I met my husband, and we were married. My husband worked in Heidenau near Dresden, and we found an apartment and moved there. That was after 1938, when preparations were already being made for war. The trains had stopped running. My husband was not a member of the Church, and he didn't much like it when I went to Church every Sunday. My husband was killed in 1944. He was called up into the army in the summer of 1943, quite late in the war. He had always been retained by his factory because he was an engineer, but that was no longer possible, so he had to go to war. He was there about only nine months when he died of pleurisy and lung infection. Just yesterday I was reading his last letter. Could I read part of that?

G. Davis: Yes, please do.

Wilfreide: "My dear Wilfriede! I send you my greetings. I hope a plane can get out to bring them to you." They were hemmed in, but I think he was already sick. He wrote this letter on April 9, and five days later he was dead. So he must have been sick even though he didn't mention it in the letter. He just wrote at the bottom, "Don't write to me." He died; there was no need to write anymore. That was his last letter.

It was hard when I received word about the death of my husband. But death came to so many in those days. However, I always said my prayers. I always remembered that I was a member of the Church even though I had married out of the Church. I always remembered.

In 1941 we had a daughter, Karla. That is Sister Liebscher. After the war, the suffering in the GDR and the other parts of Germany was terrible. The cities were destroyed. There was no money. They had no widow's pension or survivor's pension then, so I received nothing from the government. Then when the Communists took over the government, all the men who had been in the German army were declared war criminals, so we women received nothing from the Communists either.

In the apartment above me lived a woman whose husband also did not return from the war. He was declared missing, and they assumed he had drowned in the Danube when the army was retreating across the river. She didn't have any income either, and she had two children. We made an agreement with one another that we would do sewing for other people. I had been taught to sew, and she had learned some on her own. We were able to earn a meager living, enough to keep us alive. Of course, the people we sewed for didn't have any money either, so we worked very cheaply. But I must say that I never went into debt. I always managed to get what we needed. Of course, we never had a full meal; that was understood. That lasted through 1945 and into 1946, an entire year.

One day I heard from an old acquaintance, Sister Dünnebeil in Dresden, that they had a new meeting place on Dr.-Kurt-Fischer Allee. She invited me to come, and I went. From the first moment, I felt at home again, and from that time to this, I have been active in the Church.

N. Davis: That was a long distance, from Heidenau to the north end of Dresden.

Wilfriede: Yes, it was a long way, a very long way. I would travel on my bicycle with my daughter on a child's seat behind me. We would ride as far as Leuben. That's where Sister Dünnebeil lived. I would leave my bicycle at her house, and then we would ride together on the streetcar to the chapel on Dr.-Kurt-Fischer Allee. It took about two hours each way. I would leave home about eight o'clock in the morning in order to get there on time, and if I left right after Sunday School was over, I would get home about two in the afternoon. Then we ate our supper in place of our lunch—that is, we turned our meals around because we couldn't go so long without eating. But from that time on, I have always gone to church.

It Was the Hunger

In 1948, I was called to be the Relief Society president in the Dresden Branch. I was the youngest Relief Society president around, only thirty-four years old. I had been president for only a short time when the first welfare shipment came from the Church in America. You just can't imagine how this welfare aid helped us.

We were literally starving to death at the time. Many people were cooking and eating the grains remaining from brewing malt coffee (*malzkaffee*) [*malzkaffee* is a hot drink made from barley and other grains] with a little flour mixed in. Many of the children were not getting any supper. They were put to bed with just a cup of malt coffee. We had never been so thin, that's for sure. The children would come in around two o'clock in the afternoon and say, "Mommy, I'm hungry." Well, what were we supposed to give our children to eat? We just had to say, "Go out and play; we don't have anything to eat." That hurt right down to the soul. But we couldn't help it; we couldn't help it. We didn't have anything.

But then the shipments came from the Church in America. What an indescribable blessing that was! Of course, our chapel was filled like it had never been filled before. If you came late, you had to stand up in the back; there were no more seats. That is the truth; I experienced it myself. We had big sacks of food and got fat on it—peaches, canned milk.

The building up there on Dr.-Kurt-Fischer Allee was very large, and we had to clean it ourselves. But there were many grateful sisters who were anxious to help because of the food or the clothing they had

Ezra Taft Benson in front of the mission home in Berlin. Elder Benson obtained permission from the Russians to allow welfare supplies to be distributed to the Saints in the Soviet Zone of occupation. Courtesy Edith Krause.

received. They just wanted to do some little thing to show their gratitude for what they had received.

I lived on the side of Heidenau that was toward Pirna [on the side away from Dresden]. They told me I had to give up that apartment because there were only two of us, and we had a four-room apartment. The government said it was too large for one adult and a child under eight. So I had to get out of my apartment. It was really a nice apartment, too. Oh, how I prayed! How I prayed!

Normally it was this way—they offered you three apartments, and if you didn't accept the third one, you were just put out on the street. I turned down the third one. I turned down the fourth one. Oh, how I prayed. Then they offered me an apartment in Heidenau-North, on the Dresden side, right next to the train station, right next to the bus stop from where you could ride straight into Dresden. I wasn't doing sewing anymore then; I had found a regular job. Well, they called me, "Mrs. Kiessling. Please go look at apartment number 10 on Freedom Plaza *[Platz der Freiheit]* and tell us whether you will take it or not." I said right on the telephone, "Yes, yes, I'll take it," although I hadn't even seen it.

I was so thankful to the Lord that I had been given this apartment. It was a nice apartment on the second floor, right next to the train station and the bus stop, with stores all around. That was in 1952, and I was no longer the Relief Society president, but then I was called to be president a second time and then a third time. Each time with different counselors. One of my counselors lives in America, Sister Burde. She lives in Salt Lake City, but she is over eighty now. And then there is another sister in America.

G. Davis: After the war then, how did things go here in the Church? In the '60s and '70s?

Wilfriede: After the welfare shipments from America stopped coming, several members dropped out. Week after week, they stopped coming, they stopped coming. And from 1949 until about 1954, ninety members from the Dresden Branch emigrated to America. That left a very big hole in the branch. They were all young people, too. That was the future of the branch, wasn't it?

G. Davis: So did you stay in Dresden?

Wilfriede: In 1982, I moved over here to Freiberg. That was an exchange between nine families. We moved to Freiberg, and they took our apartments in Heidenau. And I have been happy here in Freiberg.

I was visiting my daughter once, and she said, "Mother, do you know what is being whispered about? That we are going to have a temple here in Freiberg." I said, "That can't be true. It's the Party; it must be the Communist Party who is spreading that rumor." They always knew everything that was going on in the Church before we did. I worked in the mission office in Dresden for nine months as a secretary. So one day I said to Brother Schulze, "Now tell me, Brother Schulze, there is a rumor going around that a temple is going to be built in Freiberg. Is that true?" "We are going to build a chapel there," he said. He couldn't tell me the whole truth. But the rumor was true.

G. Davis: Maybe you could tell us a little about the programs and events you put on in Dresden.

Wilfriede: We had a centennial celebration of the Dresden Branch in 1955. That was quite an event. There was such a wonderful spirit there. When it was over, we didn't get up. Someone said from the podium, "Brothers and sisters, the meeting is over." But we didn't get up.

Earlier, about 1947, we had a big event with Brother Walter Stover. The whole meeting was held outdoors in the park behind the church building. We set out chairs. There was a fish pond there with fish in it. And way back—the park went way back then, and there was a fence around it—that's where we held our meeting. It was warm. I think the meetings lasted until nine thirty or ten o'clock. We had missionaries in those days, but all from inside the GDR. They came on their bicycles from all over and did missionary work on their way to Dresden. At night we slept out in the open. It was warm, very warm. That was in June or July. And we had just received a shipment of food from America, so we set up a cafeteria, and it was like a pilgrimage. We all got a plate with cooked wheat and milk mixed with peaches. Peaches in it! Oh, that was something wonderful. Many of us were nearly starved to death and to have something so wonderful to eat. Oh, my!

G. Davis: Do you have any favorite memories from your years in the Church?

Wilfriede: That is difficult to say. Favorite memories! There is a Sister Schibblack who works here in the temple, who used to live in Pirna. She would ride from Pirna to Heidenau on the train, and then we would ride together into the branch house in Dresden on the bus and then transfer to the streetcar. It took about two hours each way. Of course, there were times when we missed the bus home and would have to walk from Sedlitz to Heidenau, and then she would have to walk from Heidenau to Pirna. Today we tell one another how beautiful those times were. And they were beautiful. We stood there at the streetcar stop in the winter, freezing. Red tail lights—we had just missed the bus. Waiting. Half an hour. Freezing, freezing. And today we say how beautiful those times were.

N. Davis: Why do you say that?

Wilfriede: The common friendship and the Spirit.

N. Davis: What kind of problems did the women in the Church have when you were the Relief Society president?

Wilfriede: It was the hunger.

N. Davis: The hunger?

Wilfriede: Yes, the hunger. And the lack of clothing. But the Church helped us so much with these problems. Naturally, there were some jealousies. Some of the members thought everything should belong to them. Of course, I couldn't allow that. I can say with an honest heart that my counselors and I divided the things according to our best wisdom and with a clear conscience.

N. Davis: Were there many single women at that time?

Wilfriede: Oh, yes, there were a lot of single sisters. In the first place, there were always more single sisters in the branches than married sisters. In general, it seems, at least with us, that the men are less inclined to join the Church. Also, there were several brethren who had fallen in the war. And then there were several sisters who married out of the Church. Either they had to marry out of the Church or remain single. That's the way things are here, and it's the same today.

I am so thankful that I became a member of the Church. Whenever I say my prayers, I always remember my parents who were prepared to accept the Gospel. You have to remember that my father was an official, and it was quite unusual in those days to have an official in the Church. People used to point at him and say, "He is a Mormon. He goes to the Mormon Church."

Once, in 1945, my father had a lot of business with the Federal Railroad Headquarters in Dresden; he was on the phone, and in the middle of the telephone conversation another voice came over the line and shouted, "Mormon!" They never forgot it.

My father was baptized when it was about twenty below. There was ice on the river. They had to dry him off immediately so he wouldn't lose his skin. He just said, "If the Church is true, I will suffer no ill effects." He didn't even get the sniffles.

G. Davis: Did you experience any difficulties with the government because of your membership in the Church?

Wilfriede: For me, personally, no. Once I was coming home from Dresden on my bicycle late at night, about ten o'clock. We had received a shipment of food, and I was carrying it on the back of my bicycle. I didn't have a light on my bike. There weren't any. Whoever had one, had one. Whoever didn't, rode in the dark. Anyway, here came this voice out of the dark, "Halt! Get off your bike!"

I thought, "Oh, now they've got me for something."

"What have you got on the back of your bike?"

I said, "I'm a member of The Church of Jesus Christ of Latter-day Saints, and we have received a food shipment. The State knows all about it."

"Sure, sure," he said. "We'll just take that. If it's authorized, you'll get it back."

I said, "You know what?" I was a little more aggressive in those days, although generally I am quite shy. "I want to tell you something. If one can is missing . . . Everything there is authorized. The State already takes from our church 60 percent of all the food we receive, and everything we get for ourselves is authorized."

"Well, we'll check that out." Three days later, the Heidenau city officials or the police called and said I could come and pick up my rucksack. Not a thing was missing.

N. Davis: The State took 60 percent?

Wilfriede: Sixty percent. They kept more than half of what we received from America. The upper ten thousand got that, but we were helped with this arrangement. It was worth it. It came in boxcars, not only to Dresden, but to every branch.

G. Davis: It was President Benson who made all of this possible.

Wilfriede: He spoke to the Russians and told them that the Church wanted to send food and clothing to the GDR to help its members. He paved the way.

G. Davis: Were you there when President Kimball spoke in the church in Dresden?

Wilfriede: Oh, yes, I was there. He was scheduled to arrive at twelve, but the plane was delayed for a few hours. He had to be picked up in Berlin. Many of the members were already there by nine o'clock in the morning in order to get a good seat. We had to wait for such a long time. It was beautiful in spite of all that.

Part II

Rebuilding Zion

While serving as missionaries in Dresden, we received the following letter, dated October 10, 1989:

Dear Elder Davis,

Several weeks ago in Dresden, we were conversing about the history of the Church in the GDR, in particular about the old branch house in which you are now living. We agreed that too many of the experiences which ought to be preserved were in danger of being lost.

At that time, I mentioned that I was in the process of collecting and writing a few things as a CES project, and you expressed an interest in reading this material when it was completed. I am now finished, and I am enclosing a copy of this work for you to read. Perhaps it will be of interest to you even though you will not be familiar with the brothers and sisters discussed, nor with the places which lie outside the Dresden area. But much of what you find here is representative.

Keep it as long as you wish, and return it to me when you have an opportunity.

Greetings from a brother in the gospel,

[signed] Manfred Schütze

With the exception of "My Mission" by Käthe Würscher (which was translated from a manuscript given us by John W. Welch), all the material in part II, "Rebuilding Zion," is translated from the "few things" mentioned in the letter above. Manfred Schütze was at that time president of the Leipzig stake and director of the institute program for the Church Educational System. With his kind permission, I have translated this material and publish it here. The reader will recognize from the shifting between first and third person that President Schütze has combined commentary and journal entries.

All of the persons who report their experiences in this section are from the "war generation"; that is, they were old enough to have experienced the war and its immediate aftermath, including the consequent struggle to "rebuild Zion."

Inga and Manfred Schütze. Manfred Schütze collected most of the materials in part II. Courtesy Manfred Schütze.

5
If the Lord Needs Me, I'll Go
Walter Krause

Walter Krause has become a legend in his own lifetime. The reason for this will become clear to anyone who reads the stories in this book, where his name appears again and again. A faithful member of the Church his entire life, Brother Krause lives with his wife, Edith Schade Krause (see chapter 1), in Prenzlau and serves as patriarch of the Leipzig Stake. The following material was edited by Manfred Schütze and Norma Davis.

The name Walter Krause always comes up whenever the Saints talk about how they were reunited after the war. Many things would have been different or would not have come about at all, without his influence. As a young man, Walter Krause joined the Church against his parents' wishes. He was disinherited and had to leave his home. An active member of the Church from that moment on, Brother Krause was a soldier during the war and ended that service as a prisoner of war. He was released on July 2, 1945, from a POW camp near Cottbus, a town on the Polish-German border. The country was in shambles. Two refugee camps, one in the Erz Mountains on the western border of the occupied area and the other in Cottbus on the east, were crowded with people who had been uprooted by the war and had left their homes with little more than what was on their backs. Homeless like the others, Brother Krause and his family lived in the refugee camp in Cottbus and began to attend church there. He was immediately called to lead the Cottbus Branch of the Church.

Four months later, in November of 1945, District President Richard Ranglack came to Brother Krause and asked him what he would think about going on a mission for the Church. Brother Krause's

Walter Krause. Courtesy Manfred Schütze.

answer reflects his commitment to the Church: "I don't have to think about it at all. If the Lord needs me, I'll go." Brother Krause described the beginning of that mission as follows:

> I prayed about it and then set out on the first of December 1945, with twenty marks in my pocket, a piece of dry bread, and a bottle of tea. One brother had given me a winter coat left over from a son who had fallen in the war. Another brother, who was a shoemaker, gave me a pair of shoes. So, [with these and] with two shirts, two handkerchiefs, and two pairs of stockings, I left on my mission.

He was sent first to Leipzig, armed only with the information that the branch met on Tauchaer Street and that Elder Alfred Kirchert was serving as branch president. He had been told to go to the house of a member who lived on Kreutz Strasse [Crossing Road]:

> When I came out of the train station, there was a policewoman standing at the corner directing the traffic. I went up to her and said, "Could you please tell me where Crossing Road is?" "At the next crossing," she answered. I liked the humor of her answer and haven't forgotten it to this day.

He was disappointed when he finally located Crossing Road and found the brother he was supposed to meet. The man was full of advice and instructions, but he apparently had no idea what the duties of a missionary should be. Elder Krause was wise enough to recognize this and to realize that this brother had no authority over him.

> So I took my leave of him after asking where other members of the Church lived. He sent me out to Wahren, to the Naegler family. I made my way there and arrived in the late afternoon. The members were happy to see me. There was a cottage meeting set up for that evening, and I was happy to participate. At the meeting, I found the spirit that was absolutely necessary for me to have before I could be fruitful in the work of the Lord. Sister Beyer took me in, so I finally had a place to stay.

However, he had little time to work in Leipzig and to become acquainted with the members there, since within a few days his assignment was changed to Naumburg. This was the branch closest to the one in Leipzig, and it was in the same district under the direction of another full-time missionary who served as district president.

> In January 1946, I came back to Leipzig, and Sunday I went to the meetings. The place where they met was unfriendly and cold. The war had just ended, and the members were not in the best condition, physically and emotionally. I sensed that there was a lot of fighting among them. They were accusing one another of things that had happened years ago. So I invited them to come on another day for an open discussion.

Brother Krause had been told to bring order to the branch. Rather than disrupt the spirit that is supposed to attend Sunday worship, he promised them a chance to air their complaints at another time. When the appointed time came, he asked each person to express his or her feelings. He listened patiently to all they had to say, silently pleading with the Lord for his Spirit so he could really help the people.

> Just before the close of the meeting, I said something like the following: My dear sisters and brothers, I have just now gotten acquainted with you. If I am to believe everything that I have heard here today, then no one is right, and nothing is in order. But perhaps I can help you out with a few verses from the poet Endrikat. Then I quoted the following poem:
>
> > An oxen went before a wagon
> > Loaded with manure and full.
> > He complained to all and sundry,
> > That it was too much to pull.
> >
> > Then the people all around him
> > Said he had no right to moan
> > If the load seemed double heavy,
> > The manure was his own.
> >
> > He with patience had to bear it
> > When the people did recall,
> > If he made so much manure,
> > Whose fault was it, after all?
>
> My final words were, "Why are you Leipzigers making so much manure?" This surprised them. A few smiled or snickered, some frowned and cleared their throats and started to grumble, but seeing that they were outnumbered, they kept quiet. As it turned out, they all began to examine themselves, and this little satirical poem helped them see their problem more clearly. It did its job with humor, without attacking anyone personally. With a few exceptions, peace was restored again.

Within a few months after he came to Leipzig, Brother Krause was transferred to the north, to the province of Mecklenburg. He began to gather the Saints together into branches in Demmin, Wolgast, Neubrandenburg, and Prenzlau. Few railroad lines were left undamaged, so he had to walk from one town to the next, depending on the Lord to lead him to the homes of the members. The distance between the meeting places of the Saints was often as much as fifty kilometers. He often had to walk twelve or thirteen hours to reach them. He would start early in the morning from Demmin and wouldn't get to his destination in Wolgast until three o'clock the next morning. For over a year, he traveled and worked alone without a missionary companion. He now looks back on the time as one of pure blessings:

> Once, in the middle of the winter, I walked from Prenzlau to Kamin (a little village in Mecklenburg), where we had up to forty-six members at our meetings. I arrived long after dark that night after a six-hour march over roads, paths, and finally across plowed fields. Just before I reached the village, I came to a large, white, flat area which made easy walking, and I soon arrived. The next morning the game warden came to the house of the member where I had spent the night. "Do you have a guest?" "Yes." "Then come and take a look at his tracks." Some time earlier, the warden had chopped a large hole in the middle of the lake for fishing. [The large flat area Brother Krause had crossed was actually a frozen lake.] The wind had driven snow over the hole and covered it so that I could not have seen my danger. My tracks went right across the edge of the hole and straight to the house of this brother, without my knowing anything about it. Weighed down by my backpack and my rubber boots, I would certainly have drowned. This event caused quite a little stir in the village at that time.

Few can imagine the difficulties the Saints faced. The Russians were struggling to gain control of a country that had been left in ruins. There weren't enough buildings left standing to shelter those who had survived the war or the soldiers returning from prisoner-of-war camps and from the battlefields. In addition, refugees from Poland were flooding westward in hopes of finding conditions better in Germany. Transportation was nearly nonexistent; food and clothing were scarce. Few people had work. Often they would be conscripted to clean and rebuild without receiving pay.

Within a relatively short period of time, Brother Krause organized eight branches in the Mecklenburg area. He helped the members purchase land for buildings, often supervising more than one building project at a time. He organized the youth and planned youth conferences so they could come together and strengthen one another's faith through friendship and testimony. More than one hundred young people gathered at those first conferences.

While he was away, his family lived in the refugee camp, and he had no source of financial support. He had to rely on the members he found to take him in and share their meager supplies with him. "I just lived from what the members had to offer me." Still he considers this time spiritually rewarding:

> My testimony was greatly strengthened at the baptism of a sister who now lives in West Germany. She had instructions from a doctor that because of her ears she was never to go into cold water. The day of her baptism was cold—ice and snow. I was in the water six times to baptize people, including this sister. There were no health problems; no one even got the sniffles.

Eventually, Elder Walter Krause was released, and he went home to build up his own family and the Church. In the 1960s, he was made a counselor in the mission presidency, and in 1973 the GDR government allowed him to attend general conference in Salt Lake City. There he was set apart by President Spencer W. Kimball to serve as patriarch to the mission.

June 15, 1969, in Dresden founding the Dresden Mission with GDR brethren as mission leaders. *Back row:* Elder Thomas S. Monson, Stanley Rees (former Hamburg Mission president), Henry Burkhardt (new mission president), Percy R. Fetzer (patriarch), Gottfried Richter (second counselor), and Walter Krause (first counselor). *Front row:* Helen Rees, Inge Burkhardt, Thelma Fetzer, and Edith Krause. Courtesy Edith Krause.

After all he had experienced—the war, the prison camp, the refugee camp, the long and strenuous mission, and his continued efforts over the following thirty years or more—his health was failing, and he felt such a calling to be nearly impossible. He told President Kimball, "You are ordaining a deathly ill man." President Kimball answered, "You will yet give blessings to thousands." This statement was truly prophetic. By 1989, at the age of eighty-one, Brother Krause was within two dozen blessings of reaching his first thousand. Undoubtedly he has passed that goal by now [1994]. He has enjoyed good health, continued to serve the Lord wherever he has been called, and has often been across the Atlantic to attend conferences and speak to members of the Church in Utah. He was among those who stood with President Thomas S. Monson on the hill outside Dresden to rededicate the GDR to the work of the Lord, and he was present when the government gave the Church permission to build a temple in what was then East Germany.

Walter Krause writes:

> When I look back, I have to say over and over again, it is a good thing we have a kind, merciful, and just God. His kindness and mercy is closest to my heart, because if I were to be judged according to the strictness of every work, then I would be in trouble.

Manfred Schütze summarizes Brother Krause's life in these words:

> For many decades, Brother Krause has been an example of faith and strength to all the members. Today he is still a man of God to whom many turn for help with their problems or when they need counsel. They are certain to find understanding and to receive an inspired answer.

The First Conference

Now we had another mountain of rubble and stones in our large assembly room. There was nothing to do but to unite, get out the rubble, and go on. So we went to work. Sisters who were fifty or sixty years old carried out huge blocks of stone weighing forty to fifty kilograms [twenty to twenty-five pounds].

An even more difficult task lay ahead for the members. They had to replace the missing roof over the hall. They managed somehow to get the materials to do it. Even more difficult was the work it demanded of the small group:

> We had to get four heavy iron beams up to support the adjoining wall. Each of these beams weighed 400 kilograms [about 200 pounds]! And we had to do it with our own inexperienced efforts. The job seemed enormous, but as usual we began by laying it before the Lord in prayer. Every evening before we went home exhausted, we met together and sang a hymn. We believed that the songs of Zion had never been sung more effectively than we sang as we finished our work late at night. It was in this spirit that the brothers and sisters prepared themselves to get those heavy beams up by themselves.

These beams were moved into the building and lifted onto the pillars through the efforts of eight women, two deacons, and two older brethren. Sister Edith Krause says that there was an iron monger there to supervise the work. They got the beams into the hall by putting one on rollers, moving it slowly forward, then taking the roller from the back and putting it ahead of the beam so that it could pass over the rollers again. She doesn't say how they got it up the stairs in the first place. They managed to place the first two beams and were working on the third when, as Brother Krause writes,

> a young deacon was supposed to remove one of the rollers from underneath the beam. Just as he grabbed hold of the roller, the brothers and sisters gave out and the whole weight of the beam, 400 kilograms, rolled right over his hand. We were all terrified at his painful scream, but we quickly lifted the beam so that he could pull out his hand. A missionary immediately took his wounded hand and said, "Come on, brother; everything will be all right. You will not have any damage from this." The two went into the priesthood room and looked at the hand. There was a little blood, but the elder promised him that he would not loose so much as a fingernail and that he would heal perfectly.

This almost unbelievable promise actually came true. Within a short time our young brother was helping again—carrying tiles and shaking hands. There was a man who was not a member of the Church present, and he was quite shaken by this experience. The next day the construction engineer came by on some building business. While looking over the construction, he said, "One can truly say that the blessings of God are with these people and their work." The members heard these words and were very much moved by this confirmation from an outsider.

With the help of God, work which seemed impossible was completed. And it was done with joy and harmony, something possible only to children of God. The greatest testimony and proof that we were working with the Lord was our spirit of harmony and unity during those weeks. Very often our daily ration of food for this heavy work was just 100 grams of bread [about one fourth of a pound, or four slices of good, thick bread] and a few potatoes. When we finished, we all fasted for a successful conference. We felt it a great blessing that here in this destroyed city we could now occupy these wonderful rooms.

Interior of the Dresden Chapel on Dr.-Kurt-Fischer Allee. Courtesy Manfred Heller.

Meanwhile, the conference had to be organized. Apparently, the Russian occupational government did not exercise heavy control over them at this time.

> This morning, Monday the 29th of April 1946, posters with an invitation to attend a great district conference of The Church of Jesus Christ of Latter-day Saints appeared on 420 bulletin boards throughout the city. They announced the general themes of the conference: "The Purpose of Man on the Earth," "A God Who Speaks," and "The Return of Christ." The people of the city also found flyers inviting them to our conference when they got into the streetcars. This was the beginning of a program to bring the people of the city of Dresden the clear message of the true gospel once again. For many years, we had been terribly restricted and suppressed in this city because of the political climate [under Nazi rule]. As evidence that our posters and flyers did not fail to make an impact, there were 750 persons in attendance at the morning session of Sunday School and 780 at the general session.

Brother Krause does not indicate how many of these people were members of the Church and how many were curious visitors. Certainly, the message proposed by the flyers and posters, coming just a year and three months after the devastating bombing of Dresden, must have seemed amazing to the people of the city.

> Our members and investigators were overjoyed. . . . One could see the happiness in their eyes because once again they could publicly announce the message Mormonism had for this city and for the world. Our motto, "Ye shall know the truth, and the truth shall make you free," had become a veritable symbol for all of the members in the recent days and months because we of this city had only one desire—to be free to speak to the inhabitants concerning the truths of the gospel.

The conference was prefaced with a leadership and teacher training session at four o'clock. They began by singing an old German hymn not found in the English edition of the LDS hymnbook. It can still be found in the German edition:

> *Mutig, ihr Brüder, im Kampfe*
> *Wehet die Fahne ja noch!*
> *Ob es auch brause und dampfe,*
> *Siegen, das müssen wir doch.*

Zion soll herrlicher grünen,
Ist es ja treulich gepflegt.
Das werden Völker noch rühmen,
Da keine Ahnung sich regt.

Schelten auch feindliche Zungen,
Welche nur Gutes entweihn:
Wisst, noch ist's keinem gelungen,
Jedem ein Liebling zu sein.

Gutes und Edles zu schaffen
Lohnet die härtesten Mühn,
Lasset uns nimmer erschlaffen
Niemals der Pflicht uns entziehn.

Chor:
Auf, frisch auf! Es muss gelingen,
Schöner lichtet sich die Bahn!
Der geheissen, hilft vollbringen,
Trauet ihm, der walten kann.

[Courage, brethren, in the battle
The banner yet waves!
Regardless of how furious it rages,
Victory must be ours.

Zion shall blossom as a field
If she is faithfully tended.
People yet unaware
Shall praise her.

And should enemies' tongues mock,
And desecrate that which is good:
Know this, none has ever succeeded
Who tries to please everyone.

Good and noble work is the reward
Of the most strenuous efforts,
Let us never slacken,
Never fail in our duty.

Chorus:
So, to work! It will succeed,
Our path is bright before us!
Put your trust in him who reigns,
He will help us accomplish our task.]

Walter Krause reported that as they sang this beautiful hymn, "there were many eyes wet with tears of gratitude and joy and one could see how deeply our brothers and sisters were moved that now we could say that with the help of the Lord we had finally done it."

City officials and many investigators came to the Sunday morning session, which was given in the form of a dramatic presentation by the Sunday School. By the time the general session was to begin, the newly restored hall was filled beyond its capacity. The choir was placed in the balcony and could not be seen by the congregation in the hall below. Brother Krause reports that during the congregational singing this placement "had a marvelous effect as if the angels of the Lord were singing with them." Messages of hope were given by a people who were suffering from loss and need. They were given to visitors and members who had little to eat and were living in less than adequate conditions. The people of Dresden were still struggling to clean the rubble of the once beautiful city on the banks of the broad Elbe River. Here they sat in the casino which, until recently, had been used by the Nazi soldiers and only eight weeks ago was nothing more than a bombed-out shell. Now they looked around a hall which had been restored by a handful of people to a state which few buildings, if any, in Dresden could boast. Above them a choir sang messages of hope and joy. No wonder Brother Krause remembers the enthusiasm of the visitors:

> Many appointments were made for the missionaries to visit these people in their homes, and there were many requests for copies of the Book of Mormon. Unfortunately, we did not have enough on hand. We could have easily used a thousand copies of the Book of Mormon. The request for Church literature by the investigators was so strong that it was apparent that their greatest happiness this Sunday would have been to possess a Book of Mormon.

The conference was followed by a district missionary conference. Because the enthusiasm and dedication of these missionaries was so strong, the meeting which began at eight in the morning was regretfully ended at two that afternoon. No one wanted to break away from the strength, peace, and security of the conference to return to the chaos of their everyday world. That evening the Mutual Improvement Association presented some entertainment followed by a dance. The members were reminded of the spiritual and social joy made possible through the Church's programs which they had experienced in the past. Those who were visitors must have recognized the vast contrast between what Brother Krause describes as the "dignified and virtuous" atmosphere of this evening and the previous gambling and dancing this hall had witnessed. The principal accomplishment of the conference was to strengthen and encourage the weary members.

When we sang the last song, we all had the feeling this was not the end of the conference, but only the beginning—that the conference would continue to live in our prayers and in our hearts. This feeling continued with us as we said farewell to one another at the train station with more singing. I believe it could be said that the Dresden train station had never experienced such beautiful singing throughout the terrible war or in the great confusion following the destruction of the city. So we had a joyful parting as the last members boarded the trains for their homes in Cottbus, Leipzig, and Naumburg.

The people standing about were amazed and asked, "Who are these people?" Our missionaries could answer, "We are Mormons. People with the same ration cards you have, but we are happy, very happy." And we could enthusiastically sing at the train station, "I might be envied by a king, for I am a Mormon boy." This was the most beautiful payment of fulfillment and satisfaction for the members of the Dresden Branch for all their sorrow and heavy labor.

7

Odyssey to Find a Chapel

Elli Polzin
Edited by Manfred Schütze

There was no branch of The Church of Jesus Christ of Latter-day Saints in Schwerin, Mecklenburg, before 1945. Toward the end of 1945 or early in 1946, a branch was founded consisting of members who had arrived there as refugees. Sister Elli Polzin (seventy-three years old in 1989) remembers the early years:

> I arrived in Schwerin with our children and my mother from Stettin in February 1946. We stayed first near Ludwigslust, about twenty-three kilometers from Schwerin. My husband was in a POW camp. Along with another member family, we turned for advice to the mission headquarters in Berlin. As a result of that, one day two missionaries arrived to help us get in contact with the Church again. One of them was Brother Walter Böhme from Groitzsch. They encouraged us to move to Schwerin, where there was a branch of the Church. I found work there as a secretary in the city hall, and after much difficulty, I was able to move my family to Schwerin. For years we lived there in a single room until we received an apartment. My husband returned from prison in December 1949, one day before Christmas Eve.
>
> We were happy to find a branch of the Church there. Our first meeting place was a rented room on the square called Pig Market *[Schweinemarkt]*. The first members were old Brother and Sister Meyer from Königsberg and Sister Christel Kowitz and her husband. Brother Walter Schmeichel, a refugee from Schneidemühl in Pommern, was our branch president until 1952. By that time, we had exchanged our meeting place for one on Schloss

Street. My husband was now the branch president, and the branch had to move again, this time to a place on Bornhöwitz Street. But we weren't able to keep this for long, and the branch leaders had to start looking for something else. We rented rooms in a restaurant on Goethe Street. At the Church's expense, we had to remodel them to fit our needs. After two years, this restaurant was taken over by the government, and we were obliged to give up our rooms once again. This time we were without any meeting place for more than a year and had to hold our meetings at the home of Brother and Sister Schüller, who made their living room available to us.

Following the advice of the district president, Brother Walter Krause, we tried to buy a piece of property for the Church. After many attempts, we succeeded in 1956 in buying a piece of property from a private owner on the Schlossgarten Allee, number 18a. Since the Church was not allowed to own property, it was bought in the name of the branch president, my husband, Brother Hans Polzin. Naturally, this caused a multitude of problems. On the property was an old business establishment which had one apartment and an old horse barn. When we bought the property, we intended to tear down the old building. But the application to tear down the building was denied because it contained an apartment with a family living in it. Our plan was to build a chapel on the property.

An account from the branch history of the time gives some details about this project:

> Toward the end of 1956, the branch acquired an old workers' barracks, 12 meters x 20 meters, which we could tear down for material to build a new chapel so that we could finally have our own place to meet. On June 11, 1957, the work of tearing down the old barracks began. In a pouring rain, all the brethren set out on their bicycles for the barracks, which was about eight kilometers out of Schwerin. The work was under the direction of our district president, Brother Krause, and of Brother Wiese from Wolgast, whom he had brought along to assist us. The brethren all assembled for prayer to ask the Lord for protection and help.
>
> With the help of all the members of the Schwerin Branch, we put in an average of twelve to fifteen hours a day. Brother Krause and Brother Wiese stayed at the site at night in a tent. The sisters were also active. A meal for the working brethren was prepared in Schwerin and was taken out to the work site on a bicycle by Sister Edith Schade. All together we hauled twenty-three truckloads of material to our building site in Schwerin. On Saturday, June 15, 1957, this difficult and dangerous work was completed

without accident through the help of the Lord. Now all the members assembled at the building site in Schwerin to clean up and stack the building material.

On June 25, 1957, the branch presidency submitted their request for permission to build the branch house, indicating that they already owned the property and already had the necessary building material. In order to solve the problem of the apartment on the property, Brother Polzin offered the following proposal. Behind the branch house, they would erect a small building about thirty-five to forty square meters (one and one-half

Hans Polzin, branch president. Courtesy Manfred Schütze.

rooms with kitchen). This building would eventually become a little garden house, and Brother Polzin would live in the house himself, temporarily, until a new apartment could be constructed. In the meantime, while tearing down the old building, he would give the renter his own apartment on Geschwister-Scholl Street; that is, there would be an exchange of apartments.

Unfortunately, this application was denied by the authorities. Consequently, the members turned to the local government officials with the request that they be permitted to remodel the horse barn into a meeting place. The branch record from this time contains the following entry:

> All of the members and the district presidency fasted and prayed that this request would be granted, and it was granted.
>
> Since the horse barn was old and falling apart there were many difficulties to be overcome. We laid up blocks for new walls and a new chimney and built door and window frames. A new toilet including drain pipes and water connections had to be installed; we paneled walls and ceilings, brought in floor joists, and laid a new floor. Two new stoves for heating were installed. Most of the material came from what was salvaged from the barracks.
>
> The property itself was terribly overgrown and in a wild state and had to be completely redone. We planted hedges and landscaped. With the exception of some specialty work, the brothers

Everyone pitching in. This scene is typical of the times the Saints, such as those in Schwerin, built or remodeled meetinghouses through their own labor and minimal equipment. Pictured are the members in Wolgast building a branch house after the uprising of June 17, 1953. Courtesy Edith Krause.

and sisters of the branch did everything themselves. The work on the branch house took up nearly all of their free time as well as all of the money they could possibly spare.

It was not so easy to get the necessary building supplies such as cement, drain pipe, window frames, etc., since all of these things were controlled by the state building authorities. But it was all done with the help of the Lord, and things that often seemed impossible were made possible, which greatly strengthened our testimonies. So our own branch house approached completion toward the end of 1957. The chapel was thirty-two square meters large, and there was an adjoining room for the MIA and Relief Society. It also had a tiled toilet and a room with a washbasin that also served temporarily as a coatroom. We planned to add an entry later which would contain a coatroom.

To tear down the old building and build a new branch house, the members of the Schwerin branch put in 3,800 hours of voluntary labor and contributed 2,800 German marks in cash, which was a considerable amount for approximately thirty active members.

On January 5, the first Sunday of 1958, the branch house was dedicated under the direction of a counselor to the mission president, Brother Henry Burkhardt, and the district president, Brother Walter Krause. Brother Burkhardt gave the dedicatory prayer. In the fast and testimony meeting, all the members expressed their gratitude that they now, finally, had their own branch house. In the afternoon, they held an impressive service with many investigators present.

But their difficulties were not yet over. Because of some jealousy between the county and the city officials over the legality of the building permit, the branch house was closed for a period of time, new fees were assessed, and Brother Polzin was fined a penalty of 500 marks. When he appealed, the fine was reduced to 200 marks. Continuing from the branch record, we read:

> Now, finally, the branch had their own home. The rooms were sufficient for about a year, but as the branch grew, the rooms were soon too small to carry out all of the Church programs. In 1963, Brother Pawlowski was called as branch president. Since he was a construction worker, he had, in the intervening years, been able to do a lot of work on the building. In 1973 the brethren received permission from the mission to add a room made of prefabricated

Schwerin Branch meetinghouse. Using a wheelbarrow as a delivery truck and the hand labor of all the members, the Schwerin Branch converted an old barn into a meetinghouse. Courtesy Edith Krause.

material. These prefabricated sections were to be delivered from Dresden, but for various reasons, the delivery was delayed. In the meantime, Brother Pawlowski went to one of the building commissioners, Werner Herbert, who was also associated with the Evangelical Church, where Brother Pawlowski had been employed as a construction hand. Mr. Herbert advised him to give up the idea of the prefabricated plates, and since he liked Brother Pawlowski and the Church, he obtained for the Church in the name of the Evangelical Church a commission for 4,000 building stones from the city building authorities. Brother Pawlowski was able to get an additional 2,000 bricks privately from a citizen's commission for people's building needs; thus we could begin a massive building expansion for another room measuring fifty square meters. The members all volunteered gladly for organized work parties, so the work could begin right away.

By the summer of 1974, the new branch room could be handed over to the branch in a small dedicatory service presided over by district president, Brother Gerd Skibbe. There was great joy among the members. We soon acquired a new electric organ, and everyone was happy to donate their share.

Of course, the building had not all gone as smoothly as it sounds in these few words. There were a number of problems getting the building materials. Those who participated in this had many unusual experiences in which they felt the hand of the Lord to a special degree.

The city building commission had openly given permission to build because the branch would not have to request building materials. That would have been the case had they built with the prefabricated sections that were to have been provided by the mission. Now, however, they needed cement, lime, gravel, and lumber, all of which could be obtained only from the Commission for People's Needs *[Bevölkerungsbedarf]*. That meant that the branch president, Brother Pawlowski, had to pick up everything in small quantities by standing in line and by carrying it off in a wheelbarrow. He could not do this himself since he was working. Because all the other brethren in the branch were also working, the branch president's wife, Sister Elfriede Pawlowski, said she would take charge of getting the building materials. Always, everyday, the material was there when it was needed.

During this time, Brother and Sister Pawlowski found little time to spend with one another or to do anything with the family, but since Sister Pawlowski worked with her husband everyday or brought his meals to the building site, this did not seem to be such a big problem. When he returned home from his normal work and had refreshed himself, there stood the wheelbarrow full of building material, and they set off together to go to work at the Schlossgarten Allee.

Sister Pawlowski's family doctor, who also lived on the Schlossgarten Allee and who had seen her going by several times, stopped her one day and asked her how long she thought she could continue this manual labor, and he admonished her to ease off. But both Brother and Sister Pawlowski were well aware that their strength came from a higher doctor, and this doctor received their thanks many times daily.

After the addition to the branch house was completed, they wanted to remodel the old building still standing on the property and begin landscaping. But before that could be done, two large chestnut trees had to be taken down and cut up into wood.

In the old building, there lived a family who did not belong to the Church and who were, in fact, not particularly friendly to the Church. Brother and Sister Pawlowski made an agreement with this family to exchange apartments. This took place in April 1976. This exchange of apartments was an advantage to the branch and a great relief to Brother and Sister Pawlowski because it saved them the daily travel to the branch house. But the apartment was in terrible condition. The doors and windows had to be replaced. Brother and Sister Pawlowski spent eight days sleeping on a mattress in the branch house and living in one room so they could move in little by little. After the construction work on the apartment was finished, the young women in the branch went to work diligently cleaning the rooms, and in three weeks the move was completed.

Walter Krause, now the mission counselor who was responsible for buildings in the Church, came by a few times to see how things were going and to give advice. One time he commented on the solid work that was going on and said that Schwerin was the only branch that was doing things right without his personal intervention. He was overburdened with building matters in other branches.

A building project requires many crafts and skills. It was certainly a blessing from heaven that there was one man in the branch who had all of these skills. This was also well understood by Brother Pawlowski and prayer was his constant support. The joy at seeing the progress day by day gave him the strength, courage, and enthusiasm to continue.

It was truly a relief that Sister Pawlowski was now living in the branch house so that she could accomplish something every evening. Everyone was learning, and Sister Pawlowski often mentioned that in these years she had become a carpenter.

The work progressed, and there was always talk about which improvements were necessary. A larger room was erected on the grounds for housing overnight guests. Every summer brothers and sisters from other branches come to spend their vacations here. The beautiful location and the large plot of ground are very conducive to this purpose.

Since 1977 the building has been in the name of the Church. As mentioned earlier, Brother Hans Polzin, who was branch president when the property was first bought, was the legal owner. Although they had often tried to change this, again and again the government raised legal objections to naming the Church as the legal owner. It took about ten years to bring this change about.

Once in 1961, on a private trip to Hamburg, Brother Polzin was encouraged to remain in the West. He mentioned his responsibility for the property of the Church in East Germany, which property was worth about nine thousand marks. One of the brothers who was there replied, "The door alone to the Hamburg Stake House is worth that much." Obviously, he could not understand that Brother Polzin's responsibility went beyond the material value of the property. Brother Polzin still says today, "What terrible harm that would have been to the Church." Not only would the property have been lost, but it would also have greatly harmed the Church's reputation.

Brother Pawlowski had been branch president in Schwerin for sixteen years and was able to complete all the building before, in his seventy-first year in 1979, he was released. But his help and advice were needed still. Since he was living in the branch house, he took care to see that no damage occurred.

How thankful we are that there were such brothers and sisters as the Polzins and the Pawlowskis in those days. Looking back, Brother Polzin says, "We risked many things in order to help the Church make progress, but the Lord was with us. We had no serious difficulties. In all of our problems there was always a good spirit of cooperation and love."

8

If God Is for Us, Who Can Be against Us?

Elfriede Pawlowski

I first heard of the truth of the restored gospel from Sister Ida Korth in Schwerin, Mecklenburg. During a visit, she told me of the First Vision, the Prophet Joseph Smith and his calling to be a prophet, the Angel Moroni, the Book of Mormon, and the restoration of the true Church of Christ. She told me about the "last days," in which we are now living, and the necessity for all people to repent. Her words were so lively and convincing that I did not doubt for a moment that these things were true.

This was on a cold Sunday in February, and because I was so interested, she invited me to attend a church service that very afternoon. I hesitated for a moment, thinking of another event I wanted to attend, but then I went with her to the church service.

It was very cold, and the simple room in the tavern where we held sacrament meeting at that time was not terribly inviting, but the friendliness with which I was welcomed by the members made a great impression on me. Although everything was so different, I was very taken by the procedures as far as I could observe them in my first sacrament meeting.

The two elders, Franz Meyer and Walter Schmeichel, spoke with great conviction, and it seemed to me as if I had heard this all sometime once before. I felt so insignificant and imperfect that tear after tear ran down my face. I was so impressed by all I had heard that I thought about it all the way home, and when I arrived home, I immediately had to discuss this experience with some friends.

I visited sacrament meeting as often as I could, and I began to learn. Among other things, I learned that alongside the good there was an evil power and that this power was doing everything possible to prevent me from accepting this newly found gospel. Every time I sat in a sacrament meeting to listen and to learn, there seemed to be an unknown power trying to hinder me. I could actually feel it, and it was frightening.

Sister and Brother Pawlowski. Courtesy Manfred Schütze.

A few months later, in 1953, our newly called counselor in the mission, Henry Burkhardt, visited our branch for the first time. Once again I was overcome by this strange power which I could not explain. I fought against it with all my strength, and I prayed fervently that the Lord would free me from this power so I could understand the gospel and in particular so I could follow the words of Brother Burkhardt. Then something happened that I will never forget. A new skin almost seemed to be drawn over me. It began with the top of my head and went down over my shoulders and over my entire body right down to the tips of my toes. At first, I was somewhat frightened, but a feeling of freedom came over me, a lightness, and a deep feeling of gratitude, which I cannot express in words. The Lord had heard my prayer and had given me a witness of his help and his nearness. From that moment on, I had no more problems concentrating, and I felt joy in understanding and learning the gospel.

On October 22, I made a covenant [of baptism] with my Father in Heaven, and I was happy that I had before that time been able to overcome many things and set many things in order which had been a hindrance to me. As an investigator, I had already borne my testimony in a testimony meeting, but on the day of my baptism at an MIA meeting which followed, I was able to pray before the entire branch. That experience filled me with great joy.

Because the rooms in which we held church meetings were not very satisfactory and because we were often disturbed in an unpleasant way by the people in the tavern, our branch presidency, under the leadership of Brother Hans Polzin, began a diligent search for another meeting place. In 1954 we were able to rent a room in a hotel at 64 Goethe Street. It was at the back of the hotel, and we could not hear the noise from the street or from the bar. We went through a great deal of trouble to arrange the room for our purposes, and everyone helped. The branch was not obliged to share this room with anyone else, and everyone was happy to have found a peaceful place where we could hold our church services undisturbed. Activity in the branch increased, and the auxiliary organizations could hold their meetings at the normal times. It was a time of activity and progress in the branch.

Through a series of fortuitous circumstances, I was able to get a little two-room apartment at the front of the same building just shortly after the branch moved into the room on Goethe Street. From that time on, my life was closely tied to the life of the branch. Unfortunately, this joy over our new meeting place was not to last for long. After about three years, a new problem emerged for the branch.

The daughter of the woman who owned the hotel and tavern wanted to get married, and in those postwar days, she could not get an apartment. Consequently, the owner wanted the branch room back so she could have it remodeled into an apartment for her daughter. All of the members were very distressed, and the branch presidency had several conversations with her to find another solution. So the owner offered us the following exchange: if I would give up my little two-room apartment, with kitchen, on the third floor and move into a basement apartment just beneath the area where the branch met, she would let us continue to use the back room.

As a new member of the Church, that was not an easy decision for me. The basement rooms were dark and damp, and I had to think about my thirteen-year-old son for whom it would also be difficult. But I knew how much the branch needed this room, so I agreed to the exchange. Everything was promised, and the arrangements were made, even though several members could not understand my decision. But I had promised and was determined not to go back on my word in the firm conviction that my Father in Heaven would prepare another apartment for me.

When our branch president, Hans Polzin, announced this in a sacrament meeting, he said that our Father in Heaven would accept my sacrifice and that this decision should go down in our branch history. But I did not see it as a sacrifice myself. In my heart, I was happy that through this little deed I was able to thank the Lord for his help.

Our Father in Heaven must have considered my determination to go through with this exchange to be sufficient, because, before the move took place, the young bride and groom one foggy night escaped across the border into Hamburg. So the problem was solved, and I could stay in my apartment. Everyone was happy that it had turned out this way and that I did not have to move into the basement apartment. For me it was once again proof of the love the Lord had for me.

9

The Story of
My Patriarchal Blessing

Elfriede Pawlowski

When our counselor in the mission presidency, Brother Walter Krause, returned from a trip to general conference in Salt Lake City and it became known that he had been called to be a patriarch for the Dresden Mission, we were all very moved and thankful. We learned about his calling while we were holding our spring conference in 1973 in Neubrandenburg. The news went from mouth to mouth even before it was officially announced.

Very few of us knew anything about the significance of a patriarchal blessing because very few had ever received one from the visiting patriarchs. But now this possibility was open to all of us, and the joy we had was great. The members talked with one another about it, and we were instructed to make arrangements for a patriarchal blessing through our branch presidents. My husband had already received his blessing on March 25, 1973, in Dresden from Brother Percy Fetzer, and since my husband was branch president in Schwerin at the time, my greatest desire was to receive my blessing also.

Just as I had the previous year, I was participating in the annual genealogical week in Dresden at which Brother Krause was also present. He announced that at the close of this genealogical work week, he would give his first blessings. I was sure there was a long list of persons desiring a blessing, and I hoped in my heart that I could be one of them. He and I were both from Mecklenburg, and he had been our district president for many years. When Walter Krause came up to me the day before and told me that I would be the first person to whom he would

Members participating in Genealogy Week in Dresden, June 1973. It was during this week that Elfriede Pawlowski (probably second from the left on the third row) received her patriarchal blessing from Walter Krause (front row, far right). Edith Krause is on the third row, third from the left. Courtesy Edith Krause.

give a blessing, I was overcome with an indescribable feeling of gratitude, but I did not yet suspect that this day would turn out to be one that would bring a special testimony. During a short conversation, he told me that the appointed time was Saturday, June 22, at ten o'clock.

It was a beautiful summer morning, and I wanted to prepare myself spiritually so that I would be in harmony with the Spirit of the Lord. I had fasted and prayed, and I wanted to be alone, but since there was so much activity going on at the branch meeting place, in connection with the work week, I went into the woods across from the chapel. I thought about the Prophet Joseph Smith, who had also gone into the woods to pray for a special reason. It was very quiet, and there were no other people there. I found a suitable place to kneel and poured out my heart to the Lord. I asked him for his forgiveness and prayed for worthiness to receive the patriarchal blessing.

After my prayer, I felt very happy and I had a feeling of peace in my heart. I sat for a while on a bench and could not hold back my tears.

A verse of a song came into my mind: "Thy walk today with me Has made my heart within me burn as I communed with thee" ["Abide with Me; 'Tis Eventide," hymn no. 165]. I will never forget for as long as I live this blessed moment when I felt the peace of the Lord in my heart in such abundance. The only sound was the singing of the birds.

I still had plenty of time, but when I looked at my watch, I had the feeling that I should leave the woods and go back to the branch meeting place. I went back, but I didn't know why. I really didn't want to talk to anyone before I received my blessing, so I couldn't understand why I went back, but the feeling that I should go back became stronger and stronger. When I reached the steps of the building, Sister Edith Krause, the secretary to the patriarch, came hurrying up to me and said, "I was just going out to look for you. Come with me. My husband wants to begin with your blessing right now."

I was very surprised and wondered if that was the reason I felt I should return from the woods sooner than I had planned, but I had no time to think about it then because I had something more important to do at that moment, which made other thoughts seem trivial. When we entered the room in which Brother Krause was waiting for me, he said very quickly: "Sister, I would like to begin now." It was not yet nine o'clock.

Then the blessed moment came, which I think back on with reverence and gratitude. I felt that a man of God was speaking, who told me things that could be said only through the Spirit of the Lord. Every one of his words is inscribed in my heart. Later, I thought about the feeling that had urged me to return to the branch house much earlier than I had planned, and I wondered if I would ever find an answer to this question. I received the answer several years later.

Much later, I was attending one of the last conferences to be held in Dresden and listening to a talk by Brother Krause. While listening, I learned why he had moved the time for his first blessing up and why I had been impressed to return from the woods. Neither Brother Krause nor I knew of one another's experiences on that morning, but from his talk, I learned that the Spirit of the Lord had communicated to both of us.

Brother Krause told of how he had struggled on that morning to be capable of fulfilling this important calling. I learned that he, too, had felt his inadequacy and had called on the Lord many times in prayer. I learned that Brother Krause had prayed that the Lord would give him the power to give the blessings because he did not know what he should say. He was praying at the same time I was praying in the woods. Then the answer of the Lord had come to him: "Just start giving the blessings, right now." Having received this answer from the Lord, he had sent his wife to find me, and we had met on the steps of the ward building.

While Brother Krause was giving this talk, I listened intently to his words and recognized in them the answer to my question. I was very thankful that I had gone to this conference. Four weeks earlier, I had broken my foot and had just had the cast removed. The foot was still quite painful. My first inclination was not to attend the conference, but if I had not gone, I would never have heard this answer to my question. This was a new confirmation that the Spirit of the Lord and His blessings were with me on both occasions. It was another testimony to me of how wonderfully the Lord treats his children when they obey his commandments.

10

They Shared the Last Crumb

Eberhard Gäbler

At age eight, I was baptized by my father. At age twelve, I received the Aaronic Priesthood and was ordained a deacon. At age fourteen, I was ordained a teacher. At age twenty, I was ordained a priest, and a few weeks after that, I was ordained an elder.

Before being called into military service, I was first the secretary of the Sunday School and then a counselor. At the end of 1945, when I returned from a POW camp, I was called to be the MIA leader of the newly organized branch at Forst.

In June 1947, I received a mission call. Without the least bit of financial support—we were refugees from the eastern part of my homeland and had only what we wore on our backs, the little that I earned went for food—I accepted the call without giving it a second thought, with firm faith that if the Lord needed me he would also support me. My faith was not disappointed.

I spent a full thirty-eight months in the East German Mission participating in the building of the kingdom of God. On June 9, the mission president, Walter Stover, set me apart as a missionary, and Brother Richard Ranglack ordained me an elder. The same mission president gave me my release on July 17, 1950, after I had worked in the following fields of labor: Erfurt, Gotha, Döbeln, Bernburg, Köthen, Aschersleben, Dessau-Delitsch, and Naumburg. The postwar period placed a variety of responsibilities on missionaries that were quite different from those they are normally given. The food shortage meant that the members often shared the last crumb they had in the house with us. It was a time of grateful giving and receiving, and we all considered ourselves richly blessed.

The branches to which we missionaries were sent were not self-sustaining as a rule. Almost the entire administrative organization lay in the hands of the missionaries. We were the branch presidents, the MIA leaders, the Sunday School leaders, the Primary workers, and teachers in all the organizations and did everything that had to be done in a branch. We received the welfare donations and distributed them. I remember hauling a ton of herring from Aschersleben to Bernburg in a handcart. In spite of all the work in the branch, mission work was not slighted. We held special worship services, firesides, and entertaining programs. I have never worked with so much joy in all my life as I did during those first postwar years during my mission.

The numbers attending our meetings grew and baptisms increased. I baptized fifteen persons myself during my mission and participated in many more. We also had the responsibility of caring for the many refugees from the East, who were scattered far and wide in the little villages. We also gave our sweat, digging the foundations for the branch in Berlin-Dahlem [in what was then the American sector of Berlin]. Those were times of great demands, and we were permitted to feel the Spirit of the Lord in large measure according to our diligence.

To celebrate the centenary of the arrival of the pioneers in Salt Lake Valley, we missionaries traveled from all parts of the mission to Dresden and preached the restored gospel all along the way in the branches and groups that lay in our paths, holding church meetings and firesides.

For me this was the most beneficial time of my life. My testimony grew for further important assignments. I found a wife to stand faithfully by my side as I accepted further callings in the Church. And so in 1953, when Brother Birth was our district president, I was called to be one of his counselors. In 1955, Brother Birth was called to be the mission leader for welfare work, and I was called to take his place as district president. In the Dresden District, there were the branches of Bautzen, Bischofswerda, Cottbus, Dresden, Forst, and Görlitz, with altogether about eight hundred members. The responsibility for the Dresden district lay on my shoulders for twelve years, until 1967. The following brethren helped me bear this responsibility at various times as counselors: Fritz Scherzer, Georg Dräger, Erhard Jelitto, Herbert Kaden, and Reinhold Noack.

I received the calling to be district president when I was twenty-eight years old. At this time, my wife and I had two children, ages two and one, and soon two more were added to our family. When I was called, my wife was set apart as district secretary. I am so thankful to my Heavenly Father that he has blessed me with a wife who has helped me

Eberhard Gäbler. Courtesy Manfred Schütze.

fulfill my responsibilities with complete understanding, dedication, and joy. For many years, she had to be alone with the children Sunday after Sunday and still hold many offices in the branch and in the district. This was the only thing that made it possible for me to fulfill my calling with integrity.

In the first two years, I visited the branches by train, then for many years on a motorcycle, and for one year with a car. When I went by train, Sunday started about 4:00 A.M. and often ended after midnight. It was a time of great stress for me but also a time of great blessings. Many young people were called to serve missions, and they filled them in a way that brought progress to the kingdom of God and to themselves.

In contrast to the times when we were the Soviet Zone of Occupation and were often given large halls for our conferences (the zoological lecture hall in Leipzig, for example), the work in these later times was made difficult for us. The branches had to apply to the local authorities for permission to hold church services, supplying the name of the speaker and the topic that was to be treated. Nevertheless, the members were happy and willing to serve and to support the work of the Lord. Nearly all members were in attendance at our district conferences.

After my release as district president in 1967, I was active in various callings in the branch and the district. I never knew a time of "vacation" during my membership in the Church.

When the Leipzig stake was formed, I was set apart as a high counselor, and a short time after that I was called to be temple worker. I feel myself blessed by the Lord for being a tool in his hands to participate in the building up of the kingdom of God.

11

My Mission, 1953–1974

Käthe Würscher

The following is Norma Davis's edited version of a short autobiography that Sister Käthe Würscher wrote for her children, a copy of which was given to John W. Welch.

Sister Käthe Würscher grew up in Berlin and experienced the war in that city. By the summer of 1944, there were only five priesthood holders in her branch, including her two sons. By the end of the war, both sons had died on the battlefield, her youngest child had died of an illness, and the family business was destroyed. She and her husband were left without any means of earning money to support their remaining family. At the same time, they had the additional responsibility of caring for her ailing father and mother. Their only means of income was the pension given to her parents. Five years later, in 1950, her mother died. Referring to all of these problems, she wrote:

> Especially during these difficult times, we felt the help of our Father in Heaven. Whenever the need was most urgent, his help was there. In my heart, there burned the quiet desire that I would be allowed to dedicate my entire time to the Lord when my earthly responsibilities to my family were over.

The opportunity to give intense service to the Lord came, however, during the years of her heaviest family responsibilities. In February 1953, she was called as a counselor in the presidency of the East German Mission Relief Society. When the president, Sister Berger, emigrated to the West, Sister Würscher became president and served in this capacity for twenty-one years. She considered this to be her mission, just as much as any other mission calling given the saints during these difficult days. Two months after her call to the Relief Society, her father died:

> Both my husband and I had a secret desire in our hearts that our Father in Heaven would preserve the life of my father for a long time yet. He was no longer able to be active in the Church, and I was thankful for my calling. But God's ways are not our ways, and the Lord had decided differently. On April 29, 1953, our father was released from his terrible suffering, and we were left penniless through the loss of his pension. But we felt strongly that we were under the protection of God, and today, after my long mission, I can say the Lord was with us in spite of all our trials and afflictions.
>
> We found ourselves in a very difficult situation but unexpected help arrived. There was a great deal of heavy machinery left over from our business, and in spite of all our efforts, we had been unable to sell it or even to get rid of it without cost. Within a very short time, quite by accident, or more truly, through the help of the Lord, we were able to sell it. This made it possible for me to buy a typewriter, which helped me very much in doing my Church work. This was a great testimony to me.

In this condition of extreme financial need, Sister Würscher was asked to visit the Relief Societies throughout the southern part of East Germany: Erfurt, Karl-Marx Stadt, Leipzig, Zwickau, and even the town of Annaberg up in the Erz Mountains along Germany's border with Czechoslovakia. Somehow, she managed the cost of transportation. She had to depend on the hospitality of the Saints for housing and food. However, her financial need became the least of her worries. The visits were timed to coincide with district conferences held in each city, and she was expected to speak. Her first assignment was in Erfurt, where her extreme anxiety was apparent to the sisters of the branch. After the meeting, she wrote:

> Sister Lange came up to me and said, "Sister Würscher, don't you have any confidence in us?" From that time, I knew that I was not alone, that I had the sympathy of the sisters. This knowledge brought me real joy and strengthened my self-confidence. I also had a good relationship with the priesthood. They included me in their prayers, and in their presence I felt safe and secure.
>
> My first trip lasted four weeks. I had not planned to be away that long, but in that time, I became acquainted with four important large districts of the mission. In order to take advantage of the time during the week between the individual conferences, I went with the local Relief Society leader to visit the members of the

branches and the sick in each branch. I will never forget the sick for whom the greetings from the mission presidency were like a stream of sunlight. In Zwickau, I visited a ninety-year-old sister who was confined to her bed. Attended to by the Relief Society sisters of the branch, she bore her suffering with great dignity. With her cracking voice, she sang her testimony for us:

> "When amid the conflicts,
>   whether great or small
> Do not be discouraged
>   God is over all. . . ."

This went directly to my heart, and I felt the strength of God so strongly that I was deeply impressed with the greatness of the soul of this dear, afflicted sister. How marvelous is the power of the gospel.

Käthe Würscher. Courtesy Manfred Schütze.

Still other challenges had to be faced. In order to visit the Saints in Annaberg, she had to get permission from the government to travel so near the country's border. She applied at Karl-Marx Stadt, but when the time came to go, she still hadn't received permission. Realizing she had to go no matter what the political situation might be, she managed it through what she termed "roundabout ways."

> The joy of the brothers and sisters in that area was overwhelming that they could finally have visitors once again from the mission, and I felt very happy among the dear sisters. The conference was held in the tavern *Zum Erbgericht*. Brother Burkhardt, who was still single at that time, bore his testimony, along with the young elders, with great enthusiasm.
>
> Today Annaberg has a beautiful chapel, probably the most beautiful in the GDR. And through the diligence of the members, it was possible to build a baptismal font in the building. I have been able to experience many wonderful conferences there.

Through her visits in the districts, Sister Würscher learned the conditions of the members and could assess the ways in which Relief Society could help alleviate their needs. As the priesthood worked to bring order once again to a war-torn country, organize branches, and find places for the members to meet, the Relief Society saw to the needs of the elderly, the sick and wounded, and the widows young and old. Sister Würscher wrote this testimony concerning her initial trip around the mission:

> During my first trip of four weeks, I spent only 185 marks. I was very happy about that because I lived very frugally and this money covered my travel costs. I fasted a great deal during this trip and prayed that I might be able to serve the Lord. I needed his help and support in order to be able to help others. The Lord guided and directed me in wonderful ways. I was under his protection, and my joy and thankfulness inspired me in my work. How thankful I am to our priesthood under whose protection I felt so comfortable.

The crowning experience on this trip came in Leipzig, the final stop planned for the tour:

> The meeting place was located on Gerber Street, not far from the train station. The conference also took place there. There was a rich outpouring of the Spirit. Because of the Leipzig Fair, General Authorities received permission to enter the country, and so we were able to enjoy their inspired messages, which greatly strengthened our testimonies. We felt a strong union with the other hemisphere and were so happy that we had not been forgotten. Especially in Leipzig, I felt the strength of testimony that made it possible for me to work with the Spirit of the Lord.

At first, the East German Relief Society was under the direction of the wife of the mission president, President Arthur Glaus. By the time President Glaus's mission ended, Sister Würscher had gained considerable confidence in her calling, as is clearly evident in the following example:

> I will never forget President Glaus. Before I left on my trip to the conferences, he gave me wonderful advice and help. It was customary to invite the Relief Society sisters to the district conferences if it was in their interest. And so, when it came time for his release and the district leaders were expected to be at a farewell for the president but not the sisters of the Relief Society presidencies, I became a little forward. Since an Apostle of the Lord was also expected to be there, I went to the mission home and lodged a complaint with the mission presidency. My request was denied with the excuse that the district leaders represented all of the organizations. That was true, but I didn't give up. As President Glaus and his counselor,

Brother Pettschlag, were standing up with their coats and hats on ready to leave the mission home, I just sat in my chair and waited. Suddenly President Glaus said, "Sister, now what's on your mind?" I just answered, imploringly, "I am still thinking of the dear sisters who would so love to come." At that he gave his permission, and we had such a wonderful reunion with the sisters. President Glaus is no longer living, but to us sisters his goodness will never be forgotten. We also had a very good working relationship with Sister Glaus.

When Herold L. Gregory was called to preside over the mission, his wife was within weeks of delivering her second child and could not direct the work as Sister Glaus had done. From that time, Sister Würscher carried the responsibility alone. Her confidence to lead the sisters of the Church was continually strengthened through necessity, as the following exemplifies:

> At that particular time, we were expecting a visitor from Utah. The general president of the Relief Society [Belle Spafford], who was also vice president of the World Women's Organization *[Weldfrauenbund]*, was traveling to get acquainted with other countries. She spoke first to the women in Helsinki. Her arrival in Berlin was planned for Saturday. In order to give many sisters the opportunity to meet her, we planned a district conference and invited about forty sisters to Berlin-Dahlem to meet her. President Gregory and three of us from the Relief Society presidency waited for her at Tempelhof Airport—unfortunately in vain. Our guest had been held up in Helsinki and could not arrive until Sunday. This was when I was very new in my calling, and we met at the same time as the priesthood leadership. I was totally unprepared. We had hoped to be instructed by our expected visitor, but unfortunately that had fallen through. It fell on my shoulders as Relief Society president to conduct the meeting. In spite of everything, it was a spiritual time as we sisters met together. There was a good, cooperative attitude between East and West.
>
> On Sunday morning, we met Sister Spafford and came to know her as a woman of high intelligence and benevolence. I learned a great lesson from this experience. Never again did I go to a conference unprepared. Of course, I seldom prepared my talks, that is, I seldom wrote them out, but from then on, I studied diligently and especially read a lot. Fasting and prayer helped me overcome my weaknesses.
>
> I like to think back to those times. It is truly elevating to be under the influence of God and to feel his help. So I visited almost

all of the branches, became acquainted with the sisters, and had the great joy of giving help where it was needed.

Until the Berlin Wall was erected in 1961, the Saints were able to travel to West Germany. However, crossing the border meant they had to use West German currency, and they were not allowed to exchange money. As Sister Würscher's responsibilities demanded travel to the West, she was once again dependent upon the Lord, through the aid of the members of the Church. She went many times to the branches in northern West Germany: Flensburg, Kiel, Hannover, Bremerhaven, and Hamburg. She was accompanied by her counselors, who included Sister Demanowski, Sister Galand, and Sister Ranglak. During these visits, they learned about the duties of the presidency and the organization of the Relief Society. They also had many opportunities to speak at conferences there. Still, the experience was not gained without much sacrifice on their parts:

> It is strange how the Lord leads us when we put our entire trust in Him. I once arrived in Bremerhaven totally unknown and without a bit of money in my pocket. To my relief, another traveler gave me 30 cents [pfennig] when I asked him for directions. I was trying to find my way to the branch when I saw two young men walking up ahead of me. I immediately recognized them as missionaries. I felt I just needed to follow them, and my intuition did not fail me. As I mentioned, I knew no one there, but in the society of the Saints I felt right at home. It was like that everywhere. The members were wonderful with their support and their willingness to help. I spent several nights with some Saints who had not been blessed with many worldly goods, but in their homes I felt the spirit of the gospel in rich measure. My heart is filled with gratitude for all of the love contained in the blessings of God. It was that way in Flensburg, in Hannover, in Kiel, and in Hamburg.
>
> Those were unforgettable conferences and the cooperation between East and West was moved forward by them. It was quite amazing how everything came together. We had many difficulties to overcome as a result of that godless war. One time Sister Demanowski and I drove to Templehof Airport early on Saturday and from there flew to Hamburg. The meetings were held in the beautiful stake building. All of the important items were discussed, and many things were improved by the combined experience of all who were present. We were scheduled to fly back on Sunday evening, but a terrible storm would not allow it, so we had to spend the night in Hamburg and fly back on Monday. At that

time, I was working as a salesperson in a store in Berlin, Unter den Linden, and had to be to work at 9:30 A.M. I arrived right on time, and no one suspected that I had come directly from Hamburg. We were in the Lord's hands, and even today I think of the anxiety I felt about getting back on time.

Mission headquarters were in the Dahlem district of Berlin. Because the Relief Society was under the direction of the mission president, Sister Würscher and other Relief Society leaders had many occasions for crossing the border dividing the Soviet sector, where she was living, in order to go to Dahlem, in the American sector. This was a source of great strength to the women of the Church in the GDR.

> I would like to mention one very special event. It was when the Tabernacle Choir came to Berlin. We had a district leaders' meeting in Dahlem in the mission home. All the leaders from both East and West were present. At the conclusion of the meetings, which were truly inspiring, we all went together to the train station to await the arrival of the members of the choir. The atmosphere was overpowering. In the main entrance hall, a large banner had been hung up with the word "Welcome." The area to the steps had been blocked off. To the right, the Berlin Choir had taken their place. At the cry, "They are coming," our choir greeted them with one of our most beautiful songs. Then something wonderful happened. Several in the front row rushed toward the choir and embraced friends in a joyful reunion. As they passed through, we automatically divided into two rows of honor. We shouted welcome to them, and there were shining eyes and great joy. Our choir then sang the hymn "Let the Mountains Shout for Joy." Then the members of the Tabernacle Choir stopped on the stairs and sang along in their language, and we all joined in. It was a marvelous outpouring of the Spirit, and I have never experienced anything greater.
>
> The Choir later sang in the Schöneberg Palace in Berlin, and many of the Saints from East and West had the opportunity of hearing them. It was a powerful, wonderful, unforgettable experience for everyone.

There were other opportunities available to the Saints before the erection of the Wall and the closing of the borders between East Germany and the rest of Western Europe. Some Saints were able to go to the temple in Switzerland. Sister Würscher was among these:

> In the year 1956, I was able to go through the temple. I took my young sixteen-year-old daughter with me to Switzerland. We drove

as far as Frankfurt. Since we had almost no means of support, we were put up by members at the mission home in Bettina Street. We arrived very late in the evening. The apartments were already occupied, but then we saw what gratitude can do. After a few moments thought, Brother Ihls, who had just arrived from the Erz Mountains, said, and this is word for word, "Once Sister Würscher took us into her home when we arrived hungry and with no place to sleep. She and her daughter can stay with us." So, everyone squeezed in a little, and we were given a place to stay.

All of the members there were traveling to Switzerland. My daughter and I traveled via Karlsruhe and then continued on to Switzerland. We were able to spend the night in Karlsruhe. The Church owned an old-folks home there, and we were given one bed. I had always wanted to see this home. At that time, it was a lovely, well-kept house. The director gave me a tour around the place, and I had a very good impression of it. The branch met in the same house, so the old people staying there had an ideal situation and were taken care of with great love.

From there we went on as far as Konstanz [the city of Constance on Lake Constance—known in Germany as Bodensee]. Here I remember a good and pure family who took us in. Brother Hermann was the branch president in Konstanz. He and his wife did everything in their power to help us, even though they were not blessed with the things of this world. The next day we arrived at Zollikofen.

What a wonderful feeling I had as we stood there before the temple. Its simple beauty brought joy to my heart. When I read the words over the door—"The House of the Lord"—I felt the tears welling up in my eyes. I was so aware of my insignificance. I didn't know if I was worthy to enter. It was the greatest blessing of my life to be in the house of the Lord and to receive all of the ordinances. I was sealed to my dear ancestors who had passed on, and I had the blessing of doing the work for others. My daughter performed a blessed work doing baptisms for the dead. But the most beautiful thing is that she could be there for the sealing and could be sealed to me.

The days flew by. We returned to Konstanz and stayed with Brother and Sister Hermann again. And we had the opportunity to visit with my departed cousin's son, who had received a head wound in the war and was doing very poorly. When I left, Sister Hermann promised me she would take care of him, and she fulfilled this promise in a wonderful way until the day of her death.

This poor, neglected human being found a home with her. She was an example to us, and the gratitude of this sick man was the most beautiful monument in her honor. Twenty years later, I was able to visit her grave.

The blessing of attending the temple given to some of the East German Saints brought about yet another need that had to be met by the Relief Society. Clothing of any kind was extremely scarce, and it was impossible to obtain temple clothing. No one had West German marks to buy these items in Switzerland or in the branches in West Germany. Several sisters were called to be instructed in sewing their own.

A sewing room was set up in the mission home in Dahlem to sew temple clothing. Once a week, we five sisters met together to do this work. Sister Galand had first learned to sew temple clothing in Switzerland, and thanks to her dedication to the work of the Lord, we were able to prepare others to do this work. I remember especially Sisters Poppily and Heimerl from Karl-Marx Stadt. At that time, the borders had not yet been closed for those dear sisters. Later, they did this same work in Karl-Marx Stadt with great love and enthusiasm, which was a blessing to all who had gone through the temple. The calling of these sisters was an inspiration.

How joyful and fortunate we were to be able to help in this way. Today I think back and wonder how it was possible for me to feed these sisters with my sparse means. Fortunately, they received a good lunch in the mission office. By the time the borders were closed, this work was already in good hands in Karl-Marx Stadt.

Finding material for the garments gave us a great deal of concern, but here, also, we found a way. There were some looms in Cottbus, and we were able to weave some rather coarse material which we then had at our disposal. We were pleased and happy to have solved this problem.

Later we received help from President Walter Stover, whom I think of in this connection as a dear and kind brother. He was always there with a helping hand when needed. He sent crates of material and clothing for the brothers and sisters in the East. So many members who were in need were helped in this way. We also received huge supplies of garments from him. Many remember him with gratitude and love.

The needs of the Saints in the GDR were many. One of Sister Würscher's most persistent duties was to see that the numerous elderly sisters scattered throughout the mission were cared for. This responsibility demanded continuous travel at her own expense.

In Blankenburg, I went to visit an older sister, Sister Blank. She was a faithful member. She had served the Lord from her earliest youth and had worked a lot as a teacher in the Sunday School. She had beautiful handwriting and also wrote beautiful poetry. She had lost her home in Köningsberg [East Prussia] during the war. As a refugee, she had been taken in by the Evangelical Center for the elderly, and here she was in her last years living in that lovely home. But she sorely missed her association with her brothers and sisters in the gospel. The joy was great when we saw one another again.

There is a poem that was written during these times by Sister Blank. It goes:

Du lieber Engel breite Deine Flügel aus
Und komm noch einmal in mein Haus,
Eh' ich von dieser Erd' muss gehen,
Möcht' ich dein lieber Antlitz sehen!

Dein Antlitz hell wie Sonnenschein
Der Spiegel Deines Herzens Schrein
Es leuchtet wie ein Diamant,
Der nur aus höhern Sphären stammt!

[You, Dear Angel, spread your wings
And enter my house once again.
Before I must leave this earth,
I would like to see your face once more.

Your face as bright as sunshine,
The reflection of the shrine of your heart.
It shines like a diamond
That could come only from higher spheres!]

Her joy was understandable because she was lonesome, and someone from The Church of Jesus Christ visited her. I will never forget this patient sister. She was hard of hearing and in addition suffered pains in her ears. All attempts to help her had failed. Because of this, we brought her to Berlin. I cared for her in my home. But neither the doctors in the West or in the East could help her. So a week later, I took her back. Years went by before she was released from her suffering.

From Blankenburg, I traveled on to Pöpenik. Sister Henning lay ill there for many years with crippled legs. The mission provided all of the emergency help possible. She had two children, about six and eight years old, whom she had to care for. This mother was a hero in our eyes. Since she couldn't stand, she took care of her children as well as she could from her bed. Everything she needed was placed on a bench by her bed—a little electric cooking plate and some pots and pans. Each day a woman came to help her by doing the shopping. When the children came home from school, the mother had their dinner prepared. Whenever I visited her, she had some work at hand, such as washing vegetables. She even did her washing, sewing, and ironing in bed. With all of this, she was in great pain. Now I want to mention an event that illustrates what great faith this sister had in the help of the Lord.

In 1952 the Prophet David O. McKay visited Berlin. This mother, suffering with pain, sent her two children to the prophet with the request that he visit her and give her a blessing. Unfortunately, this was impossible because of the political circumstances. His visa was valid only for Berlin. But he gave the children his handkerchief to take with them, and his blessing reached the mother, and she was relieved of her sufferings. Later, when the children were grown, she became the leader of the Relief Society in that little branch. She was an intelligent woman and liked to share her knowledge with others. It is amazing to me what faith can do and what strength it can give to the weak.

President David O. McKay in Berlin-Dahlem, June 29, 1952. The President's son, Lawrence McKay, and Sister Emma Riggs McKay are on the left. Sister Lawrence McKay is next to the president. Courtesy Käthe Wöhe.

> With Sister Krause, the first wife of our patriarch, I had the opportunity of visiting the members in Mecklenburg for the first time, and it was always a shock to me to see the sick and afflicted in their misery. Their strong trust in God and their faith gave them the strength to bear their affliction and to hope. It was at that time that the determination grew in me to dedicate my entire strength to the work of the Lord, to stand by the suffering, and—with the help of my counselors to support and strengthen me, and with the generosity of the mission presidency—relieve their suffering. We were allowed the closest working relationship with the mission. We always found a listening ear and a sympathetic heart.

During the twenty-one years of her mission, Sister Würscher served as Relief Society president under these following mission presidents: Arthur Glaus (1951–53), Herold L. Gregory (1953–57), Burtis F. Robbins (1957–60), Percy K. Fetzer (1960–63), Joel Tate (1963–66), and Peter Loscher (1966–68).

> Unfortunately, the borders were closed in 1961. We could no longer travel to the mission headquarters, and things looked dark. Today I can say that the Lord was always with us.
>
> President Tate was the right man to replace President Fetzer. He and his wife, like their predecessors, were prepared to do their best. President Tate had great love for all the people of the mission. He was never a respecter of persons when it came to his kindness. How often he exerted all his energies to bring help. Those were difficult times for us. Many were sick. We had very little proper medicine. At that time, the help of the mission was accepted with gratitude, and help was always forthcoming. The mission even paid for operations when they were necessary in critical cases. The mission was able to help many people by providing medicine, and I was, on occasions, the fortunate one chosen to bring them over the border, which was not without its risks. The Lord was always with me when I was on an assignment to do good.
>
> After the borders were closed, we were under the leadership of the East German Mission. President Burkhardt was always there to help us. The district leadership meetings were now held in Dresden. The mission leadership was reorganized. I think of my counselors. There was Sister Demanowski, Sister Richter, Sister Voigt, and later Sister Agathe Ortlieb. We tried to do our work very diligently, and there was a very cooperative spirit in Dresden. I remember with gratitude the sisters who were an example to me.

I also want to remember a brother who was always there when help was needed. That was our patriarch, Brother Krause. I remember with fondness how he helped me move my furniture into a small apartment. He helped many, and he was a true and an important companion to Brother Burkhardt.

Sister Käthe Würscher ends her short autobiography with what she felt was the highlight of her "mission"—accompanying President and Sister Tate on a visit to the Saints in the southern part of East Germany. They made Karl-Marx Stadt their headquarters, because President and Sister Tate were allowed in the country as western tourists and had to stay in a specific hotel, where they were expected to return each evening:

> I have already mentioned that President Tate and his wife had a very sensitive heart for the poor and the sick. He visited us in the East as often as he could, and this was not without its difficulties for him.
>
> At my request, just before he was released, we visited all of my sick in the mission that I could find, going before and after conferences. There was never such a great joy for them. President Tate and his wife picked me up in Berlin, and we drove to Karl-Marx Stadt to Brother Burkhardt's. . . . This was such an honor for our older sisters. They had never had the experience of being visited by two mission presidents, that is, President Tate and President Burkhardt. Sister Tate, Brother Krause, and I, as the leader of the mission Relief Society, were with them. It was unusual that five persons came. President Tate had his camera along, we took a photo, and it was a blessed time for everyone.

They traveled from branch to branch visiting the Saints, sharing their testimonies, singing hymns together, taking photos, and blessing the lives of the members. Each night they returned to Karl-Marx Stadt and then continued their visits the following day. In the tiny village of Wilkau, they visited the branch. Sister Würscher remembers:

> A marvelous spirit drew us together. I thought about the mother of the prophet Joseph Smith when her son was taken prisoner. This mother, who had been so severely tried, was terribly shaken at the news. She left everything and hurried to her son's wagon. At her request, Joseph spoke to her briefly, "God bless you, Mother." This event has always made a strong impression on me. What a wonderful mother she must have been. We sang the song, "We Thank Thee, O God, for a Prophet." It was a heavy parting.

> On Sunday we visited the branch and the regular Sunday School. On this day, however, there seemed to be a resplendence of joy over everything because of the presence of the president and his wife and the other authorities.

The visits to towns, branches, isolated members, and invalids in nursing homes came to an end on Monday.

> It was an impressive time. The Lord was with his children. . . . On Monday we said good-bye to Brother and Sister Burkhardt and began our return journey. We visited Brother and Sister Cirpka in Neuenhagen. The visit was unexpected, and we had a pleasant reunion. From there we went on to Woltersdorf, where we visited Brother and Sister Demanowski. We were heartily welcomed and experienced a joyful hour together. But then it was back to Berlin. Our trip was over. We were gone for four days, and it was the crowning missionary trip for me. All of the sick who were so dear to us and who could not attend the meetings were made joyful by the visit of the mission parents and the authorities. Unfortunately, Brother and Sister Tate had to leave us shortly after that. They returned to Utah, their mission over. But I am sure they found their visit to the sick a fitting conclusion to their work.

With this, Sister Würscher concludes her brief history of twenty-one years of devoted service as president of the East German Mission Relief Society. One more excerpt from her writing can serve to summarize her feelings about those years of her "mission":

> How great is the goodness of our Heavenly Father. How often I have felt his hand when I was traveling and arrived late at night without any lodging, the hotels overbooked and my funds very low.

12

A Second Mission

Herbert Schreiter
as told by Manfred Schütze

He sat across from me in his little apartment on the temple grounds in Freiberg. In May 1986, Herbert Schreiter had been called, along with his wife, Dorle, to an eighteen-month temple mission. He had never been a temple missionary before, but there is scarcely another calling he has not held in his seventy-seven years. And this is his fourth full-time mission. During our conversation, he mentioned being branch president in Chemnitz from 1937 to 1941, Sunday School president in Salzburg [Austria] during the war, district president in 1948, two times branch president in Leipzig, Sunday School president of the branch, the district, and the mission, high councilor, sealer, and counselor in the temple presidency.

Brother Schreiter has strong faith and great determination to serve God. He has often felt the hand of the Lord:

> One experience took place in the courtyard of the Hoffmann and Aurich company, where I was an apprentice locksmith-metal worker at the Fleischerei Machine Factory in Chemnitz, No. 3-5 Wettiner Street. Another apprentice and I were using a hand-driven elevator. We were moving machinery from the assembly room on the second floor to the paint room on the third floor. Mr. Hoffmann and the chief metal worker were watching us. The two of us were lifting the weight up, each turning on a long handle. When they were taking one of the machines off, the double steel hook by which the entire weight was hanging came loose and came crashing down into the courtyard. I was standing in such an unfortunate position that the heavy hook fell just behind my head and bounced off the concrete

floor. Those who were standing around gave a scream of terror, and I felt the rush of wind just behind my head. It was a miracle that, with the help of the Lord, I was not injured. It was not my time yet, and I thanked my Heavenly Father for this divine protection. The others there were also greatly relieved. It was strange, but on the next day I received a letter from my uncle to whom I was very devoted and who lived in Grossolbersdorf. I had lived with him for two years, and he treated me like his own son. He was also my guardian because my father had died on the battlefield in France in 1916. The uncle was very concerned about me and asked if anything had happened to me. He had had a bad dream in which I was lying across a railroad track and a locomotive had stopped just a few centimeters from my body. I consider this event as an example of the divine providence of our Heavenly Father, and I testify of this in the name of Jesus Christ, amen. This happened in Chemnitz when I was sixteen years old.

When I was nineteen years old, I accepted a call to serve a mission. This was in the year of the great depression, 1929, and I gave up a secure job with the likely prospect that I would never get it back again.

This turned out to be true. When Brother Schreiter returned after twenty-five months, he was unemployed and had to sell newspapers to make a living. But he did not regret these two years which, as the following will show, were the determining influence in his life.

There were highs and lows to his mission. In Stopl (in the former Pommern), a superintendent gave a public warning, "The Mormons are coming," and paid for the rent on a tavern himself to prevent the missionaries from using it to preach. But they were successful in spite of this opposition. About forty members came by night with lanterns from the neighboring village of Wobeste to hear the missionaries. In Küstrin (Pommern) were ten Relief Society sisters who held a bazaar to display handicrafts and attracted about 130 investigators. Brother Schreiter reports that there were even official journalists at a baptism.

These highs and lows experienced by the missionaries of those days impressed the young missionary for his later life in a positive way. He remembers with gratitude the financial support he received from his mother and sisters in this depressed time.

From 1937 until he was drafted into the army in 1941, he served as the president of the Chemnitz Branch with more than five hundred members, which brought him both joy and toil. At the same time, he had personal problems to deal with. His own illness, plus his wife's life-threatening illness, along with the terrible war experiences, tried him and gave him the maturity he needed for the job the Lord had picked out for him immediately after the war.

On Pentecost Sunday 1946, there was a missionary conference in the Congress Hall in Leipzig. Herbert Schreiter from Chemnitz was among the thousands who were able to attend this first great conference of the Saints after the war. One of the events that changed his life is described in his journal:

> After the Saturday evening meeting, which was dedicated to the MIA, Brother Richard Ranglack called me to him and asked me if I was ready to go on a mission. As surprising as this was, after Brother Ranglack had told me that no family had ever died whose husband was out working for the Lord and after he had asked me which was more important, working as a metal worker or working for the Lord, there was only one answer for me: of course, I am ready and am happy to have this honor.
>
> I felt the entire burden of this responsibility resting on me, just as I had felt it seventeen years earlier at my first missionary call, when, on November 4, 1929, I was advanced from deacon and ordained an elder and sent out into the mission field. Brother Ranglack answered, "I hereby call you on a mission. Put all of your affairs and your family in order and open your mouth to preach the truth of the Gospel."
>
> I had to split the wood I had on hand and put many things in order. I was quite surprised that my mother took the news of my mission call so calmly, especially because of her worry about the physical condition of my wife, Lisbeth, and our meager finances. Lisbeth suggested that I start my mission on March 26, my birthday, to which Brother Ranglack agreed.
>
> 19 March 1946: Took my mother's handcart and went gleaning with Hans Schumann. Arrived home about 10:00 p.m. with 80 pounds of potatoes, 10 pounds of wheat, and 2 pounds of peas.
>
> The rest of the week spent with garden work, dentist, visiting, repairing shoes for Lisbeth and the children.
>
> Sunday, 24 March 1946: Visited Sunday School for the last time, spoke a few words of farewell, closing song: *"Wir bringen dir, o Bruder hier."* Sat by my mother. After the Sunday School, I received the large sum of 130 marks from those in attendance.
>
> At the sacrament meeting of the Chemnitz Central Branch, I had my official farewell. A farewell poem by Sister Ilse Böttcher, words of praise and gratitude by Brother Alexander Franke. Donations from those in attendance, 260 marks.

A Second Mission

Herbert Schreiter. Courtesy Manfred Schütze.

Monday, 25 March 1946: Putting final things in order, paid the light bill, did some visiting, got a cover for my bicycle. While Lisbeth was getting my things together, I spent some more time repairing my children's shoes and then packed my bags. Went to bed late. My daughter, Irene, cried when she said good night.

26 March 1946: Lisbeth cooked my farewell breakfast and then accompanied me to the train station. I'm glad that Lisbeth is so brave and good. She says, nodding at the baby buggy in which she is pushing part of my luggage, "I have pushed all my happiness in this buggy, and now I sending you off on a mission with it."

On April 3, 1946, Brother Schreiter was transferred to Bernburg. While he was there, along with his other duties he organized a special meeting, which was attended by my [Manfred Schütze's] mother and my grandparents. This was the beginning of the conversion of my family, who in the midst of the war's confusion had left Schlesien and after much suffering had ended up here.

After his mission, he served the Church in the district and the branch of Leipzig. As branch president, he experienced his greatest disappointment on Christmas Eve 1968, when he was informed by the city authorities that the Church would no longer be permitted to use the branch house, which had just been newly remodeled by the members. The branch would have to vacate the house they had occupied for so many years since the war. The building was to be demolished. After the war and after much difficulty, the branch was offered an old, rundown movie theater to meet in. It was part of a building that was actually in ruins. After months of labor under the direction of Brother Schreiter, it had been turned into an acceptable meeting place for the members. Shortly after the beautiful dedication, they were told it was to be condemned and could never be used again because of a supposed violation of the building police regulations.

Under Brother Schreiter's leadership, the branch stayed together, and in the end, he was able to reobtain the use of the branch house. It is hard to explain how much spiritual strength this took.

In 1978, Brother Schreiter received a new calling, a third mission. But this time he was with his wife and in the Leipzig District. As with all of his assignments, he took this one also very seriously. He and his wife were able to convert and baptize seven adults and one child. The Schreiters had many wonderful experiences together; therefore, Sister Schreiter's death in December 1983 was very painful for him.

In 1984 he married his former sister-in-law, and in 1985 at the dedication of the temple in Freiberg, he was called to be a temple sealer by President Hinckley.

In 1986 he was called to his fourth mission, this time in the temple. For him the expression "Once a missionary, always a missionary" has a special meaning. He fulfilled his temple mission honorably, and President Monson called him to be a counselor in the temple presidency. He is also active as a stake historian.

Whenever the question arises—how was it possible for the Church to exist and to develop in the eastern part of Germany after the war, how could faithful members and active youth grow when the tie to the headquarters of the Church had to be so nebulous?—then there is only one answer: because of leaders like this!

13

Twenty-five Years a Branch President in Neubrandenburg

Otto Krakow
as told by Manfred Schütze

Conditions were bad when Brother Otto Krakow (born in 1910) returned from Stettin at the end of the war to his hometown of Neubrandenburg, where his mother was still living. He came, supported on crutches, to get his family to safety. Just as everything else was in a state of destruction and disorder, so was the Church in Neubrandenburg. The branch no longer existed; no responsible brethren were left. One man, who had once held a responsible position, had turned away from the Church and saw meaning in life only in collecting bread to survive. So it was not surprising that when Brother Ranglack of the mission presidency arrived in Neubrandenburg, he approached Brother Krakow and offered him financial help to alleviate his material needs. The answer Brother Krakow gave to this offer is typical of him: "You cannot help us with money. You can help us only by sending us missionaries."

The first missionaries soon arrived; among them, arriving on foot, was Brother Krause from Wolgast. Brother Krakow took him and others in and fed them. They held cottage meetings and, later, sacrament meetings in a public trade school.

The Church acquired its first rented rooms on Pfaffen Street. Brother Krakow was among the brethren who repaired and beautified the rooms so they would be appropriate for the meetings of the Church. When the branch president, Brother Roloff, married and moved to Cottbus in 1951, Brother Krakow replaced him—for the next twenty-five years.

He experienced many highs and lows in these years. He was, in his direct, honest, and humble way, a good leader, an example, and a blessing to all the people. The fact that the members of the Neubrandenburg Branch were able to acquire and remodel their own branch house in such a time is one of his great accomplishments. He insists he only allowed his Heavenly Father to lead him in all of his decisions.

When the Church was informed by the owners, a tailors' guild, that they would have to vacate the rented rooms on Pfaffen Street, Brother Krakow arranged for the Church to buy a neighboring building. This called for courage! Builders

Otto Krakow. Courtesy Manfred Schütze.

pointed out to him the dilapidated condition of the building in general. In particular, instead of collecting the rainwater, the valley tins and rain gutters dropped it through the many holes in the roof. The building had been part of a carriage house, where wagons were stored. It was next door to the quarters for the servants and attached to a splendid house at the front. There was even a smithy's forge in the building.

"We are not afraid of work," was the branch president's curt answer. So all of the branch members went to work, and help arrived from others. Brother Brokatzki, a carpenter from the Werdau Branch, came and put the roof in order. Brother Pawlowski from Schwerin, a skilled bricklayer, and Brother Krause alternated between Prenzlau and Neubrandenburg to provide the necessary building materials. "We had good support from the authorities in getting the building material," Brother Krakow remembers with gratitude. "No problems."

In 1967 the first meetings were held in a part of the building. In 1970 they moved into the chapel area. The rooms were needed; the branch had grown. Brother Krakow remembers many great events that took place in those rooms in the following years. One of these was the visit of a General Authority, Elder Theodore M. Burton, who came at Easter in 1972 to dedicate the property. Another was a concert by the Mission Youth Choir in August 1972. There were over one hundred people present. In the years that followed, many district meetings and other special meetings were held there. The branch house was always the center of Church activity for the members of the branch.

Branch house in Neubrandenburg, a former theater. Many members came to the conference there by bicycle from 60 to 80 kilometers (37 to 50 miles) away. Courtesy Edith Krause.

When Brother Krakow was released in 1976 and turned his calling over to a younger brother, he turned over a solid branch with good leadership, young couples, and very active members with a strong spirit.

When asked what the most painful experience was during his calling, he quickly mentions the death of his wife.

> You can imagine how I felt sitting up there on the podium, shaking, after my wife died suddenly of cancer in 1973. I was finished. My wife had been the strength of our faith, stronger than I. She is the one who had often encouraged me. For example, my clerk, Brother Roloff, died and I had to also take care of the reports in the evenings. Many a night I sat there until my wife came and said, "Come on, sweetheart. Come to bed. Things will look better in the morning. Just get your rest first."

Brother Krakow tells about his humble origins and his conversion:

> I am a simple man; only went to grammar school. I was the son of a widow with four children, of which I was the oldest. No one to help me with my school work. And if I can do anything today then I have to say that everything, even my speaking (I learned only a low dialect at home), I have learned in the Church; everything has come from my activity in the Church.

I was baptized by a missionary, Wendel G. Allen, on December 27, 1927, here in Neubrandenburg in the Tollense Lake. My mother was somewhat opposed to it. Later I became the Sunday School secretary. One day she found my record books and a few tithing receipts. She threw everything in the stove, which made me so mad that I spit at her. At that she threw me out; my violin, my accordion, and my books came flying out after me.

But later we made up. When she was seventy-eight years old, I baptized her, and she brought me great joy when she said, "If only all my kids had been like you." That's something I will never forget. But I had long since forgiven her. Just imagine, I've been a member for so long, sixty years—but I'll never be perfect. No matter how old we get, as old as the stones, we will never understand everything. The Gospel is so rich, we can never comprehend it all.

During my last visit, I saw a freshly renovated classroom and saw how neatly it had been papered. A brother next to me said, "Yes, Brother Krakow did that recently." He still comes, Sunday after Sunday with his *Trabant* [a small, East German automobile], as he lovingly calls his bicycle.

14

A Dollhouse for a Chapel

Renate Ritter
Edited by Manfred Schütze and Norma Davis

The little city of Groitzsch, about thirty kilometers south of Leipzig, would have remained unknown in the history of the Church had it not been for one brave family that moved in there decades ago, the Böhmes. Their influence extends down to the present through several generations that carry names well known in the entire region: Bauerfeind, Hachenberger, Ritter, Sickel, Winkler.

It all began with a school teacher and his wife who became members of the Church. Leipzig was the closest branch, and they attended the meetings there with their children. That meant they had to be on their way by 6:30 A.M., travel a long distance by train, and finish off with a long walk. Sister Renate Ritter, now sixty-three years old [1989], was one of these children. Her parents' dedication to the Church taught her to have a great love for the gospel. As a young woman, Renate would stay in Leipzig overnight in order to attend MIA. She took the train home the next morning and went directly from the train station to school.

Later, when she had to participate in the so-called year on the farm near Eilenburg and had only one Sunday off every month, Renate did not go home but met her parents at church, where they brought her fresh clothes and supplies.

The opportunity to be in a Berlin conference in 1938 when the prophet, Heber J. Grant, was there strengthened her desire to remain true to the gospel. "The last sounding of the trumpet" was the theme of the conference. "At that conference I was deeply moved in my soul. Even today I can hardly restrain my tears when I think of this wonderful experience. I recognized with gratitude what a great blessing it was for us to belong to this Church." Soon after this, all foreign missionaries had to leave the country. World War II had begun.

The family survived the war, but the father, a former school principal, no longer had a profession; he was among the unemployed. The brother, Walter, returned from the war without a penny in his pocket and was immediately called on a mission. But Renate had completed her schooling and could support her brother from her wages. "And so the Lord assists and leads us in His marvelous ways."

The son of a knighted family with a large estate wooed her at the time, but Renate did not marry him: "a member of the Church—my Wolfgang—was dearer to me." He also was a knight—according to his family name [*Ritter* means knight]. The fact that he had the same ideals was more important to her than the other suitor's money or estate.

Renate and her new husband moved to Leipzig. They brought his father with them, and Renate's husband opened a cleaning establishment. Before long she was caring for four men—her husband, her father-in-law, and her two sons, Roland and Lothar.

> I loved my father-in-law as I loved my own husband and my children, so with God's help everything went well. What a blessing it was to have him there to take care of our children when we were carrying out our Church duties or when we wanted to go to a concert or to the theater. On Tuesday I was busy as the president of the Primary and as a teacher in the Primary. Thursdays I was a teacher in the MIA, and in the meantime, I was going back and forth to Groitzsch.

Her frequent trips from Leipzig to Groitzsch were necessary because of the growing branch there and because her aging parents needed her help more and more. The Böhme family was still the heart of the branch. Church meetings in Groitzsch meant sacrament meeting in the Böhme living room. Each Sunday the living room had to be set up, the other rooms had to be cleared out and made ready for classrooms, and afterwards everything had to be put back in place again. This went on for years. Getting their own meeting place was out of the question. They had tried many times to get permission to build something, to add on somewhere, or to rent something—always in vain.

That was until Sister Ritter—undoubtedly after much fasting and prayer—came upon the solution one day. Her parents had a large piece of property, and she wanted to build a "weekend house" for her father-in-law behind their house. Her request to the building authorities brought the city building inspector to her parents' house. During the week, Renate's mother used her house for a "doll clinic." Various village

Renate Ritter. Courtesy Manfred Schütze.

children's organizations like kindergartens and preschools and even private citizens brought their broken dolls to Sister Böhme to be repaired. Since she had no workshop, everything was stored wherever there was room in the house. And so it was that on the particular day of the inspector's visit there were many dolls to be repaired, and it looked like the entire house was full of dolls. "You don't have a house here, you have a dollhouse," the astounded building inspector said. "You are going to have to build a workshop."

When the "doll clinic" was finished, the branch had a place to meet. It had recently been declared illegal for church meetings to be held in private homes, so it fell out quite naturally that when the branch asked the authorities where they could meet they were directed to the doll clinic, which was under construction. To revise the building project to correspond to the needs of the Church was now only a matter of labor. The members put in many hours of hard labor until they finally held their first sacrament meeting there in May 1977.

In the meantime, the father-in-law and Renate's mother died, and the Ritters moved to Groitzsch. Now a different type of work became the central activity of the family—genealogy.

In Karl-Marx Stadt was a man who was an amateur-archivist and collected many family trees, pedigree charts, and family chronicles. He had published some of these. Each time after visiting him, Sister Ritter returned home with the fixed idea that she had to get all the names from that man and prepare them for temple work. "I fasted and prayed many times that I could obtain those books," but things were delayed until one day the owner died. They bought an entire washtub full of legal documents, pedigree charts, family coats of arms, etc., from the widow. Several members of the Church immediately went to work sorting out this material and preparing the names for the temple, and it was a good thing they did. When a later will was read, all of his records had to be placed into a state archive. But the work was already done. "This is the way our Heavenly Father hears our prayers and fulfills our hearts' desires."

Sister Ritter became known in her little village as "the angel of Groitzsch" for another type of service. It all began with two unmarried sisters named Graf, who were core members of the branch. Because they were growing old and more feeble, one day they asked Sister Ritter if she could help them. She went to their home to help them three times a day until 1973, when one of them died.

> Since Liesel [Graf], the surviving sister, was completely exhausted, I took her straight home with me. At a family counsel, it was decided to keep her there. In 1985 she suffered a broken hip while in a hospital, and later she shattered her right elbow in a fall. She should have gone to a nursing home, but I prayed for strength and took care of her.

Then two more women were added to the Ritter household. For many years, Brother and Sister Ritter spent all their vacation time in Leipzig helping an eighty-seven-year-old sister in the Church, Sister Liebing, and her crippled daughter. On Pentecost Sunday 1978, they were with them again, and Sister Ritter describes what occurred:

> It was at a Mothers' Day service in 1978, Pentecost Sunday. Famous mothers were remembered, and words of gratitude were expressed to all the mothers. One brave mother had brought eleven children to the world and raised them all to be good members in the gospel.
>
> That evening, as it had come so often, the thought came to me once again: "Only two times have you fulfilled your partnership with the Lord." The doctors had advised me against having another child because of the RH factor. A third child would likely be mentally retarded. I did not want to tempt God.
>
> Nevertheless, after discussing it with my husband, I asked the Lord if it might not be possible the next time we came to Leipzig to go to an orphanage where I could find a child who would call me mother. But then I spontaneously prayed, "Or would you prefer, Lord, that I take care of Sister Liebing?" I ended my prayer: "Whatever is your will, O Lord."
>
> I had just lain down to sleep when I heard a scream from the bedroom. "Renate, help. My mother is on the floor, and I can't lift her up." Yes, she had had a sudden stroke and should have been taken to a nursing home. But we held a family counsel and decided to take care of them. I had both mother and daughter at my home for the next three years, when the dear mother died in her sleep on her ninetieth birthday.

We had prayed for a third and a fourth child of our own, but our Heavenly Father sent us instead his helpless, feeble, and crippled children to take care of. We learned to bow to his will. We learned how to love and sacrifice. How could we do all of this and maintain our family unity? During family home evening each case was discussed, and we held a common prayer for wisdom and understanding in caring for these dear sisters for an indefinite time. We had to vacate rooms and make time for others. We were suddenly no longer just ourselves in our home, but we were there to care for others, to appreciate them, to help them, to love them as we loved and understood the members of our own family.

After having lived with Sister Ritter for fifteen years, Sister Graf died. During this time, Sister Ritter's husband died unexpectedly. Renate Böhme Ritter's service to others is a perfect example of "pure religion and undefiled before God and the Father" (James 1:27).

15

All They Have Left Is an Organ and a Window Drape

Paul Schmidt
as told by Manfred Schütze

I wonder if we who were born and grew up after the war can realize what it meant in the summer of 1946 to be called on a mission that was to last for fifty months—to be forty-six years old, to leave behind a wife and two children still in school? The story of Paul Schmidt is not so much about the intense concentration on converts as it is about how, out of the total confusion after the war, one had to worry about bringing the branches back to life, finding the scattered members, creating a place to meet, and helping the destitute survive.

On Brother Schmidt's arrival at the mission office, the mission president said, "You will go to Gera. All they have left is an organ and a window drape. You will build up the branch." And thus his worst fears were realized, because he had told his wife when he left, "The worst thing that can happen to me is that I will have to find a branch meeting place and furnish it." He learned that it often turns out in life that one has to do exactly that which one does not want to do. He added:

> I was successful in all of this because in principle I followed the mission rules. I had studied them thoroughly. The rules said that a pair of missionaries should have a room with two beds. When I told that to the branch president, he told me we would be lucky if we could find a room with one bed. I replied that that was also my opinion, but that my mission rules were of a different opinion and that I intended to follow them.

Paul Schmidt. Courtesy Manfred Schütze.

He and his companion went to work, and after a long, strenuous day, when they were ready to give up, they were led to a family who had a lovely house. Soon the family heard about their problem concerning a room and spontaneously made them an offer of a room with two beds. The price was agreeable, and the lady of the house remarked a short time after they had moved in that she had never had such neat guests.

With this one contact, they solved all of their problems: food—the family owned a butcher shop; a place to meet—the family ran an inn which rented rooms; furnishings—the innkeeper loaned them chairs and gave them wood to make a podium, etc. Summarizing, Brother Schmidt emphasized:

> All of our success in Gera was dependent on following the rules, which were based on experience and inspiration. If they had been based on experience alone, then we could have done nothing, because in 1945–46 no one had the kind of experience that was necessary. But it depended also on inspiration. We could follow that without worry, and we were successful.

Brother Schmidt and his companion were invited to eat in homes where their hosts didn't know what they were going to feed them because they had nothing to eat themselves. But the families had faith that they would be able to do it, and they did. He was once given the bedroom of a couple, temporarily, until the missionaries could find an apartment of their own. When he moved, he learned that the host family had been sleeping on a mattress in the washroom.

As missionaries after the war, they were also responsible for storing and distributing the welfare supplies that came from the American members. This program brought joy as well as problems, such as when a delivery would be temporarily confiscated as "black market" goods. These and other experiences—such as the organization of the *Freundecho* [a magazine] in 1948 or a camp-out in Berlin in 1950 with eight hundred participants—helped bring the members together and provide stability in the Church after the devastating experiences of the war. These were not small duties in a time of poverty and deprivation.

After returning from his mission, Brother Schmidt faithfully filled many callings. For almost seventeen years, he served as president of the elders quorum and as a counselor in the branch presidency. He is especially proud that he served for almost fifty years as a teacher in the various organizations of the Church and as a teacher trainer. Not only is he active today, he is dynamic in the best sense of the word.

Part III

Living with the Communists

The following excerpts are mostly from interviews with younger members who were born shortly before, during, or after the war and who went on missions in the 1950s and early 1960s. These are the members who grew up in a communist country, went to communist schools where atheism was officially taught, and had to wend their way carefully between church and state. Some of them hardly mention politics, the State, or communism in their interviews; for them politics were merely a background to their normal life in the Church. In some cases, this silence was, they informed us, out of a habit of avoiding any discussion of a political nature. Others were more anxious to talk about their confrontations with a political system that was in large part antagonistic to their religious beliefs. The following excerpts are from the members who kept the Church together in the 1960s, '70s, and '80s and who lived to see "the dawning of a brighter day."

Branch house in Wolgast, 1965. As District President Walter Krause had prophesied, members now had their own cars. Courtesy Edith Krause.

16

All the Promises Have Been Fulfilled

Ilse Kaden and Herbert Kaden

Ilse Kaden and Herbert Kaden live in an old section of Dresden known as Freidrichstadt. Across one wall of their sitting room, a modern-styled storage cabinet stands as evidence of Brother Kaden's abilities as a master cabinetmaker. A block from their home, the Kadens have a small garden plot where flowers, vegetables, fruit trees, and berries grow in neat rows in front of a small garden cottage. These were the settings of our interviews with the Kadens. What stands out in our memories of them is Sister Kaden's sparkling brown eyes and radiant smile and Brother Kaden's gentle humor.

The original interview with Brother and Sister Kaden took place in May 1990. A subsequent interview took place in April 1994, providing additional information.

Ilse: We were both born in Grosshartmannsdorf in the Erz Mountains. There used to be a branch of the Church there, but it was closed when they formed the stake. The old branch house is now used as a dormitory for temple visitors. I was born in 1914 and went to school there. When I was a child, I used to go to Sunday School, but only when my father was at work. There was a Sunday School teacher who lived in our apartment building, and she took me to church, but I had to be back before my father came home because he then took me to the children's service of the Lutheran Evangelical Church. That's the church to which my parents belonged. So, in 1929, I finished school and moved to Karl-Marx Stadt. Now it is called Chemnitz again. I went to church there one Sunday, and that's where we met one another. We had gone to the same school but had never become acquainted.

G. Davis: Brother Kaden, when were you born?

Herbert: I was born in 1910, and I was baptized in 1921, when I was eleven years old. My mother was a member. My father had been killed in the First World War in 1914, and my mother was alone with us two boys. She wanted to be with her husband again, and it was because of this hope and this faith that we came to church. In Grosshartmannsdorf we had a lovely branch, about seventy members, which was quite a few for a small village. It was wonderful.

Ilse: At Christmas time, we always put on a play, and we used to have bazaars. We had big exhibits, we had all kinds of handicrafts, we baked cakes and made potato salad. The whole village turned out—the baker, the shopkeeper, they were all there.

Herbert: So, I chose a very worldly girl to be my wife, and she is still my wife. We were married in 1938, and then in 1940, I had to go to war. My wife said, "If my husband comes back from the war all in one piece, then I will be baptized."

G. Davis: And where were you living at the time?

Ilse: We were living in Grosshartmannsdorf.

N. Davis: Was there heavy fighting going on there?

Ilse: Yes, there was! We fled when the Russians came. We got on the last train out. We saw the Russians coming, and there was this military train at the railroad station. My father worked at the post office in the train station. Everyone climbed onto the train, and we left because the Russians were coming. The train was heading toward Sayda and Mittelsaida, that direction.

Herbert: That's down on the Czechoslovakian border.

Ilse: And then a troop of soldiers on horseback came toward us, and there was a volley of gunfire. We saw the men being shot off their horses, and I held my hand over my children's eyes, and we just kept going and going. My father said we wanted to get off at Olbernhau. We had relatives there, and that's where we wanted to get off, but the train couldn't stop, so we just kept going and going and landed up in Czechoslovakia as refugees.

I had my two sons with me plus my parents and my brother's two little girls, and there we were in Czechoslovakia in a town called Eger. That was the first place the train stopped. We were all exhausted, and they took us to a schoolhouse, where we were divided up into the various classrooms. There was another family from our area with us who were also Mormons. Then a man from

Ilse Kaden and Herbert Kaden. Dresden, 1991. Courtesy Herbert Kaden.

the area came in and said, "Someone in here has to be in charge." They chose my father. He said, "Would you help me get things under control here?" Everything was really in a state of confusion. My father said to me, "Would you help me, sweetheart?" I said, "I'll help you," and so we got things in order, and there we were for eight days.

A woman lived next door in a little house, and she told me, "If you need anything, you can come to me with your children, and I will help you." She came to see me one night and said, "Listen, Mrs. Kaden. They are going to put the men into a barbed-wire enclosure and the women in another one. I don't know if they will let you keep your children, but I can help you if you want me to."

I told my father what was happening, and he said, "Well, if that's the case, we will give all the money we have if we can get home." And I said, "Father, we have to tell the others from our village." So I told the Reicherts, and they came with us through the "night and fog" [*Nacht und Nebel*, sneaking through fields and over the border to avoid being seen by guards]. This man put us in a boat to get across the river; it was like a ferry. There were my father and mother, myself, the four children, and the Reicherts. We had a large handcart and a baby buggy. The man had his small son as well as a bicycle. He told us, "I'll lead you over to the place where the forest ends, and when I turn around, you run for it. Run to the house; they know you are coming. They will open the door and let you in."

He watched until the guard went by, and then he turned around, and we ran for it. My father had the handcart; my mother had the baby buggy. I put a pacifier covered with honey in the baby's mouth so he wouldn't cry. The people opened the door, and we went flying in with all our belongings. When we peeked back, we saw the guards coming back. But let me tell you, we fell to our knees. Every one of us fell to our knees. And then we went on. It was about six o'clock in the morning; I remember it so clearly. We had arrived just at dawn and left at six.

And so we made it to Brambach with prayer as our guide. My parents were not members of the Church, but they went down on their knees with us. There was nothing else we could do. From there, we went to Hohendorf, where I had an aunt. This aunt had a restaurant, but the SS used it for their meeting place, so it had been taken away from her. When we got there, she had only one room left for herself. We stayed there overnight, and then my father said, "Let's go home. Let's go back and see if our house is still standing." So back we went again to Grosshartmannsdorf. My mother stayed behind in Hohendorf with the three children, and my father and I and our oldest son, Rainer, walked back to Grosshartmannsdorf.

Herbert: They walked the whole way.

Ilse: There were no trains. Nothing was moving. Of course, some Russians caught up with us, and we were afraid. I took an old shawl and put it over my head so that I would look like a grandma. They didn't bother old women, but if they got their hands on a young woman it was bad. Finally we got back to Grosshartmannsdorf. Our house was still there. My mother-in-law had saved everything she could, because the Russians had occupied it. The next day we had to report to the city hall and tell them that we were back. A man, who had been put in charge by the Russians, said to my father, "Now tell me, Max, how could you just run off like that?" My father just turned blue in the face and just screamed at the man.

But back we went to get my mother and the other children. When we were returning with our handcart, there came a truck full of Russian men and women with stuff piled high. They stopped, and someone took my little Berndt out of the baby buggy and handed him to someone up on the truck. I nearly fainted. I only remember my father trying to hold me up, and when they saw that I was fainting, they came down and said they only wanted to hold him. They weren't going to take him away from me. Then they all got back into the truck and drove off, and we just stood there and bawled. Then six months later, Herbert came back from the war.

Herbert: I got out of an American prison camp in Bavaria in 1945. I was in prison for three days. I was a medical orderly, and that's why I was released after three days.

G. Davis: And then you came back to Freiberg?

Herbert: It wasn't so simple. In 1945 we had to sneak our way across into the Soviet Zone, in "night and fog," as we say.

Ilse: He had to see whether or not his family were still all there. I kept my word and was baptized a week after he came home from the war. I always knew that it was true, but I couldn't join because of my parents. They were always so good to me, and they were Evangelical-Lutherans. I was always telling myself, "You just can't do it," but then I decided to be baptized anyway. My husband didn't even know. On the first Sunday after he came back, it was announced that Sister Kaden would be baptized in the lake. But my parents already knew about it.

G. Davis: What did your parents think about it?

Ilse: Well, it was done then.

Herbert: Things had changed, they had become much calmer about it. And besides, we were our own family then; we had our own apartment.

Ilse: At first, you see, my parents knew nothing about the Church but polygamy. That's all they knew. They said, "Yes, you will take a handsome husband, he will never be faithful to you, and you won't have him to yourself." That's all they knew, but, well, he proved them wrong.

Herbert: I returned home from the POW camp in September 1945. I applied for a job at the prison in Waldheim and got a job there as a master carpenter. We moved the family to Waldheim in 1946, February, to an apartment that was for employees of the prison. In June the Soviet Occupation Army came in and occupied the prison.

Ilse: They moved out a lot of the workers but kept the supervisors. "You, specialist, you stay." So my husband stayed. I was so frightened when he had to go to work early in the morning and then when I had to pick him up and there were those strange guards there. And then they made us move out of our apartment.

Herbert: The Russians processed the entire group of prisoners, assembled them in Waldheim, and sent them off to the East. Then they gave orders that every apartment had to be vacated. There were forty-nine apartments there, and they had to be vacated—immediately!

Ilse: We moved out in a pouring rain, a regular downpour. Then the order came that all freestanding clothes closets, all lamps and ceiling lights, and all overstuffed furniture had to remain in the apartment. Fortunately, we had got our things out the day before, so we didn't have to give up any of those things.

Herbert: We had to be out in three days.

Ilse: And we weren't the only ones.

Herbert: Fifty-five families had to move out . . .

Ilse: All at once. But we were lucky. Most of the people had open trucks, like the farmers have, and the furniture was just piled in, in the rain! We had a closed furniture truck, and our Rainer stood by the truck and told the movers where everything went. He would say, "That's ours, that comes over here." He watched them when they brought things down. So when they had all our things in the truck, we were moved into the house of a dentist, where we were given the servant's rooms. They had had a servant who occupied two rooms.

Herbert: Everything was done according to orders. We had no choice.

Ilse: So there was all our furniture stacked up in the entry and hallway so that we could get by. We had our own cooking stove, and the first thing my husband did was make a hole for a stovepipe and set up our stove. A lot of our things were wet, and we had to dry them out. Then the dentist's wife saw the stove and said, "Oh, that's wonderful, you won't have to share the kitchen with me." I said, "No, my husband has taken the liberty of setting up our stove." She said, "Oh, I'm glad, that's very nice." You can understand why she was happy.

N. Davis: You mean she just had to take another family into her house? The State just said, "You go here?"

Ilse: Yes, yes. That's the way it was.

Herbert: If a room was empty, the State would just confiscate it.

Ilse: And that room was empty, so they confiscated it. And the people didn't get any rent, either. That was hard on them. But we had a very good relationship with the dentist and his wife. Every morning she would say to my boys, "Aren't you going to come in and have breakfast with me?" Then she took our two boys in and gave them breakfast. We didn't have much to eat, so that's why she always took our boys in for breakfast.

N. Davis: Explain what you mean when you say you didn't have much to eat.

Ilse: Everything was rationed. We got rationing stamps, but we got very few. Bread was rationed, butter was rationed, meat was rationed. There was really very, very little to eat. But we had it better than many. I set up an exchange with some farmers. I darned their stockings. You can't imagine how their stockings stunk when I got them—from the cow barns. I had to soak them in water and then beat them because we didn't have any soap. We had some canned soap called *Bimstein,* but it wouldn't even make suds. So first I washed all the socks and hung them up to dry, and then I darned them, even though they weren't really clean. And then I took them back to the farmers in a big sack, and I got butter, cottage cheese, eggs, milk. I never took money, never.

Once I knitted jackets for a miller—for him, for his wife, and for his son. I often knitted all night long in order to finish them on time, and I got a sack of flour. They asked, "Do you want money or flour?" Who would have said money in those days? No one! I took the flour. I still had my parents to take care of, and I had to share our food with them.

And then it came out that the miller had been with the SS. A big politician, and he had cheated a lot of people at the mill. So he was taken to Waldheim, where my husband was foreman in the cabinet shop and my uncle was the warden of the prison. All of the new prisoners were interviewed, and my uncle said, "Well, Mr. Hempel, would you like to work in the kitchen. Since you were a miller, I think you belong in the kitchen." "No," he said, "I would like to work in the cabinet shop." "Why in the cabinet shop?" my uncle said. "Because I know Mr. Kaden. I helped his wife once when they were desperate." That's what he said because he had given me that flour. My uncle asked him, "What great things did you do for them?" I ask you, who would have worked for money when they were starving to death. No one!

N. Davis: Money was of no value?

Ilse: Useless. There was nothing to buy. We got some *Zuckerrüben* [sugar beets] from some members in the Döbeln Branch. We scrubbed them thoroughly, and then we cooked them. We made syrup, sugar-beet syrup. And again I had good luck in that I didn't have to do all the work by myself. My husband sent some help over from the prison, and they helped me scrub and cook the sugar beets. Well, they ate a lot of them, but that didn't matter; I was glad to share them. We had a big washtub, the kind we used to boil our clothes in, and we used a tub like that to cook the sugar beets. We took off the water and spread it on our bread. We would take dried potato flour and mix it with a little oil and smear it on the stove top and bake things on it.

N. Davis: Did you have a garden then?

Ilse: We didn't have a garden, but I had some connections with a man who raised vegetables. But then we finally got another apartment in Waldheim and moved out of the two little rooms. We were given an apartment for employees; the Russians had occupied it. That was a real catastrophe, what they had done to that apartment. They didn't understand running water and had poked pipes into the walls wherever they wanted. We planted rows of beans in the backyard and had them growing on stakes. The blossoms were a fire red, and the Russians came along and thought they were flowers. They broke the blossoms off and made bouquets out of them.

Herbert: We belonged at the time to the Döbeln Branch. They met in the back rooms of a building there in Döbeln, and all the members from Freiberg and Karl-Marx Stadt attended there. There were a group of refugees from Silesia who had settled there, so we built up a branch. There were about eighty members.

Ilse: But we had to get from Waldheim to Döbeln . . .

Herbert: By bicycle.

Ilse: There were no trains running then. So we went by bicycle, each one with one of the children on the front. He took the older boy, I took the little one, and we had our lunch sack hanging off one side. There was nothing there to eat; we had to take our lunch with us. We could not eat with the members; they didn't have anything either. And then back home again, and you could always count on it—one of the bicycles would break down, and we would have to walk the rest of the way. Oh, that was something.

My husband had a position in the branch there, and when there was bad weather, I couldn't go with my little children, but it never stopped him. Sometimes the weather was really bad, and I would say, "Oh, Herbert, you had better stay home today," but he went anyway, on his bicycle, and I stayed home with the children.

One day I went with my son Rainer from Waldheim to Döbeln because some welfare supplies had arrived from America. We got bags of wheat, canned peaches, salt, canned herring, and powered milk. We loaded everything into this four-wheeled hand wagon and pushed it the eight kilometers back to Waldheim.

G. Davis: Was the wagon covered?

Ilse: Well covered, so that no one could see what we had. On the way back, our Rainer kept saying, "Mommy, if the people knew what we had in this wagon!" We couldn't let them know. They would have taken much of it; they would have confiscated it. We got home safely, and what a joyful day that was. We could live well for a while. I didn't have to tell my children, "No, you can't have a slice of bread." In the apartment next door was a family who kept a lock on their bread box. Only the father had a key, and at night he would cut off a slice for each of the children. That was hard. Whenever the children came to our apartment, I gave them something to eat.

And then in the fall, I went to Grosshartmannsdorf, where my parents lived, and helped harvest potatoes for the farmers. They turned them up with a machine, and then the women came along behind and put them into baskets. My parents took care of the children while I worked in the fields. For a day's work, I got a hundred pounds of potatoes.

N. Davis: How long did you have to work in a day?

Ilse: We started at six in the morning, had an hour off for lunch, and worked then until six in the evening. That was long enough. You could feel it in your back.

Herbert: In 1950 we moved to Bautzen. I was employed by the prison there, and that is where our Elke was born. In Bautzen the branch was very small, about thirty members.

Ilse: They were so happy when someone moved in.

Herbert: When they got new members. But we didn't want to stay in Bautzen. The prison system had been under the Department of Justice, but now the State Police had taken them all over, they had become political institutions, and I didn't want to work for the police. Then the director of the prison called me in and said, "I'm sorry, but I am going to have to let you go because you belong to that American church." And then he said, "If you sign this document that certifies that you do not belong to that church, then everything will be all right."

Ilse: "If you belong to that American church, you can't work for us anymore."

Herbert: I said, "Well, I'm sorry, but I really enjoy attending my church."

Ilse: You told me about it. "I can't sign that, and I'm going to go to church no matter what you say." Right? And then he had to spend his vacation looking for another job, and we had three children then.

Herbert: So I went looking for work and got a job with a firm in Dresden. That was in 1952.

Ilse: But you couldn't start in an administrative position. You had to start out supervising the apprentices.

G. Davis: Now was this a problem when one belonged to any church, or was it a problem only for the Mormons?

Herbert: No, anyone. If you were Lutheran, no administrative position.

Ilse: More particularly the Lutheran Church . . .

Herbert: Because we were not so well known.

Ilse: The Evangelical Lutheran Church was so active, they couldn't study at the university, they couldn't do anything.

Herbert: I was a cabinetmaker, that is, carpenter or cabinetmaker. We did all the work for the big communist buildings here in the GDR. You have seen some of those big buildings in Berlin, the Congress Hall? We did all of the interiors.

Ilse: He had seventy workers under him in his department. He was the foreman.

Herbert: For a time, we were doing the interiors of airplanes. They wanted to start up an airplane factory here. They built only one plane, and it crashed, and that was the end of it. I was permitted to do the interior construction, but I was not permitted to work on a plane when it was at the airport.

Ilse: Because he was a Mormon. And then he was supposed to sign a document that he was not a Mormon, and he lost his job.

Herbert: I had to go looking for work.

Ilse: After he looked for about three months, the mayor of Dresden finally had four jobs available. So that's when you applied at the Hellerau

Furniture Factory. And they hired you, but not as a foreman, which you really were, but you had to go back to the workbench.

Herbert: So now I was in a large firm, the Hellerau German Furniture Factory, and I had a chance to work my way up, but only because of my professional experience.

Ilse: He couldn't start out as a foreman. They told him he had to supervise the apprentices, but he said no, he would rather go back to the workbench. Then later they had to beg you to become the foreman, right?

Herbert: I stayed there eight years, until 1975, but only during the later years was I the foreman.

Ilse: And you were given high recommendations and awards, several, and in spite of the fact that you did not belong to the party.

G. Davis: So, tell us about the branch then. You were in the branch house on Dr.-Kurt-Fischer Allee then, right?

Herbert: When we came here in 1952, the Dresden Branch had about three hundred members, on the books.

Ilse: But how many active?

Herbert: In the years right after the war, 1945 to 1950, there were many added to the membership list because of the welfare plan.

Ilse: We got peaches, shortening, and wheat.

Herbert: And the branch grew because of the "canned-goods Mormons," and then they dropped out, but we still had about three hundred members. From 1953 until 1955, I was the branch president here in Dresden. That was when we celebrated the one-hundredth anniversary of the Dresden Branch.

N. Davis: 1855 to 1955, right?

Herbert: Right. And that was the first time we had the opportunity of having an American mission president visit us in Dresden—Brother Gregory. We printed beautiful golden invitations, which, of course, had to be approved by the Russian Commander. He approved everything.

G. Davis: So who was supervising the missionaries during this time?

Herbert: We didn't have any missionaries from outside the country. Later, Brother Burkhardt, the first counselor to the mission president, supervised the missionaries for fifteen years, from 1954 until 1960. Brother Schulze and Brother Ortlieb were missionaries.

Ilse: After 1982, when the first stake was organized, we had stake missionaries. Look how full our new chapel is now, how many attend the meetings. We might have 260 or 280 members in attendance. There was a time here around 1960 when we had been reduced to about fifty members at our sacrament meetings.

G. Davis: What had happened to all the members?

Ilse: All emigrated or died.

Herbert: We used to have only one organist here in Dresden. Now we have several. That was Brother Hilde. He did what he wanted and didn't let anything bother him. The organ was up in the loft, and the choir was down below. The choir director had to follow him.

Ilse: He could play beautifully.

Herbert: We experienced everything here in the Dresden Ward, from the depths to where we are now.

G. Davis: Would you say that those days were difficult or beautiful?

Herbert: Difficult.

Ilse: Well, yes, they were difficult, but beautiful, too. For me those were the most beautiful times; I have to say that. We had very little, but how I remember Easter, Christmas—we always had the youth conferences here in Dresden. Those were wonderful times.

Herbert: Yes, in spite of everything.

Ilse: The way we stuck together was beautiful. Oh, the excursions we took! And what plays

Members of the Schwerin Branch costumed for a play from the Book of Mormon. Branches in the German Democratic Republic built unity through drama. And drama-related practical jokes lightened the members' lives. Neubrandenburg, 1984. Courtesy Edith Krause.

we put on! We even did a big production of *Hanneles Himmelfahrt* [*Hannele's Ascention*] by the German playwright Gerhart Hauptmann]. That was supposed to be a serious drama, and when Hannele was lying in her casket—that was Sister Moskva—she got to laughing so hard that the casket was shaking. I played a deaconess. That was wonderful. The productions were marvelous. Of course, we didn't take it all too seriously; at practices we laughed and had a good time.

We had a director, Brother Böhme, and he expected everything to be perfect. Sometimes, when we didn't pay attention, he would throw the script down and say, "That's it, I'm through." Then we would be very humbled and repentant and say, "Please don't leave, Brother Böhme, we'll do it right." "Alright," he would say," and we would go on with the rehearsal, and the performance was always a big hit. It was wonderful.

Then we did Christmas plays, manger scenes. My husband was a shepherd; Brother Strauch was also a shepherd.

Herbert: And Brother Höhle was one of the actors.

Ilse: Yes, Brother Höhle. And something always happened; it was always something. Brother Strauch had this long staff, and he used it to scratch his head. That was so funny to see, and just at that moment Brother Robert Höhle gave the cue, and the shepherds were supposed to sing. But they just stood there with their cheeks puffed out, trying to suppress their laughter, and when Brother Höhle gave the signal, not a sound came out.

Herbert: The whole branch broke out laughing.

Ilse: Then Brother Robert Höhle said, "Alright, we will just begin again." Then everyone got control of themselves and sang properly. But the audience, all of the guests, they laughed and laughed and couldn't stop laughing. Brother Kempe, who played Joseph, was so angry afterwards. Well, we just made a comedy out of the whole thing. It was the shepherds' fault. But that's the kind of fun we had putting on plays.

Herbert: And I was the branch president.

Ilse: Oh, we had some great theater. Once we were doing a drama, and Anneliese or someone came up to me before the performance and said, "Watch out, Brother Höhle has some trick in mind." During the dress rehearsal, everything went fine. But during the performance, he said to me, "Well, my lovey-dovey" or some silly thing like that. He was just supposed to say, "Well, dear." Everyone else knew that it was a joke that didn't fit at that point in the play, and oh, how they broke out laughing. It was just too beautiful.

We used to be at the church three times during the week. I was the president of the Primary then; that's when we still had our children at home. Then I went to Relief Society and then to Mutual. And Papa was everywhere all the time. I don't know where we found the time in those days. I was working then, and we had all of these meetings during the week. Sometimes I would run out of clean clothes and would have to do the washing on a Sunday. My neighbor was always saying, "Ilse, how do you keep it up? You are running off to your church at least three times every week." Well, we did it, and it was wonderful.

On Saturday we used to have outings in the woods or to Sonnland. Once the men decided they wanted to get off by themselves, and so we said, "Fine, they can go off by themselves if they want to." But one sister, Sister Herta Moskva, got out of her husband where they were going. The men were going to take a hike to Sonnland. So we decided that we would take a hike to Sonnland but didn't tell them anything. You should have seen their mouths fall open when we showed up with all the children. We had a wonderful time. We played games. Of course, I had to be everywhere and in everything and ended up spraining my ankle, and they had to carry me to the bus. I couldn't walk. But it was fun anyway.

And we used to go swimming in the Elbe. Then Sundays we were all together at church, Sunday morning and then again Sunday afternoon.

Herbert: We spent more time at church than we did in our apartment.

Ilse: Yes, yes, yes, yes!

G. Davis: Did you ever feel a little overburdened?

Ilse: Never, never!

Herbert: She just didn't notice.

G. Davis: Did the members here feel somewhat isolated from the Church in Salt Lake City or from the General Authorities?

Herbert: Yes, certainly we did.

Ilse: We didn't have many visitors, but when one came, the building was packed. Of course, Brother Burkhardt was always here. He was everywhere, and everyone loved him so much. That was a big advantage for us. He did so many, many good things for us. Those were beautiful times. I would not have wanted to miss them. Of course, it is nice now, too, but. . . . It would be so hard on us now if we had to go to church twice on Sunday, to say nothing of the expense. But in those days it wasn't hard, not at all. And if you sang in the choir, you had to be there an hour earlier.

N. Davis: Then someone had to get the building ready.

Ilse: Oh, the heating; that was hard. That was Brother Heller. Sometimes he had to be there all day long with just a short lunch break. There was a big furnace, and he had to keep shoveling the coal in so that the building would be warm when the brothers and sisters arrived.

Herbert: But we didn't have the large furnace then, just the old small one. Sometimes the brothers had to work all night long on Saturday until Sunday morning just to get the building warm.

Ilse: That's right. Our boys had to help, and sometimes they set up a cot and took shifts shoveling coal through the night so that the rooms would be warm for us the next morning. And then, the cleaning! We didn't have a janitor; we all had to pitch in. We sisters had to get down on our knees with scrubbing brushes and scrub the entire building while the brothers carried and changed the water. Oh, that was hard.

And downstairs we had the kitchen. We had such a big kettle to cook for the conferences that I couldn't get up high enough to stir the food. Brother Krause had to make a platform for me to stand on so that I could stir the food.

Herbert: Brother Krause could do anything. He was a carpenter, plumber, he was everything.

Ilse: There were stairs leading out to the big park beside the church, and to call the young people in for breakfast or for lunch, we had a big gong. All the little children fought over who would get to strike the gong. That was fun.

Then we always had a genealogy week here. All of the genealogists from the country came here for a week. They worked and slept right in the chapel, and we took care of feeding them. We had a breakfast and then a little snack in the middle of the morning, then lunch and another snack in the afternoon, and then supper. There were usually four of us in the kitchen. There was Sister Wöhe, there was Sister Pfeil, and there was Sister Hagen. And we didn't have any machinery; we had to do everything by hand—scrubbing and peeling and slicing. Not like at this last Youth Conference where we had an electric stove and oven and a machine that peeled the potatoes. We used to sit in a circle around a pot and sing songs and peel potatoes. Then my little grandson Kai would come along and throw a potato in and splash water all over us. Oh, that was fun. But then we were often worn out for two weeks after. Papa would come along and say, "You said it didn't hurt then, but now you are moaning and groaning." Oh, those were beautiful times.

Herbert: We stuck together. We knew one another. We worked side by side year after year. That was better.

Ilse: We used to get packages of used clothing from West Germany, which were given to the Relief Society to distribute. That was nice. Of course, sometimes we got things that we couldn't pass on to anyone, but we got many, many nice things.

G. Davis: What kind of a relationship did you have with the government?

Herbert: During the years when I was the branch president, we had to report every sacrament meeting, every meeting of any kind to the police. I had to turn in a monthly report of every speaker by name. One time I didn't report a branch party *[Faschingsvergnügen]*. I was informed that it should have been reported within one week.

Ilse: He had to go to the police station, and I was afraid they might lock him up.

Herbert: It wasn't so pleasant. I appeared before this official, and he said to me, "I know you very well. I know everything about your branch. I attended the big celebration you had."

Ilse: That was our centennial celebration.

Herbert: "But," he said, "there has been a crime committed, and I am obligated to punish you." I had to pay a fine of eleven marks. That was it.

Ilse: Practically nothing.

Herbert: "I understand your situation," he said, "but I have to punish you." He was a very nice official. But those were difficult days. They were always checking on everything. The secret police would go to the neighbors and ask about us because we belonged to an "American church." They were not supposed to say anything, but they always came to us afterwards and said, "Listen, someone was here from the secret police again."

Herbert: We were always being watched. You had to behave yourself. They probably had me on their list because I was the branch president at the time. But I never had any trouble at work. They would ask me why I never drank coffee, and I would tell them honestly why. "Oh, it's forbidden for you." "No, it's voluntary." They used to tease me at first, but then things were OK.

Ilse: I never had any trouble at work, none at all. I was the head saleswoman for our floor in a department store on Ernst-Thälmann Street. When I left, one of the saleswomen said to me, "Do you know what we used to call you? We used to call you the Good Samaritan; we always called you Ilse, the Good Samaritan." "That's nice," I said. I did what I could, but it wasn't much.

We didn't have much. Sometimes the people would want a little wool yarn, and I would feel so sorry for them because we had wool in our warehouse, but we weren't allowed to sell it, just because we had to have a supply in our warehouse. Well, sometimes I would just snatch a little of it and give it to someone.

We used to tie our bathrobes here around the waist with a cord. Well, this woman had been everywhere. She was going on vacation to the Baltic with her children and couldn't find any cording for her bathrobe. We had the material. I told her, "If you could just wait a little while until I have my lunch break, then I will braid you a cord." She waited very patiently, and I got the yarn together and went up to the next floor and braided her a cord. Our boss looked in and thought, "What's she up to now?" Well, there was an article about this in the newspaper. The lady said she thought she was living in paradise; the saleslady braided a cord for her bathrobe.

I was trained in textiles. I went to work later in a butcher shop only out of desperation, at the time when there was nothing to eat.

N. Davis: We have heard about your problem of getting teaching manuals for the Church.

Herbert: Not allowed. If we could get a teaching manual from over there [West Germany], it had to be copied sixty or seventy times so that the branches could have at least one teaching manual.

G. Davis: Brother Albrecht told us about an occasion where President Burkhardt instructed you to destroy all unauthorized material.

Herbert: There was always the danger that these things would be confiscated, and it became important that all the branches not have any written material that had not been explicitly authorized. So everything was burned. We spent day and night in front of our stove burning the stuff.

Ilse: That was sad; that was really sad.

Herbert: But I didn't burn any of my private literature.

Ilse: The first time I was permitted to go over to West Germany, after I was on a retirement pension, that was the only thing I wanted to bring back—teaching manuals and copies of the *Stern* [Church magazine in German].

N. Davis: Did Herbert go over with you?

Ilse: No, that was not permitted. That was before his retirement, and I had to go by myself.

N. Davis: So how did that come about?

Ilse: I was a clerk in a grocery store, and I had to have permission from my supervisor. My supervisor said to me, "But you don't have your authorization from the City Hall." I had to have permission from the authorities to travel because I had to make a monthly report of sales. Anyone who accounted for money had to have special permission to travel. Normally, I would have had to wait three years, but my supervisor stamped my request anyway, and then I could buy a ticket to Stuttgart.

I had a "cousin" over there; we just say cousin, which means a member of the Church who helped sponsor people from the East. We didn't even know one another; she had only written to me. So we said we would tie a red scarf to our purses, and that way we would recognize one another at the train station. I was one of the last persons to get off the train. I saw this enormous fat woman, and I thought to myself, "Can that be her?" It wasn't. Then my "cousin" came up to me and gave me a big hug. We had a wonderful time together; I will never forget it. I was invited out to see so many members. Everyone wanted to meet me. I made so many friends. A few years later, Herbert was able to travel with me.

G. Davis: So, what did you bring home with you from Stuttgart?

Ilse: I brought copies of the *Stern* and teaching manuals so that we could type off copies. And I brought a children's Bible. My cousin was so generous. She was always putting money in my hand and saying, "Here, buy whatever you want." But what did I buy? Things for the children and grandchildren. She was always saying, "What did you buy for yourself?" No, nothing. Only for the children and grandchildren and a watch for Herbert. And the teaching manuals. I packed them between my clothes in the suitcase and put something in every pocket.

Anyway, she said, "You can't take that with you. What if they check your bags at the border? I'm going to pray for you until I know you are across the border." She was more afraid than I was. Well, they would have taken it all away from me and detained me there. But I was a disobedient citizen. I said, "Father in Heaven, it's not a sin to smuggle these things in." They didn't check me, not once. In our train compartment, they always pointed out someone and made them unpack everything, but never me. Heavenly Father knew that we needed these things I was carrying in. Oh, that was wonderful. And I made so many new friends over there.

G. Davis: So you always brought teaching manuals with you.

Herbert: I was coming across once from West Berlin, and they checked my bags, and I had a bunch of Church forms. The guard looked in: "What is this?" Then he didn't say anything more. That was it.

Ilse: Those things weren't forbidden. But I didn't have to open a bag.

Herbert: It was always a frightening experience.

Ilse: We prayed a lot at the border; that's for certain. We prayed until we were over. I really prayed to my Father in Heaven that they would not want to see what was in my bags. It worked every time.

When we were both retired, we could cross the border together. We would go to visit Brother Schlevoigt in Frankfurt, and he had everything, all the teaching manuals. We knew him quite well. "Here," he would say, "I'll gladly give you everything, but will you make it across the border?" Yes, that's the way it was in those days. Nowadays we say, "Oh, those days weren't so bad," but I can remember how my heart would be pounding.

Ilse: It was 1981, when the two of us traveled to the temple in Switzerland. At that time, we had no idea that we would have a temple here. But we didn't have any money. We were allowed to exchange fifteen East marks for fifteen West marks; that was all. But we were fortunate we got to go at all.

Sister and Brother Ringger were here in Dresden and Sister Ringger said to me, "Tell me, Sister Kaden, have you ever been to the temple?" "No," I said, "we're not allowed to travel. How could we go—how could we do that?" "Sister Kaden," she said, "this is not right. You leave it up to me; I'll see to it somehow."

I will find a cousin for you in Switzerland." In about four weeks, I had a cousin.

N. Davis: Another cousin!

Ilse: Another cousin. That was Brother and Sister Litscher. She is Sister Ringger's sister. The situation was, you had to have a letter from a relative in the West before you could get permission to travel, even if you were retired. The relatives had to say that they would provide for you, and you had to take this letter of invitation to the police. So she wrote me this nice letter: "Dear Ilse, we are so happy that after so many years we will be able to see you once again. It is such a pleasure for us to invite you," etc. So that was just fine.

But then I went to the travel bureau and ran into another problem: "You can pay from here to Basel with East marks, to the Swiss border. But you have to have West money from there and for the return trip." "Oh," I thought, "I had better talk with my husband." So I called him at his office and said, "Papa, the Ringgers will have to pay for the return trip because we are not allowed to pay for it with East marks. He said, "Well, then we'd better let it go." But Brother Burkhardt said, "We will not let it go; that's out of the question." "Good," I said, "I won't give up."

I went down on my knees to my Father in Heaven. "Let me find a way," I said. "I want to go to the temple." I thought about it. Wednesdays there is a different shift on duty at the travel bureau. So back I went, and I was a little bold. I put two marks over the counter and said, "I would like some information." "Yes, what would you like to know?" "We would like very much to go to Basel, then on to Zollikofen, then on to Zurich, and then home. How can we arrange it so that I can pay for the entire trip myself with our East marks? Is there some way, or do my friends in the West have to pay for us?" "Come a little closer," he said, "I will let you in on a secret. Go over to the airline office; they have a way."

So I took my letter and papers and went to the airline office. "Just a moment," she said. "I'll see if there is any space available. Yes," she said, "but you can stay only thirteen days, and it will be rather expensive. You can go there by train, but you will have to fly home and do so one day earlier than you had planned." "I will have to talk to my husband about it, but please hold our reservations." "Yes," she said. "I'll take care of that for you."

So I called my husband. I said, "Herbert, she says we can pay for everything ourselves, for the plane, for the train, for everything. Shall I book our travel?" "Of course," he said. "Do it." So I went back and booked our travel, and we could pay for the entire trip ourselves. Sister Ringger met us in Basel and drove us to Zollikofen, where we had a wonderful room right by the temple. We went to the temple every day.

The first time we went into the temple, I said, "Herbert, this is where I would like to work someday." He said, "Here we are in the temple for the first time in our lives. Now you have finally got your wish, and you already want more." On the evening of the day on which we were sealed, the temple president took us on a tour of the entire temple. We came out about eight o'clock and wanted to do something special on our "wedding day," but all we had was one apple and a small piece of sausage. We went down to the waiting room, where there were tables. I saw a sister watching us and then talking with the others who were there. I said, "Papa, that woman is talking about us." Then he said, "Oh, the strange things you imagine." When we came to the temple the next morning, the temple president handed us an envelope and said, "I am supposed to give you this anonymous gift." This sister I had seen the night before had taken up a collection for us because she knew we were from the East.

I met her later, and we developed a good friendship. Her name was Sister Jaeger. She had had a husband who would never allow her to go to the temple. After he died, she went to the temple, and in the temple she met a single man from the Erz Mountain region, near where we lived. They married and were very happy together. It was while we were in the temple in Switzerland that we learned we were going to have a temple of our own.

G. Davis: You learned about that in 1981?

Ilse: In Switzerland. No one here knew about it, oh no. And we couldn't say a word about it, and we didn't say a word. It hadn't been announced yet. It wasn't finished until 1985.

Well, we stayed a week at the temple in Zollikofen and then flew from Zurich to Prague, and from Prague we took the train back to Dresden. And we paid for the entire trip with our East money. That was the only time we were permitted to do that. After that they stopped this practice, and no one else was allowed to travel with their own money. Was that a miracle or not? Just that one time. Many tried after that, but no more.

Herbert: My wife wanted to stay over there in the West.

G. Davis: I was going to ask you why you didn't stay.

Ilse: I wanted to, but my husband said, "I'll just say one thing. You have your parents here. You would be so homesick for your parents, and whether they would let us come back again or not, that would be a real question." We could have done it then. We could have done it later. Herbert could have flown out for the Church. We could have done it. But it was good that we stayed here.

Herbert: I have never regretted it. We have experienced so many things. If all the members of the Church had gone to the West, we would have had no temple, nothing.

Ilse: We would never have had our temple mission. I might never have been a Relief Society president. Over there I might never have had the callings that I could fulfill here. My parents needed me here. And the Church needed us; that was also very important.

G. Davis: But you did get your wish to work in the temple.

Herbert: Yes, I'll tell you about that. I retired in 1976. I wanted a rest from my professional work. It had all gotten too political, you see. One day Brother Burkhardt, who was in the mission office at the time, came up to me and said, "Brother Kaden, can't you help us out in the leadership of the mission?" So I worked in the mission office from 1976 until 1982.

Ilse: And I cooked for the mission.

Herbert: But then I was released. I said, "They are going to organize a stake here, and that will be too much work for me." But when the temple was finished, here came Brother Burkhardt again. "Brother Kaden, wouldn't you like to work in the temple?" From that time on, we have been working in the temple. I was a temple worker until 1986, and then we were called as temple missionaries until 1988, and then I was called as a counselor in the temple presidency.

Ilse: So all the things I wished for came true. We had to get up early; the train to Freiberg left at five o'clock. We went with the five o'clock train and then had to walk from the train station in Freiberg to the temple. There was no bus.

N. Davis: That is a long walk!

Ilse: Yes, and then at night we had to walk back to the train station and ride back to Dresden on the train and take the streetcar back home. We did that three times a week for the first year and a half, and then we were called to be temple missionaries. Then we lived in Freiberg, in the temple dormitory behind the temple. Our mission lasted for eighteen months, but because Herbert was called to be a counselor in the temple we stayed on longer. How long was that Herbert?

Herbert: Not quite another year.

Ilse: We traded off with the other counselor and his wife. We stayed in the dormitory for a week, and then they stayed for a week. In the meantime, we celebrated our golden wedding anniversary. Just a few years ago, we were called to be temple workers again until last March [1994], when we were released. That made me a little sad. No other release ever made me as sad as being released from our temple work. Of course, we can still go to the temple, but it's not the same.

Herbert: Our legs gave out.

Ilse: Now we can go only when someone takes us. It is too hard for us to take the streetcar to the train station and then the train to Freiberg and then the bus out to the temple.

We had to tell them that our health wasn't so good anymore. We just couldn't travel that far. Well, I can understand it, being released, but it still hurt. That was so wonderful. But it's such a joy now to see all of your old friends, the brothers and sisters you have known for so many years, the ones you love so much. "Oh, Sister Kaden, we miss you at the temple. Oh, Sister Kaden, when are you coming back?" Oh, those were wonderful days. I treasure them so much now. Our temple is so small, but we have the same ordinances and everything, it's all the same. We got to know the Swiss Temple and the Frankfurt Temple, of course. That was a nice experience. Well, those were our days, and I would not have missed them. I take every opportunity I can to go to the temple still, if it's possible. There are so many waiting for their salvation.

G. Davis: So what lies in your future now?

Ilse: The future? We'll leave that to our Father in Heaven. It will be good if we can stay healthy.

Herbert: Enjoy a little rest.

Ilse: And it's nice that the children still need us, and the grandchildren. That's the real fulfillment of life.

G. Davis: What other assignments have you had here in the Church?

Herbert: After 1945, I was a counselor in the district for two years, and then I was in the presidency of the Sunday School for the mission. I can't remember all the jobs I had.

Ilse: He had a bicycle and was gone all the time.

Herbert: We always had a job in the Church.

Ilse: I was, let's see, first I was a teacher in the Primary. After half a year, I was the Primary president. After the Primary, I was the Relief Society president for nine years. Then I was with the Young Women. And I was a counselor in the Relief Society again, and after that we started working in the temple. Oh, yes, and once I was even a counselor in the Sunday School.

Herbert: We were never lacking for a job in the Church.

G. Davis: To say nothing about all the work you did with the youth conferences.

Ilse: Oh, that was the most fun of all, the cooking for the youth conferences. Sometimes we had as many as 150 young people. Oh, that was fun. The whole bunch were here. At first Brother Krause did the cooking. Then one day he said to me, "Ilse, wouldn't you like to help me with the cooking?" "Gladly," I said, "gladly." So then we cooked together for all the youth conferences. Brother Krause was so popular with the young people that he wasn't in the kitchen much after that; he was out with the young people.

N. Davis: So, what did you cook?

Ilse: Stews in a giant pot, meatballs, roasts.

N. Davis: And where did the young people come from?

Herbert: From everywhere in the GDR.

Ilse: We either put them up in our own apartments, or they slept out there in the branch house. I remember one time we had ten young people staying with us in this little apartment—six people slept in the living room there, two here in the dining room, two outside.

N. Davis: Outside, in the yard?

Ilse: Yes, right out there. It was like a barracks here. I had to warn them to keep quiet so they wouldn't wake up the people in the other apartments. Herbert had to go to work early, and so I had to see to it that they all got up. I said, "When I start cooking breakfast, you all have to get up."

Herbert: And our children were still with us then, too.

Ilse: There was a Brother Kohlhase who slept right over there. He came in the kitchen and said, "Sister Kaden. You'd better have a look in your children's room; they have all broken out with black pockmarks." Blackpocks is a very serious illness. So, of course, I went right in and about died laughing. He had taken shoe polish and had put black marks on their faces, a mark here and a mark there. And my laughing woke the others. Oh, how funny they looked; I couldn't stop laughing, it was so funny. Then the others came to me and said, "Sister Kaden, help us play a trick on Brother Kohlhase." I was always ready for some kind of nonsense, so I said, "OK, I'll help you, but I won't tell in advance what I am going to do." Oh, they were excited.

At the Post Office square, we had to change streetcars, and there was always an ice-cream wagon right there. I had sewed up Brother Kohlhase's pockets, here, behind, and here, in his jacket, so that he couldn't get to his billfold or to his money. So, when we got to the Post Office square, I said, "Brother Kohlhase, be a sport and buy us all an ice cream." He was always very generous, so he said, "Of course, all of you come over here, and I'll buy you all an ice cream." So, now we all had our ice cream, and I said, "So who's going to pay, Brother Kohlhase?" He couldn't get into his pocket here; then he tried here and couldn't get in. Everyone standing around the ice-cream wagon broke out in a roar of laughter. "What are you all laughing at," he said. "What's the matter with my pocket here?" We left him there, and he came along later, after he had paid for the ice cream.

All day long at the church, in every meeting, someone was saying to him, "Brother Kohlhase, would you buy me an ice cream?" That was so much fun. It helped relieve the tension. We were younger then and could work at the youth conferences from six in the morning until ten or twelve at night. We spoiled the young people a little in those days. We would have more ice cream after the meetings and then a dance. Always something going on. That was something wonderful!

Herbert: I don't regret that I stayed here instead of going to the West.

G. Davis: Another question. How do you feel now about the political changes and how they have affected the Church?

Herbert: Well, if you look at the promises of Brother Monson when he dedicated our country, you can see that everything, literally everything, has been fulfilled.

G. Davis: You have a temple. And new chapels.

N. Davis: You have all the blessing of the Church now.

Herbert: Yes, and we used to be behind the rest of the Church in everything. We were not recognized by the State, but today we are known everywhere and are looked up to.

G. Davis: And today the young people can go on missions again; they can even leave the country.

Herbert: Yes, that's just wonderful. And it's a great support to us to have full-time missionaries in our ward again. All the promises have been fulfilled.

17

I Saw the Russian Tanks Coming

Günter Schulze

Günter Schulze—tall, soft-spoken, and unassuming—has been quietly behind all the important events which contributed to the reestablishment of the Church in East Germany after the Second World War and the reopening of the area to missionaries in 1989. It would be impossible to estimate the miles he has driven (and walked) in the service of the Church. During the time of our interview, he was serving as bishop of the Dresden Ward.

I was born on March 15, 1937, in Dresden and was placed in an orphanage. I was an illegitimate child. Apparently that was not a problem under Hitler, but it was still a scandal, and my mother had no financial support, so she had to go to work during the day, or we would have both starved. Apparently I did a lot of crying when she was away during the day, so I am told, and I was reported to the welfare office. They took me away from my mother and put me in an orphanage in Frankfurt-Oder.

My adoptive mother had been looking for a baby—this was before the war—and I was her third or fourth offer. I was so weak that when I was eleven months old I couldn't even hold a bottle or sit up. I couldn't eat by myself, so she told me. My new mother would have to have a lot of patience with me, but she took me anyway.

When I was one year old, I was given to my adoptive parents, and it was through them that I became acquainted with the Church. I was raised in the Church, and I was baptized in a river on March 18, 1945, when I was eight years old. The river was frozen, and it was very cold. We had to break a hole in the ice with an axe. I was baptized by Elder Karl Wöhe, who was the branch president in Dresden at the time. We lived at the time in Bischofswerda, approximately fifteen miles east of Dresden. Since there were no priesthood holders in Bischofswerda at the time who could baptize me, he walked from Dresden to Bischofswerda. This was just at the end of the war, the bridges had all been blown up, and no trains were running. He baptized Moroni Haas and me, and then he walked back to Dresden. This made a great impression on me as a young boy, that a man of his age would walk from Dresden to Bischofswerda and then back again just to accommodate us two boys. I learned a great lesson from this that has served me in my personal life.

I can remember as a child, when the war was over, riding from Dresden to Bischofswerda on a train, and the train was so full that we had to sit on the roof of the cars. Whenever we came to a viaduct or a tunnel word was passed back, and we had to lie down on the roof. Of course, the train was not traveling very fast, but still, you had to be careful.

The trains were always overfilled. One day a Russian soldier was sitting on the car with us, and he told me and my mother that Hitler was very bad but that Stalin was even worse. He was probably right as we are able to judge such things today. Saying something like that in those days was very strictly forbidden, and he was taking a big risk, but he was undoubtedly right.

Toward the end of the war, in 1945, we had to flee. We could hear the artillery in Bautzen, and we quickly loaded up our handcarts. I had a small handcart made from a box, and my mother had a larger one. We packed a little food and especially some warm clothes in two feather comforters, then set off with our handcarts for Putzkau. There were long lines of refugees, and we could still hear the cannons. Then we were taken as far as Königstein in army trucks. From there we and our handcarts were taken down the Elbe on a ship. We met our relatives at the ship landing in Dresden and went through the streets with our handcarts, about fifteen or sixteen of them, with a horse leading the way. We walked as far as Hainsberg, and then the horse had to pull all the handcarts up the mountain. There on the mountain I saw something that I will never forget.

It was during those final days of confusion. We lived high up on the hill, and one day I saw the Russian tanks coming up the Freital Valley toward Hainsberg. On the other side of the valley, I saw the German soldiers climbing up the mountain with their rucksacks full of ammunition on their backs. That was a spectacle I will never forget.

Later we returned to our home in Bischofswerda, riding on the roof of the train as I mentioned. The bridges in Dresden and in Klotsche were held together with wooden braces. When we got to Bischofswerda, we saw our house, burned to the ground. The Polish army coming through Bischofswerda thought they had found a uniform of Hitler's SS officers in our house. It was actually a uniform of one of the people who worked as an undertaker and must have been similar to the uniform of the SS. Anyway, in their confusion, they thought that the SS lived in the house and burned it down and the houses next to it also. So, everything we had in the house was gone.

As fortune would have it, one family never came back to Bischofswerda but went on to America. That was my mother's half-sister, Sister Haas. She was the mother of the boy who was baptized the same day I was. So, we had a roof over our heads once again. We had a few dishes and a pad to sleep on.

In 1946 the first welfare goods came from America. My mother was the Relief Society president, and since there were no priesthood holders around, the entire shipment was stored in our tiny apartment. When we wanted to go into our bedroom, we had to crawl over sacks of grain. That part was not so pleasant for me, but we were happy to have something to eat and happy we could help out many other people with these things. Cooked wheat, peaches, and good milk were delicacies in those days.

I remember a visit from Brother Fritz Lehnig and Brother Byrth, the first district authorities from Cottbus. I remember the authorities from the district spent a night with us. We took some mattresses from the beds and put them on the ground so that we would have more room. Everyone slept on them, men and women, in a long row.

One thing essential for my progress, for my education in the Church, was the advice given me by Sister Martha Scharschuh, who was the Primary leader at the time. Back in 1947 or '48, she told me I should learn to play the piano. We needed an organist in the Primary. At the time, my mother didn't have any money to give me for piano lessons, so I wrote the letters of the notes on the keys of the piano and learned to play "Scatter Sunshine" and "We Love You, Dear Father, in Heaven Above."

When my father came home—he was released early from a POW camp because he had edema and malaria—we were able to get him into a hospital. We had somehow gotten our hands on a large container of coffee and were able to bribe a doctor with it so we could get father into a hospital for treatment.

I had been learning to play the piano, so this is what my father did for me. After his recovery, he went into the forest, and with the permission of the forest ranger, he rooted out tree stumps. My mother and I then helped him get these large stumps out of the forest. We brought them home, sawed them up, split them, and then we sold sacks of firewood. I don't remember what we got for a sack of firewood, but with the money my father bought me a used piano. Anyway, in this way, I learned to play the piano and became the branch organist and also accompanied the choir in the branch. That gave me a great deal of pleasure.

In 1949 my parents officially adopted me. I could no longer remember my real mother. I had only known her briefly, and I couldn't remember what she looked like. When I was nineteen years old, I went on a mission. I didn't know how to teach a discussion. Once I had given a talk; my mother had written it out for me, pages long, and I had to memorize it. If I stumbled over one word, I was in trouble. I was very naive and very uneducated, but I had a wonderful man for my first companion. He instructed me and trained me so that I soon became acquainted with the basic principles of the Church. I learned how to conduct a meeting and how to teach a lesson. Of course, while I was on my mission, I had to continue playing the organ or piano in the meetings because organists were very rare. I also played for the missionary meetings and conferences. It was always expected of me, but I was very happy to do it.

Shortly after I came home from my mission on May 10, 1958, I took a young wife to the marriage altar. This was on May 31. I had become acquainted with her in Bernburg, where I spent nine months as a missionary. While I was there, I said nothing to her or to her mother or her grandmother. Her father had come home sick from the war and had died in 1948. When I left Bernburg, I said, "I want to finish an honorable mission, but I will be back. Take good care of Hannelore for me." They didn't take me seriously, but I meant it, and she is still with me today.

So, we began to make our way together, and it was very difficult. When I was released from my mission, I could not find work because I had missed out on two years of training while I was gone. It took six months to find a job. In the meantime, my wife went to work at a flour mill in Bernburg handling sacks of wheat and flour and managed to earn a few *Groschen* [coins] which kept us alive. After a year, our Olaf came along, the second year our Berndt, and the third year our Elke.

After my release from the mission, I was the branch president in Bischofswerda for three years, until 1961. The next ten years were bitterly hard. It was a serious situation for us. We had very little money and three children, but we always paid our tithing. There was one time we couldn't afford to travel to Görlitz to conference. It was simply impossible. Afterwards, I was asked why I hadn't been there. It was very embarrassing for me to have to say why, but there was no way we could have gone. That was not our custom, to miss a conference.

My next calling was in the district MIA presidency, and then I was called to a leadership position in music for the entire region. We organized and built up a youth choir, which brought a lot of joy to many members in the region, and we also brought many investigators into the Church. We had about sixty or seventy members and two directors, Brother Lehrig and Brother Baasch. I was the accompanist.

In 1976, I received a surprise, a real shock. I had never believed I would be called to be a counselor in the mission presidency. Elder Wirthlin was here, and I was busy doing some work in the church building. We had been doing some cleanup on this particular evening. I had on an apron and was very dirty when President Burkhardt called me into the office. That's when Elder Wirthlin asked me if I would accept the calling. So I spent the next eight years as a counselor in the mission presidency.

I had worked a lot with our patriarch, Walter Krause. After work I would take him in my car along with the necessary building materials to the various branch houses where he, because of his carpentry skills, did a lot of repair work. He repaired carpets and built stages and did this and that. I helped him many, many times. Also during these days, I must have traveled to Poland about forty times. Once I went with President Burkhardt, some other brethren, and Brother Krause.

There are two experiences I should perhaps relate, one in Upper Silesia and one in East Prussia. As I was traveling to East Prussia, the car broke down along the way. The motor just stopped, and I simply couldn't get it started again. I called home. Brother Krause was very sick—he had blood in his kidneys—but he came anyway with his delivery truck. We met one another there on this country road and determined that the motor was gone. His first question was, "What have you done wrong? How could that have happened? You were driving for the Church, for the Lord, why did that happen?" I had been approaching an area of deep forest where it might be up to forty kilometers between farmhouses. As we drove on, we found there had been a terrible wind storm; trees and telephone poles lay across the road. Where I had been driving, I hardly noticed it, but it caused a real disaster here in the forest. If I had been in the forest, it would have been very bad for me, so we were pleased that the motor had stopped, and nothing had happened to me.

We continued on and visited the branch in Selbongen. It was our habit to visit the members over there once a month to take care of their needs. Over the course of time, we made arrangements for some of them to emigrate to West Germany. Others came to Dresden, and eventually no members were left in Selbongen.

There was another occasion when we were traveling in Upper Silesia to find members whose names and addresses had been given to us by the international mission. We were mainly just supposed to find out if the members were still living. From the birth dates, it appeared that this was possible. We found only two old sisters. One was Sister Herod, who had at one time lived in Breslau and the area around there. She had been the district Relief Society president. We spent a long time visiting with her. My son Olaf, who was only a schoolboy at the time, was with me and Brother Erich Sellner from the Werdau Branch. He worked at the time for the regional office.

So we two adults and Olaf had an interesting experience. Sister Herod pulled out a long stocking from behind a kitchen cabinet and began untying several knots. She made a dish of her hands and filled them with money from the stocking. "This is my tithing. Even though it has been twenty-five years, I knew that the priesthood would visit me some day." That was in about 1974 or 1975. So from then on, she was cared for by the district president, Brother Rudi Lehmann, who is now our stake patriarch. The members in the border city of Görlitz took care of the members in Upper Silesia. I went back two or three times, but I never experienced anything like that again. I will never forget it.

We used to take a lot of things into Poland. We took furniture; we took toys. Once, for example, we took in a large dollhouse with two floors and several rooms all furnished with doll furniture. We took donations from members. We took shoes. We took in literature so they could study the scriptures.

Once I was with my father and with Brother Lothar Ebisch. We arrived at the border at Görlitz on the Neisse River about one in the morning with a big truck. It was in the middle of the winter, and we were in a blizzard. We had to unload everything at the border and weren't allowed to load it back in until six o'clock in the morning. We had to take some things back to the train station and to Brother and Sister Lehmann before we could continue on our way. All this because we had household goods and such things, and they wanted to know where they were going, and why did we have this thing and that thing? Five hours in the middle of the night from 1:00 until 6:00 A.M. in freezing ice and snow. But we were glad to do it.

In the meantime, I became acquainted with my real mother. She had spent several days looking for me in Bischofswerda until she found a man who told her I had joined a church and didn't live in Bischofswerda anymore. He didn't know where I had moved, but he advised her to go the Mormon Church and ask there. She found Brother Koschnicke, and, of course, he could tell her where I was. She must have learned my name from the welfare office or from the orphanage in Frankfurt-Oder. Anyway, she found me.

She was originally from Görlitz and must have kept up a little contact with her people there. But when she came to our apartment on Bergmann Street in Dresden, she sent her husband up, and she waited below in the car. I invited her to come in. At first we were very formal with "Mr." and "Mrs.," which was a rather strange situation. But then we dropped that and got along very nicely.

I have done a lot of work in the Church, often after work, on weekends, and on vacations, until at times it was simply too much for my wife. Then there were all these trips into Poland. I finally had to tell President Burkhardt that it couldn't go on like that, that I couldn't keep up with my work. Then he made the suggestion that I go to work for the Church, and since 1979 I have been employed by the Church.

We often had business in the office of the state secretary for ecclesiastical affairs *[Staatssekretariat für Kirchenfragen]*. One day an officer in the Secretariat spoke to us and asked us if we wouldn't like to have a temple for our members in the German Democratic Republic. For years the state secretary had been aware of this problem, that we wanted to travel to our temple in Switzerland and were not allowed to. Now they offered us the chance to build a temple here and offered us three plots of ground in Saxony. We in the mission presidency decided on the hill where the temple now stands in Freiberg. It is a lovely location. The other locations were in Freiberg itself, but they would require a lot of tearing down of old buildings, etc.

But why am I telling you this? In 1979, President Monson crossed over Checkpoint Charlie with President Ringger. We were in a private car, President Burkhardt, President Richter, these two brethren, and I. There in the car, President Monson informed us that the First presidency had given their approval for the building of a temple here. But he also told us that he would like to have our promise to say nothing of this to anyone, not even to our wives. That was really hard.

Then in 1982 or 1983, the preliminary work was begun with the state authorities. Several members of the Church were involved, so naturally, the news spread, and several members knew about it before my wife did. Then my wife asked me if there was any truth to the rumor. I said, "If you have heard it, then yes, it is true. But perhaps you should wait until it is announced officially." After that no one asked us to keep it confidential anymore, but I can say with a clear conscience that I personally kept it confidential. That was something that cost me a lot of energy.

At the ground breaking of the Freiberg Germany Temple. Thomas S. Monson, Robert D. Hales, and Günter Schulze are second, fourth, and sixth from the left respectively. Courtesy Käthe Wöhe.

But the work was not any easier, and finally in 1984, President Burkhardt was called to be the temple president, and I was released as his counselor. Then I became the group leader of the high priests in the ward. Since I have been in Dresden, that has been my favorite job in the Church—high priest group leader—except for my job as organist. Working with the brethren, taking care of the older brothers, and visiting them when they were sick was a beautiful experience.

At the spring conference in 1989, I was called to be a member of the high council, and the stake president put me over music and singing once again. He told me that as long as he was stake president I would never be released. Half a year went by. In the middle of November 1989 at a seminar in Zwickau, he told me that I was to be the bishop in Dresden. That just about turned me inside out. I hadn't the slightest desire to get involved in statistics and organizational matters. I wanted to be with the high priests, but somehow I had to find a way to convince myself that I was not too old. So I said yes, and when I received a blessing at my ordination, all the shyness and disinclination for these things essentially disappeared.

There is a lot of work in the Dresden Ward. We have new members almost every week, one to three baptisms, sometimes more. All of these new members have to be fellowshipped. They have to have an interview with the bishop. They have to work with the stake missionaries. They must be introduced to the temple, and before that they often have to receive a testimony, and a lot of detailed work is connected with that. They have to be continually strengthened, and one has to be their friend as well as their leader.

I am very thankful for my family, for my wife, that we can be so happy together. There are so many things one could talk about, the experiences I have had with President Burkhardt, Brother Krause, and Brother Richter, how one or the other of us was sick and how we supported one another, how we slept out on the highway some nights, and how we complemented one another so well. When you can read anothers' lips or read it in their eyes and see what they need or what they want and know that you can fulfill their needs or their wants, it is a wonderful feeling.

Just the day before yesterday I said in the sacrament meeting that there are people who have come to us from a distant country who have helped us so much, who have strengthened the members in their homes, who have helped us put back into shape things that had become misshapen, who have helped many members make rough things smooth again, who have not shied away from any work they could do for the Dresden Ward, physical or spiritual. For these things, we are grateful with all our heart.

18

Book Burning

Joachim Albrecht, Kurt Nikol, and Marianne Nikol

We interviewed Joachim Albrecht, Kurt Nikol, and Marianne Nikol in Bautzen, a city overshadowed by its infamous prison. Yet, as we sat in the Nikol's apartment, their quiet dedication made it difficult to imagine the misery and horror represented by the prison walls only a few blocks away. The easy flow of conversation in this interview is the result of their long life of friendship and service together in the Church. At the time of the interview, Sister Nikol was serving as the stake Relief Society president.

Joachim: I was born in Königsberg, in East Prussia. My parents were not born in the Church. My mother was converted by the missionaries, who then came to see my grandparents. My grandmother then raised her three children in the Church, although she was not baptized until some time later. They went to the Church meetings every Sunday, but my grandfather fought against it. He didn't want to be a part of it and would not allow my grandmother to be baptized. In 1935 my mother married a man who was not a member of the Church. My father had been a soldier. After his twelve years in the military, he went to work for the Customs Bureau, and the family moved to the Lithuanian border because my father was assigned customs duties there at the border. In these years, from 1938 until 1944, we were quite removed from the Church.

In 1944 we had to leave our homeland because the front was getting closer and closer. I was nine years old at the time. We went back to Königsberg but lived there for only a few weeks and then moved to the area near Elbingerode. There we thought we would have a little peace. My father's brother was a forester in the area and owned a large farm at the edge of the forest. We felt more secure there than in a large city because of the bombings, but we had to move on again because the front was coming across southern Prussia.

It was January 1945 and bitter cold. We had to make the trip to Danzig with a horse and wagon. From Danzig we were to take a ship across the Baltic to Schweinemunde. The ship was part of a convoy of several ships that were bringing refugees out of East Prussia. One of the ships was the *Wilhelm Gustwerf.* It was a wonderful luxury liner that had been commandeered during the Hitler period as a transport ship. We did not get on this ship because on the way to Danzig my feet had become frozen. My toes and heels turned completely black from the frost. I couldn't walk, and my mother took care of me in an old factory, where she rubbed my feet with gasoline to bring life back into them. The pain was terrible. Then a short distance before Danzig, we stopped at a military hospital, where they treated me. They wanted to amputate my feet but finally decided it would not be necessary. Life came back into my feet, so they wrapped them in heavy bandages and gave me two crutches to walk on. That was the reason we arrived too late at the harbor in Danzig. The liner *Wilhelm Gustwerf* was already overloaded with refugees, so we were put on an old, rusted-out freighter that had been used to haul ore. The refugees were placed below decks, and we were given some wood shavings to make a bed on.

We began our journey across the frozen Baltic. One night not far from Danzig, which was a freight harbor at that time, the sirens sounded the alarm that we were under attack. We were not hit, but the next morning we learned that within the convoy the *Wilhelm Gustwerf* had been torpedoed by a Russian submarine. The ship had sunk through the ice with all six thousand refugees on board. We picked up a few the next day who had somehow got into life boats, but very, very few. That was my first real experience with suffering and mourning.

My mother had been a little angry with me when we were hurrying to reach the Danzig harbor. We had spent the night in a schoolhouse, and when the sailors told us that the ship was already loaded, it was a great disappointment. But then when we learned that we had escaped certain death because of my problem, we were very happy, and we reached our destination, Rostock, on this old freighter.

However, we could not find an apartment in Rostock because everything was packed with refugees, so we made our new home in a little village near Rostock called Neubuckow. There was a branch of the Church in Rostock, which was an answer to our prayers. My mother had been trying very hard to find the Church, so right away we started attending the meetings. In the first two years, we met in various places, first in a school and then in a tavern. We had meetings there on Sunday, and on Monday they served beer and schnaps in the same rooms.

In 1947, I was baptized. The decision to be baptized was made when we traveled to Dresden for the big centennial celebration of the arrival of the pioneers in Salt Lake Valley. This took place in the old branch house on the Dr.-Kurt-Fischer Allee.

In the large park, we had an open-air celebration, and there I got to meet all the members and was introduced to two missionaries who were to be transferred to Rostock after the celebration. One of the brothers who was to come to Rostock as a missionary was Rudolf Wechsteter. He asked me, "Have you been baptized yet?" And I said, "No, I have not been baptized." "That's wonderful! We will have our first baptism when we get to Rostock." And that's what happened.

I was baptized on August 10, 1947, along with my brother and my grandmother, who had brought our entire family into the Church. My grandmother's decision to be baptized became fixed after she had been cut off from my grandfather three times. He had stayed behind in Königsberg because of the war business that was going on there, and then he had been interred on a ship from Königsberg to Denmark. Next he was put in an internment camp. His family was scattered everywhere. My grandmother was with us because she had to take care of the children while my mother was at the doctor's, and then we had to leave East Prussia in such a hurry. Grandpa said, "Well, it won't be so bad. There will be a lot of people on the boat, and things are getting so hectic here." So he stayed behind and had to be transported out later with this ship and ended up in an internment camp in Denmark. While he was in Denmark, we heard from our uncle in America. We had first heard from him in 1939. He told my grandpa that rather than go back to Germany after he was released he should come directly over to America from Denmark, so my grandfather had gone to America. And he wanted to know what was going on and asked my grandmother if she had really been baptized. My grandmother told him that after all the experiences they had been through she assumed he would no longer have anything against her baptism. So my grandmother was baptized with us two boys on August 10, 1947.

I was actually supposed to take my grandmother to America a little later since she couldn't travel there alone. I went on a mission in 1953, and after my mission, I was going to go with my grandmother to America. But then grandpa died over there in 1954, after a separation of almost ten years from my grandmother, and that sort of settled the matter for me and I stayed here.

I was on a mission from 1953 to 1956, and my last area was in Bautzen. I met my wife and decided I wanted to set up camp here because I didn't really have a home in Rostock anymore. I didn't want to go back to Neubuckow, where my home had been, because I would be so far away from the Church. There was a little group of members in the Bautzen Branch. As a missionary, I had been called to be the branch president, and when I was released from my mission, the missionaries still had to take over the branch leadership. So in May 1957, I was set apart as branch president again. I was released in 1980.

G. Davis: Was there a branch in Bautzen before the war?

Joachim: Yes, but I must say that the branch was shuffled around a bit, here and there, because of the things that were going on. For a time we had no meeting place, no rooms. Meetings were held in members' homes.

G. Davis: That was in the thirties?

Marianne: Early in the thirties there were missionaries from America here, and they stayed until just before the outbreak of the war. Then suddenly, overnight, the missionaries were gone. Through Sweden or Norway, gone, overnight. And here we stood, without leadership. At that time, we had a large building on Münz Street. It was a lovely chapel, but we had to give it up. I don't remember why anymore. During the war, we had a room in a tavern. Then that wasn't allowed anymore, so we had to meet in a private apartment, one room, on the fourth floor. We were there for a long time. I can remember that well. Saturday evening I had to go heat up the room so that it would be warm. The meetings were at 7:30 at night. But we didn't have any missionaries then. My father, who was branch president, did it all. Then the war and all that brought us a lot of trouble. We didn't have any meetings at all.

G. Davis: Was Nikol your maiden name, too?

Marianne: Yes, I was born a Nikol.

Kurt: We are, if you like, sort of related because our fathers were half-brothers. Our grandmother on our fathers' side had these two boys out of wedlock, and yes, in that way, we are actually half-cousins. As children we had a little contact from this relationship.

I didn't grow up in Bautzen but in a little village about ten miles from here. My parents were farmers. I finished out the war, and I had received my discharge papers from the German army just as the war ended, after May 8, 1945. At the time, I had been with the communications service on the Yugoslavian border in an old building. So we tried to get home on foot through Austria. Well, we got as far as Klagenfurt and had to decide which way to go. Toward Vienna and through Czechoslovakia? The Russians were there, and we didn't want anything to do with that business, so we decided on the longer route, through Salzburg and Bavaria, but the English were there. The options became fewer and fewer. We couldn't get through the Bündering Pass anymore, so we had to go this way and that way through meadows and finally found ourselves spending several weeks in a so-called internment camp run by the English. After about eight weeks, we were turned over to the Americans there in Bavaria. We were taken to Donau-Eschingen for final release. That was the plan. Then one day I was *not* released.

They learned I had been with the communications division, and communications people were not to be released. Everything had to be put back together—all of the telephone lines and telephone connections, etc. I told them I was no high-wire man. I didn't have the slightest idea about telephone lines and things like that. I was a telegraph operator. Didn't help. I didn't go home. Instead I was given to the French and taken from Donau-Eschingen to a POW camp high in the Western Forest. For six weeks, I was put to work for a farmer in a slaughter house–butcher shop. I was then sent back to the camp, and from there I was transferred to a POW camp in the south of France. With one other prisoner, I was sent out to work during the day for a farmer who owned a vineyard. Two others were already assigned to work in the vineyard, so that made four of us. The conditions in the camp were not good. We were put into two small rooms with slab cots, so we made plans for our escape, but a few false starts fell through when the farmer got wind that we were trying to get away.

We weren't taken back to the POW camp every night because it was over sixty kilometers away, so we had to spend some nights at the vineyard. Finally, in October 1946, I and the others who were with me at the vineyard did manage to make our escape. We made it from the Spanish border all the way to Austria. One of my companions had relatives on a large farm there, and from there we made contact with our families and requested the necessary civilian papers to get home. We actually smuggled our way across all the borders until we were home.

My first stop was here in Bautzen. I had come all the way by trains, but the connections were not so good, so I stopped over here in Bautzen for a while. Marianne and I were always good friends as children.

Marianne: But that's not the whole story. I have to add a little. When they escaped from the vineyard, the next day he had blood poisoning in his big toe because he didn't have any good shoes, only those heavy boots. It turned red, then black.

Kurt: Yes. That happened when we were running away from the vineyard to get to the closest train station. That was about sixty kilometers away, and we couldn't let ourselves be seen during the day, so we had to walk at night. Actually we wanted to ride the freight trains. We had gotten hold of a schedule, so we knew where they were going and could make our way home. We had to keep hidden during the day. We needed water during the day so that I could cool my foot off so that I could walk a few kilometers the next night.

G. Davis: So you two became reacquainted here in Bautzen?

Kurt: Yes. We got a little better acquainted here, and then in April 1948 we got married. On November 16, 1948, I was baptized in Bautzen in the Spree River. There were at least eight people baptized that day, some of them from here and some from Grünewalde.

G. Davis: How large was the branch at that time, in 1948?

Marianne: In those days, we had a good-sized group.

Kurt: We became acquainted with the branch here, and held the meetings at the home of Sister Hänsel. She was the widow of a dentist and had a fairly large apartment.

Marianne: We had at least twenty-five.

Kurt: In those days, we had meetings in Bautzen and in Grünewalde, because they couldn't always get over here, and also in Doberschau.

G. Davis: There were no foreign missionaries here during this time?

Marianne: Before the war, they were all pulled out and since then, none. It's been fifty years now, that is until last year, when the missionaries came back.

G. Davis: But you always had your own local missionaries?

Kurt: There were the local missionaries. The first ones we got to know were Brother Schieck from Annaberg and Brother Plietschau. I don't know exactly where he came from.

Joachim: Those were the missionaries in the first years after the war. Then for a long time, there was nothing here in Bautzen. In 1954, Bautzen was opened up again for missionary work with Brother Meier. At that time, the missionaries lived in our branch house. We had rented a branch house here in Bautzen, on Korn Street. Everything had to be remodeled, and the missionaries lived in the same building. We turned one of the classrooms into a room for them, and we had missionaries here until 1957.

Marianne: The very first ones were called right after the war to get the branches back together and see that everything got going again. There were many people who were out of contact with the Church. We didn't even know where they were anymore. They called these men right away so that they could gather the sheep into branches so that we could get together again.

G. Davis: Do you think there were many members who were lost?

Marianne: Yes, yes. Many were in POW camps, the cities had all been bombed, and there was great confusion because of the war. There were many who went over to their relatives or emigrated some way or another. No one knew for sure where anyone was.

Joachim: Here in Bautzen, many members joined after the war; many were baptized. It became sort of a test of faith when we started receiving welfare goods from America; this attracted many people. We had a saying among us in German that these were the "canned-goods members" *[Büchsengeschwister, Büchsenmitglieder],* who kept a sharp eye out for canned peaches. And when the welfare goods stopped coming, we noticed that the members became less and less active. We didn't, of course. We visited and took care of the members we had here in Bautzen, but we couldn't get them back into activity again.

Marianne: But we always had a good relationship with those members. Two sisters live just a little ways away, and they are always happy when someone comes to see them. They were always glad to have a visit, but they never came back. They always admit that everything they know they learned from us. One of them goes to another Christian church occasionally.

Joachim: Before the branch on Korn Street became self-sufficient, we were dependent on the Bischofswerda Branch. The brothers came over here from Bischofswerda on Sunday to conduct the meetings. That must have been before the new missionaries came, before 1952.

Marianne: We met at Sister Hänsel's place until about 1950. Then Brother Habicht came and took care of us, I remember, with his young wife. They came around 1952.

Joachim: In any case, a bunch of members were up in Grünewalde, about fifteen kilometers away. The missionaries were active up there and baptized a few members, but it was very hard for them to come into the city to the meetings. There were a few older sisters among them, including Sister Fietze, a local sister who made her home available. We held meetings in her apartment on Thursdays and Sundays. I went over there as a missionary Thursdays by bike and on Sundays by train or with the bike. These visits were very important, and the missionaries after me kept them up.

When the sister missionaries came, they didn't go over anymore. A few of the members had moved away or died, and the group became smaller and smaller until we stopped holding meetings. Sister Frieze's brother, Brother Gleizmann, let himself be made a secretary in the Evangelical Church and turned out to be very antagonistic toward the Mormons. He was a member himself. He had gotten a little upset over a few things, but that was mainly a matter between him and his sister. Then he left for the West, and we wanted to clean things up so we invited him to a Church court. It didn't help. The man wouldn't talk with us. But he came back because things didn't go so well for him over there. He was very homesick and was all alone. But he never showed up at church again and was never taken back. We learned that he was back only when his sister died, and even though she didn't even mention him in her will, he got most of her estate and actually made a lot of trouble for the Church there in Grünewalde because of his attitude.

We were just getting a little activity going in the genealogy program. Brother Tschislig, who lived in our branch, had some ancestors from Grünewalde, and he wanted to look them up in the archives of the Evangelical Church. One day when he went over to the church office, he ran into Brother Gleizmann. They didn't know one another, but when he said that he was a Mormon and wanted to look up some ancestors, Gleizmann had him thrown out of the church offices and arranged it so that no other members could do research there. That was not easy for him to do, but I would say that he hurt himself more than he hurt us. The members who were still there in Grünewald drew a clear line. They knew whom they had to deal with and decided to whom they would go. But they eventually all died out, and there are no more members there.

Once we had great success there with conversions because a large group of Swedish refugees moved in. The local people were not so interested in accepting the gospel; it was more the refugees in those days. One of the enthusiastic members in Grünewald was Brother Koschrücke, a refugee. He was one of the younger brothers in Grünewald when we were holding meetings there, and he took over the missionary work.

Later, after 1957, the branch was no longer under the direction of strangers. By strangers I mean the full-time missionaries, who were the branch presidents and who were changed about every six months. In 1957, I was set apart as branch president, and since then the activity in the branch has been good. I was branch president until the organization of the stake, when we were put together with Bischofswerda. That was because we had to give up our meetinghouse on Korn Street when the city started rebuilding the area. They offered us another place on a side street. The place was large enough for us, but it was old, with damp walls. There were a lot of construction problems there. We made it as attractive as we could, but it wasn't a permanent solution. It was supposed to be only a temporary move, but then they never gave us another place to meet. So on Pentecost 1952, our branch was dissolved, and we became part of Bischofswerda.

We had always had a good relationship with Bischofswerda. There was one common elders quorum between the two branches, and when they rebuilt their meetinghouse, we were very active in helping them during the construction. Brother and Sister Nikol both shoveled lime or dirt out of the lime pit onto the conveyor belt when they were digging out for the drainage tanks. That was hard but beautiful work, and by doing that we were laying the foundation for our own branch house, right? That was two years ago.

Marianne: The work started at eight. We traveled over to Bischofswerda by motorcycle.

Joachim: We belong to the Bischofswerda Branch but live in Bautzen. We have about twenty-two members here in Bautzen.

Marianne: That's quite a few. More than when we had our own branch.

G. Davis: And how many members are there in Bischofswerda?

Kurt: There have always been about forty.

Joachim: About one third to two thirds. And it's still about that.

G. Davis: What sort of problems did you have in directing the branch? I understand that you had many problems getting manuals.

Joachim: Yes, that was a big problem, teaching materials. After a while, we got better organized and helped ourselves. There were relatives or friends over there in West Germany who sent us their leftover manuals from the previous year, and we duplicated them on the typewriter. That was very, very, hard work. But then this work was taken over to a certain extent by the mission office.

That was the teaching material, but there were other things such as the *Stern* [Church magazine in German]. Until about 1949, we were permitted to bring these things into the country, but after that it was strictly forbidden. When I was on a mission and was working in Rathenow, near Berlin, we had a lot of contact with the mission office in West Berlin, Dahlem. We local missionaries had to take the manuals in our pockets and get them from Berlin into East Germany. This was always done with a certain amount of fear and trembling and with a pounding heart. But then one day our mission president, Henry Burkhardt, said, "No more of that. That's forbidden, against the law; we simply can't do it. Period."

Before that we smuggled in a lot of teaching materials. We had a saying in the mission, "We go out without purse or script but come home with a box of books." I remember that I was sending new books here to Bautzen and had a box so big I couldn't get it to the train station because it was so heavy. I had to unpack it and put the books into three boxes when I sent all my things home from my mission.

Suddenly one day I received a message from our mission president that all of the manuals, books, tracts, etc., we had smuggled into the country somehow, illegally, could be very harmful to the Church. The authorities had already searched a few of our apartments, and we were instructed that we had to destroy all of these materials. I sat down in front of our open stove with a big pile of books and kept telling myself, "You have to keep that one" and "You have to keep that one" and "You can't burn that one," but for two days, we kept the fire going without coal, just paper. It was pretty warm. But in the end, I did keep one book. It was four years of priesthood manuals I had saved and had bound into one volume. "I don't care if they throw me in prison," I thought to myself. "This is one book I am not going to burn!"

I can say that at that time I was obedient. I did it because I was told to. But somehow I couldn't see how anyone could get into trouble because of these manuals. Then one day I received an unexpected visit from a certain office.

G. Davis: Secret police?

Joachim: Of course! They asked me a few questions about the branch and wanted to know this and that. Then they wanted to have a look at my bookcase and wanted to know what kind of books I had. I was able to open my bookcase without a pounding heart and show them what books we had.

G. Davis: What about those four years of priesthood manuals?

Joachim: I didn't show them. But I had the *Stern,* which we were permitted to receive up until 1949, and they wanted to see the later volumes. I told them I didn't receive them. Then they asked me if anyone from "over there" [West Germany] was sending them to me, relatives, etc. "No," I said, "you can see that this is all I have." I was so happy that I was finally shown a reason, some sense, for burning my books. I must say that I really mourned over my books. But in the end, this actually gave us more encouragement to study our lessons more thoroughly from the standard works. The whole thing made us a little sulky, but it taught us a good lesson.

G. Davis: Do you think now that it was inspiration, that you should burn your books?

Joachim: Of course, I'm convinced that it was inspiration. I had to learn from direct experience how to understand the whole matter. They sent these people to us to search our apartment, and the order to burn the books came from our mission president, Brother Burkhardt.

Marianne: At the time, everyone here was saying, "Well, religion, that's going to be abolished. In this country, there will be no more churches. Religion will be abolished." That was really the big concern we had here, that there would be no more religion. Especially those in the government were saying it. We had a relative, a brother-in-law, who was a big party member. He was always spouting this rubbish. "Sooner or later, mark my words . . ." And when we were interrogated, it was always a frightening experience. What do they really want? Where did they get that information?

I remember once I was at home alone with my little boy when this lady came and introduced herself, saying she was from the bank. I was working in the Relief Society at the time, and she wanted to do an audit of the finances for the bank, she said. I asked her if she wanted to know about my private finances or just what it was she wanted. No. She said she knew everything about what I did in the Church, and she began to tell me all about it. I'm not certain whether she said she had already spoken with Brother Albrecht or not. But she knew a lot of details. I just told her, "I'm sorry, but I don't know anything about the Church finances." We had been instructed, essentially, not to give out any information. "That's the business of the branch president." But she kept on. "You must know that. You're an active member of your church." She also asked me if I was happy in the Church. I said I was, but she wouldn't leave. She kept asking and asking and asking. I don't remember if I called my husband, but she wouldn't let me alone. She wanted to know all about the Church finances. Then she started in on tithing. I ought to know how much tithing I paid, I ought to know that, and how many members there were. I kept saying, "I'm sorry, I can't help you, that's what the branch president is for. I don't pay any attention to those things. I can't help you."

Kurt: But in general, they didn't try to make a lot of trouble for us here in Bautzen. They knew that we belonged to the branch here and that we had to report on our meetings every week. We reported everything about all of our meetings to the police and that seemed to satisfy them, except for these special things, which they really put under the magnifying glass.

I had a similar visit once. I hadn't been a member for very long, and he began asking me about Church "taxes." I told him we didn't have any church taxes, but then it became obvious that he knew all about our law of tithing. I told him it was one of the laws of the Church, but that it was all based on voluntary contributions. If I pay my tithing, that's my own business, and if I don't pay, I won't be kicked out of the Church. Well, that's what it was all about, I think, whether or not our tithing was a form of church "taxation." The other churches have a fixed taxation, which is taken, in part, from their paycheck. So that was the conversation I had with this man. He introduced himself by name, but I didn't recognize what office he came from.

Marianne: Could I say something else? One evening we heard the doorbell ring; that was after June 17, 1953 [the day of a major uprising of the citizens of East Germany against the oppressive communist government; the uprising was harshly put down by the Soviet army], and after we had been told the Church was categorically forbidden to provide refuge. During the uprisings, several political prisoners had escaped from prison. I remember we had been told that what we did privately was our own business, but that we shouldn't do anything like that in the name of the Church. As I was saying, just after supper one night, the doorbell rang. That's when we were still living with the Ottos in Lichtenau, and the man at the door asked if he could come in—he was a fugitive. Then he told us he knew the missionaries, and he named a name. Brother Schiebold was a missionary in our branch at the time, and I don't remember the other one anymore. He was supposed to meet a Mr. So-and-so, but he didn't meet him.

Kurt: He had been to see Grandpa, and Grandpa had sent him to us.

Marianne: Oh yes, that's the way it was; that's what came out. He claimed that he was a fugitive and a member, that he came from Hamburg and that, of course, he was in hiding and had no money to get home. Could we help him? He gave us his name and address and everything. "I can trust you with this. I am a member." And he even told us how long he had been a member. He knew the addresses of members from Cottbus, people that we knew so that we were supposed to believe that he was a member. We gave him some money. We really couldn't afford it, but my husband had received some money from his mother as his inheritance. At that time, this was our sacred treasure, and we gave him the money for his transportation. I remember very clearly we told him, "What we are doing we are doing as private citizens because we feel sorry for you, but this has nothing to do with the Church." We had been warned to say that, and that was probably our salvation. I gave him some soup to eat. He slurped it down so that one was to assume he hadn't eaten for days. Then I said to him, "Now tell us if this is too dangerous; maybe I should get the ticket from the train station for you, and you can rest a little." "No, no," he said. "I'll worry about that." He didn't want anyone to go with him. No one! We never heard from him again. That's the kind of man he was.

Kurt: He passed himself off to us as a fugitive.

Marianne: He escaped from Görlitz. That's where they were doing time. We were glad we never heard from him. That meant the whole matter was done with.

Joachim: There was a lot of that going on. Someone who had a little record with the police would turn to people who had a little sympathy left in their hearts, usually religious people. They would go to them and try to raise some feelings of pity. We had people who would come right in the branch house and in the meetings and start asking questions. We didn't know what to think of them. Were they enthusiastic investigators? That's the way they represented themselves. But in the end, they would turn out to be clever people who were supposed to spy us out. We experienced a lot of that.

And not only men; there were also women who showed up during the week at MIA. They joined right in, everything was wonderful, and then someone from the Church recalled seeing her somewhere. They were working for the police or for someone and just tried to slip into our circle. It was usually pretty hard to just slip in; we were, after all, a pretty small group. It wasn't so easy. We all knew one another. We could tell they had spent a lot of time studying us from the outside.

The reports we had to turn in on our meetings varied a great deal. In the first few years after the events of June 17, 1953, they handled things very, very strictly. We had to file a report on our meetings every week. Who were the speakers? Who was presiding? Everything had to be in the report. Later, we only had to turn in a monthly report. In the last few years, they just told us, "We don't care what you do in your meetings; you can do whatever you want. You just have to tell us when you hold your meetings, what are the starting times." And this happened only once or twice a year, whenever we had some contact with them. They handled things very differently then.

Then the district officials set up an office that was responsible for church affairs, and I was often invited to attend forums conducted by them. They invited the various church leaders, asked them what kinds of problems they were having, whether they could do anything to help, etc. Usually that was in connection with an upcoming election, when they wanted to attract a little sympathy from the people.

We even invited one of the city councilors who was up for election to come and meet with us. He informed us about his goals and plans. That was a good thing. At least I considered it a good thing because then the members could talk very openly with the man. He was a functionary of the CDU [Christian Democratic Union, one of the political parties in the GDR]. His job was to represent the interests of the Christians to the authorities. That was nice. The members asked some good questions. They kept him so busy he couldn't even squeeze in his propaganda. He had time only to answer our questions. And we were able to come out in the open and tell him, "We're ready to help out. We're ready to support our country, but on the basis of free agency." And we were able to scatter in a lot of criticism at the same time. I thought it was a good thing that we became a little better known. I have always had the feeling that these people come around only to give us their opinions. As it turned out, he got a little instruction from us. That was pretty satisfying to me. At least I know that after this kind of open meeting with the officials we had a better relationship. We had fewer difficulties.

G. Davis: Would you say that the insurrection of 1953 was a turning point in your relationships with the government. Did they become stricter? Did they curtail your missionary work?

Joachim: More and more it began to reach a head. That went on until 1959. To begin with, after June 17, 1953, the day of the insurrection, the government began to give us a little air, a little breathing space. They said, "OK, maybe we were pulling the reins in a little too tight; you were shoved around a little, etc. Now you can have a little more room to spread out." For a while things were fine. But we noticed that systematically, little by little things started coming back. They reintroduced regulations concerning our branch house, reports on our meetings. All written material that came from outside the country was inspected. Each local area handled it a little differently. Then they seemed to be very concerned about the fact that we served missions and thereby robbed the state of workers. That was the reason they gave. They could not afford to let people be unproductive. The missionaries were workers without work, they produced nothing for the state, and the government couldn't allow that. So, missionary activity had to go. We could do missionary work in our free time but no more door-to-door. After that we called retired members to serve full-time missions.

G. Davis: Were you able to have stake missionaries after the stake was organized?

Joachim: Yes. We already had district missionaries, but the kind of work they were permitted to do restricted them a bit. We were not allowed to do any missionary work in public. We could not set up any street displays. All of that was declared illegal. We saw that other churches had a window display, but when we came into the center of a city, they said, "No!" Those who already had something, that fell under the laws of customary behavior. But when we turned in a new application, we got a very strict "No!"

Also printing of any kind was strictly controlled, even for invitations or for little tracts. Of course, the missionaries were also clever. They said to one another, "If you don't get permission in this area, go try somewhere else." The various officials in the various areas were very different. In Bautzen they were very strict. They were a little afraid to make any concessions to us because of the higher officials. It was the same over in Görlitz, wasn't it?

Marianne: It was bad there. We were not even allowed to write "Until we meet again" on an obituary. They gave you a selection of prewritten verses, and you could choose one. That was all pretty stupid, but there was nothing we could do.

G. Davis: How did you maintain relations with the Church?

Joachim: We took advantage of every opportunity to get together with any of the authorities who came in. When I was a missionary, I had the opportunity to meet Henry D. Moyle in West Berlin. I even had a personal conversation with President Kimball at the chapel in Charlottenburg. There were a few from the Quorum of the Seventy, but the most beautiful time for us was when they had the Leipzig Fair. When the fair came around, many foreign visitors came as guests. Many of the Church authorities took this opportunity to come to the fair, and then we were all invited to a special conference at the chapel in Leipzig. We would have a meeting for all the leaders of the branches the day before, and on the next day, a meeting for all the members. The branch house in Leipzig in those days was an old factory building on Gerber Street. We stood on the steps and anywhere just to be there. It was really an inspiration to see someone from the leadership of the Church again.

I will say that the brethren from over there in the West did everything possible to make contact with us, and I must also say it was a great inspiration to us. The members from Bautzen and Görlitz got together and rented a bus and rode together to Leipzig. That was really an event. It was only a meeting, but it was a place to meet one of our leaders, and that was always a high point for us; it was like a conference.

Kurt: But, as we have said, that was possible only until '61. In 1961 came the Wall, and then it was all over.

Joachim: When the Wall was built, we were completely isolated.

Kurt: After that we didn't even have these good contacts in Leipzig. But when the Tabernacle Choir sang in West Berlin and the president of the Church was in Berlin, we were there.

Marianne: But the leadership did everything—a special train, right? So the members somehow made the arrangements. But maybe that was arranged from the other side, from the leadership in America. Because, a special train!?—You have to get permission for that—so that all the members could go over. But that was also before 1961.

Joachim: With the building of the Wall, it was as good as over with us. All contacts were shut off. And then, then we began to develop an entirely different attitude. All I know is that the Brethren told us that we had to live according to the laws of our government. We could not break the law in order to solve our ecclesiastical problems; that wouldn't do. On top of all that, we had this problem: we wanted to go to the temple.

There were many members who were already retired and were permitted to travel to West Germany for a visit, but the temple was in Switzerland, and their travel visa did not permit that. Of course, it would have been possible. You just had to climb into the car of one of the relatives over there, and they could have taken you to Switzerland with them. But then you wouldn't have a temple recommend. Our mission president could not write out a recommend because he couldn't give the impression he was breaking a law of the state by approving travel to a foreign country when the person had no papers authorizing such a trip.

So that was our problem. When the Brethren began to say that we would live to see the day when our wishes would be fulfilled, when we would travel to the temple, we always thought of the Swiss Temple as our temple. Someday they will open the borders, everything will be possible, and we will be permitted to travel.

When this kind of talk was going on, something began happening with us. Maybe not even consciously at first, but we began to be aware that the government was beginning to show a different attitude toward us. They were saying, "The Mormons want to travel to their temple. But they accept the fact that this is forbidden, and they don't go." There were even cases where members went to the police and said, "I want permission to travel to West Germany. I am retired. But I also want to travel to Switzerland." And then they got permission. Even though they had no relatives there, they got permission! Those were exceptions. But by this, we recognized that they were showing us more trust. Like they were saying, "If you are open about it and have not broken the laws, maybe we can make a little exception in your case."

Later we noticed that more and more things began to develop in a different direction. We noticed that the government was becoming very anxious to get capital, to get hard currency into our country, the German mark, the American dollar. In 1976 my mother flew to America on a visit, and she was given instructions on the general rules of behavior. She would not do anything to harm our country when she went abroad, they told her, because she would certainly tell her people there what living conditions were like here, etc., and it was important that they receive a good impression. And my mother said, "Oh yes, we can certainly do that. Things are going well for us here, and I will tell them that. And if they give me some money over there, may I then bring the money home with me?" "Bring as much back as you can! There is no limit."

They kept a sharp lookout for this kind of currency, and when we began to build the temple, it became very clear why they were actually treating us so nicely. We had always demonstrated that we lived a decent life and that we supported the state, but behind it all, behind all this special treatment, lay the fact that they wanted our hard currency from the West. And because of this, they may have permitted us many things that they may not have permitted other people. I am thinking in particular of travel permits. I heard from many brothers who had been permitted to cross the border just by asking for a travel permit. And they got it, even though they could not demonstrate they had relatives over there. They just said in all honesty, "I want to visit a friend. We have worked together for a long time, and now he is over there in West Germany. He is working in my Church. We are both active members." And they gave them permission. But that really began to develop for us in a positive way only in the seventies.

G. Davis: And what did you think when you heard they were going to build a temple here?

Joachim: I was so surprised that the temple problem was going to be solved in this way, that we were going to have a temple in our own country. From my point of view, I was overjoyed that such a thing could happen. And in this connection, I think I began to see a little further into the future. I began to see that because of this a new era was beginning, where we could also rearrange our missionary efforts. Of course, the consequences have been that we now have full-time missionaries and that we have been able to send missionaries abroad. But the fact that the state has declared itself so favorable to us, that was a real surprise, and I must say that credit is due to the good leadership we had here in the Church.

Marianne: I would like to second that. We were always taught that if we received permission to cross the border, whether retired or not, we should not take advantage of the situation and say to ourselves, "I'll take this permission to travel, but I'll stay over there and never come back. I'll emigrate out the back door." And I think the government authorities must have noticed that we, as a Church, accepted the principle of being subject to authority, supporting the government, etc. There may have been a few individuals who reacted differently, but that's what we were taught.

Kurt: Although they knew there were very few Communists in the Church.

Marianne: You might as well say none. But I believe that doing good does help the State, and if the government notices that these are people who have been taught by their church to do an honest day's work, to do their best, to be diligent, then that has to help the State. And they must have noticed over time that there was no subversive activity against the government going on. They see that this is the case, that we are serious about it, and that there really is a religion which teaches its people to do good.

G. Davis: Why did you decide to stay here?

Marianne: I can tell you. When the demonstrations came in '53, many left, good members, leaders in the Church. I remember those times very well. I was very confused and said to myself, "Maybe we should just take a trip over to Berlin and ask . . ." We asked ourselves, "Should we stay here or get out?" and we decided our place was here. I was very nervous. First this family left, then that one. We didn't want to lose our chance.

Kurt: There were a few members here who, I think, started a regular stream of emigration. I remember, it was in 1960, '59 or '60, before the Wall went up. There was such an uproar among the members. We were coming home from a conference in Dresden, and during the conference, the members had been talking among themselves a little and saying they had the strong feeling we ought to get out, and they influenced others. Here we were sitting on the train with our brothers and sisters, and they were saying to me: "You've got it made. You've got relatives over there in America!"

Marianne: That really made us nervous. Should we get out or not?

Joachim: We simply had to make a decision; in any case, we were very agitated. And I said, "Why leave? Somebody has to stay here. We can't all just take off. We can't do that." And I really had to exert myself to calm my little flock at the time, because such a strong mood had swept over us to just get out. There was one brother who started a regular hysteria with his attitudes. Of course, he couldn't say anything openly in the public meetings, but he would tell someone, and then they would say the president was of this or that opinion. It was terrible. Then one day the whole family was suddenly gone, and they had a lot of children, too.

Marianne: His last daughter, she was on a mission and had to quit her mission early to join her parents in the West. But we didn't want to leave; this was our home. Earlier, after the insurrection, I could have gone over, but Mother said, "Well, we may have a little less to eat here, but we're all together, and if we stick together, we'll get along." That was right. It really wasn't such a great thing, going West. One day you're here, and suddenly you're in a big whirlpool of confusion. Then when Father said, "Our place is here," that was the end of the matter. "They can all go if they want to. We're staying here." And we did.

G. Davis: Have you looked on staying in East Germany as a sacrifice?

Kurt: I have to say that I have not considered it a sacrifice. We found our Church callings here. In such a small branch, everyone has to have several callings. When someone can't be there for one reason or another, things don't run so smoothly. It all depended on each and every individual, and we had plenty to do here. There was scarcely a Sunday when every brother in the branch did not have to speak or teach a lesson either in the Sunday School or in priesthood meeting or with the younger brothers in the Aaronic Priesthood. We didn't get many visitors here. We were so used to this activity that we didn't look at it as a sacrifice.

Marianne: Somehow I was quite happy in our branch.

G. Davis: Did you have the feeling that in spite of the difficulties the Lord was blessing you here in this branch?

Marianne: Yes, we were such a small branch; I was always happy here. We were like a family.

Joachim: We had a lot of work. If there was only one person responsible for the MIA, that person had to organize something for every meeting. Even if we didn't do something terribly exciting every time, neither did we just study the gospel. We concerned ourselves with educational things of a general nature and interest. I was looking back over some of the themes we had in the MIA in the past, and I must say they were wonderful.

Kurt: It is somewhat difficult for us because we live in Bautzen, and the branch is in Bischofswerda, and it takes a while to get there. In principle, if there are meetings during the week, it is possible to get to them only if you have your own car, because public transportation doesn't come and go according to our needs. It regulates itself according to work and shopping schedules.

When we had our branch here in Bautzen—our little group—and when we knew one another intimately, we could tell just by looking at one another what each one needed. We had no problems then. As has been said, that's the way things were. We didn't have a lot of choices. We couldn't have a different calling every few years. Brother Albrecht was the branch president for thirty years, and I was for the last two, before we became part of the Bischofswerda Branch. I was the branch clerk for twenty-five years and, of course, at the same time a counselor in the branch presidency.

We didn't have a big selection of brethren here, so each one had his calling and filled his calling. There wasn't a lot of opportunity for us to see how things were done outside. It was only at conferences and the like, when we met with other members, that we could hear and experience things and see how others were doing it.

Joachim: But I have to say that this new organization of our branch, being transferred to Bischofswerda, has also been a good thing. It was an intelligent decision that corresponded with the times exactly. It was also a blessing for us. That's the way I look at it. We had improved our family finances to such a degree that we could afford the trip over to Bischofswerda. Our family got a car. We were then able to take the brothers and sisters with us, the ones who live in this area and had to go by train. We solved the problem with the members here in the city. We couldn't have done that a few years ago. We were prepared for it. We had the cars; we could drive over.

I have also said that if we would do our missionary work here then we could become an independent branch again. It's a problem when we have to send our investigators over to Bischofswerda. After you are converted, you accept all the difficulties and problems, and you overcome them. But before someone is converted, to take them out of the comfort of their apartment and tell them they have to take the train over to Bischofswerda and will get back at eleven o'clock at night—that's difficult.

Marianne: That is really a difficulty. We are members, and for us that is understandable and normal. When I want to attend Relief Society, for example, I have to leave here at four o'clock and get home about eleven o'clock at night. And if there is no one to pick me up at the train station, I have an hour's walk to get home. And it's dark, and I'm afraid. It's pretty lonely, and things happen now and then. You can't always be calling on our Father in Heaven, making demands of him. It's not much fun. I leave here at four and get there at five-thirty. But Relief Society doesn't begin until seven-thirty, so I have two hours with nothing to do. Sure, I can clean the branch house or take along some knitting, but somehow that is . . . Seven-thirty to eight-thirty, and then you get to the train about ten. We have a good time when we have to take the train. There are three of us, sometimes four. Now one of the younger sisters has a car and can take the four of us over. That's a lot of fun. That's nice. But if we have an investigator, we don't have enough room.

For two years, I took the train so that Papa could load everyone up and take them over in the car.

G. Davis: Brother Albrecht, what were the big problems you had to solve when you were branch president?

Joachim: Keeping the branch house clean was the problem that got on my nerves more than anything. The building we were in with those big, thick walls! They were built from some kind of stone, granite. The building was at least five hundred years old. Earlier there had been a little brewery in the basement. The basement had vaulted arches, and all of the groundwater had gone up through the stone walls. On the main floor of the branch house, the water crept through the stones right up to the ceiling. We had really wet spots on the wall. When it was lovely outside, summer, one would naturally think that it would be nice if the dampness would go away, but it was in the walls. They were so wet you could pull the wallpaper off. And the dampness had so much saltpeter in it that it was continually flaking off. So we had to clean them or put wallpaper over them, or they would just go on dripping.

Then we covered the chapel with large panels. We screwed some furring onto the walls and attached these plates to the furring. That provided a space so that air could circulate. In this way, we hid the wet walls, so to speak. It looked lovely, but the walls began to smell. And if we didn't air the place out during the week—but we couldn't be airing it out all the time, could we—when we came, well, this musty, strange smell was not too pleasant. I guess I could say we pulled our hair out over this building.

Kurt: That is the only thing in the Church that I have not really understood. President Burkhardt knew what was coming up in the future. This putting the two branches together—that wasn't planned overnight. And we worked, literally, up to the last day on those walls. We built in a timed thermostat and tried everything else; then suddenly the word came out from the authorities: that's it, shut the doors, close it down. They knew what was coming in advance, didn't they? We turned in our budget every year, didn't we? All of our remodeling plans had to be approved by the mission headquarters, and they let us work right up to the last day.

But, I guess we had to leave it in good shape. There's a grocery store in there now, and if it weren't for us, they wouldn't be able to sell their groceries.

Joachim: We did our duty there right up to the last minute. We invested thousands of marks in cash and our energy and our time and our ideas.

Marianne: I'll tell you something lovely, something wonderful. I'll never forget it. When Brother Albrecht was replaced by Brother Nikol, Brother Albrecht said, "I know that Brother Nikol is not able to do much physical work anymore"—he knew that the whole building project was coming up—"so I will support and help him as much as I can." I find that quite beautiful. When one has done all he could for so many years, when he has got everything going, and then another comes along to finish it off—that he could have such thoughts. I find it beautiful when people cooperate like that.

G. Davis: How do you feel in relation to the future? Are you optimistic?

Joachim: Yes. I have my own particular visions when I see what is happening here in our country, in our city, in relation to the Church. Now I can speak more openly and more freely with people, and even though they have their own ideas and plans, I have the feeling that some I have spoken with we will one day accept as members. Many of them.

G. Davis: Do you believe that the Lord is behind all of these great changes that have come about this past year?

Kurt: We have talked about that. In every country where the Church gets a foothold, where the Church can carry out its missionary work, a new world will open up for the people. We have certainly experienced that here in East Germany—ever since the temple was built. Over ninety thousand people came through in two weeks. Since then we have been working in Freiberg as temple missionaries—we go over every two weeks. At first we worked primarily in the Information Bureau in Freiberg. After Brother and Sister Birsfelder went home and before Brother and Sister Müller arrived, the tours were directed by the temple missionaries. We learned then how hungry people were to really learn about us.

Marianne: The people infect one another with their curiosity; it doesn't come from the members. The ones who were there come back with their relatives. They say, "I was here once," and now they are there with relatives from West Germany.

Kurt: In the business where I worked, I was the only member of the Church. I had a colleague there; she is now an official guide for the East German Travel Agency and takes tours around every weekend. Whenever she is in the area, she arranges it so that she can come by the temple. In the last five years, she has brought many busloads by and has given the people much information. It's simply amazing.

When I was in the war, there was suddenly this kind of an atmosphere. There was a different relationship. My comrades would come to me and say, "Tell me about your church." Many were becoming more and more dissatisfied with the system. They were members of a church but had no real association with it and hardly ever went to church. But they were very interested in our way of life.

G. Davis: We have baptized many people who had their first contact with the Church at the temple. I don't know if you are aware of this or not, but in the 1970s, when President Kimball was the prophet, we were asked to pray often that the borders to the Eastern countries would be opened so that missionary work could be carried out there. And now, beginning in July [1990], we will have new missions in Warsaw and in Prague.

Marianne: In Czechoslovakia? What is the world coming to?

19

The Border Guards Often Confiscated Them

Erich Ortlieb and Marianne Zwirner Ortlieb

When we first interviewed Erich Ortlieb and Marianne Zwirner Ortlieb, the street on which they lived was called the Ho-Chi-Minh Strasse, a constant reminder of communist rule. Nevertheless, their apartment has witnessed the progress of a large family raised in love, warmth, and good humor. It has housed weary visitors who came to district conferences in Dresden and has been the setting for wonderful meals given often to every missionary serving in Dresden since the mission was reopened in 1989.

Marianne: I come from Breslau in Silesia. My grandmother had already become acquainted with the Church when she was a young wife. American missionaries came to their home, and they started right in on genealogy, which was just the right thing for my grandma. She was actually Catholic, but she was a black sheep in that church because she wouldn't believe that little children would be thrown into the eternal flames if they were not baptized. She had a sister who died before baptism, or, maybe it was the sister of her mother, I don't remember anymore. In any case, she said that she wanted to be together with all of her loved ones and that if they went into the eternal flames then that's also where she wanted to go. So, when the American missionaries told her about the genealogy program, she said, "That's the right church for me," and she was baptized within four weeks.

Her husband took a little longer. That was at the end of the nineteenth century. After that many of the missionaries came to their house. They always felt right at home with my grandmother. My mother was the fourth child. When she was four years old, her father died.

When my mother became acquainted with her husband, he was not a member of the Church, but he let himself be baptized just because he didn't want to lose her. He was afraid she would drop him, but then after the wedding, he didn't go near the church. So my mother didn't go to church for twelve years.

In 1945 we had to evacuate Breslau with just a suitcase because Breslau had become a fortress. The Russians were getting closer and closer, and there was real warfare. I don't remember exactly, but about five o'clock in the evening, we received orders that women and children were to leave immediately. We were lucky. We didn't have to walk. Many left on foot, and many of them died because it was a very cold winter. We were able to ride in an open truck. My father arranged that. He was serving in Breslau with an antiaircraft group that was right in our neighborhood. But during the night, the truck broke down, and we sat there for three hours. Everyone else got frostbite, but we didn't, not a thing. Not my mother, not my brother, nor I. We didn't even catch a cold.

Then we were put into a camp. Before we came, there were Polish people there, prisoners. There were so many bedbugs it was terrible. One night my mother had to attend a meeting. We children were alone, and someone lost a key. He went crawling around under the beds looking for it with an open candle, and the beds were covered with straw mattresses. It's a miracle we weren't all burned to death.

Then my mother became attached to the Church again, and we became very active. My father stayed in Breslau during the fighting because of his responsibility for the fortifications there. He said to my grandmother, who had stayed behind, "If I ever get out of this, I am going to become active in the Church." We had always hoped that would happen. In 1949 he came home from captivity. He had been a POW in Russia and had become a Marxist, so he would have nothing to do with the Church. In 1951 my parents divorced.

By this time I had gained a testimony of the gospel, but when I turned seventeen, my father insisted that I join the FDJ *[Freie Deutsche Jugend]* or he wouldn't let me go to church anymore. The FDJ is a communist youth organization. I protested, but in the end, I had to go so I could attend church.

Many times I went out walking in the evening, and I thought to myself, "Is there really a Father in Heaven?" I was taught quite differently at school. You can belong to both the FDJ and the Church because the FDJ is just a youth organization, but you cannot belong to the Communist Party and also go to church. I didn't want to go to the youth organization. When I am forced to do something, then something in me resists. So I began reading extensively in the Book of Mormon. Whenever I read the Book of Mormon, I became very calm, I felt a genuine peace, but when I stopped reading, anxiety rose up in me again. I didn't realize what was happening. About a month later, I had such an overwhelming feeling of joy while reading I can't even describe it. I felt so happy, and from that moment on, I knew I was in the right church, I knew the meaning of life, and I never doubted these things again. I knew them.

In 1955 I went on a mission. While serving in Nordhausen, I met my husband. He was not a missionary but was living in the branch there. The mission president, President Gregory, told me that one might meet his or her future spouse while on a mission, but one should not respond to these feelings. If it became too difficult, the missionary should request a transfer. He also said that if I would fast and pray about it everything would turn out the way it should. That was what I did, but I was very nervous; I was always hoping that I would marry him. When I was released, we found one another again, and I was very happy.

I had always wanted to have twelve children. That part didn't happen; I had six. To me, having children seemed to be my stewardship in life. As a child, I was always playing with dolls; that was my life. Even today I often ask myself where the other six children are. I fulfilled only half of my task, but if I get six daughters- or sons-in-law, I will have twelve children. I am very happy. I have always said I was prepared for any sacrifice. The main thing is that my children remain faithful to the Church and all return someday to our Father in Heaven. That is the real desire of my life. So far I am very happy that my children are on the right path. I am also very, very happy I have a son on a mission. I feel the strength of the Spirit whenever I think of him.

Erich: When you have filled a mission yourself, you know the kind of experiences you have had, and you want them for your children. It doesn't matter what country the children go to or what happens to them. The spiritual values that one receives on a mission cannot be obtained through any other calling in the Church. I think it is one of the most important callings a young person can have—as a preparation for life, for marriage, and for later callings to serve the Lord. There is no better work than missionary work; therefore, I can understand why my wife is so happy.

Marianne: And now Coni can go! There is no way I could be sad. When Luka went, everything was different, and I was somewhat sad. [In May 1989, their son Luka was one of the first missionaries permitted to leave the GDR to serve a mission outside the country. He served in Argentina. Their daughter Coni was one of the first sister missionaries permitted to leave in March 1990. See chapter 31.] There was the uncertainty about going to a foreign country and all; we just didn't know what to expect. In spite of all that, I *was* happy, but now I am really happy because I know how happy Luka is and because Coni had such a desire in her heart to go. She cried because Luka was allowed to be a missionary and she wasn't.

I was just telling you about the period of transition, the time right after the war. We had so little to eat that I fainted in the street one day. We were foreigners. We landed in the little village of Geithain, which is located between Leipzig and Karl-Marx Stadt, and we were treated like foreigners: "You don't belong here. Why don't you go back where you came from?" They were so hateful. If there was a garden where we could get something to eat or where lettuce or other vegetables were being sold, they were always just sold out when it came our turn. We had nothing. We had so little to eat I was literally close to starvation. I couldn't learn in school anymore. I could no longer do the simplest mathematics. It was all gone out of my head, and I couldn't understand what I was supposed to learn. It was my uncle who saved us.

He was a member of the FDJ. He was a group leader in a castle and was also a leader in an indoctrination school. He took my brother and me into his home, and he and my aunt really pampered us. They kept us there for four weeks, and everything came back. My memory came back, and I felt totally refreshed. We ate so much there they must have been embarrassed to watch us. They had sliced cucumbers, and they always had to give me a second plate. They were my salvation.

Then in Leipzig we began to get cans of fruit and vegetables from the welfare program of the Church. We were living in Geithain, but we belonged to the Leipzig Branch. (I was baptized in Leipzig when I was twelve years old.) We went to Leipzig, and I received a sack with things like clothing and soap and grain and canned vegetables. The trains going there were packed.

Erich: The trains were so full that people stood on the roofs and on the bumpers between the old railroad cars. There was a lot of hoarding going on, and the people from the cities were going to the villages and selling their carpets and rings and anything because the farmers would give them potatoes or bread for them.

Marianne: One time, my mother and I left Leipzig at night, and the train was not so full. We were dead tired, and we fell asleep. Suddenly, I looked out and said, "We're already there!" My mother didn't even look out. She just grabbed up our sack, and we jumped out. Then we saw that we were at the wrong train station. Bad Lausick it was called, I think. It was late in the night, dark, and cold. It was in the winter. So my mother and I wandered through the streets and found some sort of a pension where they gave us a bed. We didn't dare go to sleep for fear they would steal our sack. It was terrible. We caught the first train the next morning, but it was so full, like my husband just said, that we had to stand on the running board on the outside. My mother tied the sack on somehow, and I had to stand out there in the cold on the running board. There was such a strong wind, and it was so cold. I had to close my eyes. If I looked down, I got dizzy. I kept thinking, "I'm going to fall off." I kept telling myself, "Just hold on." I was like a block of ice, and I thought, "If you fall off . . . !" When the train finally arrived in Geithain and nothing had happened to me, I felt like I had been reborn. That's an experience I will never forget. It was terrible. We got home, and I got a slice of bread with sugar on it and went off to school. I was so happy that we returned home safe and sound.

Erich: A lot of things happened in those days. Brother Krause was a missionary then, and he was working with Brother Lehnig. One time when Brother Lehnig was a missionary, he fell off a train. After he fell, blood came out of his ears and mouth and nose, and everyone said he was dead. Brother Krause carried him into the little house of the signalman and kneeled down and prayed for him and gave him a blessing. A short time later, Brother Lehnig stood up and dusted himself off. There was nothing wrong with him. He could walk, he could run, he could continue his mission. Brother Krause told me that story once when we were talking about how the trains were so packed.

There was also a lot of fear around. The local police and also the Russians took everything away from the people who were hoarding things. There was a lot of profiteering going on. If someone took a good vase or a picture or something and gave it to the farmers and got bread in return, then when they arrived back at the city, they might find controls set up at the train station. They would say, "I gave this or that for the bread," but the police would take their bread or their potatoes away from them because that was profiteering. That was against the law. There was also a lot of stealing and black marketing going on.

Marianne: My mother once sold a ring and a necklace to get some meat and sausage. We lived up in an attic, and we left a little lard out in a cupboard, and it was stolen. We had practically nothing, and the people who stole it owned a vegetable market, and they weren't poor at all.

G. Davis: Tell us about your missions.

Marianne: I went on a mission first. My first field of labor was Leipzig. The missionaries were about half sisters and half elders. That was in 1955. We had ration cards to get food. Actually our mission field was Delitzsch, but we couldn't find a room there, so we lived in Leipzig. When we arrived, the people we were supposed to stay with had just moved out. Since we had to have authorization for an apartment, we could stay there only a few days and then had to move out. Brother Burkhardt told us that if we could not find an apartment in Delitzsch he would have to close that part of the mission.

Once a week, as soon as the housing office was open, we went to Delitzsch. The men in the housing office were very nice to us, and we finally got a room. In the meantime, I had been living in the missionary apartment in Leipzig, but I was not a registered resident with the police, so I had to be there as a guest. The worst part of that was I could not have a ration card for food. You had to register with the police and state where you lived in order to get a ration card for food. But the owner of the apartment was gone, and even though the apartment was unlocked, I was not authorized to live there, so the police wouldn't let me register. I couldn't go on like that. The lady who gave out the cards said to me, "Well, you can't starve, you have to get something to eat," and so she gave me a food card, even though it was against the regulations. It was a testimony to me that I got a food card anyway, and then we found an apartment.

In Delitzsch we met a lot of very nice people who listened to us, and one of them, a Catholic woman, was baptized and did a lot of genealogy. Back then it wasn't like it is now, when so many are being baptized. In those days, we were happy to baptize anyone.

We also did a lot of work in the branches during our mission—teachers, leaders in the Relief Society, and so on, but we also did a lot of tracting.

Erich: I was twenty when I was called on a mission. That was in the spring of 1958, but I didn't want to go on a mission. I never wanted to go on a mission because I was never very good in school. I liked to study, but outside, in nature. I watched the animals. I knew where all the squirrels were, where there was a woodpecker, where there was a bullfinch. I knew every tree and knew how to climb it. That was my world, and when my mother went looking for me, she always found me in the forest. I had little interest in school. At church I met many missionaries. They were always my idols. They were perfect. They could do everything. They could write correctly, they could read properly, they could handle numbers. They could even play the piano and lead the branch. I told myself I would never be able to do those things.

And then our district was divided. The Thüringen district was dissolved, and we were put in the Leipzig district. The district president, Walter Schiele, didn't know me very well. He said to me, "We're sending you on a mission." I told him I couldn't go on a mission. "Why not," he said. I told him I had problems, and I didn't know how I would get the finances together. He told me to fast and pray about it, and I would find a way.

So I went home and talked it over with my mother and father. My mother said, "Well, we can help you out a little, maybe twenty-five or thirty marks." My father was very ill at the time. He had a problem with very bad rheumatism, and he didn't earn much money. So I fasted and prayed about it. I was earning a little money at the time and had saved a little over a thousand marks. So I fasted and prayed for two days. On the third day, I left our house and went to the park in Nordhausen, where I prayed again. When I finished praying, I knew that if the leaders of the Church said I should go on a mission then I could go on a mission. I went to President Schiele and told him I was ready to go. But I still didn't know where I was going to get the finances.

Then I had a conversation with Brother Burkhardt, who was a counselor to the mission president, Brother Robbins. [Burtis F. Robbins was president of the North German mission 1957–60.] Brother Burkhardt said, "Brother Ortlieb, just don't worry about it. The Lord will help you." So in April 1958, I went on a mission.

I still had six hundred marks left, but I had to buy myself a new suit, new shoes, and a coat. I didn't want to go on a mission in old clothes, and because my father didn't earn much, we were a very poor family. As a young man, when I earned a little money, I always quickly bought something for my parents, a new radio, for example. We had never had a radio at home. We didn't know what it would be like. Since we all wanted to have a radio but no one had the money for one, I bought a radio for us. And once I bought them a couch, not a very big one. But now there was no money, and I wanted to go on a mission.

My first area was Gotha. I had a very good companion who did a good job of teaching me. At that time, there were still food ration cards, but not all food was rationed, only some things like butter, meat, and sugar. All the other food items were not rationed, but the things that were rationed were very cheap; I could get them for very little money. When I got to my first area, Brother Burkhardt sent me one hundred fifty marks. I didn't know where the money had come from. He told me there was an elders quorum in the United States who would support me. But, he told me, "Each month you must write a letter to this quorum."

That was very hard for me. I had never liked writing letters except to my fiancée. That was before I went on my mission and only to show my fiancée (the woman who is now my wife) that I really liked her, that I loved her, so that she would feel secure. We became engaged before I left so that I would be sure of her and she would be sure of me and know that I truly loved her. I had never written a single letter to anyone else.

Well, there I was in my first area, and every month I wrote a letter to an elders quorum in Idaho. The quorum president was a former German, Brother Hans M. Bötscher, who is now working with his wife in the Freiberg Temple. Imagine my joy when I went to the temple this year on the Day of Pentecost and when I entered the reception area and saw a brother with a name tag that said "Temple Missionary, Hans M. Bötscher." I embraced him and said, "I know you." He said, "But I don't know you." I said, "But I have written many letters to you. You never liked my letters; you were never satisfied with my reports." He said, "Well, I don't know about that. Why wasn't I satisfied?" I said, "I just had this feeling that you weren't satisfied." Then I told him I was the missionary correspondent whom he never knew. I told him I wanted him to thank all the brothers with all my heart for supporting me for two years on my mission.

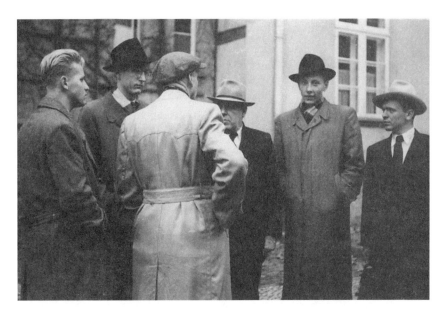

German Democratic Republic missionaries in 1956. Henry Burkhardt is second from the left. Courtesy Edith Krause.

I sent all the letters to Idaho, and I hoped they all got through. That was out of my control. But Brother Bötscher never said my letters were not coming. Usually he answered all of my letters, which was a very nice thing. I wrote to him of my testimony, and I told him what I was doing in the Church. I was the MIA leader while I was a missionary, but we also did missionary work, going from door to door. I explained to him our method of making a map of the streets we had covered and marking the names and house numbers so that we could come back in the evenings and catch the people we had missed during the day. We often caught people home in the evenings, but we didn't have a lot of success even with this method. We found very few investigators. At that time, in our country, there was so much pressure on the people from the Communists and the Marxists that many people just didn't dare join a church, even if they had an inner desire to do so. They didn't dare because they were afraid of the reprisals at work or wherever it was found out. We didn't have much success, so I wrote more about my church work than about my missionary work, and Brother Bötscher was not as satisfied with my reports. He wanted to hear about more missionary work. Now I have explained all of this to him.

I must say I learned a great deal on my mission, and I met a lot of people. But we, as missionaries, had a lot of problems. The criminal police and the secret police visited us in our apartments several times. They inspected the books we had, especially the Books of Mormon we were passing out. And we had several little tracts at the time which were forbidden. But we always had a few that we had picked up at the mission office in Berlin, *The Joseph Smith Story,* for example, or *What Do the Mormons Believe?* And, of course, we distributed them to investigators wherever we went.

We had more success in Werdau. My companion there was Brother Frank Apel, who is now our stake president. We gave out the Book of Mormon, and the people there were quite interested. Werdau is a little branch out in the country, and the people were not as restricted as they were in the cities. They were much more interested in the Church and in the Book of Mormon, so we gave away a lot of them. But we didn't have many books, and when we ran out, we had to travel to West Berlin with a big suitcase to get our books. But as missionaries we had to pay for them. Each book cost, at that time, eight marks. We didn't have much money. We could get the money back from the mission office, but we had to pay for them in advance.

We were also afraid that when we came to the border with a suitcase full of Books of Mormon that they would take the books away from us. They always asked if we had any West literature or if we had this or that. Where were we going, and where had we been? Did we buy anything in the West Sector? We couldn't lie. We couldn't say we hadn't bought anything. We just told them we were working for the Church and we had picked up some literature, the Book of Mormon. When they saw we had thirty or forty copies in one suitcase, they wanted to know what we were going to do with them. The border guards often confiscated them, but we usually got them back again.

Often we could get misprints from the mission office. Those were Books of Mormon that were not printed properly; maybe there was a typo, or the title page was upside down, and we could say that the books were a gift, that we had not bought them. They were a gift, and they were allowed in the German Democratic Republic, and that's why we were bringing them in. We then distributed these Books of Mormon to investigators, especially in Werdau.

The authorities in the GDR knew our methods, how we went from door to door and from street to street. In Werdau, for example, we went through every street. We would hand out the

Book of Mormon, and the authorities would come behind us and tell the people, "Give us that Book of Mormon" or "Give us that literature that the people from that church have just given you." We handed them out, and they collected them.

Sometimes we were called in by the authorities and told it was forbidden to be missionaries. I always said that my authority came from the Lord and I wanted to be a missionary. When they forbade us in one city, we got permission from President Burkhardt to go to another city. We were not only in Rathenow, but also in Stendal. That was the next largest city. Then we went to Werdau an der Havel, or we worked in Potsdam. I was always looking for cities where we could do missionary work and the authorities could not say it was forbidden. Because it wasn't forbidden by law at that time; the laws against missionary work came later. That's the way I worked, even with the threat that it could cause us some difficulties.

I learned a lot of things while I was a missionary. I served in Gotha, in Weimar, in Gera, in Rathenow. It was a good experience, but it cannot be compared with the kind of work the missionaries do today. We were too busy doing the work of the branches. Often we couldn't go out teaching investigators because we were the branch presidents. In almost every branch I served in, I was the organist because they simply had no one else who could play.

Marianne: I was a missionary in Weimar, for example, and one of our responsibilities was to reactivate the youth. None of them was coming anymore. I think our efforts went quite well, since many of them started coming again. We held a lot of firesides and programs. In Gänsemarsch we took all of the young people collecting wild flowers.

Erich: I won't say our work at that time was not necessary, but the missionary work now is much more productive in finding investigators. Of course, politically and socially, things have changed greatly, and the attitudes of the people have changed, also. Clearly, with the political turnaround going on here, a policeman, a soldier, or even an officer in the army can become a member of the Church. That could never have happened before. He would have been discharged from the army immediately. And he would not have found a job, either.

I have a good friend, for example, actually a good brother in another city, who was a civilian employee with the army. As such, he was forbidden to have any contact with anyone from a western country. One day he gave an old school chum a ride in his car.

He was found out—these things were passed along—and he was dismissed from his job and for several months could not find any work. No company would hire him. Of course, this was very hard on him. He finally got a job as a garbage collector. That was the only job he could get. He was paid well enough, but it was not something he liked to do, and it was hard on him. I just mention this to demonstrate why people were afraid to join the Church.

G. Davis: Were there any missionaries from outside the country during those years?

Erich: No, there were none. In short, no foreigners were allowed into the country in those days. There was a possibility that the mission president could get permission to enter the German Democratic Republic when the fair was held in Leipzig. Then the mission president or the Brethren who wanted to enter the GDR—at that time we said "behind the iron curtain" or "Russian Zone"—these leaders could get a visa in West Berlin or in the Federal Republic of Germany somewhere, and with this special visa, they could enter the country. Then we always had a special conference in Leipzig.

I still remember that old branch house in Leipzig. It was on Gerber Street right by the train station. That place was always packed. I saw Ezra Taft Benson with his wife and two daughters at one of these special conferences. These special conferences were always held twice a year, during the spring and during the fall fairs.

How it was for the regular citizens of the West, whether they could come in or not, I don't know. We had the feeling that the majority of the members of the Church in the West were afraid to enter our country, to enter the Russian Zone. They were afraid they would be arrested and they would never get out. But that wasn't true. Actually, foreign visitors were treated quite well. The authorities never did anything to bother the foreign visitors if they behaved themselves. We never had any trouble in Leipzig. The visits were well known to the authorities because the letters of invitation to the special conferences always went through the authorities so they knew about it.

No one is to be blamed for being afraid to enter the GDR. I am just telling you how it was. There were some mission presidents who were quite fearless. One of these was President Joel Tate. He was here all the time. He was always coming into the GDR. Others came only during the spring and fall fairs. Whenever the leaders of the Church came in to see us, it really gave us spiritual support. It renewed our ties to the Church so much.

At a 1963 conference in Leipzig. Joel Tate (mission president) with his wife, Frances; daughter Nancy; and Walter Krause on the front row. GDR members considered President Tate their guardian angel. Courtesy Edith Krause.

G. Davis: Did having visitors cause any difficulties for you?

Erich: For us there was no danger. But when we wrote a letter, we never knew who would read it. We just didn't know. But the Church had nothing to hide. Often I would write a letter with statistical information in it—especially during those years when I was in the mission leadership—and friends would come to me and say, "Mr. Ortlieb, what's going on? Someone from the authorities was here to see me and asked me about you." And I told them, my neighbors or people in our apartment building, that I was responsible for the statistics in our church. I evaluated them and sent them on. The authorities knew all about it, but they just wanted to know if I was behaving myself. We were being watched.

Marianne: When Luka went on his mission, they asked our neighbors about us.

Erich: The Church has nothing to hide because we don't break the laws. And this fear—it's often all quite needless, not only with us, but maybe with the other churches, too. Naturally, there were problems in Czechoslovakia and Hungary, and the mission presidents were thrown out by the officials, and contact with the Church was broken, but I have actually never felt anything like that here in the GDR. I must say that except for the time when I was on a mission I have been nicely treated by the authorities.

Marianne: Yes, in Dessau, for example, when I was there on my mission, we went door to door. One day the police came along and said, "Can't you just go to your investigators or to your members? The people here have complained that you are bothering them." But it was no bother when we just asked them if they wanted to learn about the Church or not and if not we went on our way.

There were a lot of party members who were playing this game with us, but the police themselves were very nice and just said, "Go on; do what you like."

Erich: Generally the authorities thought well of us, but there were, of course, others—there are people like this in every country—who couldn't stand the Mormons, and they tried every way possible, especially if they were employees of public officials, to make problems for us. There were several years, for example, when we had to apply to the police for permission to hold every meeting. We had to write down who was going to speak in the sacrament meeting. So we wrote them down. Then the police wanted to know what they were going to talk about. There were times in some branches when we had to report every sacrament meeting every week, and in others, every month. They wanted to know what we were doing. They wanted to know the times of our meetings, how long they lasted, etc. They wanted to know when we had a dance at the church house.

For several years, young people's dances were forbidden. The excuse was that dancing did not belong to a cult or to a religion. You can do whatever is appropriate for your cult, but if it is not appropriate, you have to do it with the FDJ [Free German Youth] organization or the official youth organizations. Then our young people started going to Free German Youth organization, where we didn't want them. So several times we reported our branch or district youth programs as a young people's worship service. We didn't say "dance." It was a worship service, and only a part of it was a dance. We reported it as a worship service to the authorities, or we didn't report it.

I don't know how that went every time; I was not always involved. I only want to say we had real problems in the GDR that had to be solved. They couldn't be solved by the Church authorities overseas but had to be solved by the Church authorities who were right here in the country. It is very important to us that people understand that.

The first person who really implemented this idea when I was in the district presidency was our current area president,

Hans B. Ringger. Whenever he came to Dresden for a meeting with the district presidency and we sat down in the mission office, his first question was almost always, "Brethren, what are you doing to let the Church operate in public, and how are you getting along as leaders of the Church with the regulations of the State? What relations do you have with the mayor and other state authorities?"

Actually, we had kept ourselves very closed and withdrawn for the following reasons. Every activity that the Church sponsored in public, regardless of the nature of the activity, would immediately be used politically. It would be turned into political propaganda to the advantage of communism or the existing social system. So, for several years, we had isolated ourselves as a church.

Of course, that was also fine with the authorities, but what we were saying was that we didn't want to identify ourselves with Communism in any way. And, the state authorities had placed real obstacles in our way. We were not permitted to construct any buildings in the country. For many years, that was forbidden. We were not allowed to build chapels for ourselves. Therefore, it was actually a good thing when Brother Ringger came on the scene. He brought us new instructions directly from the leaders of the Church that we should open a dialogue with the authorities and invite them to our functions, especially to our sacrament meetings.

Brother Ringger challenged us. And from that time on, things began to open up. The separation between Church and State that we promoted did not break down, but we did develop a good relationship. Things were no longer so stagnant. The authorities approached us in a more friendly way. They had a more friendly attitude toward us, and we didn't have to report every little meeting. As a Church, we were invited to special state functions that had a bearing on church affairs, functions to which we were never invited before. Before, only the big churches were invited—the Catholics and the Evangelical Lutherans. After that, we were invited along with them.

Erich: Once there was a youth conference that was always in August. I was responsible for the youth in the Church, and the young people were supposed to do some community service, either something that the Church took care of on an ongoing basis or a one-time project like cleaning up a playground or cleaning up a park. I had the responsibility of talking with the individual organizations or with the authorities.

I asked around in the city hall, and the man who was responsible for such things suggested I talk to the individual state organizations. The office of state organizations said there was nothing for us to do, and that was the end of the matter. Then I went to the People's Organization for Parks of the City of Dresden [*VEB Grünlagen der Stadt Dresden*]. They kept the parks in order and so on. They were very shorthanded, and the man in charge was very enthusiastic. He told me what a wonderful thing this was and asked how many young people would be involved? I told him there would be about eighty. "Oh!" he said. "I don't know what I would do with so many. We don't have enough tools; we don't have enough supervisors to train them and supervise them."

But I brought the negotiations along to the point that we had an assignment cleaning up a very busy street. Everything was organized. Then he went on vacation and told me to give him a call when he got back. When he got home from his vacation, I called him, and he said simply, "No! We can't do it. We can't use your young people." "Why," I said. "Why can't you use us?" But he wouldn't give me a reason.

I was not allowed to place the young people in another area. I asked the man why, but he wouldn't give me a reason. I asked him, "Why are you calling it off now; there is so much work to do in the city?" But he didn't want to be involved. Maybe he was afraid of the authorities or of the public, I don't know. So we used the young people to clean up the park and the land attached to the Church, which is, as you know, a very large area. And then we sent them to help the members—older sisters and brothers, those who lived far out, and some in the city. They were supposed to help out a bit, to visit with these older people, so that the young people would have something constructive to do that would give them some pleasure.

When we had the youth conferences, most of the young people were really enthusiastic that they could do something. I think it is so important our young people learn that true love grows out of practical service and of activity. So, if this kind of service was denied us by the state, we tried to do something on our own property. The young people really took good care of it. Of course, it was a problem for us to get our hands on enough tools for ten or twenty workers. But the service was always a great thing, and we tried it at several youth conferences.

A lot of people were aware that the State was trying to put the brakes on it, either the state leaders in the factories or in the administration. They didn't want a youth activity such as the churches were promoting—not only our church. They were always trying to put us down. They didn't want any church groups of young people showing the Free German Youth communist organization how people can actually work together for the common good.

Once we buried an old sister in Nordhausen. It was in the fall, and the rain was pouring down. When I got out of the train, old Brother Gulla was standing on the platform waiting for me because we had to dig the grave ourselves. There was no one else there, and we also had to lower the casket into the grave. When he saw me, no hat, a ragged, old coat—I didn't have a hat or any money to buy a hat—he said, "Brother Ortlieb, where is your hat?" I was probably about fourteen or fifteen years old. He was a very strict man, and I learned a lot from him, from the old Brother Gulla. He was truly full of love.

Marianne: When I was released from my mission, I went back to work at the same job where I had been before. The foreman went to the personnel office and arranged everything for me. But when I changed jobs because I could get more money in another position, my mission came out. They took a close look into my files to see what I had been doing for a year and a half. They noticed I had been a missionary, which was something that hadn't come to their attention before. Then the new job was no longer available, and my old company didn't want to keep me.

After a while, I went to see a colleague with whom I had worked before I went on my mission, and he was able to help me. We had worked at a small branch office of a big firm in Karl-Marx Stadt. The department head at the branch refused to sign my hiring papers. But then he became very ill, and my colleague took advantage of the situation and went to the temporary department head and told her that the papers were complete but needed a signature. So she signed them, and I could go to work.

A short time later, the party secretary from Karl-Marx Stadt showed up and said he would have to meet me and see what was going on. So we took a little walk, and he listened while I told him what our Church is all about and what I had done on my mission for eighteen months. He was very nice and told me that if I had any problems in the future I should know why. The reason was that the word "mission" was in my file. I wrote it in there myself. I was honest, so I thought, Why shouldn't I? I didn't want to lie about it. He told me he couldn't understand it. That's the way things were here. There were some missionaries who had real problems getting a job after their mission.

Erich: Brother Fischer, for example, and Brother Schulze. He couldn't get a job for four months. He used to have a tough job, a dirty job. He is a trained foundryman. Do you know what a foundryman is? He's the one who pours the hot metal into the forms. That is a very hard and a very dirty job. He was trained to do it. Before he went on his mission, he had a good job, but when he was released from his mission, he couldn't get a job anymore. And that is not the kind of work where you might peek into documents or something like that. It was all just because he had worked for the Church.

G. Davis: When did you move to Dresden?

Erich: I came to Dresden in 1960, when I was released from my mission. I didn't have much money, and we had to travel back and forth. My wife lived here in Dresden, and I lived in Nordhausen. That's 250 kilometers away, and we wanted to be together. At first the plan was that my wife would come to Nordhausen because it was just a small branch of the Church and I didn't want to leave. I owed so much to that branch. I grew up there. I don't say this to boast, but as a young man in the Church, I learned to bless and pass the sacrament, and on a single Sunday to give a talk, to teach a lesson, and to play the organ because there was simply no one else. In a small branch like that, you learn an enormous amount, and I didn't want to leave.

My parents were also members. My mother joined the Church in 1937, and that was a rather strange event. The missionaries had gone to a small restaurant to have their lunch. It was a small private restaurant. My mother came in to eat. The missionaries began tracting out all the tables. Each day they would sit at a different table; it was a good method. One day there were some investigators there, and when the missionaries came in, they said, "Go talk to that stout lady over there; she is really interested in the Church." My mother says, "I don't know where they got that idea, but the next day they came over to my table and began to tell me about the Church." She was interested in the Church right away, and in a very short time, she became a member. At that time, I was about to be born.

My father drank a lot. He comes from South Germany, and that is an area where they drink a lot of wine. They say that Nordhausen is really not Nordhausen, but Boozehausen. Before and during the war, there was a liquor distillery on every street. When the missionaries came to our house, my father refused to let them in. He said they could not enter his house. About three months later, when I was born, my father came into the maternity clinic, and a little baby blanket was lying there. My father asked where it had come from. My mother told him the missionaries had been to see her and had brought it. They had been to see her before my father had. They were very conscientious missionaries. So my father said, "Well let them come back." From then on, they were permitted to come to our house, and my father later joined the Church.

I owe a great deal to my father. He always made me adhere strictly to the teachings of the Church even though they were very hard for him. He always had trouble with the Word of Wisdom, but I learned a great deal from him. In particular, he taught me that a man has to get up after he has fallen, that he can never give up.

So, in 1960 I came to Dresden. At the time the stake was founded, I had been a counselor to the district president, Brother Lehmann. Then the district was dissolved, and I was made the first bishop of the Dresden Ward. All in all that was a wonderful calling, because from 1983 on, two years before it happened, we knew that a temple was going to be built here. There were many members who had been true and faithful for years and who had always had the desire to go to the temple. I had the marvelous duty of helping them prepare themselves to go to the temple—myself included.

Of the 125 members whom I considered to be active, 84 of them received a temple recommend. I am still so thankful that I was able to serve as bishop at that time and help the members prepare themselves for the temple. That was a wonderful blessing for me.

G. Davis: What did you actually do to prepare the people for the temple?

Erich: Of course, that was a very difficult situation for us because none of us here had ever been in the temple, or very few. The members who had been to the Swiss Temple were mostly so old that they couldn't help us very much. We received instructions from the leadership of the Church, and we had a manual which we used with all of the members who attended the temple training seminar. All of the members were invited to the seminar, not just the new converts, but also those members who had been in the Church for many years. There was nothing new in the temple seminar for many of these people, but we tried to prepare them with as much concrete information as possible because we had never received the temple ordinances ourselves. This was a unique situation in the history of the Church. We were, for example, ordained as high priests but had never been in the temple. It was the same for those called as bishops. I'm sure that this was a situation peculiar to East Germany. Many of the Church leaders couldn't understand when we explained this to them.

We knew after Elder Monson had given us his blessing—he rededicated the German Democratic Republic here in Dresden, actually in Radebeul near Dresden—we knew that this blessing would be fulfilled, not only with the building of the temple but in many other ways that had to do with the state authorities. We knew that things would move forward and that ways would be opened. For example, we can now have Church literature, manuals for the classes, and programs for the young people, the single adults, the Sunday School, and the Primary. Our contact with the Church itself has stabilized since that blessing spoken by Elder Monson.

Marianne: In March we celebrated our silver anniversary, and in June we were sealed.

G. Davis: Could all of the members go to the temple at the same time?

Erich: The temple wouldn't hold so many people. As far as I know, it is the smallest temple in the world. The Freiberg Ward was first and then came Dresden. Not all of the Dresden Ward could go together. There were too many, so we had two days reserved for the Dresden Ward. On the first day for the Dresden Ward, I took all the ward leadership, that is my counselors, the quorum presidencies, and the ward mission leader and their wives and families into one session. On the second day, I took all the members that had not yet been.

G. Davis: How did everything proceed?

Erich: Well, it was this way. We, as a ward, were instructed to be at the temple at seven in the morning, and we didn't come out until seven in the evening. We were in the temple for twelve hours until the endowment and all the other ordinances had been completed, including the sealing of the children to their parents. We didn't do any sealing because our son was in the army and we wanted to wait until the fall, when he would be home. But the families who had children did everything in one day. That was just for the families where this was possible, and, of course, everything took a long time. We had to learn everything for the first time, but there were many workers there to help us.

Marianne: The more often one goes, the more beautiful it becomes, actually. At first our heads were spinning. I thought, I'll never learn all of that. But then, as we went more often, peace seemed to prevail, and it all became more beautiful.

The first "foreign" missionaries to enter the GDR. *First row, left to right:* Ruth Schult and Hans Schult (members living in the GDR), Jeffrey Engelke, Christopher Karpowitz, William Powley. *Second row:* Wolfgang Paul (German Dresden Mission president), Stephen Anderson, Christian Yost, Craig Miles, Steven Tree, Steven Smith, Manfred Schütze (Leipzig Stake president). Courtesy Christopher Karpowitz.

G. Davis: How was it for you when the first missionaries arrived?

Erich: When they first came in, we were overjoyed. We never learned ahead of time when they were coming. We in the ward would have given them a real welcome. But they just came sneaking in. There was a wedding reception in the chapel, and suddenly there they were.

Marianne: We were thinking, "That can't be the missionaries!"

Erich: That was a special experience for us because of what we had heard from our parents about the missionaries, about what they had meant to them. Toward the end of the war when Nordhausen was bombed, my mother escaped with the pictures of her family and of the missionaries. That's all she took with her. She talked about the missionaries all the time. She loved the missionaries who were in Nordhausen converting people. That's why my expectations were so high, and then suddenly, there they were. They just dropped in.

Marianne: In any case, when they came to visit us, Elder Smith came first and taught us how we could invite friends into our home. And there was always such a special spirit when they were here. It was like light coming into the room. There was such a feeling of freedom. If you were feeling depressed or something, that all went away. Those were really joyful times. Even when they came to eat. It was always so natural. You noticed it when they came. They seemed to glow.

20
Political Isolation
Erich Ortlieb and Marianne Zwirner Ortlieb

The following interview with Erich Ortlieb and Marianne Zwirner Ortlieb took place four years after the previous chapter and after the fall of the Berlin Wall and the reunification of Germany. Perhaps the reader will detect a slightly different tone to the conversation.

Erich: It is very important that the history of the Church be complete. I believe that the history of the branches in the German Democratic Republic is already a special history because of the people in the GDR. The group was relatively small and was always isolated. We were not isolated because we wanted to be, but because at first the people in the government wanted to isolate us. They didn't want people to believe in God. They didn't want people to have ideals.

Later on they decided that our ideals were not so far from their political aims, and then they tried through the media and also through individual politicians to get the Church to go along with them. That's the point at which we remained neutral. The Church teaches—and this is an important point which I consider correct—the Church says that the state and the church should remain completely separate from one another. And so, if we as a church attempted to have a strong influence on the politics or on the economy of the state in which we, as members, became politically engaged, well, in the GDR that would have meant that we identified ourselves with Communism or with atheism, because Marxism is fundamentally atheistic. And as members of the Church, we didn't want that. So that is why we

Marianne Zwirner Ortlieb and Erich Ortlieb. Dresden, 1990. Courtesy Norma and Garold Davis.

withdrew ourselves, and as a consequence, we were naturally quite isolated for several years.

Now as a result of this isolation, not only could we not get permission to build regular church buildings, but it also meant that very few members of the Church were allowed to attend the universities or choose the profession they wanted to follow. There were, of course, many young people in the Church who were interested in a very broad spectrum of studies, but they were simply not allowed to attend the university. Wanting to become a teacher, for example, was out: "Maybe you could be very good teachers, but you could never educate the children properly in the Marxist philosophy." That was the program of all the schools, in all educational institutions. It was that way in the preschool, kindergarten, elementary school, high school, trade school, and university. This Marxist philosophy was always in the foreground, was always the basis for the educational methodology.

Marianne: Yes, that was more important than anything else. If you got an "A" in these areas, then it didn't matter if you did poorly in your other studies; that was no sin. But if your grades were the other way around, that was bad. You couldn't continue.

Erich: And because of this, many members of the Church were held back. Yes, and are so to this day. Not everyone. I never wanted to go to college and made no demands on the State. I can truly say that I have been satisfied with the offers I received from the individual companies or businesses in our country. I am happy that I could accept them without compromising myself, so that no one can say today that I have obligations to the State. It used to be that when a person in the GDR wanted to study, to go to college, then the State said, "Well, you want that from us? Then you are obligated to give us something in return."

Marianne: Students at the university were actually obligated to spend three years in the army. Everyone had to spend one-and-a-half years anyway, but if you wanted to study at the university, they wanted you to do three years and become an officer. Olaf, our oldest son, really wanted to go to the university. At first they wouldn't let him, and then he applied again and applied for an area where they really wanted students.

Erich: Construction engineers who specialized in equipment installation.

Marianne: Yes. And he was accepted, and then they wanted to make him serve three years in the army. He had already served his one-and-a-half years before he went to the university. That was obligatory, and now they wanted another year and a half from him, and he was supposed to enter officer training. He wouldn't do it, and there was a big fuss about it. They called him in for consultation. In the end, they finally let him become a student, but they told him that he would never receive a leadership position in the profession. There was nothing he could do about that. Someone who goes to church and does not follow the party line would never get a leadership position. But now he has become a manager. Now that we are no longer the German Democratic Republic.

G. Davis: Did a person have to be a member of the Communist Party in order to attend the university?

Erich: No.

Marianne: It wasn't absolutely necessary, but it was . . . well, they just didn't want to admit him because he was a member of the Church.

Erich: You see, as a church, The Church of Jesus Christ of Latter-day Saints, we were a very small group inside the GDR. And it was quite natural that the State authorities who decided on the admissions policies for the university looked on us as an American sect. The Protestant and the Catholic churches had a lot more influence in these matters, in political matters. They took advantage of this influence insofar as it was possible, whereas we, as a church, were quite isolated. In the early years, we never attempted to make any contact with the local or state authorities, and consequently there was no possibility that we could do anything in the way of influencing them. That was simply not possible for us. In the beginning, we were only about four and a half or five thousand members in the GDR, and that is a small percentage out of a population of seventeen million.

G. Davis: You never had the feeling that you had been forgotten by the Church?

Marianne: No. On the contrary. It was actually somewhat of a disadvantage to us that there was always someone coming over from

America. The police could think they were spies and think that we were agents or something. Our Olaf, when he was in the army, always had trouble when he attended a stake conference, because there was someone there from America. You see, it was like this. Whoever was in the army, the army of the GDR, was not allowed to have any contact with foreigners from the West. And when we had a conference and there was a General Authority there or visitors from the West, then he was never allowed to speak to them. And in case he did speak to them or came in contact with any of them, he was required to report this contact to the authorities at his army base. And that was actually something of a problem with the young people who were in the army. Either they didn't report, or they got in trouble for not reporting. Of course, it wasn't always known. Not always. But we never had the feeling that we in the GDR were isolated from the Church as such.

Erich: On the contrary. I think that today we receive fewer Church authorities than we did in those days. There was a time, however, when no one could enter the country. That was after the building of the Berlin Wall. For the first two or three years after that, no visitors from the West were allowed to enter. That was when they were trying (by "they" I mean the people in the socialistic camp to which the GDR belonged) to achieve complete isolation in the areas of economics, culture, science—you name it. They wanted a complete isolation in order to make us independent. They had always believed that an economic dependence on the West brought with it a political dependence, and they couldn't have that.

I really think they were correct. If I trade with you and we have some kind of common economic interests, cultural and scientific exchanges will follow, and that's what they didn't want. And so there was a time, a number of years, when we had very little contact [with the Church].

G. Davis: So what kind of difficulties were there for the Church here in this country?

Marianne: We could never do what we wanted to do.

Erich: Well, there were difficulties. For one thing, we could not do missionary work. The government forbade missionary work. And they didn't say it was because we were political agitators, but they based this decision on the idea that young people who were working for the Church were not part of the socialistic work force and they were therefore hindering the productivity of the State. So they didn't put it in direct political terms. They just said that they couldn't spare young people from production to work for the Church. We were not in the factories for two years. That was the reason they gave, and of course we as a church had to go along with it.

Another difficulty was that we couldn't have the *Stern* [Church magazine in German] and we couldn't have any teaching manuals. We had to copy them off with the typewriter, but that was illegal. For a while, we as teachers had a very difficult time, but there was also a good side to it.

Erich: It was a blessing.

G. Davis: Why was that?

Marianne: Well, it took us a lot more time to prepare a lesson, but we really had to study. We studied a lot more intensively than we do now. Now we have the prescribed lesson, and you have to read it and learn something in order to understand it and so on, but the lessons are so carefully worked out that you don't have to do much. I used to teach in the Primary. We just had a title for a lesson, "Keep the Sabbath Day Holy" or one of the commandments. And we had to make a lesson out of that. We had to figure out how we could make that apply to the children, and so we had to draw on our own experiences. It was a lot of fun then to be a teacher. Of course it still is. And that's what's funny about all of this. It's hard to imagine how it was anymore. Now we are happy that we don't have to spend so much time preparing, that we have everything prepared for us.

Erich: But it was a terrible disadvantage when the literature of the Church was not available for the teachers or for the priesthood leaders. We didn't have any handbooks! Just try to imagine that. There are specific handbooks and specific instructions that tell you how to run a mission. And if anyone had a handbook, it had to be Brother Burkhardt, who was first a counselor to the mission president and then became mission president for the GDR. And if anyone had a question, they had to contact Brother Burkhardt or someone who eventually had a handbook. So it wasn't only a problem with teaching; it was also a problem for the administration of the Church.

A lot of people were afraid to join the Church because then their neighbors would see that they were attending church. "Oh, you're a Mormon now." Then they lost their jobs, or were ridiculed at school or at the university. Many people, when they join the Church, do not yet have the spiritual strength to stand up to this. It's being locked in like we were that causes this uncertainty and this insecurity. We are living in this large camp, and we hear that America is the land of unlimited possibilities—which must have its negative as well as its positive side. But we didn't have anything like that. We had only the one perspective, and that is what caused a lot of unrest in the branches.

Marianne: We were talking about the difficulties we had here in the GDR because we were members of the Church. We had them alright. You were always a little bit afraid. When your children went to school, you were always afraid that they might say something that could be to your disadvantage, that could get you in big trouble, because they spied on the children. They could learn from the children if their parents watched Western television, which was not permitted. We lived in what the other Germans called the "valley of the naive" because we couldn't get Western television here in Dresden. But in other cities they asked the children what TV shows they had seen, and then they knew if the parents had been watching Western TV, and that could get them into big trouble.

Erich: Actually, the problem was that the kids in the schools would talk to one another about TV shows from the West, and then the authorities could say, "Mr. Ortlieb, your children are making propaganda for Western TV." That was the problem. It was always interpreted falsely. A child could suddenly get enthused about a particular film or TV show, and they interpreted that as propaganda. They never actually said that it was forbidden to watch Western TV. They only said that it was forbidden to talk about it in public. And a child who is in a school is in a public facility. And when these kids talked about a TV show or even made gestures they had picked up that were typical of the West, then that was Western propaganda.

Marianne: If a child wore a T-shirt with any kind of advertisement from the West, they had to take it off or at least, never wear it to school again. Or if they got a sticker on a package from the West, they weren't allowed to show it at school.

Erich: A school bag, the kind that is common now, if it had any advertisement such as Solomon Skis or Herti Sporting Goods, even if it just had the child's toys in it, they could not bring that to school.

Marianne: Or, they would be told never to bring it again.

Erich: The entire socialist ideology was actually supposed to be supported by the smallest unit of society and in every family. And that's why the people always felt they were being watched.

Marianne: But now, the children can talk about God openly and about their attitudes. It didn't used to be that way. We always taught our children to speak their opinions freely, but many parents wouldn't do that because they were afraid that their children wouldn't be able to get into a decent profession.

Erich: Or they wouldn't be able to attend the university. It was this way. Our daughter Maja had good grades, and the director of her school recommended her for the university. That was always a privilege to be recommended, and it made a difference if one was recommended or just made an application. If one was recommended, it was as good as certain that the child would be able to attend the university. If one made an application, it was always questionable. And Maja, she brought this recommendation home and said, "Look at this, they want to send me to the university." Actually she wasn't so excited about going on with more school.

Marianne: Yes. Yes. She wanted to go.

Erich: Well, maybe then. But she had this recommendation in her records from the fifth grade on, and every year or two the children were asked what they wanted to study. And Maja wrote that she wanted to study medicine. And I was called to a conference for parents at the city hall where we parents were to be clearly informed that our children were going to the university. And there at the city hall they told me that there were other students who were better than Maja and that the State could not guarantee that Maja would be able to study medicine. And so they didn't process her recommendation.

Marianne: But my husband knew the school director, and he asked him personally, and the school director told him it was because of the Church. He said clearly and openly that it was because of the Church that she could not go to the university. But they said, "No, it was because there were so many other children." They tried to find an excuse.

Erich: Yes. Yes. They said, for example, that they had a number of applicants, young men who wanted to attend the university whom they had obligated to spend more time in the army. The army always came first. What that meant was that if my boy had bad grades at school and if I applied for him to become a career officer, he had the best chances of getting into the university. And many of them did this, and afterwards their parents would tell them to go to a doctor and get a statement that they were not physically fit to go into the army. But once they been accepted, they could study something else. But our family and the other families in the Church didn't want to use these kinds of underhanded methods.

M. Ortlieb: But a lot of families did.

G. Davis: Now, tell me about the problem of getting to the temple.

Marianne: There was a time when we could go to the Swiss Temple.

Erich: This is the way it was. There was a particular time in the GDR when people from the GDR were allowed to travel into West Germany. They received a visa for West Germany. And the Church in West Germany made it possible that certain members who were older and who could afford it were allowed to travel to the Swiss Temple. But this was actually illegal. It was not officially sanctioned by the Church here. Officially the Church here was not allowed to issue a temple recommend for the Swiss Temple or for any other temple because the members could not receive a visa from the State authorities to travel into these countries.

Marianne: But there was also a short time when they could go to the temple, before the Wall went up. My mother wanted to go, but it was just at the time when I was on my mission, and she was happy when she was able to give me a little financial support. She wanted to go to the temple, but she didn't have any money.

Erich: Yes, I can explain that. There was a time when it was permitted to travel from the GDR into West Germany without a visa.

Marianne: That was before 1960.

Erich: That was before 1960. Long before 1960. We had permission to travel into West Germany, but when the United Nations recognized the Federal Republic of Germany and the German Democratic Republic, we had to have official State visas. And we couldn't have a visa to travel to Switzerland or to London or to America. We could have a visa only to travel to the Federal Republic of Germany, and there was no temple there. So we couldn't go. Members could cross the Swiss border without a visa, but they had to have a temple recommend, and no bishop or branch president could issue a temple recommend that authorized the person to attend the Swiss Temple. It was just impossible.

Marianne: Brother Burkhardt did it. He filled out recommends for Switzerland.

Erich: Yes, Marianne, that is true. We filled them out too, but that doesn't matter. He knew that when he filled it out he was going against official instructions from the State, and that's why in the later years he stopped giving these temple recommends.

In the '50s and '60s, we always had the feeling that the Church was a blessing for us. That was very important. Otherwise, we wouldn't have remained faithful to the Church. A church that has nothing to give its members has lost its value. And we members of the Church understood that. But these problems really come about when a church or a country is isolated. The leaders of the Church have always talked about the "iron curtain." And the leaders of the Church have always tried to get around it so that we have never really felt that we were alone. There was never a time when we had to say, "Well, they have forgotten us." That never happened. Of course, there were times in the small branches where the people felt they were alone, but that is probably true also in America.

The fact is that we here in the GDR were only a small unit of the Church, and we were together for special conferences and meetings for more than forty years. If there was a conference here in Dresden or we had to travel to Leipzig, in Leipzig they would announce that three hundred or five hundred members of the Church would be coming and that they would need housing. The members in the GDR were not able to pay for a hotel. So they would say, "Sister Davis, how many people can you take in?" And Sister Davis would say, "Well, two can sleep in that corner, and two can sleep over there." Then that night she would have ten members to take care of in her three-room apartment, members from Rostock and from Erfurt. That's the way the members inside the GDR got to know one another and how they grew into a beautiful unified group.

We, as a family, the Ortlieb family, the Zwirner family, we felt this to be a wonderful thing. We never gave this a second thought; we just thought this is the way it has to be. It couldn't have been better. Whenever there was a conference or a special occasion here in Dresden, we always had guests in our home. There were even occasions when members of our own family who came for the occasion were offended because we had the house full of guests. They wanted to stay with us, but they hadn't told us they were coming, and there was no place for them to sleep. But this is the way the Church family in the GDR grew together.

And there were also the youth conferences, where the young people for the entire GDR came together. Then they all stayed at the chapel.

Once when we had a youth conference, the young people from Dresden or those from Leipzig got an assignment to build a large Sphinx. You know, there by the pyramids in Egypt there is this big lion or Sphinx. And they told us, you have to build a Sphinx. And then they came. And the big room at the ward house it would be decorated like a robbers cave.

Marianne: Or like a pond with fish.

Erich: Or there would be a festival at the court. All the young people would have on courtly costumes.

Marianne: Like a court festival.

Erich: We put on a court festival, and all the young people brought their families with them.

Marianne: And everyone participated. It's not that way anymore, at least they tell us that they do this and that. And sometimes the young people don't even come. And we used to dance. Not at all like they do now where a bunch of them stand around in a corner.

Erich: Maybe I could say something. When I was responsible for the young people, we had a youth conference for the Dresden district over in Bischofswerde. And Bischofswerda had a meeting place that had a high ceiling, but the ceiling was covered with wood panels, and the bishop over there said, "You can't go home until drops of water start falling from the ceiling." By that he meant, that we had to get so warm from our activities and sweat so much that moisture would drip from the ceiling. And it really happened. The young people were so enthusiastic, and, I'm sure those things happen today, but you asked how things were inside the GDR in those years. A very strong spiritual and emotional feeling developed among us in the Church in the GDR. It developed because of the isolation we felt from the State. We said, "We have to take care of ourselves. There is no other way." And many things happened. And the young people always felt very secure.

Marianne: In the old chapel, there was a room up there in the second floor which we called the Celestial Kingdom *[Himmlische Herrlichkeit]*. That's where we wanted to sleep when we had the youth conferences. The room wasn't so large as it was down on the main floor, where most of the young people had to sleep. Someone would always say, "Let's make a place up here for the Dresden group." We would spread our things out so we had room to sit and to sleep. Oh, those were beautiful times.

Erich: And you have to understand that we who were in leadership positions were interested in offering the young people something in contrast to the offerings of the State. The State had many things to offer the young people not only for their cultural and scientific development, but also for their social life too. As leaders in the Church, we wanted to fill this cultural and educational void for the young people in the Church in the GDR, to close the gap. So Brother Burkhardt and the leaders of the Church were always seeing to it that the young people had not only the opportunity to get together, but also the financial support that they needed. And the young people looked forward to the next youth conference for a whole year.

21

Church or School?

Wolfgang Zwirner and Karin Zwirner

Wolfgang Zwirner is Marianne Ortlieb's younger brother. He and Karin Zwirner, his wife, are articulate and well educated. They have raised their three daughters to be active both in their community and ward. Shortly after the missionaries returned to Dresden, Brother Zwirner served as a very active, involved ward mission leader. As Relief Society president at the same time, Sister Zwirner not only carried the ordinary duties of this calling, but also found herself welcoming and integrating an average of four or five new convert sisters into the ward every Sunday.

Wolfgang: I came into the Church because of my parents. My mother joined the Church with her mother in Breslau through two American missionaries. My grandfather also joined but died a short time later. My mother's brother and a sister also joined.

My father joined the Church in the 1930s through my mother, but he was never very active. He is a very nice man, very nice. He is still living, but he never received the priesthood. During the war, my father ended up in a Russian prison camp. He had something to do with Marxism, with Communism, but he didn't have any trouble with the National Socialists as far as I know. But he was still thinking about these things when he ended up in the Russian prison camp somewhere beyond Brünn. He was sickened by the war and had seen so much suffering. The suffering of the children was particularly abhorrent to him. He wanted to do something for peace so that there would never be another war.

Well, the Russians had their own ideology. He said he was standing in a row of POWs, and he was called out. He didn't know

Outside the Dresden branch house on Dr.-Kurt-Fischer Allee, December 7, 1953. Dorothea Condie (top row, second from left), Wolfgang Zwirner (next to bottom row, third from left), Heinz Wöhe (bottom row, fourth from right). Courtesy Käthe Wöhe.

why they selected him, but he was sent to the party school in Moscow, so he went in that direction. He became a Communist. But he is a good man. He has never said anything negative about the Church. He has kept the Word of Wisdom. He has never smoked. He told me once that he always spoke well of us with his party comrades. In 1949 he returned from his prison experience, and we have always had a good relationship with him, but he no longer came to church. He has never been excommunicated; his name is still in the records, but his experiences have led him in another direction.

My mother stayed firm in the Church throughout the war, and I was baptized in 1946 in Leipzig. At the end of the war, my mother and I and one sister (Marianne Ortlieb) had to flee from Breslau. In 1949 we arrived in Dresden, and my mother was very active from that time on. She was a missionary and the Relief Society president. Her entire life from 1949 to 1963 was one of continuing Church activity, and that, of course, influenced me. She was a very clever woman. She never tried to force me, never.

I used to play a lot and for a long time, and it was often hard for me to go to church, but we went regularly. One day she gave me the following advice, which really helped me. She said, "If you will concentrate very hard during the first talk at sacrament meeting, you can play after that." I tried very hard to be obedient and concentrated on the first talk, and then I played. But as time went by, I began to get interested in the other talks, and in this way, she never had to force me at all.

We came to Dresden in 1949, and in 1950, I was ordained a deacon and experienced a normal growth in the Church. When I was eighteen, I was ordained an elder, and I wanted to go on a mission. I don't remember why anymore, but I had to wait. Finally in January 1958, I was called on a full-time mission. We could serve full-time missions then, but I was one of the last ones to be called. Shortly after 1960, the State would no longer allow missionary work. They said it took two years away from productivity for the State. I was happy that I could serve a mission for The Church of Jesus Christ of Latter-day Saints, and that this was on my record.

In Rathenow, my first area, I was a companion to Brother Johannes Schiebold, who later emigrated to America and became rather well known. I believe he studied art. Anyway, he was my senior companion for the first six months. One day we came upon a man; he must have been a writer. At any rate, he was very impressive, and I was afraid of him. We were not supposed to discuss politics, but a few expressions slipped out in our conversation. He became very excited, went upstairs, and brought a friend down with him. Then it was bad. I wasn't the one who had said anything, but I tried to defend my companion. I just said, "You have misunderstood him," and he said, "Oh, he can defend himself." Apparently these were two pretty high officials, and he said, "This is impossible! We can't have this, you running around from door to door saying things like that."

We left and went down the street, and suddenly we were approached by a man from the State Security—what we used to call the secret police. He said he was a police officer and turned us over to a uniformed policeman. I don't know how my companion felt, but I was pretty scared. We had to go with him to the police headquarters, where the sergeant was fortunately not alone. There was a young lieutenant there from Potsdam, and he was the senior officer. We had a very casual conversation. He asked us a few questions, what we were doing, and so on. I said that what we were doing was not forbidden. And he let us go. He was very tolerant. He sent us home, and we went on our way.

The Church was not suppressed everywhere, in every city. You can see how arbitrary it was. It all depended on the local authorities, on their attitude. This experience was very typical.

A short time later (I remember the day well because our toilet was stopped up and we were trying to repair it), someone suddenly appeared and told us we were to report to police headquarters again. Off we went without any idea what it was about. But this time the lieutenant was not there, just his subordinate, and he was red in the face: "Why are you still going about doing what we told you was forbidden?" We told him that the man who had interrogated us told us it was not forbidden, but he didn't go along with that. He forbade us to go door to door. We could never do that again, period! So you see, there was no clear line. Either the first man was staying in the background or this man had received other instructions. I don't know, but that's what we had to experience. We couldn't go door to door anymore. We had to find other ways to approach people. I don't remember what we did after that; I was soon transferred to Gotha. I spent six months there, and we went door to door every day.

Naumburg was my third area, and from the first day, we were informed by the previous missionaries that we would not be allowed to go tracting. It was forbidden there, so we obeyed the law. Those were our instructions from our mission president,

Brother Burkhardt. We went to the neighboring city, Weissenfels, which was just twenty minutes by train. There tracting was not forbidden. Here we were, native Germans in our own country, and there was no clear line from one city to another. And the officials would never give us anything in writing. Everything was by word of mouth. They were likely afraid that we might have copied something and sent it off and caused some international trouble.

And so we went door to door in Weissenfels. And one day we had an experience that shows how we were guided by the Spirit. We started at the top of an apartment house and worked our way down. When we were on the ground floor, we saw a door open a little, which meant there was someone at home. But we just walked on by. There was no reason why we shouldn't have rung the bell, but we didn't. Then suddenly someone came up behind us and pulled an ID out of his pocket—secret police. He told us to come into the apartment.

But we knew who it was and why he wanted to get us into the apartment. They would have someone sitting in a neighboring room, or they would have a tape recorder. They would get us into a conversation where we would say something that we ought not to say, and they would have us. We had seen this before and were not so young and inexperienced now.

We told him we were not doing anything illegal, and where tracting was forbidden, as in Naumburg, we didn't do it. But he gave us an appointment to appear at police headquarters anyway. So we went, and once again there was a young man in charge. The young people were, in general, somewhat more tolerant. We described to him what we were doing. We told him we introduce ourselves and ask the people if they would be interested in our message. We never put our foot in the door. We didn't force ourselves on people. And he just said, "You can go." Nothing in writing; always word of mouth. So we went.

Then I was transferred; my last area was Mittweida, and there again we had the typical experience. We went tracting. We were the first missionaries there in a long time. The members of the branch were wonderful to us. There were some large families, the Jentzsch family, for example. We were taken care of; we were something special. In some of the larger branches, missionaries were not so uncommon. Anyway, there we were, and we went door to door. We also lived in the branch house, which was also illegal, but they left us alone for six months.

My mission was almost over when one morning there was a knock on the door, just as we were eating breakfast. It was the police. They told us we had twenty-four hours to leave the country, leave the GDR! I knew right away something was wrong. We were citizens of the GDR. Besides that I didn't want to go. The Church had told us we should stay. My mother was here. This was before the wall went up in 1961. Anyway, we were taken to police headquarters again. They said that "people" had complained about us going from house to house. In my opinion, that was all a lie. It may have been that some of the Communists complained, but not the people. That was just their way of doing things, to say that "the people" have complained.

Then the second blow fell. You can't live in those rooms. That is not an official apartment. I explained to them that I was nearing the end of my mission and that we were going to be transferred in a few days, a week at most. I told them we would move somewhere. "No! You have already exceeded your time. You have to be out of here before midnight. Either leave Mittweida, or leave the country." So, we left. At eleven o'clock that night, we happily marched away and went over to Döbeln. There were members there. We spent a few nights there, and then I was released. Those were my two years as a missionary, and they were happy years. Of course, we couldn't serve in a foreign country, but we served. That was the main thing.

In 1960, I came home and went to work in a factory as a toolmaker. In 1964, I married. But let me go back and tell you something interesting. It was the first time I stood up for the Church. It was in elementary school. The teacher said something against the Church—the Church in the Middle Ages. I raised my hand and stood up. My legs were as heavy as lead, but I told him that the things he had said did not apply to my church. Nothing happened to me.

But later, when I was in high school—that must have been 1953, when I was seventeen—those were hard times. I remember it was just before the uprising of June 17. The authorities were pretty hard on the churches, and several young people had to leave school but were brought back after the political climate changed.

I was in the tenth grade, and I really didn't like school much anymore. I wanted to quit. We had a conference coming up, and the Church had permission to print flyers announcing the conference. I was given the assignment of distributing the flyers, which was something of an honor to me. So I passed them out at school.

I came up to one of my teachers—he was a fine man—and I gave him one. He said to me, "Watch out. You can give that to me, but don't give them out to anyone else." He warned me, but I was too thickheaded to pay attention. There was no explicit reason for not distributing them, but I shouldn't have done it.

The next teacher I gave one to, a white-haired woman, went straight to the director's office. While I was in biology class, in the class of the teacher who had warned me, someone came in from the director's office and said that I should see him during the class break. I went but didn't realize what was up. When I entered, there was the white-haired teacher and right beside her was the secretary of the FDJ [*Freie Deutsche Jugend,* Free German Youth]. They laid into me, first about distributing the flyers—What did I think I was doing?—and so on.

Then it occurred to them that I was not a member of the Free German Youth. They knew my father; they knew that he was a Communist. He was a loyal Communist. A fine man. He really believed in what he was doing, that he was fighting in his way for peace, and I have to emphasize that here since nowadays it is easy to defame the Communists. But he was very sincere in his beliefs. He wanted to give. I know that he would not even take money for his lectures. Well, anyway, they knew him and thought that since I was his son I should have been in the Free German Youth from the time I was fifteen. But I had never joined. I was a member of the Church.

And there had been another matter. My class had gone for a weekend into the country. My teacher was a very nice woman, and she wanted everyone to go. But for me the problem was that we would be gone over Sunday, and I wanted to keep the Sabbath day holy. Looking back I know that was a little pharisaic on my part, but that's the way it was. What was I supposed to do? I wanted to be at church on Sunday. I should have talked to my teacher about it. She would probably have fixed it up for me so that I could keep the Sabbath holy even on this outing; I could study or something. She was a nice woman, but I didn't do it. What a thick skull I had then.

Anyway, this all came out, and my teacher told me I would have to choose. Either I would have to go with the class on Sunday, or I could go to church. She couldn't force me to make this decision, but why had she sent me to the Director's office? She probably had her instructions, and they wanted to put some pressure on me. They said they would never forbid me to go to church, but they never gave me any instructions in writing. Anyway, they gave me the alternative, school or Church. I left school and never went back. I didn't graduate; there was no going back.

So, first I became a mechanic, and then I got into a trade school, where I spent three years learning to be a machinist. And another thing happened to me there. The section leader came up to me one day (he probably had some instructions from somewhere, or so I heard), and he told me that I wouldn't be allowed to stay because I belonged to the Church. But nothing ever came of that, and actually I graduated with distinction in both areas—practical and theoretical—and received my diploma. Then he said I could not graduate with distinction, but they had to let us graduate with distinction, there were four or five of us. And then this guy who was always after me, always on my back, fled the country a year later, went over the border illegally.

I really had no problem because of Church there, none at all. On the contrary, I remember I had to give a report in class one day; because I was always speaking out so freely. I had to have a debate; I defended the Church and my opponent defended Communism. It was all very official and lasted almost an hour. After it was over, one of the students started to mock me, and the teacher stepped in and said, "We'll have none of that. Neither from one side nor the other."

It was after this schooling that I went on my mission for two years. After I got back, I went to work in a factory in Karlswald, and I had no problems there because of the Church, because of my belonging to a religion—none at all. And then I went back to school. That was interesting. First I studied Russian at an evening school, and then my wife and I studied English.

While we were there, we met an instructor, a very nice man. He had gotten into some political troubles. He was a Germanist, and he said, "Mr. Zwirner, you know what you should do? You should get your high school diploma and then you should go to the university." He knew very well why I had not gotten my diploma; he knew all about it. I think they were all glad to have gotten rid of me at the high school without a big fuss. If I had really been forced to confess why I had not received my diploma, I would have had to say it was because of my religious convictions, and there might have been a fuss. They were glad that it turned out the way it did.

I had to participate in an M-L Institute, a Marxist-Leninist Institute, and while I was there, I had to be a "referat" for a research paper of another student, that is, I had to give a response. In the course of my response, I said something about the Church, something about the Mormons, and so that, of course, labeled me as belonging to a church. But I also said that divorce was criminal. The professor later took me aside and said, "What do you mean by saying divorce is criminal?" I had to give a spontaneous response, and I believe it was pure inspiration. "You see," I said, "what I meant by criminal was taking something for which one has not worked, that is, taking something for oneself without social justification." And then I added, "In a marriage, if one only wants to get and is not willing to give, then that person is not justified. If one takes something, one should be obliged to give something in return. So, you see, if one demands a divorce on this principle of taking without giving, the divorce is criminal." He was satisfied and went his way.

That was just a little incidental thing. When it came time for examinations in this Marxist-Leninist Institute, he examined me, and I came out with a B grade in M-L. Then he took me aside and said, "Now that the examinations are over, let's talk about something else." He wanted to know all about the Church, and we had a long and interesting conversation about God. He was very honorable about the whole thing and didn't cause me any trouble. He was genuinely interested. The examinations were over, and he wanted to talk about these other things. He truly wanted to know. He was apparently interested because of my referat. He knew that I was religious and wanted to know more about the Mormons. I told him that the Mormons were not political in the same sense that we in the GDR were "political." There are Mormons who are Republicans and Mormons who are Democrats. Religion is a private matter in the United States, and each person can decide for him or herself. Anyway, that was my answer, he left me alone, and everything turned out all right.

I applied at various schools and was finally accepted at a medical academy. That was a real blessing as I still have a position there. At first I wanted to study other places. I applied at the German Technical University and at the State Library, but neither of these worked out.

There came a time when I ran into serious difficulty with my supervisor. I was often—I may as well be honest about it—I was often inclined to take an extreme position, and sometimes I may have gone too far. But that's the way I was. That was my nature, and it has caused my wife no little anxiety, for which I am sorry. This incident had to do with a subscription that was taken up among the workers to buy weapons for the Palestinians. It was called a Solidarity Subscription *[Solidaritätsbeitrag]*. It was all written up in the *Neues Deutschland* [the official newspaper of the Communist Party]. I had always paid my Solidarity Subscription, but when I read what this money was going for, I refused to pay anymore. I thought it over very carefully, and I went down on my knees about it, right here in this room. I had to think carefully about this matter, because it could have caused serious consequences for my family. There were always the secret police to consider. One never knew for sure, but we always had this insecure feeling that they were watching. And they were watching; we know that for certain today. Anyway, I knew that if I stopped my contributions it could have serious consequences. So I prayed about it. I still remember some of the words of my prayer: "Father in Heaven, I do not want to continue paying my Solidarity Subscription because I cannot buy weapons to be used against Israel." Inwardly I had always been for Israel, and I had tried to make compromises. But we have to think these things over, don't we? I mean, where is the border between cowardice and wisdom? There is always this gray zone. It was not so easy for us.

Well, in the case of this subscription, I tried to apply the instructions in Doctrine and Covenants 9. I didn't ask God, "What should I do," but I thought about it, prayed, and then made the decision not to pay the subscription. I felt peace in my heart. I wanted to be right with God, and, I mean, if I had gotten into real trouble, maybe I would have paid it, but I was at peace.

I was called in. I understand now that supervisors have their own problems with these matters. He took me aside in the men's room: "Mr. Zwirner, please don't do this." I must say that my supervisor was anxious to be helpful. Politically, we were at odds, and there was nothing that could be done about that. He had given up on me. But I remember when my wife had our third child he was there to help. He did what he could; he tried to help, you understand, but the party had him under a lot of pressure. I picked that up later in a conversation I had with him when he told me, "You know what? They will send me back to the Middle Ages if I don't go along with socialism. They will do the same thing to me they did to my boss."

Anyway, I said, "I can't do it; I simply can't do it. I can't finance weapons that will be used against Israel." So this is what happened. He had to report it, that much was clear, and then the director himself had to get involved—the top man in the firm. He was really a fine man. Well, he called me in, and we sat across from one another at a small table, and he said, "Mr. Zwirner. Now tell me how an intelligent man like you can put yourself into such a situation. Why are you doing this?" and so on. So I told him everything. I said, "You see, in the Bible"—I think I quoted Isaiah or someone—"it says, whoever fights against Israel will die." I told him that I felt I belonged to Israel. "What kind of a friendship would that be," I asked him, "if I went along with this subscription? I do not agree with everything that Israel is doing," I told him. "There is a militarism there I don't like. But when I have a friend who makes a mistake, I can't just declare him to be my enemy. That's not right." He heard me out very calmly, thought about it, and said, "Mr. Zwirner, I accept your position."

But before I tell you what he proposed, I have to tell you something else that made the whole thing much more difficult. I was a member of a "Socialist Brigade." Our entire section of the library was in this brigade; it was obligatory. And whenever a subscription came up, our brigade was obligated to contribute 100 percent, regardless of what the subscription was. And so now they were all in trouble because I wouldn't participate.

I told him, "You see, it has nothing to do with money. I don't care about the money; you can have it. I am not doing this for the money; but I cannot contribute when the money is going to buy weapons." So he said—he was a clever man— "Mr. Zwirner, could you accept the following? Suppose you pay your subscription just once a year instead of paying it monthly as you now do. Pay it all at once for a particular purpose but not for weapons. Would you do that?" I said, "Yes, I would do that. I don't care what the money is used for as long as it is not used for weapons." So he had made his chess move, and the tension was relieved.

Once a year, in the fall, toward Christmas, a list was sent around for a particular donation. It was usually for forty or fifty marks. So I signed up for fifty marks for the victims of the earthquake in Romania and specified what the money was for. The next year it was for the suffering children of the world (that was the Year of the Children), and I wrote what the money was to be used for. It became a joke, because on the list where my name appeared they began to write at the top, "Collection for the Earthquake Victims" or "For the Hungry of the World." Right at the top. So I never paid a monthly subscription again; I paid it all at once, once a year.

Of course, they noticed that, too, and someone would inevitably say, "Everyone is paying for the Solidarity Subscription but one person." Me! But that's the way I paid, and that's the way we broke the log jam. So I can at least say that I acted according to my conscience, and if they used the money for something else, that was their responsibility. I had my own morals, and if they used my money for something other than what I donated it for, they falsified my money, so to speak. Anyway, it was a moral decision, and I tried to make the best of the situation I could.

Well, there was another affair I got involved in that, to be honest, made me quite nervous. The situation was this: There was a petition sent around that had something to do with the oil crisis in the world. That must have been back in the 1970s. We were called out for demonstrations, and there was a big protest about oil. It had something to do with what the Western nations were doing against the Eastern nations, and it had to do with oil. Well, they sent around the petition, and I refused to sign. I admit I was afraid, but I said, "This is all part of some secret diplomacy, and I don't know a thing about it. I never know what is going on. They don't give us the necessary information."

Then I got scared. Something my boss said frightened me, or maybe it was someone else, I don't remember who, but I was afraid. So when they called me in, I turned the whole thing around. I told them—and now I was really afraid—"The problem is we are given too much information. It makes it hard for us to come to a decision." That was my chess move, and they left me alone. I didn't have to sign their petition. I don't remember how the whole thing turned out, but I know that I was afraid, and I didn't make the mistake again of saying, "I don't get enough information." But the whole experience was very negative and left a bad taste in my mouth.

Of course, I didn't get enough information. I mean, they never gave us all of the information; they gave us only a part. They left out the other part. Maybe they didn't directly lie to us, but in my opinion, they printed only half-truths. They always gave us photographs about what Israel had done but never anything about what the Palestinians had done, never. They wouldn't report that, or they watered it down. That just drove me mad. Oh well, that's politics.

I remember an occasion when we had to vote by a show of hands (and we had to vote), but I said to myself, "You can't raise your hand in favor of that." So I bent over and pretended to be tying my shoe when the vote was called for so that I wouldn't have to raise my hand. I was always trying to get by with these kinds of tricks. If they had called me out, maybe I would have had to vote against the proposal, maybe not. But I tied my shoe instead, and no one noticed me.

There's another story I can tell you that might be of interest. A man started coming to the branch when I was the branch mission leader. It was a strange situation, and he was very likely from the secret police. Actually, I suspect that he was spying for both sides. Ours was called the State Security Service *[Staatssicherhheitsdienst]*, and theirs was called the Federal Information Service *[Bundesnachrichtendienst]*. Anyway, the branch president asked me to visit him and put him in contact with the missionaries. He was presumably interested in the Church. We invited him here and went to his house. Then his wife showed up here one day and warned us not to have anything to do with him—his own wife, although they were divorced then. Actually by that time, the whole affair had about run its course, but it was strange business.

We often went walking together in the Great Garden and talked about this and that. One time I might have said too much, I hope not, but I tried to change the subject, thinking I might get someone into trouble. I don't think I would have, but I can't say exactly now how it was. It might have been quite harmless. But he kept coming back.

One day I put a notice on the bulletin board at church listing all the missionary programs we had planned for the year. He showed up that evening, and at the end of the evening the notice had been ripped off. We all assumed he had taken it.

One day at a conference, one of the brothers was talking about "the vision," meaning, of course, the vision of Joseph Smith. Right after the conference, another of our brothers was called in to the police station. "What kind of an organization do you have in your Church?" he was asked. He tried to explain everything, the missionary program and all. "No, you have a division," they said. He had no idea how they thought we were divided into divisions, but we assumed it must have been our investigator from the secret police who understood "the vision" *[die Vision]* to be a division in a military sense.

Well, there were other things that gave him away, but one evening he showed up at my apartment building about nine at night. He called me on the intercom and asked me to come down. I came down to see him, and he told me he had to have an emergency baptism. He said he was being hounded by our secret police, who suspected that he was working for the Federal Republic of Germany, and he wanted to have an emergency baptism. He wanted me to take him down to the Elbe and baptize him. I told him, "No, we don't do that. God knows if your conversion is sincere, and it is not necessary for you to have an emergency baptism. I can't do that. It's not done." He disappeared.

A few days later, a stranger showed up at my apartment and wanted to come in. I invited him in, and he wanted me to deliver an envelope to this other man. He said, "You have contact with him." Actually I didn't have any real contact with him anymore, you see, and I had nothing to hide. I had never been that clever, so clever that I could have managed this kind of an operation. God was really with me this time. The man must have told his wife that I was too clever for him, but he was wrong about that. I had nothing to hide, and I was actually a very harmless man. I could never have gotten involved in these matters.

Karin: You were too naive.

Wolfgang: Exactly. Naiveté is a principle with me. But this stranger with the envelope said I was playing games with him, you understand. I wasn't playing games; I was being honest. I never heard from him again, and I certainly didn't take the envelope. He tried to pass it to me over the table, and then they would have had me. The man they were trying to contact was probably from over there [from the West]. Anyway, he had told me as much, that he was an officer in the paratroopers. It was all rather bizarre. His wife had told me that she had found a secret code in one of his books. That was when she warned me, but her warning wasn't necessary. And that was the end of it.

G. Davis: It was good that you didn't take the envelope.

Wolfgang: No, I didn't take it. No way. I had never worked for the secret police, but then they would have had me. I assume they were just putting me to the test to see if I was still having contact with him, but I really wasn't. Still, I had to be very direct in refusing to take the envelope.

Karin: They wouldn't have had you if you had taken the envelope. They would have had you only if you had passed it on to this Brother Meier.

Wolfgang: But Karin, if I had taken it, they would have had reason to suspect me. My innocence would have been lost. Oh well, maybe not; I'll never know. Anyway, I didn't take it. I just said, "I have no idea where he is." And he said, "Well, he will show up here again." I said, "I don't know; he's gone somewhere. I don't know anything more about him." It was all very strange, but you have to understand, Karin, that even an innocent person can get involved in these things. You just let yourself in a little bit, and immediately they suspect you, you see. Maybe they offer some money. This stranger gave me a name and told me to contact that person, but I never did. Well, that was that.

I can say that in this country I have never felt any of this pressure in the Church. I have always felt at ease in the Church. There were occasions when I was a student when I would bring up something about Marxism in one of my lessons, but I always got a little tap on the shoulder from the branch president. "This is not the place for that!" He was right, of course. But as young people, we were always trying to justify our position, and if you spoke freely, something of that was bound to come out. Then he would tap me on the shoulder. That was the only restraint I ever felt, and as I matured, I learned that one didn't get into these things at church. It was good that I learned this. The branch president was never unkind about it; he only said, when I went a little too far, "Wolfgang, you can't do that here." Just a little suggestion, you see. That was probably the only area in the Church where we were a little touchy.

Once I had to take a tour of the mission, and I brought back an armful of newspapers with me. Oh, I was naive in those days. I brought them all to church to point out what the Communists were saying in their newspapers. You see, you had to look in several newspapers to find one good article. Well, one of the leaders of the Church told me, "You just can't do that anymore," and I never did. That's the way it was then. I really didn't mean any harm, but I was naive. I had found something in the newspapers about Israel, and I was telling the members, "Buy this newspaper, this one." That was not a good idea. I mean, I shouldn't have been making propaganda, either for one side or for the other.

I remember another occasion when I was working with the young people in the branch. We wanted to decorate the hall like a medieval castle, and we made some weapons out of cardboard or something to hang on the wall, just some crossed swords. Some police official came along and told us to take them down. That's the way it was in those days—just a little thing like that and we had to take them down. We made a castle tower, and we had a drawbridge at the entrance, but we couldn't hang these crossed swords on the wall—forbidden. I think someone must have squealed on us; otherwise how would the police have known about that? It was completely harmless.

And then there was the time when we were forbidden to have a pioneer trek. We were going to have this pioneer march through the whole mission. I had even made some special insignias at the factory where I was working. I still have one of them, a covered wagon with the oxen and everything. We were going to pass them out. We were going to march from here to Freiberg and then from Freiberg to Karl-Marx Stadt and then on and on. We had a real journey planned out. Forbidden! We weren't allowed to do it. Well, we did do a little trial run to see how it would go, from Hainsberg to Freiberg. We had a lot of fun on that.

And the reason it was forbidden was because of the name "pioneers." You see, the Young Pioneers is a branch of the FDJ, the Free German Youth, a communist youth organization. I had been a member of the Young Pioneers when I was a child; my father used to take me. I liked it. Then we let our children join the Free German Youth if they wanted to.

This might be of interest. Uta, our oldest daughter, came home one day and wanted to know if she could become a member of the Free German Youth. I knew all about the Communist Manifesto and their attitude toward Christians, so I told her, "Look, we can do this. If you will join openly as a Christian and will do only those things that are allowed by our Christian ethic, then you can join." That's what she did. She announced very officially that she was a Christian, and they accepted it. She became a member, and they told her she had to do only what her conscience as a Christian allowed her to do. I mean, this was our way of making a compromise.

Karin: But no compromise on the Sabbath.

Wolfgang: No, not on Sunday. That's what we always told our children. I think we let all of our children participate in the Young Pioneers so that they wouldn't get into trouble. You see, the little children had to decide about that in their first year of school. So we always said, "You can go, but church comes first. On Sunday we go to church and if there is a meeting during the week, then church comes first and then the Pioneers." We couldn't force our convictions on our children. Little children of six or seven can't be responsible for political things, and if all the other children got to participate and wear their little blue neckerchiefs and our children didn't, we had no strong convictions that they shouldn't be part of the Young Pioneers, so that's what we did.

But when it came to the Free German Youth, then they had to decide for themselves. I've told you how it was with Uta. With

Grit, it was pretty funny. They just took her in, no questions asked. So first Uta was a member and then Grit—all very official. They both announced that they were Christians, but there were a few incidents.

Twice they had to recite a poem in which they were supposed to curse God and the Church. I wrote into their study book that they could not say that because of our religious convictions. They accepted it, and we didn't have any difficulty. But on another occasion, Grit refused to sing the "Communist International."

Karin: She and Franzi.

Wolfgang: Yes, she was with her girlfriend, Franziska Fürll, and they both refused to sing. The teacher said something about them being enemies to the State, so I went straight to the school. I made an appointment and was there the next day. The teacher wanted to know why I had come, and she changed her tune a bit. She had probably asked the principal what she should do about it. She said to me, "Oh, no, they don't have to participate. I won't require it of them because we understand that their refusal is because of their personal convictions and not intended as a provocation. No, Franziska and Grit will not be asked to sing alone, and when the choir sings, they don't have to sing along." That's about what she said, so there was no further difficulty over that incident.

That's what it was all about. They said our daughter and her friend were enemies to the State because they wouldn't sing the second stanza of the "International" in which it says, "We need no God, none." So they wouldn't sing that. When things like this came up, we as parents stood up for them, and the authorities accepted it. I always had to speak out in defense of all my children. There was always something with Grit or with Uta. Either we had to respond in writing in the school notebooks, or I had to go to the school and talk with the authorities. But you have to do something. Either you have to go in, or you have to do something else; then you don't have serious problems.

I've been talking a lot because I thought you might like to know how we got along in this country, broadly speaking. I must say I did not experience these forty years as if I were in a prison because I am not that type. I am not a wanderer who is always wishing he were somewhere else. As far as reading material goes, we had access to the basic things. Of course, I often wished I could get my hands on some different literature, and once in a while, I could get something. Sometimes we could have someone send us something, and sometimes it would get through. In recent years, it got a little tighter so that I couldn't get the books from over there [in the West] that I dreamed about. I wanted those books. That was a real disadvantage.

But I must also say that because of our life in the Church, I never felt restricted, that I couldn't develop myself. I never had that feeling, that's the truth. It may have been only my naiveté and maybe the guiding hand of God played a role, but all in all I have always been able to get along with people. Either they have approached me, like the teacher I mentioned, or I have been able to go to them for advice. I have never been forced into a situation where they might have put me in prison or where they really put heavy pressure on me, where I was really frightened. Well, I did mention one episode where I was frightened, but all in all, I have felt comfortable here. Maybe in conclusion I can give you an example of what I mean, a rather typical example.

Recently a doctor came up to me, one I had known for some time who had been a strong socialist. I got into a conversation with him, and he said, "You know, Wolfgang, some of those things we did earlier were not right." Now he was beginning to see that things were not totally in order. He was beginning to change. Socialism was not so wonderful for him anymore. But I just said, "Well, things aren't so wonderful now, either, are they? But I was happy back then when the socialist state was everything, and I am happy now." "Yes," he said, "that's what I don't understand. That gives one something to think about."

And this will be interesting to you. The temple was dedicated before all the political changes took place, and I took our entire section, including my boss, to the open house. You see, I was in the presidency of the seventies quorum and had to spend a lot of time at the open house for the temple, conducting tours and talking with the people, and so I had to ask for time off from work. We had no idea that so many people would come to the open house. Then some in my department complained that I was getting extra vacation time. That made me so mad. So then they said, "You can have the time off, but you have to get us tickets so that we can see your temple; we all want to go." No problem! I got tickets for all the doctors. And I got them tickets to see the Lamanite Generation when they came, too.

Then, shortly before the political change [1989–90], we got a new supervisor, and he was very tolerant. I could even put up posters for concerts at the church on our bulletin boards at the hospital. But I must tell you this: the supervisor was a Communist, a member of the Socialist Unity Party. During that time, I was a counselor in the bishopric, and I often had to attend funerals. He always gave me time off, but I always made it up. I could have gotten the time off without making it up, but I didn't want to owe them anything. I never asked for free time. He was a dedicated Communist, but I could talk freely with him. He was very tolerant.

Well, one day there was a little incident. I told him that I would not be at the May Day Demonstration. I had never missed before, and he was rather upset that I would not be there because that would cause trouble for him. He said, "Mr. Zwirner, I thought for sure I could count on you to be there." But it was on a Sunday. So, I said, "Look, here's what I will do. I will come just for your sake. I will come early, before our church service, and I will march for a while, for your sake, because you have been so nice to me and because you have been so tolerant. And I will also march out of gratitude to the State for allowing us to build our temple." It must have been about the time we were building the temple. "I will come with you, but then I will go to church." He accepted that. So I marched along for a ways. Otherwise, I would never have done it on a Sunday. He was pleased with that because he had to turn in his report, and he would have had to report that one of his employees was not present at the May Day Demonstration. That would have been unpleasant for him. We understood one another. But now I am going to stop talking and let my wife say something.

Karin: Well, I had these same experiences that my husband has told you about, but to a lesser degree. I was a twin. My sister and I always had a special role at school, and we were always very good at school. We always said that we believed in God, and actually, we never had any problems because of that.

N. Davis: That was in Annaberg?

Karin: Yes, in Annaberg. We were always accepted. As children we were also in the Young Pioneers; I remember that well. I was always so proud of myself. But I was never afraid of saying that I belonged to a church. I have heard others say, however, that they suffered some disadvantages because of their church membership and were always a little anxious. To be honest, I must say I didn't experience that, not even later when I studied to become a medical assistant at a professional school. I never suffered any disadvantage because of my membership in the Church. On the contrary, I always experienced a certain recognition for my openness about my religion. So I can't offer you anything dramatic in that direction.

I worked for five years as a radiology technician, and after five years, I was given an administrative position as a radiology assistant, and then I ran into a little trouble. I can't say it was entirely political; it was just something that came up. At that time, we had these Socialist Collectives. This was a movement where the colleagues from a particular department were supposed to get together in a group and express their political convictions.

G. Davis: Sort of a socialist testimony meeting?

Karin: Yes, something like that. We had to express some sort of political creed. My husband was studying at the time in Berlin, and I was alone with my two children. First it was just Uta, but then Grit came along during my student days. I was doing some course work on the side to become a professional assistant, which would make me eligible for a promotion. I was very busy, and I was very happy with what I was doing. I often had to get someone to fill in for me in my position as the chief radiology technician in order to go to these classes.

As a Mormon, one is always a little outside the regular social circle, so to speak, and there was this obnoxious colleague who had joined our Socialist Collective. As the head of our department, I was also supposed to be the head of the Socialist Collective, the two sort of went together, but I turned down the position as head of the collective. I told them I didn't want to do it. Well, this colleague began a little witch hunt, and I lost my job.

So, after five years in a government hospital, I went to work in a private hospital, run by the Evangelical Church, as the secretary to the chief physician, and I had a little rest from political affairs.

Then something very paradoxical entered into my life. At first I had a few difficulties with the Evangelical-Lutheran Church because I was the first Mormon there, but it was not serious because everyone knew where I stood. I told everyone that I was a Mormon and that I didn't smoke or drink, not because of the health benefits, but because of the blessings. But after a while another Mormon came to work in the same department, and she was very pushy with her religion. So the rector, the head of the hospital, issued an edict that there would be no missionarying going on. Somehow out of this it was insinuated that I was a member of the secret police. I, of all people! Then I had real troubles, but here is the paradox. I had left the government hospital and moved over to a private hospital and was so happy that I would have a little rest from political intrigues, and now I was accused of having changed jobs because of political motives. I have to assume that this all came about because of my father-in-law, because the name Zwirner was well known as that of a man who was very politically engaged. I couldn't think of any other reason why they would suspect me.

I noticed that when new doctors came into the hospital they were at first very friendly, but after a time they became quite withdrawn. I thought, "Something is wrong here." After they got to know me better, they would tell me they had been warned that I was an informer for the secret police. That was a very unpleasant situation.

I stayed at that hospital for seventeen years, and then, another paradox, my membership in the Church lost me my job. The rector had made it known that Mrs. Zwirner would be the first to go. I was very good at my job; they couldn't complain there. But when the political change came, I was very sick. It was a very unfortunate time, and as soon as I recovered from my illness, they gave me my notice. I was told that it was because of my membership in the Church, because I was a Mormon.

But, as far as the State was concerned, I never had any difficulties. They didn't give me any trouble when I was a student. I was always open and honest, and it was never a disadvantage. The Church along with my family has been my life, and because of that I can truly say I have never felt oppressed.

G. Davis: Were there other problems in the Church during these years? Emigration, for example? And I have heard about the problems you had getting teaching materials, and Brother Albrecht in Bautzen told me of an occasion when you had to destroy some of your Church literature.

Wolfgang: Yes, when I was a missionary, there were dates established, and anything we had that had been published during that time had been brought into the country illegally and had to be burned. And I have to confess that I was disobedient. We had a teaching manual that was called *Signs of the Times.* I tore off the cover and kept it. And I believe I kept some other things. But, yes, we had to destroy everything that had been printed during this time. Those were the government instructions. It was sad. But I didn't burn everything. Not everything.

Karin: I was right in the middle of this because I had wearily copied these teaching manuals. Brother Burkhardt had provided us with a typewriter, and Doris Menzel and I had to copy the teaching manuals. Oh, that was hard. With carbon paper, six or seven copies, and they were hard to read. But then Brother Burkhardt got some good carbon paper from the West, and they were a little easier to read, but it was still a wearisome work.

Wolfgang: We had instructions during this time that we were not to take any teaching material with us into the classroom. But that wasn't so bad; it taught us to really prepare. We couldn't just read out of the manual.

But that is the way the authorities were, the way they worked. And so the Church leaders had to do the best they could, but the politics were so uneven. When they were harsh, we had to burn everything. That's the way it was then. And there were times, in my opinion, when things loosened up. I remember, for example, when we had to apply for permission to hold a dance, and it had to be reported. And then things were relaxed a little. Church dances were allowed then. And so it went.

Karin: And the most beautiful thing for us was when we could receive the *Stern* [Church magazine in German]. There was one brother who could receive them and then distribute them. Someone in West Germany paid for all of this, and we got them regularly. That was around 1985, after the temple was built. Around that time.

Wolfgang: But then there was a problem caused by another church. They wanted to smuggle some literature into Poland, this other church, and the material was confiscated and that put a stop to the *Stern* for a while. That was punishment for all of the churches because they tried to do something illegal, tried to smuggle some illegal literature into Poland. And so for a time there was no *Stern*. Well, in time it all turned out all right.

G. Davis: What about the problem with emigration?

Karin: Yes, the problem with emigration. Well, I had a personal experience with that; it was in the 1950s at a district conference. I don't remember which year exactly. Our district president left. And on the Sunday before, he had stood before the congregation and had said, "Brothers and sisters, stay here. Stay where you are; that is where the Lord has put you." And on Monday, he left with his whole family. That left a lasting impression on me. They were my friends, my same age, and they were here one day and gone the next. I will never forget that. I can still see his face as he stood there at conference. That was the first time in my life that I understood clearly that a man's word and his actions were not always one and the same thing. That was a big shock in my life.

Wolfgang: But when he said, "Stay here," that was in quotation marks, you know. He was always a good example to me. He had political problems and had to get out. They were after him. There were cases like that. They had to go. I heard that from another brother. He was really afraid. He had to get out.

But I never wanted to go. I am not a man of action. I am not one who wants to do something adventuresome like that. I am more settled, you see. I just want my peace and quiet, to be able to think and to read.

G. Davis: Is it somewhat of a paradox that I hear from people about hard times and yet hear at the same time how happy they were in the Church?

Wolfgang: Yes, that's natural. I remember, it must have been 1948 here in Dresden. I was so happy, and yet I know it was the time of our greatest despair, compared with how well off we are now. One can't really say "well off"; everything is in transition, and there is so much uncertainty. But we have more material things. One has to admit that. If you have work, you live better, or so it seems to me.

But I have to be honest. I didn't want to leave, either. Once I prayed, once I wished, "Oh, Father in Heaven! Just for once let me be able to buy all the things that the people who have been in the West tell about, all the things they can buy over there. They tell us the stores are full of everything."

A brother who was permitted to go to the West once told me that he got physically ill when he saw all the tools in a hardware store. He was a craftsman, you see, and the hardware store was full of tools, and he so wanted to just hold some of those tools in his hands. "I got sick and had to sit down," he told me. And I said, "Father in Heaven, I want to have that experience, just once." Oh, I wanted that experience. To never have to stand in a line again. Never stand in a line. Always these long lines. Well, not always, but very often, and you had to stand so long.

But now I have to say that in spite of all this I think back on these time with a feeling of joy. I can tell you now, I will never forget those times. I will never look back on my past as a lost time. No, I tell you I will never see them as lost; no, I would never say that. Not at all. I was happy in those days. I was happy.

Karin: In our country, we had problems with the secret police, but we never had any problem personally.

Wolfgang: No, we never had to experience that.

Karin: We suspected things. The way things were, you could never really talk openly anywhere. If you were in a hallway . . .

Wolfgang: You had to be careful telling jokes. You could not tell political jokes.

Karin: Yes, but that was not a problem with me; I don't tell jokes anyway. But I mean just normal conversation. That was almost never possible. Everyone was watching everyone else in one way or another.

Wolfgang: That was bad. That was really, really bad.

Karin: The Russians applied a little pressure to the whole situation.

Wolfgang: The mental pressure. The lack of freedom.

Karin: But, as he has already told you, we really had nothing to do directly with the secret police.

Wolfgang: But we don't really know. We don't know.

Karin: But we didn't experience anything directly. And after the political change when we heard all the things that had been going on, how they operated and so on, we were really very thankful that we were spared. I mean, many times it may have been very close.

Wolfgang: I believe it was.

Karin: Because we are a little naive. My husband always tells things the way they are, and that was probably also his protection. They were probably saying, "Is he really that dumb, or is he just playing dumb?" They were probably thinking, "He is just playing dumb."

Wolfgang: I have a clear conscience, you understand. I can honestly say that I have a clear conscience. I have never had anything to hide. I had an acquaintance once who told me (and he named another brother in the Church to whom he told the same thing) that there was nothing negative on my records. He must have had a look at them. I can't remember how he explained why he came to me. He was not a bad man, on the contrary, often quite pleasant to talk to, but everything was always a little hazy with him. He always told me, "Mr. Zwirner, there is nothing negative on your records." But one never knew for sure how much danger there was in situations like that. I don't think he worked for the secret police, not at all. But, on the other hand, maybe he was working for the secret police and was just trying to feel us out.

Karin: Yes. And we never had any trouble with our children at school. We always had our own strategy. Right at the beginning of the year, when they were having new school orientation, we went in with the children so they could get better acquainted with our family. We told them right from the beginning what church we belonged to, and that they shouldn't make a big fuss when they had an outing on Sunday because our children would not be there. They accepted that, and from then on, they left our children alone. That's the way we raised them, but, of course, that was not the case with all Mormons in the GDR. Our children always knew where they belonged, and they got along very well with this procedure. From the first grade on, all the other students and all the teachers knew where our children belonged, that they attended church and conducted their life accordingly. That's the way they were raised. But your behavior has to be in order before you can stand up and say that.

Wolfgang: Let me add that we had the impression that many of the teachers were also Christians. Inwardly, you understand. Inwardly they were good people and inclined toward God. I often had this impression. Many of them as much as told me so, but that they had to make a living. They were not all inhuman or dedicated atheists. They all wanted to survive. And then there were some who were, I must say, noble Communists. I got to know them and can say they were fine people. They really believed in what they were doing. I mean, they believed like Mormons and Catholics believed. And after the political change took place, many of them were mistreated by those who came to power, when everything fell apart.

G. Davis: I have heard a lot about the youth conferences you used to have.

Karin: That was the high point in the Church.

Wolfgang: That's right. The young people stayed together. They were all under a certain amount of pressure, you understand—some more, some less. Many felt it more than others. This censorship that you had to lay on yourself, at work, everywhere, that was bad. Of course, you had friends who more or less knew that things were OK, friends that you could talk to; but even so, you had to be very careful. That was not good. You could never talk freely. You know what I mean, just speak openly to people. You always had to be a little careful when you talked about the Church or about God. When you were at work, you had to ask yourself, "Can I say this or not?" You had to be wise. You always had to be on the alert, and always being on the alert is no fun.

And that reminds me of something else. We used to baptize in the open, in a lake, but the authorities could never know about it. Later we put in a font in the basement of all the chapels, and then we didn't have that problem, but we couldn't hold baptisms in the open anymore. There were several baptismal fonts then, in Chemnitz and in Annaberg, for example. So all the members could go there to be baptized, and we didn't have that problem anymore.

Then something new came along. A few of the brothers were allowed to travel to Salt Lake City for general conference. I felt that a little personally. A few of the brothers could get out, and we couldn't. Not that we wanted to emigrate, but we would liked to have traveled, you see. But that wasn't so bad.

Karin: The fact that we didn't feel the whole political situation so negatively is probably due in large measure to the fact that we had our satisfaction in the Church. We always had, what should I say, our leadership positions, where we could actually develop ourselves. We could apply our talents; we had some recognition. And I can say that I have had some positions of leadership in my profession. We were also allowed to attend the university.

Wolfgang: My director at the university, a nice man, took me aside one day on the campus and said, "Mr. Zwirner, because of your religious orientation, you will never be given an administrative position." He said, "You will be put in a subordinate role." After my schooling, I obtained this position at the medical academy and went right into public work in the information office and in the reading room. Finally I was doing what I liked, but I was never given an administrative position. I had no one under me, so to say. But I had a position where I was dealing with the public. It required a little higher training because I had to classify the books, and that's what I'm still doing. I have never been given an administrative position by my superior. If one wants to become a leader, then over time you have to work with your superior and be his representative on occasions. I have never done that, but I have never really wanted to. I am very happy with my position.

Now, with the political change, I have the chance to apply for a directorship. I have actually been trained for this. At the university, we were all trained to become library directors, trained for administrative positions. But I knew this was always out of the question for me, and to be honest, I never really desired it. I never felt restricted. I never had any desire for all of the administrative affairs, but maybe, maybe it would have come if things had been different, if the political situation had been different. Maybe then they would have brought me along, and maybe I would have liked it. But now I'm too old for that. I have no desire for it anymore. I'm happy with where I am. I'm fifty-seven years old, eight years from retirement. But it might have been nice. I was actually quite good.

Karin: That's a different problem.

Wolfgang: Yes, that is a different problem. He couldn't see into the future. I had good grades. My studies were not bad.

Karin: Not bad! He always got "outstanding."

Wolfgang: No, not in my studies.

Karin: One area with A and another with "outstanding." In information, or in technical, I forget . . .

Wolfgang: I did graduate with honors.

Karin: There was a big article about him in the newspaper.

Wolfgang: They did say something about us in the newspaper.

Karin: And they kept it very quiet, the fact that he belonged to the Church.

Wolfgang: No, they wouldn't write anything about the Church. But they did say something about the diploma. There were others, too, who got outstanding, and they wrote about them.

Karin: He was the show horse for our socialism. Evening school, factory worker, super scholar.

Wolfgang: Evening school. Those were good times. But I have only my wife to thank for that. For evening school and the university. It would never have been possible without my wife. She made a real sacrifice. Eight years. First, three years of evening school and then. . . .

Karin: Forgotten all about it. You'll have to tell me.

Wolfgang: Yes. Yes. I will be in her debt forever, for all eternity. I can truthfully say that.

Karin: Oh, don't pay any attention to him.

Wolfgang: Yes, I know.

Karin: But I'm glad to hear that you still remember.

22

Time to Put Out the Lights?

Reiner Schlüter

Reiner Schlüter, a medical doctor, is a member of the Dresden Ward. Elke Schlüter, his wife, is the daughter of Herbert and Ilse Kaden (see chapter 16). Shortly before the missionaries arrived and after years of practicing medicine, the Schlüters received their first telephone. Five years later, we interviewed them in their large, new home furnished with all the latest appliances. They have two children and have served in a multitude of callings in the Church.

Reiner: I am now forty-three years old, and when I look back, I can say that I must thank the Church and the Lord for the entire development of my life, so far as it has gone. I had the good fortune to be born into a family that had already been acquainted with the Church. My mother was the first to be baptized by the missionaries, and my father made the same decision somewhat later, after I was born. I can remember very clearly when our family moved to Dresden in 1957. I was already in school, and then in 1958 the question of baptism came up. At that time, we were baptized in a stream called the Briesnitz. There was a deep pool, and all the members came there to hold their baptisms. Interestingly, I was baptized on the same day as my wife. That indicates that the branch in Dresden at that time had some family unity. As far as I know, there were no convert baptisms, but the families were relatively strong, and all of the family members were baptized. In any case, everything went its normal course.

    The parents had developed a rhythm to their life in which attending church on Sunday was normal, as well as Primary during

The Schlüter family. Elke Schlüter, James Welch (visiting organist from the United States), Susen Schlüter, Kay Schlüter, and Reiner Schlüter. Dresden, November 1991. Courtesy Reiner Schlüter.

the week and then later MIA for the young people. As young people, we were together a lot, and those were beautiful times, especially when we had the youth conferences where the young members from the entire mission came together and had common experiences.

Of course, these activities were not without their problems. The Church was merely tolerated in the GDR. It was certainly not encouraged. Everything that we did had to be done in harmony with the laws of the land. Meetings had to be reported. When a large group of young people were together in the Church building, the State authorities automatically assumed it to be some sort of political activity, so we were carefully watched.

As young people, we didn't take all this too seriously, but the priesthood leaders in those days had a heavy responsibility. On the one hand, they had to direct the young people and get them together. On the other hand, they always had to have a corresponding relationship with the State authorities. That was no easy matter, and it is truly admirable how in those days Brother Burkhardt, Brother Krause, Brother Richter, and the other leaders could handle these matters. I am still very thankful today for those times.

As far as my personal relationship to the Church is concerned, that was not so uncomplicated either. Anyone who wanted to begin a course of study leading to a profession, or change a profession, or attend a university—anyone who wanted to receive a higher education—could not allow himself or herself to speak in public about the Church—at school, for example. That would have destroyed any chance for further education.

I was personally very fortunate, or I should say I was greatly blessed by the directing hand of my Father in Heaven, that I was permitted to get through my high-school studies and graduate without having to participate in many activities of the political youth organizations. And this continued when it came to my university studies. There are some things that, when we look at them superficially, seem to be nothing more than accidental. But in reality it was certainly the hand and intervention of our Father in Heaven, at least in my case.

When I began school, it was stipulated that on admission I was supposed to choose a trade—to become a pipe fitter for the railroad—and to study a language, Polish or something like that. But that all came to nothing, and I was able to go to another school and study mechanics and get a diploma. I wanted to go to medical school, but there were no openings in the medical field, so I had to begin my professional studies training to be a dentist. After two years, there were some new regulations, some health reasons or something; anyway, I was able to switch to a study of medicine. I do not believe this was all accidental.

So life went on. We made friendships in the Church. When I was sixteen, I became acquainted with my wife. Our friendship developed, and we both felt that it was because of Church that we understood one another. After we got to know one another well, we decided to marry. This was all a direct result of the fact that families in the various branches got very personally acquainted. Everyone watched out for everyone else. We got to know one another. Those were beautiful times but also difficult times. Some things were hard to understand.

The lesson manuals in the Church, for example, had to be copied off on a typewriter. Whenever a Church book other than the standard works got into the country, it was considered a great blessing and made us very happy. The spiritual relationships we had with one another were better. Material things were clearly pushed into the background. I cannot say that I personally ever felt any disadvantage from my membership in the Church. I had only advantages. I learned to speak out; I learned to be a leader. These things were a great advantage to me in my professional life.

When the political change [the fall of the Wall] came, it seemed a great miracle to us, but the change brought with it special experiences and possibilities. Before the fall of the Wall, the people were very hungry to learn about spiritual things. They were all searching and were very open to questions about the gospel. This was especially true when in 1985 the temple was dedicated and we held an open house to which tens of thousands of people came, after standing in line. We had the opportunity to serve as hosts on the temple grounds, to have countless conversations, to get addresses of people who were interested, and to explain the Church. That gave us a great deal of pride and joy. Somewhat later, when the political changes were complete, this enthusiasm ebbed somewhat. But right at the time of the big change, 1989–90, we had 150 baptisms in our ward. There were, of course, many people looking for something who were not really firm and later fell away from the Church.

There is no doubt that it is much easier to be a member of the Church now because we don't have to be so cautious. In our own circle, we can talk openly about the Church. That is a great advantage, and we treasure it. In spite of all this, as I have said, we like to think back on those times, the way things used to be, how we were strengthened and led by the gospel so that we could overcome those difficult times. At any rate, those are my experiences before the political change and my impressions of the way things are now.

My assignments in the Church in those days were important, and I performed them gladly. But I believe it makes little difference what calling one has at any time. The important thing is that one has the feeling one can be of service and benefits by this service, whether as a teacher in Sunday School, the song leader, or whatever. It makes no difference.

I was relatively young when they made me the Sunday School president, a calling that had heavy responsibilities. At the time, we also had Junior Sunday School, so we had a double organization, a lot of teachers, a lot of classes, opening exercises with two-and-one-half-minute talks, song practice, and special programs such as on Mothers' Day and Christmas. All of that had to be organized by the Sunday School president. Those were beautiful times. I was only eighteen; I remember it well. And all of this contributed a lot to my profession because I learned leadership skills. This experience was very important for me. In later years, I was a teacher, song leader, director of the branch chorus. Later I was a counselor in the branch presidency.

G. Davis: I get the impression that many members in the ward here have musical talent. There are several who play the organ. Is that something unusual here in Dresden?

Reiner: No, I don't think so. We made sure that many members took piano lessons or sang in the choir, but I don't think that was unusual. I don't think we have so many, but there are several families where music instruction is emphasized. And, of course, we took advantage of the public programs. There were the public music schools, where piano instructions were given. Of course, they didn't study church music, but that could be done in the family.

G. Davis: But it was unusual for a member to be able to attend the university. In America we always heard that one had to be a member of the party in order to attend the university. Is that right?

Reiner: I conscientiously avoided the party, and I went to the university anyway. Of course, I have to add, we could not come out against the State. That would have been unthinkable. We would never have had a chance. And we had to at least give the appearance of doing one's duty for the State. That would be recognized, but at the same time it was recognized if one was a Christian. It made no difference if one was a member of a church whose headquarters was in America or of any other church.

In my professional career as a doctor, it was assumed I would have certain administrative responsibilities. For that reason, they came to me and said that if I would become a member of the party [Communist Party] I would have a chance to advance to these administrative posts. Of course, I declined, and they knew exactly why. Without going into detail, I can say that I was watched very carefully. But in the later years of the GDR, say after 1984, after we had the temple, they trusted in the people who were Christian or who belonged to a church a little more. There was a clear tendency in that direction. As a result, even though I could not officially assume an administrative position, as I have said, I was unofficially given full administrative responsibilities. That was, of course, somewhat contradictory. On paper I was not permitted to do what I was actually doing, which was acceptable. It was all officially recognized. I had no fears.

G. Davis: Let me ask you about another matter. In 1988, as you know, the Church came to an agreement with State Secretary Erick Honnecker to allow the Church to open a mission here. That allowed young people to leave the country to serve a mission elsewhere for the first time in fifty years. I have heard criticism that the Church ought not to have done this because it was compromising and working with the Communists. What do you think of this?

Reiner: It was very important to make compromises at that time, or we could never have had the development we had with any security. The way it was done was the right way. In addition, I believe that such compromises actually hastened the political changes. For the Church in this part of Germany, the willingness to make compromises was the only way these things could be possible. And the results have shown this was right. I would give my approval to this procedure any time. Without question. To have taken a hard line would have made it much more difficult for the members of the Church to do anything.

It should be understood that this willingness to compromise was not done by the State only out of the goodness of their hearts. They could see the economic benefit to them just as we could see the spiritual benefit to us. They could see that we could build chapels with hard currency and that they would naturally benefit in some ways from that. On the other hand, what the Church officials told the government at that time was not unknown to them. We members of the Church had gained a reputation in our own society as people who could be relied upon, as people one could look up to, as a people who did not need to be restricted merely because of their religious philosophy. Those who performed their church service loyally were seen as people who were reliable citizens of the State. And there was no contradiction in that. Oh, in the early years of the communist state, that might have been seen as a contradiction. But the part that was unbearable was the spying and the tricks. For many people, that was just too much.

But our Church was composed of reliable people. The State officials were more afraid of other religious organizations where the leadership can exert less control. Certain parts of the Evangelical Church, for example, where the reform movement is particularly encouraged. But political reform only has little to do with religion. That is simple political engagement.

I accept the Article of Faith given by Joseph Smith that tells us to be subject to rulers and magistrates. I still accept it today as we are moving in a more democratic direction. Of course, there were exceptions, and I don't want to say that everything that glittered in the GDR was gold, but I did find this decision at that time to be the correct one. I have no criticism on this point whatever.

G. Davis: You said that the consequences prove the rightness of the decision?

Reiner: The consequences have proven it. I would say that, yes. Of course, at the time, one could not see the consequences. We didn't think, "Now the members will be able to travel out of the country." That was a very important issue for us, to be able to travel.

It's probably not possible for you to understand what it was like to never be able to travel, to see that stupid "no" whenever we wanted to get out, to escape from this imprisonment—we placed a lot of hope on that.

G. Davis: But most of the members stayed, even if they had the opportunity to emigrate. I believe most of them said, "No, we are supposed to stay here and build up the Church." Were there problems concerning emigration among the members?

Reiner: On this matter, I do not want to generalize. There was a particular time for me when this question was connected to my profession, in 1988, 1989. Things were reaching the point economically where many were certainly saying to themselves, "I have a responsibility to my children and cannot guarantee that my roots will remain here." There were certainly cases where raising this question was justified. We had discussed this in our family and, right or wrong, there was this saying going around that maybe it was time to "put out the lights" in the GDR. It would be wrong for me to say now that this question did not come up in our family. It wasn't just a personal decision. We had the responsibility for our family and our children. Under what conditions would they grow up? We haven't talked about these things yet, about how socialistic the educational system was and such fine points. At some time, one had to make a decision. Nowadays this decision doesn't have so much to do with the Church, but back then it could divide you in half.

And, of course, there were some families who emigrated, families who belonged to the Church. And I must say that the Church at the present could have been much, much stronger if these families were still here. And I don't mean only the parents, but the entire family. It's too bad they finally made the decision to get out. But, personally, I must say if that was the decision they came to then I accept it. That is, I would never say what they did was not right. That is something hard to evaluate, and I would never feel so confident of myself that I could say whether he or she should have stayed or not. There were also cases I could point to where families came back.

G. Davis: This problem was more acute in the 1950s and '60s, and just before the Wall went up, was it not?

Reiner: Yes, there were many who emigrated then, but I was just a little boy. My parents were faced with the question and decided not to emigrate to America because of the illness of my older brother.

At that time, the question of emigration was always connected with America, and this wave of emigration today is something quite different. Emigration was not encouraged by the Church. On the contrary, the leaders of the Church told us our place was here; we should stick it out somehow. But I would not like to brag because we stuck it out for so long. There are always personal circumstances where one says, "Yes, it is best that we stay here."

G. Davis: In general, the Church went on its normal course here during these years, did it not? I mean with Relief Society, priesthood blessings for the sick, youth conferences, and so on.

Reiner: Yes. Yes. The only thing which made it almost impossible was the question When will we have a temple? When will we be able to make the covenants? That was the great desire of our hearts. But then it finally came. The temple came, and then everyone had to reflect, "Am I worthy to go into the temple?" That is the problem. When one finally has everything, one sees it all in a different light.

G. Davis: What are your fondest memories from your youth when you were growing up in the Church?

Reiner: My fondest memories, on the one hand, are of my family. I come from a good family. There were six of us, four children. The foundation of our family was that we had a lot of happiness; we felt secure, mother had time for us, and father guided us. Those were the dominating things. As far as the Church was concerned, it was that, in spite of what I must call economically complicated times, it was the Church that could organize activities which were quite different from the activities of the Free German Youth organization or other State youth organizations. The Church activities were unique; there was a possibility to break out. Those are the fondest memories I have brought with me from my youth in the Church.

But I don't mean only the big things. There were also small things. When we put on plays, for example, in the branch. Sometimes we had a production that required fifteen parts. That was a big undertaking and quite an experience when we were able to do it, when it was uplifting and brought us so much joy. We had to spend a lot of time at this, but one never forgets those times—times when you put in so much effort and something good comes out of it. We put on fairy tales and Christmas plays. Then we did *The Prince and the Pauper* and *The Flying Carpet.* Those were marvelous things.

But we did fun things that went beyond the branch. We had a mission youth choir in the GDR in those days. It was no competition for the Tabernacle Choir, but there was a lot of enthusiasm there. We had some professional musicians who worked over the music so that it was singable, and then we copied off the notes and made multiple copies. This mission youth choir—that was something.

23

The Way Things Were

Hans-Jürgen Schlüter and Ursula Höhle Schlüter

Hans-Jürgen Schlüter is the brother of Reiner Schlüter. He and his wife, Ursula Höhle Schlüter, also live on the former Ho-Chi-Minh Strasse in a modern apartment a block or two away from the Ortlieb family. After raising their own family of children to be committed members of the Church, they recently accepted into their apartment a young boy in need of a home. He is a student in Sister Schlüter's elementary school class.

Hans-Jürgen: We met at our branch meeting place on Dr.-Kurt-Fischer Allee, which we can now call our old branch house. We felt very much at home there. The prophet [Spencer W. Kimball] visited there on one occasion. And we experienced many momentous events in our country while we were there. But one day the word came to us that we were to have a temple here in East Germany, and we told ourselves that we should get prepared. We tried to prepare ourselves but probably too slowly, and suddenly the temple was there. There were many who were not prepared to enter the temple and had to see what they could do to make up for lost time in their preparations.

The next thing we knew was that we were to have a new chapel. Again we told ourselves we had to get prepared, that we had to do this and do it better than we had in the old chapel so everything would work out well, so we would feel at home there, so we would worship more devoutly—and we tried. From time to time, we watched the progress of the building, and suddenly, it was finished, and we were busy preparing for an open house. Many, many people came. They stood in long lines to come

Hans-Jürgen Schlüter and Ursula Höhle Schlüter with family. *Back row, left to right:* Uwe Schmidt; Annelies Höhle, mother of Ursula (see chapter 24); Ursula Schlüter; Hans-Jürgen Schlüter; Berriet Steuer; Olaf Steuer. *Middle row:* Birgit Schmidt; Carina Schlüter, fourth from left; Edith Schlüter, mother of Hans-Jürgen, third from right; Winfried Höhle, right end (see chapter 24). Dresden, 1994. Courtesy Schlüter family.

through our new chapel, and we were very proud and very happy that we were permitted to belong to this church, to The Church of Jesus Christ of Latter-day Saints.

So we had experienced many wonderful things in our new chapel. Then one day we were told that an Apostle would visit us, Elder Dallin H. Oaks. Elder Oaks came, and many other authorities. Then we were told that we were to have missionaries in our ward, and one day there they were—two young men. The young women would say two handsome young men, Elder Powley and Elder Smith. When President Paul introduced them he called them "top missionaries." They had already been tried in another mission, and they really were top missionaries. As it says in the scriptures, they thrust in their sickle with all their might, and within nine months about one hundred people had been baptized.

Well, this new building had put me into a very interesting situation. Where I worked there were a few who worked alongside me who knew that I went to church, and they knew what church I went to. But the times were not right for me to just come out and say, "I'm a Mormon. I go here, and I do this and that." One said such things only to very intimate friends. Then one day I returned from a trip associated with my work. It was the custom where I worked that whenever there was any cultural event or outing, an announcement was passed around. It said what was up, and whoever wanted to participate just added his or her name to the list. I had been away on this trip, and when I came back, there was an announcement on my desk that said, "Who would like to come on a tour of the new church building of the Mormons of the Latter-day Saints?" It wasn't written out very correctly, but it went through me like a bolt of lightning. I thought, "This can't be." I knew that the building was under construction, and in fact the rough construction was about completed. Of course, I signed up and had to go along.

I thought to myself, "How can I do this? How can I open my mouth?" (I had prayed to the Lord many times about it.) How can I speak out without making mistakes and tell people who I really am so that everyone will understand, and in a way that will not make me ashamed of myself and of the entire situation?" Now I saw the opportunity. So I signed up, and the day came.

Before the tour, I went to the person who had organized it and said, "What is this tour all about. What do you want to see there? Are you interested in the building or also in the Church itself?" "Well, the building, and well, the Church, too." "OK," I said, "I can tell you a few things about it." "What do you mean? Are you a member of that church?" I said, "You bet, dyed in the wool through and through. Just let me know. I'll be happy to lead a group through anytime you want." But he didn't dare do that and said no more about it.

The day of the tour came, and we were all in the building. The building contractor took us around. He was not a Mormon and was just saying this and that. I prayed fervently to Father in Heaven to please help me understand where it would be proper and appropriate to say something. I kept having the feeling, not yet, not yet. We went through as much of the building as we could, saw everything, and the tour was over. The building contractor got a little tip, and we were all standing around, and suddenly it came to me, Now you have to say something. I said, "Now we have seen the rough construction of this lovely building, as far as it is completed, and I am willing and prepared to take you on another tour when it is finished." My immediate supervisor's mouth fell open. "How's that?" I said, "Sure, I'm a member of this church, and I am an authorized representative and can tell you about it. I'd be glad to."

The director of our group, like all the other group directors, wanted to finish off the tour with a drink or two, and they knew and had known for a long time that I wouldn't go with them, that I didn't drink. Now this fellow was always very interested in this part of the celebration, the drinking part, but on this particular day, he wouldn't go with them. He wanted to ride home with me on the bus because we lived in the same direction. On the way home, he asked about this and about that and wanted to know everything from me. Later I gave him a Book of Mormon, but he hinted that he couldn't change. I don't know what the reason was, maybe it had something to do with the secret police. In any case, I gave him a Book of Mormon, and after he looked at the title page and saw that it was printed in Frankfurt, West Germany, he gave it right back to me. He was probably a little nervous and cautious. But all these experiences in the ward building made a deep impression on me.

Then in 1988, I had the opportunity to visit the USA and to attend general conference in Salt Lake City. The first day after my return I was asked, along with my family, to help with the open house in the new chapel. We were very excited and enthusiastic about helping as a family with the open house. There were many, many visitors, and I saw a lot of people who knew me. There were some from my work and also another colleague who was a big member of the Communist Party. "We didn't know you were a member of a church," he said. "Well, no one ever asked me about it, but now you know, don't you?"

After that the word got around that I was a member of the Church, and several people wanted to have a tour of the new chapel. "How about it?" they said. "OK," I said. "I'll be glad to do it, but I can't guarantee that I can get you straight in. There will be a line there; I don't want anyone to get upset if we have to stand in line with the others and wait our turn." They patiently waited in line, and when we were all inside, I gave them a tour through the building. They asked a lot of questions, and I asked my group to assemble and have a seat in the chapel. That would be a better place to answer questions. In a flash, the chapel was filled. They listened very attentively and asked question after question. But then others wanted to get into the chapel, so my time was limited, and I had to break it off and then conclude the tour with my group.

We had arranged the open house so that we would get about 100 or 150 people together in the cultural hall and show a video. The visitors came out of the cultural hall very serious and then left the building. The video talked about the purpose of life, and this gave many of them something to think about. Of course, as soon as they were out of the building and didn't have the immediate influence of the Holy Ghost—maybe when someone on the bus stepped on their toe or something like that—then the Spirit left them. But at least many, many people in Dresden heard about the Church in this way.

The location of our chapel is so favorable; I'm sure this was inspiration because it is right next to the huge park in the center of Dresden, where many people go walking on the weekends, and our elders and sisters can thrust in their sickle. Many people have joined the Church, and we are very enthusiastic about the work.

G. Davis: So much for the Church today. Can you tell us something about the history of the Church in this country? What was it like to grow up here, say, in the 1950s and 1960s? What sort of restrictions did you have? What kind of a relationship to the government? How did you feel as a member of the Church?

Hans-Jürgen: Gladly. I was born in Warnemünde, right on the Baltic coast, and in my parents' house only my mother was a member of the Church. My father was not a member. He was Catholic. Before the end of the war, my mother and my brothers and sisters and I all went into Rostock together to church. There were four children in our family. We held sacrament meeting in a home there in Rostock, in the home of Brother and Sister Stöckich. The Rotenberg family was there and several others. Those were nice times. I was about seven or eight years old. My father was the chief engineer at the Warno docks in Warnemünde. He was there when I was baptized in the Baltic Sea. By coincidence my [future] wife was baptized on the same day. Brother Wächtler baptized me, and my father-in-law baptized my wife. That was a memorable day and a marvelous experience for us. My father observed all of this, and then when my sister was to be baptized (she is two years younger than I) my father said out of the blue, "I want to be baptized too."

Then we had to leave Warnemünde because of the troubles there. We went first to Oderberg—that is near Bad Freienwalde, Eberswalde—and then came to Dresden. And here in Dresden my father [Wilhelm Schlüter] was the Sunday School president for many years, and then for twelve or thirteen years, I think, he was the "branch president," as he always put it. He didn't want to be called "bishop." He was very shy, a very shy man. He was also, I would say, a good example and a very good bishop. His two counselors were both bishops in Dresden after his death. So, he had a progeny, so to speak. That was Brother Ortlieb and Brother Manfred Heller. But now back to the Rostock days.

My father came into contact with Brother Heinz Winter, who had been a missionary there, and they became great friends. He was a man who loved action, Heinz Winter was, so he said, "We can't always be traveling all the way to Rostock. We've go to see to it that we have our own branch in Warnemünde." So he bought an empty barrack and built up a branch. Those days are the most beautiful memories I have in the Church, when we had that little tiny branch.

I learned a lot in those days that contributed to my personal development, and I made a lot of progress. I think I was about nine or ten years old then, maybe eleven when I received my first calling in the Church, branch clerk. I remember so well; it is stuck in my memory that I always had to count the number present at the meetings. That wasn't much, but then I had to add them up at the end and write, "Total." I spelled "total" with two "l"s, and he corrected me, only one "l." Those are little things that get stuck in the memory.

As I said, we had wonderful times. We were like a large family.

G. Davis: How many members?

Hans-Jürgen: We were all together: my parents' family—six persons—then there was my grandmother, that makes seven; then Brother and Sister Winter—four in their family; Brother and Sister Siebert and their daughter. Brother Siebert was a pilot on a ship and was often at sea. And there were always some visitors there. Then we had another brother. I don't remember where he came from anymore, but I remember that he claimed that he never made a mistake and that he was pure. That gave me a lot to think about in those days. It also became the topic of some discussion, but then he didn't come back to church anymore. I guess he found a little worm in his apple somewhere. Some members came over from

Rostock now and then to visit, from the big branch to the little branch of Warnemünde. But those were wonderful, wonderful days, and I like to think back on them. That was the pure gospel.

Perhaps I should mention that after 1945 I learned the magnitude of the work in the Church. The Church helped to save us—I won't say from starvation, but at least helped save us from serious illness. Of course only a small part of what was sent into East Germany got to the members. Most of it was divided up among the Communists and the Red Army. But we got some of it, and even today my wife and I have fond memories of the gunny sacks and the canned peaches. And when we had wheat, we cooked the wheat in water until it turned to mush, and then we poured a little cream and some of the peaches over it. Oh, that still makes my mouth water. That was something marvelous.

I was so thankful when I later visited Salt Lake City that I could see the Deseret Industries and could talk with the brothers and sisters who were working there and could tell them about my experiences. I wanted to volunteer to work there for a day or so, but I was told that the work was all divided out. Maybe someday I can do that so that I can demonstrate a little of my gratitude in the form of work.

But then came a day that was very decisive for my parents and for our whole family. It was getting harder and harder for the Church—more and more problems. Now we know that the secret police were mixed up in it and made things difficult. We now know that there were mass arrests. People were sent to places similar to concentration camps. Many were executed; many starved to death or died of diseases. My parents and Brother and Sister Winter had agreed to leave the country. "We're getting out!" "Getting out" meant first of all getting into what was then called the Western Zone of Occupation, now the Federal Republic of Germany, and from there maybe farther away.

By some accident, I learned about their plans. I have to say that I was very patriotic about our area. I was very proud of my homeland, my Warnemünde. And when I heard about their plans, I said to myself, "You have to do something to see that they don't leave Warnemünde." I had a little cold at the time and saw my chance. When they took my temperature, I rubbed the thermometer a little so that it went up. Then my parents said, "Oh, we can't go with you now. We're sorry, but Hans-Jürgen has a high fever. He is very sick."

I have often wondered what would have happened if I had not done that. Maybe we would have been better off materially, would have had it better. But I think what I did was the right thing because we feel very comfortable here in our country now, and the progress we have made here we could never have made somewhere else. Well, if I hadn't done that, we would probably be in the United States today, but I think it was right, even if it was a little deceptive.

Then we were alone there, and my father was taken in by the secret police. He was really being pressured because he had recommended Heinz Winter at the harbor and now he was gone. He had got out—"fled to the Republic," as they say of people who went to West Germany—and now my father was really worked over. He told me on his deathbed that he never knew there were other rooms in the building where he worked. A door was closed behind him. Further down a hallway another door closed behind him, further and further in until he was in this room. There they grilled him very thoroughly. Then they made him an offer. "Well, there is a possibility, maybe you could just. . . ." He was supposed to keep an eye on one person or another and submit a report, etc. And then he said to them, my father told me this word for word, "Out of the question." He would not be a fink and rat on his friend. He used a vulgar German word *[Kammeradenanscheisser]*, which meant that he wouldn't betray anyone.

After that they made more and more problems for him, made things more and more difficult so that finally we moved away from Warnemünde to Oderberg. That was an inland dock. There we were really alone. There was no church anywhere nearby. But that also has a lovely spot in the memory of my childhood.

There was a small branch in Eberswalde, but Eberswalde was about twenty kilometers away from Oderberg. So then, every Sunday the whole family got on their bicycles very early and biked over to Eberswalde. We attended the meetings there and then biked back. There were very few days, even in the winter or even in bad weather, when we missed a meeting. We did this every Sunday, and I have fond memories of it. I was allowed to take my little brother, who is twelve years younger than I, on my bike. Along the way, we took a rest and ate a bite in order to build up our energy again. It was truly a beautiful time.

Then they began to build up the airplane industry here in Dresden and were looking for people who had experience. Before 1945 my father worked on airplane construction in Warnemünde with the Arado company, who built sea planes. He applied and was hired, and we moved here to Dresden.

And then here in Dresden, from out of the past, suddenly there was Ursula Höhle, the one I was baptized with in the Baltic Sea. At that time she was a very thin, one could say, a skinny girl.

G. Davis: [To Ursula] Is he telling the truth?

Hans-Jürgen: That's right. She wasn't too interesting to me at the time, but when I got to Dresden I thought to myself, "Hmm, there is a pretty interesting girl."

G. Davis: She came to Dresden before you did?

Hans-Jürgen: She was from Dresden. She just came up to the Baltic Sea to be baptized.

G. Davis: But why weren't you baptized here in Dresden?

Ursula: We were on vacation. It was in the summer, and I had just had my eighth birthday. I was baptized in the Baltic on my eighth birthday. And it was just a coincidence that he was there.

G. Davis: But you hadn't known one another before that?

Ursula: No. We became acquainted at church. His parents often invited us over when they had some wheat, and we ate with them, and so it came about that we became acquainted with one another. And my mother always told me that I said, "I like Hans-Jürgen. I think I'll marry him someday."

Hans-Jürgen: Yes, it's very strange how things in life turn out sometimes. If we had left then, I would not have had the family I have now of which I am so proud. During those days in Dresden, the Church took on a new meaning for me. Everything was larger, everything was better organized. Not like the little branch in Warnemünde or especially not like in Eberswalde. But even then I had my highs and lows in the Church. Maybe I can relate a personal experience from which I learned a great deal.

I always wanted to be like my father. Although he is not living anymore, he was a great example for me. Well, the young people in the Church today are probably like I was. You reach an age where you want to go your own way. Our whole family went to church, and I went through this stage. I often tell this story to youth groups in the Church, and they really prick up their ears. Well, I didn't like the fact that I had to go to church every Sunday. I was an enthusiastic biker, and so when my parents and my brothers and sisters went to church, I arranged to take a bike ride into the

Tharandter Forest. I would ride alongside the streetcar—that's nice riding, alongside the streetcar—and I would ride clear out to the Rabenauer Meadows. There was a little lake there, Lake Weisseritz, and I would cool off there, wade around, etc. And by the time I got home, my parents were already there, and we had Sunday dinner together. And my father never said to me, "You have to come to church with us." I liked that.

But then one day I began thinking that I was not really happy with the situation. I didn't feel right. I didn't have to go to church with them, I enjoyed my bike riding, but somehow I wasn't satisfied. And then, just sort of automatically, I started going with them again. I could see that it pleased my father and my mother. They didn't say much, but they put their hands on my head and ran their hands through my hair. I think that was a wonderful method of teaching and inspiring. From that day on, there has never been anything that has kept me from church. On the contrary, I have truly enjoyed it.

The branch here in Dresden was located in those days on the Dr.-Kurt-Fischer Allee. That building is very important for the history of the Church here. I mentioned that we came to Dresden all the way from Warnemünde to a meeting here. That was what we would probably call a regional conference today. Walter Stover was the mission president at the time [1946–51]. And the large park that belonged to the branch went way out behind the building. The transportation police have taken most of it now. Well, we held this big conference there and slept in the park on straw at night. And the Russians came along and made us all get up and show our identification papers. That was something I won't forget soon.

And when the conference was over, we went to the train station. We wanted to take a train to the Rheinland to visit my father's parents. At the train station, I saw how well-organized the Church was. Brother Stover had arranged it so that all the children at the train station were assembled in one place, and we were all given a bar of chocolate candy. And since I was just a little boy at the time, I got one too. We wanted to buy a ticket, but they wouldn't sell us one because my grandparents were living in the Western Zone, in the Rheinland. And then I observed how the members of the Church stand by one another and help one another. Someone, one of the Mormons who had some authority to buy tickets, arranged it so that my parents could take this trip. The Mormons have always had to help one another here.

The State Security Police infiltrated the branches here in our country, I'm sure of that. Maybe in our church here, too. But I think they eventually saw that it was not right to oppose God, or maybe they just decided to draw back a little. It was not always an easy thing to work openly and honestly for the Church. There were many who had to experience serious disadvantages. I think, for example, of Brother Krause, the patriarch of the Leipzig Stake, who visited our ward today. He has been in prison several times. He has been through a lot. And I think about Brother Pawlowski. He has told me about how he had to go to the authorities to report every Church meeting. Every meeting, all the activities had to be reported to and approved by the police. He told me that he was not a great speaker—he didn't have a glib tongue—but he told me that always before he had to go to the authorities he prayed about it and then the words would just fly off his tongue: what he believed, who he was, and that it was all true. He always came through it all right.

I remember one experience I had where Brother Pawlowski really strengthened me by placing great faith in me. I was up there in Schwerin on business and had visited the branch. A sister from the branch came to Brother Pawlowski—he was the branch president at the time—and told him she had to take a long trip into Poland, and she wanted to have a blessing. We all got together and prayed, and then President Pawlowski said to me, "Brother Schlüter, will you please give the blessing." I was very pleased that he would have so much confidence in me that he would give me this important responsibility of giving the blessing. And the sister was very pleased, and I learned later that she went to Poland, had a wonderful time there, and came back safely.

Perhaps I could tell you about an experience that greatly strengthened my testimony. It took place in the old branch house. A nephew of mine was at that time in the army stationed at Görlitz, and whenever he had time off, he would speed over to Dresden on his motorcycle to see his parents. One Sunday, it was fast day, we came into the chapel, and I saw that his parents—my sister and my brother-in-law—with his sister and with other members of the family were very distressed. I learned that the nephew had had a very bad accident on the way to visit his parents and that his life was hanging by a thread.

Of course, I also became very depressed. It was hard to watch the emotional reaction of his parents and his sister. So I began thinking to myself, "How can I help? What can we do?" There was no opportunity to give him a blessing. During the entire testimony meeting, I was thinking about how we could help him. Of course, we could speak words of comfort to the parents, that's all well and good, but it doesn't really help the one who is injured. And then suddenly I had this idea in my head, "Heavenly Father is the only one who can help him. How could he help? He could help if we would show him our humility through fasting and prayer." But how was I to tell the others about this, about what we could do?

And in the moment that I stood up to bear my testimony, it was all clear to me. I asked the branch to continue fasting together until that evening and then come to the branch house once again where we would have a common prayer for our brother, for my nephew. I was really surprised to see how many came, how many continued fasting until that evening. That was a real testimony to me—that I made this suggestion to the members and they came. And there were some who had not understood what I had suggested, who came to me later and said they would have continued fasting and would have come if they had understood it properly. But there were many members there. We went to our knees in unison, we prayed together.

Some time later I had the opportunity to go to the hospital to see my nephew. It was a terrible sight. It is such a testimony to me when I see him today. You can hardly tell that he has ever had an accident. But then he couldn't see; one eye was misshapen; his nose was gone; his teeth were completely distorted; his jaw was broken in several places. But today, he has finished college; he has a family and is very faithful in the Church. This experience has been a real testimony for me. It has helped me very much. I have learned from this that we have the possibility to talk to our Father in Heaven. It doesn't necessarily have to be through a formal blessing for the sick; it can be through fasting and prayer. And when it is right, he will bless us. In this case, the blessing was very direct and is very visible.

So those are a few experiences that tell something about my feeling for the Church, from my point of view, from my contacts with the Church. Maybe I can tell you one more small experience. I once had the opportunity, along with Olaf Schulze, to be in charge of a youth conference in the old branch house. We had a wonderful time. The conference lasted for a week, and we had a wonderful time together, a time which strengthened our faith. And the thing that impressed me was this: the old branch house had many rooms that had to be cleaned up. The next day was Sunday, and it had to be left in such a condition that the branch could hold sacrament meeting. We had only a short time to do this, and normally it took the entire branch all day long to do a thorough cleaning and put everything in order. But these young brothers and sisters worked so hard that we had everything done in just two hours, including the washing of the windows. We could give it over to the branch for their Sunday meetings. That was a real testimony to me that when we are motivated and work together for the Church, nothing is impossible.

On the opposite side of the street from the meeting house, on the Dr.-Kurt-Fischer Allee, there were apartments where many military personnel and many members of the secret police lived. They watched us through the windows when we came and went. I'm sure we were always watched. Applications had to be filed for permission to hold meetings. But after they began to understand that a very strict separation of church and state is a principle of the Church and that we were not enemies to the State, then they began to loosen up a bit. We did not have to apply for permission to hold meetings every week, and then later, when there were certain Church functions during the week, we did not have to report them at all.

Ursula: I learned a lot about the history of the Church from my grandmother. She had a very hard life. She lost her husband when my mother was four years old. He died of an illness which would probably not be fatal today—some type of brain fever. So there she was, a widow with my mother to care for. That was about 1923.

One day she went to visit a friend, and just at this moment, this friend had the missionaries at her home, and she heard about the gospel for the first time. As she explained it to me, she invited the missionaries to visit her in her home, where they gave her further instructions. She became a member of the Church.

My grandmother was very diligent and also very talented. She had to provide for herself and for her daughter all alone during the difficult years of the depression with its inflation and unemployment. During this time, she always rented one room to the missionaries, and her small apartment consisted only of a kitchen, a living room, and one bedroom. She kept a large collection of postcards from the missionaries with their photos. Brother Percy Fetzer was one of them when he was a very young man. They always wrote a greeting on the backside.

She told me that the missionaries often ate their noon meal with her, and they always asked her to make her dumplings. Those were the yeast dumplings that she put in a pot with a cloth over them. I'm sure she gained a great deal of spiritual strength from those times. I have seen a photograph where the missionaries celebrated Christmas with her. She invited a large group of missionaries, and there is my mother in the middle of them as a little girl. So my mother literally grew up in the Church.

At the time, Brother and Sister Stover were in Dresden as mission president, if I remember correctly. [Actually, Walter Stover was mission president of the East German Mission 1946–51.] My grandmother once told me that when there were meetings during the week she had to bring my mother with her and my mother was so small she often fell asleep. Then the mission president told her that the family came first and that her first concern should be for the care of the child.

But eventually my mother met her husband in the Church; I don't know when that was. He was already a member. My mother married quite young. She was just nineteen years old, and my father was quite a bit older. He is thirteen years older than my mother. Well, then I was born in 1939, and of course I don't remember much about the events when I was small. I only know that my parents told me that the branch met at that time on Königsbrücker Street, where the large grocery store is now. But I remember that the branch met for a while up the street a ways, up toward Dr.-Kurt-Fischer Allee, in a building that was back behind some other buildings. It was a little, flat building, and I remember being there with other children from the branch.

Hans-Jürgen: There was a Brother Bory in the branch at that time. He told me when I first came to Dresden that they used to hold street meetings down on the Elbe River and other places. Like the missionaries are doing now; they used to do that here.

Ursula: My mother told me that just before I was born all the missionaries had to leave the country. I was born on the last day of freedom, and the war began on the next day, September 1. And this year when I celebrated my fiftieth birthday, we had missionaries in our country again. So from that, you can see the span of time in which we had no missionaries.

In those early days, before I went to school, my father was very involved in the music programs of the Church. He conducted the mission choir, and he also played the harmonium and the piano. We didn't have an organ at the time. We had a piano at home, and it was always so beautiful when my father played during our Christmas celebrations and the whole family sang along. My grandmother had a very beautiful alto voice. Those are very beautiful memories. It was only a shame that my father didn't have the necessary talent to teach me how to play the piano. He didn't have the patience. I sat down at the piano a few times, but then we gave it up.

I remember the great conferences we used to have at the branch house on the Dr.-Kurt-Fischer Allee. The members came from Forst and Cottbus and from all around. At that time, we owned the entire park next to the branch house, all the way down to the Wall. It had not been divided up. And the members camped out there and had picnics. It was wonderful. That was before the army and the police took it over, and we owned the whole park. After my youngest brother was born, I was allowed to take him out, and I always went up there with him to the park by the Church.

We did so many wonderful things together in the Church. We participated in a lot of programs. I recently found an old program about the sower who scattered various kinds of seeds. I had a part in it, and my sister Ingrid and Helga. We all had little speaking parts. Then we all took part in a Christmas pageant. I was an angel, and I brought my friend in who didn't belong to the Church. She was an angel too. For a long time her mother talked enthusiastically about how her Inge got to be an angel in a long, white dress. I hope she will come to church with me again, even though many, many years have gone by.

But then something happened that really set us all back. Maybe it began with the fact that we always had such nice things in the Church, and through them the Church received a number of new members. For example, during the hard times, we always had something to eat; we received wheat and canned goods and other things. For example, we had a patchwork quilt at home made of colorful pieces of material over a cotton filling. You have seen them. It was made by the sisters at Relief Society. Nothing but little colorful strips sewn to one another, that kind of a quilt, so beautiful, like a comforter. It was something wonderful. When I was little, I stared and stared at the patterns. But now I have to go back just a bit.

Whenever I had to stay home alone when my parents had to go to the church house at night, I was terrified. Those were frightful times. I couldn't go to sleep until I heard the key in the lock, then I could go to sleep. Then I knew that I wasn't alone anymore. At that time, we lived about fifteen minutes' walk from the church, and Brother Wöhe lived in the apartment above us. That was the father of Brother Heinz Wöhe. I think he was the branch president then.

Then there was something, some pieces of clothing or something came from America, and a quarrel broke out at Relief Society. In any case, it was my grandmother who got into an argument with someone. Well, it got worse and worse. This person or that person was reported to have said something, and as a result my grandmother and my mother refused to go to church anymore. And of course, they kept us children at home with them so that— I don't remember exactly when all this happened—so that for several years, I did not go to church. Then I went to college, and then I became a practice teacher, and it wasn't until I graduated and became an elementary schoolteacher that I came back.

When Hans-Jürgen moved to Dresden with his parents, he began to get better acquainted with me. We met one another on occasions, and through this acquaintance, I came back again. So our children had the great good fortune that they were born into the Church. But my youngest brother, who was just at the most impressionable age when this trouble took place, has never found his way back to the Church. He is totally out of the Church. It is very hard, but my parents still hope he will come back again.

Yes, my mother came back, and that was through some very unusual circumstances, not too long ago. In 1979 her only relative died up in Lübeck. She had to go to settle the affairs. She was sixty years old and could get permission to leave the country. So there she was in this strange city. My mother-in-law had given her the address of Brother Wächtler from Hamburg, and she turned to him. Then Brother and Sister Wiborny from Lübeck came and helped her take care of the family affairs and invited her to come to church with them. Sister Wiborny—she is a little like my mother, a little reserved—they understood one another right off, and that was the turning point that brought my mother back into the Church.

My father had stayed in the Church the whole time. He always went alone, and I know there were some very unpleasant times when they grew further apart. She couldn't understand why he would keep going. But he bore it all with calmness and continued to go. I am so thankful that they are all together in the Church again—with the exception of my youngest brother. He went off and joined the Communist Party. He thought that was the best thing for the country and that he was going in the right direction. Now he has begun to think a little differently, now that so many things have begun to come out that no one knew anything about. I think that maybe he might, that sometime, he will find the way back. What is lovely is that his children all come, especially his son, and now he wants to be baptized. But he will have to wait until he is eighteen because his mother won't hear of it. She won't have anything to do with the Church.

Hans-Jürgen: Perhaps I could also say that I am happy that my parents-in-law both come again and are both very active in the Church. It is so wonderful when in the extended family everyone has the same interests and the same goals. I must say how much I respect my father-in-law. As my wife has just said, he was always there, like clockwork. He was hardly ever sick. Every Sunday he was there. He did his duty. And since my mother-in-law has become active again, we have a very different relationship. I am so happy about that.

Ursula: Could I interrupt? My grandmother also came back again. She spent the last year of her life in the Church, as long as she could walk. She couldn't see anymore, but she came to the meetings regularly, so one could say that before her death she found her way back. This has often been a good lesson for me: that in spite of some little false words and some disagreements, even though one is truly offended, one should not set the gospel aside because of these things. You can't just say, I'll worship at home, and I won't come anymore. I saw how we were all pulled further and further away. This is a good lesson, because I know where it all ends. It always happens that when someone turns aside and the children are in that age where they take in everything, then it will be decided whether they will spend their life outside the Church or whether they will remain true to the faith. It has been so good for our children that they have never had to experience an interruption like that, that they have always been in the Church.

Hans-Jürgen: Perhaps one other experience that has helped me a lot may be of some help to someone else. My father was bishop of the Dresden Branch for about thirteen years. He literally gave all of his energy to the Church, and when I close my eyes and see him sitting before me, I see him in his very common pose sitting at the table doing his Church work. He spent essentially all of his free time working for the Church. In a sense, he actually had no free time. And he had a very difficult illness that eventually took his life. He had a sarcoma, a bone cancer that has a tendency to metastasize, and he suffered very terrible pains. But as a family, we managed to take care of him in our apartment and not in the hospital. We said among one another that we would care for him ourselves. My brother and I took turns giving him his injections, and we are actually very grateful that we could keep him at home and that he died at home.

As he was lying there on his sickbed, he often talked to me about various things. Among other things, he had read a great deal. In a situation like this, when one has a difficult illness, a great deal of stress is placed on one's personal faith and testimony. We often talked about Job and his experiences and trials, and we were actually able to strengthen one another. At one time, my father told me something that has remained strongly in my memory, something I will never forget. He said, "Hans-Jürgen, even if the gospel were not true—but you know that I believe in it with all my heart—but if it were not true, the least I can say is that because of the Church I have not been such a bad fellow. But you know that I believe in the Church." That taught me a lot: that a man for whom I have a deep love had a firm testimony, and that this gave him so much strength.

This was at the time when President Kimball came here to Dresden. My father hoped that President Kimball would somehow be able to visit him, and sent a message to that effect. My father could no longer be taken to church. President Kimball discussed the possibility of visiting him, but he had so many meetings that he could not get away. But when he spoke, he mentioned my father in his sermon. That was truly wonderful. My mother had to stay home with my father, and suddenly my father said, "My name has just been mentioned." And that was at the exact time when President Kimball mentioned him in his sermon. That was something truly marvelous. And it is also a testimony to me to know that a man of God can truly be a mouthpiece of God and that one can feel the influence of the Holy Ghost over distances, can feel that someone is praying for him, that they are with him in spirit. That has meant a lot to me.

He was still the bishop at the time. I know because I was the branch clerk. For ten years, I was the branch clerk. He was a strict bishop, but a good bishop. I remember that when he died and we went to the cemetery I had never seen so many people following a casket. I don't believe there was a person from the branch who was not there. My father was very beloved. There were also a number of his colleagues from work there, and many of them said that they had really appreciated him and that he had truly been an example to them. He was a bishop to the very end. On his deathbed, he signed his last documents. My father's name was Wilhelm Heinrich Schlüter. I am very proud of that because my name is Hans-Jürgen Wilhelm Schlüter. The Wilhelm is in there, and I am very proud of it. I am very proud that we can be members of the Church as a family.

I always tell myself that we have something that can make us happy. We really have to ask for God's help in finding people who have this same desire. The mission president, President Wolfgang Paul, has said that not everyone has this desire. That's why we can't lose much time. We have to decide when we see someone whether they are ready or not. But I'm sure there are still many who are ready, and I am working hard to find them.

Ursula: Speaking of missionaries, the leader of our Pioneer Group [a communist youth organization] at school said once when I was in her room that we ought to be a little more concerned about religion and that she would like to learn a little about my church. So I told her a few things, and not long after that I was sitting in sacrament meeting, and the chapel door opened, and in she came with her family. I was more than a little amazed, since as a member of the Communist Party she was supposed to be an absolute atheist. At the end of the meeting, she greeted me and said, "I have to stay a while because my sister is being baptized today." I had to sit down for that, it was so totally unexpected. And now she always sends a greeting with me for Elder Baumann. Apparently there is more to the story because she is also receiving the discussions.

We were talking about it on Friday, and she said to me, "Well, do you know how all this came about?" I said to her, "Elder Baumann told me you have a wonderful daughter." Then she said, "Yes, yes. My sister and her husband had my daughter for a few days, and they went to the Strömerhof Restaurant to eat. There were two missionaries sitting at their table, and my little chatterbox Liese, she began talking about everything, so they got into a conversation. The end of the story is that my sister and her husband were baptized."

Now the husband has received the priesthood, and that's how it all came about. That is Brother and Sister Wolf. There was a rule among us public schoolteachers that we were not allowed to talk about the Church. We were employees of the State. It was known that I belonged to the Church, but I was not supposed to talk about it at school. I have a few colleagues whom I consider to be wonderful people and whom I would love to have with us, but I have invited them as much as I dare, and they have always had one excuse or another. They were afraid that it would be bad for them, some disadvantage. I hope now that conditions are loosening up I might be able to bring them with me. You can see from such examples as the leader of the Pioneer Youth Group that you can't say in advance what will happen. There's no use doing that.

24

Those Are Just Little Things

Annelies Höhle and Ursula Höhle Schlüter

Annelies Höhle is the mother of Ursula Höhle Schlüter (see chapter 23). She lives with her grown son Winfried in the same apartment block and across the courtyard from her daughter and son-in-law. We interviewed Sister Höhle around her table as she leafed through her photograph albums and served us the fruit dumplings for which she is known throughout the ward.

Annelies: My father died when I was four years old. After the funeral, my mother wanted to take a bouquet of flowers to the cemetery. She went by a friend's house to ask the friend if she would like to go to the cemetery with her. While she was at her friend's house, the doorbell rang; it was the missionaries. On this particular day, the missionaries had invited my mother's friend to a meeting, and after the missionaries had gone, it had become somewhat late, so my mother didn't go to the cemetery at all. She went with her friend to this meeting instead. The hymns were so consoling to her that she continued going back, and it wasn't long before she was baptized. Then I started going to church with her, and when I turned eight, I was baptized.

    I really don't remember very much about my baptism. I was baptized at the mouth of the Briesnitz. That is a little stream that empties into the Elbe. The only thing that has stayed in my memory is that two sisters who had a garden gave me a little marmalade jar full of blackberries. I have never forgotten that. It was not long after my mother had been baptized that the missionaries came to live with us. That was a fun time for me. They always had time to pay attention to me. Well, those are just memories out of my childhood. Back then the branch meeting place was on Brücker Street.

Whenever I go in that store now, I can see our branch house. We built that little chapel in 1939, before the outbreak of the war. When we started, the missionaries were still here and helped with the construction and painting. Suddenly they were gone, and we thought, well, they will be returning soon. The branch house was dedicated in early September. My daughter was born on August 31, and on September 1, the war began. Then there were no longer many of the priesthood here. My husband and Brother Wöhe were about the only ones. There were, as I said, very few of us left. That was in 1945, and our branch house was still there. That was in the *Altstadt* [old part of the city].

G. Davis: And the Altstadt Branch was destroyed in 1945?

Annelies: It was destroyed, yes. Actually, in the entire bombing, as far as I know, we lost only one sister. That was Sister Giedemann, who lived in the center of the city, right downtown. The others all showed up after the bombing. Then, because the Neustadt Branch house was too small for both branches, we looked about for another place to meet. We had a choice between two places, one on the Marien Allee and the other on the Dr.-Kurt-Fischer Allee, and we decided on the one on the Dr.-Kurt-Fischer Allee.

The day we started [with the rebuilding] was splendid, marvelous. Right in the middle was a big hole where an antiaircraft battery had been. It would have been quite dangerous for the little children, so we just filled it in. There was no shortage of rubble. They brought a horse and wagon and hauled in the dirt and rubble, and we sisters leveled it off with all sorts of tools, whatever we had.

G. Davis: Were there many of the brothers there?

Annelies: Yes, some, but they had other things to do, and this grading was easy for us sisters. It was no problem.

In 1947 we had a missionary conference that lasted an entire week. I remember one day so clearly. The Church rented some tourist steamers, and we went up the Elbe as far as the "Saxon-Switzerland" [*sächsische Schweiz,* a mountainous tourist area upriver from Dresden]. There is a "Theater in the Rocks" there, an outdoor amphitheater, and it was reserved for us. The various branches put on a show.

G. Davis: Was it a large conference?

Annelies: Yes, it was very large. There were four large ships. It was really something. And when we came back, we went to the big city

Robert Höhle, husband of Annelies Höhle, 1938 and father of Ursula Höhle Schlüter. Courtesy Robert Höhle.

auditorium, the one that is now a military museum. It used to have a restaurant. So all of the members had the entire restaurant for our dinner. We had a wheat broth. We had gotten wheat from the welfare program, you see. After dinner we had a dance, if I remember correctly. At the end of the week, we had a special conference. The members all sat out in the park at the side of the chapel, and the chorus was on the terrace. The terrace wasn't enclosed back then. It was open on all sides.

Ursula: You always told me that earlier, before the war, there was such a closeness among the young people of the Church.

Annelies: Yes, there was. This was just after 1945. We were very close at the time when we had nothing to eat. That was when one of your friends would come up and say, "I don't know what we're going to eat tomorrow." And another would say, "I've got something. Send your children over to my house, and they can eat with us, OK?" That's right. We were all like one family then. There weren't so many of us. Those were nice times, and the young people did a lot of things together. It wasn't just everyone for themselves. Those things stay in my memory. But that was in the old days, you see.

N. Davis: One story that I have not forgotten that you told us when we were here as missionaries is about the birth of your son Winfried.

Annelies: Yes. Winfried was born a month early. He was—how shall I say this? We knew about the persecution of the Jews. My husband had a cousin who was a Jew and who died at Auschwitz. So we knew about the persecution of the Jews and a lot of other terrible things that were going on. But that they were taking retarded children and putting them to death, I didn't know. Well, they had this counseling service for new mothers, and we were supposed to attend, but I didn't like it. The place wasn't clean, and you had to wait around a long time with your undressed baby. I just didn't go, and so they never saw Winfried.

It wasn't too evident right at first that everything wasn't just right with Winfried, but then I took him to a woman pediatrician; that must have been after about three months. She told me, very confidentially, that I was going to have to have a lot of patience with this child. She was right. I did have to have a lot of patience. He was a year old before he could sit, a year old. And when he was two, he still couldn't walk.

N. Davis: But were you in danger of losing him?

Annelies: Yes, I had to be very careful that I never went anywhere with him where he might stand out. I didn't take him to get shots. I just didn't go.

Ursula: That may have been an act of providence.

Annelies: I just had to watch myself. I think still to this day that it was some sort of an inner voice telling me, "Don't go out with him." An inner feeling. And if I hadn't followed this voice, I might not have had Winfried for long. They would probably have taken him away. So I never let him be seen in public. I think it was just an inner voice, some kind of a feeling—"Don't do that, don't go there."

Ursula: Otherwise, you would have done everything that one normally does with children.

Annelies: You see, Winfried was born in 1942, when things were a little uncertain, when one never knew, so I just didn't go out with the child. They were always out there checking.

Ursula: He was born at home.

Annelies: Yes, he was born at home. He was not born in a hospital. Actually, they were all born at home, even Ursula. If Winfried had been born in a hospital, it might have been bad for him.

Ursula: Well, didn't you say anything about a ration card for food for him?

Annelies: He did get a ration card for food.

Ursula: But he was older then, wasn't he.

Annelies: Yes, yes. I am happy that I have Winfried, especially since my husband is gone. Now I'm not alone. I have someone I can take care of. My sister is always telling me, "My husband would never have let me raise a child like that. He would have put him in a home." I would never have let them take my Winfried, never.

My daughter and my other son always said, "Sure, your Winfried. Your Winfried." But now maybe they understand that I had to give him a little more love than the others. Well, he's still with me, and he feels secure. He is never aware that there is anything he can't do. Of course, he always wants to go somewhere; he wants to have a girl friend. Oh well.

G. Davis: I was pleased last Sunday to see that the bishop asked him to be an usher.

Annelies: Oh, he is so proud of that. Of course, you never know. When the bishop asks him, he might just say, "No, not today." That happens sometimes. He has done that twice. Being an usher is his pride, but he is even more proud when he can sit up on the stand with me when I have to give the closing prayer or in the fast and testimony meeting when I take him up on the stand. Oh, then he is really proud.

G. Davis: On another subject. I have the feeling that the members in the United States who do not know a lot about this country are of the opinion that the people in the Church here were suppressed by the government or that they felt themselves isolated, cut off from contact with the Church. But many members here with whom we have spoken deny that. They tell us that they felt quite comfortable here. What is your opinion?

Annelies: I can confirm that opinion, that we have always felt comfortable here. Having said that, I would also like to say that we were isolated, cut off, as it were.

Ursula: Yes, we stuck together and helped one another, and in that way we were comfortable, but it was hard when we looked outward. In part it also depended on what sort of a profession one had.

Annelies: Lots of times the hard situations started with the children. It is sad to say, but our youngest son doesn't come to church anymore. He was baptized, and as a child he always came to church, but in his last two years of school, he didn't want to come anymore. He said, "I'm not going to be ridiculed anymore when my friends see me coming home from church and then the next day in school someone says, 'Oh, you went to see the Holy Post on Sunday.'" That was a derisive term they used. And so he wouldn't go anymore. And now when we talk to him about the Church, he just won't take the necessary step to start coming again.

G. Davis: But that could happen with us, too. I mean, not only in this country, that could happen in Salt Lake City.

Annelies: Yes, but here it was more intense because no one wanted to know anything about religion.

Ursula: It is no accident that less than 40 percent of the people in our area, in the former GDR, are religious at all. The large majority of the people are atheists, and this is a direct result of forty years of education. Whether a child in school was Protestant, Catholic, or whatever, the others were always of the opinion that she was a little strange. Someone who could believe in religion must not be all there. That's the way it was, and it was very hard on the children. It was not so easy on the parents either to be hearing these remarks all the time and that "those people who go to church have something wrong with them." That was the opinion. And in my profession [elementary school teacher], it was made very clear to me that I was not to talk about religion if I wanted to keep my job.

G. Davis: Yes, I wanted to ask you about that. You became a teacher. That is a little unusual for someone who belongs to a church, isn't it?

Ursula: Yes, but I became a teacher back at a time when things were not so strict. When I was a student, I put my religion on the application. They asked about your religion then, but later, in the 1960s, it started to get even harder. There was a girl who had been in my class at the university, for example, who made a little mistake. She sat down in the school cafeteria and prayed over her food, in full view of everyone. We usually did that very privately without drawing any attention to ourselves. She was told that she would have to give up her profession. This state, which was raising the children to be atheists, could not tolerate someone doing something like that in public. That's the way it was, and I must say I was always a little uneasy when I met a colleague in the streetcar on Sunday morning when I was on my way to church. Because, as I have said, we were always under a little pressure.

Annelies: Yes, my husband had problems. After the war, he was released from prison in 1945 just before Christmas, and he got his old job back. Then a little later they told him that if he wanted to keep it, he would have to join the SED [*Sozialistische Einheitspartei Deutschland* (German Unity Party), i.e., Communist Party]. So he joined the SED. But he never denied his membership in the Church. He always said that he belonged to The Church of Jesus Christ of Latter-day Saints. And after a few years, that finally began to sink in, and they called him in and told him he had to decide: church or party. They gave him a few days to think it over before he told them his decision. So he went to them and said that he had decided for his church. Then he came home and told me, "At last, I am out of the party." But he was mistaken. He didn't get out of the party. They told him that someone had come down from the party leadership and said, "Are you people crazy? Do you want to start a religious war? Do you want the word to get out that we are suppressing religion?" But that was quite late. Anyway, he didn't get out of the party.

G. Davis: What do you mean, "quite late?"

Annelies: Well, that was in the '70s. Then he did leave the party. But by then they had already taken up the problem of the Church, you see. This party leader had told them not to make a big fuss about the fact that he belonged to a church. So then he was stuck with the conflict between the party and the Church. There was no getting around it then.

G. Davis: Do you think the fact that the members had these problems brought them closer together, that the problems made them stronger in the faith?

Ursula: Each individual will have to answer this question for himself or herself. I was actually quite uncertain about my faith for a long time, and it didn't have anything to do with pressure from the outside. I was just young.

Annelies: When you were in Bischofswerda in the Pedagogical Institute you came to me once and said, "Yes, that's all well and good, but my teachers say thus and thus." I told you that someday when you became a teacher you would have to say a lot of things you don't believe yourself. You would just have to say what you are instructed to say. And that's probably what was happening to those teachers back then. They had to say what was prescribed in their lesson manuals. They weren't allowed to express their own opinions.

Ursula: Yes, but I would still like to maintain that my testimony, as it has grown over the years, has not been influenced by this external pressure. Maybe this pressure has influenced the way we talked about our testimony with others. Of course, we were afraid to talk about it in certain places.

For example, I remember well the day when a student asked me, "Mrs. Schlüter, is there a God?" Right in front of the class. It took some courage on my part to answer: "Yes, I believe there is a God." Yes. But I couldn't discuss it any further. Today, the little children are not inhibited, and they talk freely about religion. They ask me what I think about life after death, and I talk openly about it. But there is still a barrier. There are some who say, "Oh, that can't be." Atheism is deeply rooted because their parents were raised that way and have taught it to their children. It will be very hard to change that in this country.

You also hear frequently the opinion of the older people who are quite convinced that there cannot be any religious instruction in the schools, that it's all nonsense. They don't want anything to change. Many students' parents are hesitant about it. I once sent around a questionnaire in the school asking how many would like to see religious instruction introduced into the school. Two persons wanted Catholic instruction, and all the others were strongly against it. That is all very deeply rooted, but I don't think it has had any influence on my own testimony because we in the Church strengthened one another and we went to church regularly.

Annelies: I remember when Brother Karl Wöhe died. We lived in the same apartment building. Sister Wöhe wanted the casket painted white. That came from Brother Fritz Lehnig from Cottbus, who also wanted to have a white casket. So Sister Wöhe had the casket painted white. The entire apartment building, and it is a big one, ridiculed her for that. They all knew what church we went to, you see. They ridiculed her about painting the casket white. That was so strange. [Typically, white caskets were reserved for children. Adults had natural wood or black caskets. The people apparently believed the white casket was part of the beliefs of the Church.]

Ursula: Yes, and I can remember what they said about her. They said she was a hoarder. "Guess what? She has sugar and flour in her apartment. Hoarding things." They talked about her behind her back. She was just doing what the General Authorities have told us to do, trying to keep a supply of food on hand.

Annelies: Those people were quite spiteful, I must say.

Ursula: Yes, and if we want to be honest, we were also a bit cowardly. We were afraid that if we spoke openly about something that was not approved of, there might be consequences.

I know a Sister Ziegler, who is dead now. In every store where she had to stand in line—she was always telling me about this because we were both teachers in the Sunday School—she always took a Book of Mormon with her, and she always taught the person standing in front of her in the line, even during those times when they were so strict. That didn't make any difference to her. But she didn't have a job to worry about. They couldn't do anything to her. But, oh well. Maybe we were a little lacking in faith in those situations. We knew very well that one person couldn't feed the family. We wanted to keep our jobs. That's the way it was.

Annelies: Feed the family. After 1945, when we got the meeting place up there on the Dr.-Kurt-Fischer Allee, we planted all sorts of vegetables way at the back of the park. The park was much larger then than it is now. They took half of it away from us. But way in the back, we planted vegetables, tomatoes, and parsley, all sorts of kitchen herbs, and they were divided among the Relief Society sisters so that we would have something to cook. At least we could have a taste of something, and some tomatoes, even if there weren't many. But it was a supplement.

When the first welfare goods started coming in, that was fantastic. And I must say that they helped us survive. Many families were completely out of bread. I didn't have so many problems because my daughter was always saying, "Oh, I ate yesterday." But many people were having real problems with their nourishment, and when the wheat and the peaches and the salted herrings or whatever arrived, that helped so many people. And then, how our membership grew. The word went around, and members showed up we hadn't seen in years. Then they never came back.

Ursula: Oh well. That's understandable. Everyone wants to survive, and I think in those situations there's nothing wrong with that.

Annelies: It was similar during the bombing on February 13. I was down in the cellar, and I heard people praying who had never prayed before in their lives. They didn't believe in anything, and suddenly they started to pray.

G. Davis: How was it with your family? Did you live in the old part of the city?

Annelies: No, we lived in Neustadt, not so far away from the Dr.-Kurt-Fischer Allee, up there where the streetcar line runs. I was there with my daughter and with Winfried. We were alone then. And my daughter even to this day gets a strange feeling when she hears a siren. It was strange squatting down in the cellar and listening to the bombs whistling overhead. And then we heard the explosion and tried to make ourselves smaller and hoped that it didn't hit us. We were spared. The last bomb hit just two houses down from us. Only a fire bomb hit our house. Anyway, I don't ever want to experience anything like that again.

Ursula: Yes, an experience like that gets right down inside of you. You never forget it.

N. Davis: How old were you then?

Ursula: I was five years old. Winfried was two. I can still remember that we had a long kitchen and that my grandma lived right in the next apartment. That was fortunate, because Mom was quite young then. She was just twenty-five, and after the second attack, she just sat in the kitchen crying and saying over and over, "I'm not staying here anymore, I'm not staying here anymore." When I looked out the window, everything around was red, and there were sparks flying up from the fire across from us, at a hat factory. It was terrible. I couldn't tell if it was day or night because of the smoke.

Annelies: And this fire storm howled. It sounded just like an organ. It was really terrible.

Ursula: It was a powerful storm. She put me and Winfried in his baby buggy. We were both lying in there, and I couldn't see out because the top was up. I guess my legs were hanging out, I don't know. She grabbed up a few things plus my grandma and both of us and left Dresden.

Annelies: We had three attacks. The first was around 10:00 or 10:30. Then came the second one and then another around noon the next day, and I said, "I'm leaving. I'm leaving." I bundled up my children, and my mother said, "Where are you going?" I said, "I'm going to Hof" (my hometown, not far from Dresden). I loaded up my children, and my mother said, "Well, then I'm going with you." She pulled my little wagon with two suitcases.

Some things happened that really strengthened my testimony. We started out, and we had heard that the trains were leaving from Radebeul. And on the way to Radebeul, actually not far from our house, in the garden area, a group of soldiers came toward us. They were trying to get into the city. When they had almost all gone by, a soldier stepped out of the last row and said, "Young lady, where are you going?" I said, "I want to get away. I'm going to Radebeul" [a suburb northwest of Dresden]. He said, "You'll never make it that far. We were sent to help, and it doesn't matter to me whom I help."

He pulled my baby buggy, I helped my mother, and we started out, but he said, "We'll never get to Radebeul." In the meantime, the strap with which I was pulling the baby buggy had broken because of the double load. I had an uncle who lived on the way to Radebeul. I hadn't seen him for years, but the soldier said, "If he has a handcart, I could make it to Radebeul." My uncle lived right on the way, so we went to his house and asked him if he could

Refugees leaving Dresden with a handcart. After the bombing of Dresden, Annelies Höhle left under similar circumstances. Source: Richard Peter, *Eine Kamera klagt an* (Leipzig: Fotokinoverlag, 1982).

lend us a handcart. He said, "Yes, but I need it back." So we loaded everything in it and walked to Radebeul, and there was a train.

The soldier said, "I'll go find out where it is going," and he came back and said, "It's going to Leipzig. Come on. I'll get you on, and then I'll take the wagon back to your uncle." He loaded us onto the train. The train stood there for a long time, and the soldier went back. Why did a soldier out of the last row step out and say, "Can I help you?" There must have been something that spoke to the man and said, "You should help that lady."

G. Davis: Did you make it to Leipzig?

Annelies: No. We got only as far as Riesa. We arrived at Riesa at midnight, and then the sirens went off. The bombers were coming back again, so the train stayed in the station train shelter.

Ursula: Right in the station?

Annelies: Yes, right in the station. There we waited until morning, until the first train started off in the direction of Chemnitz. We rode to the second stop, where we had to get out and walk to the next village. But in the train, there was a man who knew us. He was a neighbor of my aunt, and he said, "You must be coming from Dresden." We must have been covered with smoke and soot. Anyway, he offered us some of his bread, what he had, and then he said, "I'll ride on ahead on my bicycle and tell your aunt to come to meet you, O.K?" We lived in that village until June of 1945.

Then my mother walked back to Dresden. She said she was going to inquire around and find out what was going on. After about a week, she came back and told us that there were no trains running, nothing, but that there was a ship running from Riesa to Dresden. She told us we had to get back or we would lose our apartment. It was still there, but we would lose it.

The next morning, very early, we started out for Dresden by way of Riesa. It was actually still curfew time. I had a handcart with Ursula sitting on top of my bedding and a wagon with Winfried and whatever we could carry. At the edge of Riesa, there stood a Russian guard. We just wished him a good morning, and he didn't say anything. He let us go into the village even though it was still curfew.

When we got down to the Elbe River in Riesa, we saw the ship leaving. It was already gone. You see, they had different times. In the village where we had been staying, it was normal time, but in Riesa, they went by Russian time. There was a two-hour difference. That's why the ship was already gone. We sat down there on the Elbe, and I began to cry because there wouldn't be another ship for two days. It went up to Dresden on one day and back to Riesa on the next.

Now what were we supposed to do in Riesa? We couldn't walk back. My mother said, "You know what? Let's go to the city hall. The parents of the neighbors of my aunt live in Riesa. I know the Birners, and maybe they will take us in for two nights." She went into the city hall and asked, but they told her, "We're sorry. The documents are all mixed up. We don't know anything." But a man standing there said to my mother, "You know, I know a family by the name of Birner. If you want to come with me, I'll show you where they live. Maybe they're the ones."

We went with him, and when we came around the corner and down a few houses, there was a lady poking her head out of the window, and my mother said, "That's Mrs. Birner." They did take us in for two nights and helped us get down to the ship very early so that we could get back to Dresden.

Those were all things we had prayed for before we set out. Why was a man standing there just at that time to say, "I know a Birner family"? Those are things that one doesn't think much about at the time when one is so upset, but later when thinking back on them, one realizes that help came as an answer to prayers. And those are things that strengthen testimonies.

Once there was a Danish dance group who came to Dresden, and I put up three sisters in my apartment. That night they didn't come home. They couldn't come home from the program with us because they had to get their costumes in order because they were leaving the next morning. These sisters didn't come, and they didn't come. I stood at the window and thought, "My goodness, are they lost? They went that way once." I went to my room, and I prayed. Not long after that, I stood at the window, and there came the three sisters. They said they had gotten lost. They had gone down the wrong street. Suddenly they had this feeling, "Wait a minute. What did that sister tell us when we left? One street left, then right, then straight ahead. Now let's think about how we came." So they found their way back.

These are just little things that strengthen my testimony. I said to myself, "You prayed for them, and just at that time, one of the sisters had this feeling, 'wait a minute.'" Well, those are just little things.

N. Davis: Those are wonderful things.

25

Those Were Hard Times

Käthe Wöhe

Käthe Wöhe now lives alone in a modern apartment complex in the area of Dresden known as Leutewitz. Although she is a small woman, her quick movements and sensitivity to the needs of her guests are reminders of a long life of heroic service in the name of love. Her story says little about political life under the Communists but speaks to the results of war and of the committment and determination of one woman in the face of heavy suffering and responsibilities.

Käthe: I was born in Dresden to Walter Singer and his wife Elisabeth Singer, whose maiden name was Hiller. I was born premature and weighed only three pounds. When I was four years old, I was out on our balcony and fell into a tub of boiling water in which my mother was washing diapers. I suffered third-degree burns and had to remain in the Johannstadt Hospital in Dresden for a year, after which I could go home. I had to have skin grafts. In the meantime, my brother Heinz was born in Dresden on September 24, 1929.

When I started school, I had trouble with my gymnastics class because of my burns, which made it impossible for me to do some of the exercises. Nevertheless, I did my best, and after much hard work, I was able to graduate from the eighth grade. Because of my health, it was not possible for me to complete another year at school, which was normally obligatory. In order to prepare me to be a housekeeper, my father sent me to a home economics school that was then located on Pirnaer Street in Dresden. There I learned all sorts of practical things such as cooking, baking, and ironing. I loved everything I learned there,

Käthe Wöhe and Heinz Wöhe. Dresden, 1991. Courtesy Käthe Wöhe.

and I formed a friendship with my teacher that lasted for many years. She was a very intelligent woman, well read, kind, and pious.

In those days, I was active in the Evangelical Church. In 1940, I was confirmed in the Johannis Church. After that I began an apprenticeship at the famous Lingner Company—mouthwash, toothpaste, perfume, dental equipment, etc. I worked at this from October 1, 1941, until September 30, 1944. After my apprenticeship, I took my examinations with the Board of Industry and Trade and passed with distinction, which was a very positive experience for me. But then came the great trauma in my life.

The great air raid on Dresden came on February 13 and 14, 1945, and the city was bombed to rubble. My mother, who was only thirty-nine years old, was killed as well as my grandparents and my father's sister with her two children. All in all, twenty-two of my near and distant relatives were killed. I was only nineteen at the time, and I was devastated. It was a terrible shock. My father was still in the army at the time and came home when I informed him of the tragic event. When my father got home, he went out for an entire night searching for my mother, and he left a letter with me, which I was to open at a specified time in case he did not return. But he did return and silently took the letter back. I will never forget those days. It was not easy to lose everything.

At first I tried to take care of my father and my brother as best I could, but unemployment was everywhere and living conditions left much to be desired. I had to sleep in the same room with my father and a second mother, which was just too much for me, so I decided to move in with my aunt, who lived in Landshut in Lower Bavaria. But since they didn't have very much to eat there either, I had to go looking for work. At first I got a job on a farm where I worked in the kitchen and then took care of the children. I was not strong enough to do farm labor. Every two weeks, I got a day off to visit my aunt and her family.

One Sunday she asked me if I wanted to stay home with my uncle or if I would like to go to church with her. So I went to church with her. My aunt was a Mormon. So from her I learned about The Church of Jesus Christ of Latter-day Saints and its doctrines. Since I had been raised as a Christian, I was interested in everything. I noticed right away that the Church went into the doctrines in much more depth. After a period of study and trial, I was baptized in Landshut on October 11, 1947. At my confirmation, I received a wonderful testimony. I had the feeling that strong cords were pulling me up into heaven. It was an experience I have not forgotten to this day.

Suddenly the word was out that the last train from the West to the East would soon be leaving, and I was overcome with homesickness. I wanted to get home. I loved my Dresden. Well, while away I had become a member of the true church, and when I got home, my testimony was strengthened.

I approached the church there on Dr.-Kurt-Fischer Allee and opened the door for the first time. A very handsome and spiritual young man was standing at the pulpit to open the Sunday School. On an Easter walk, I became better acquainted with this brother, and we both had the feeling that we belonged together. We became engaged in June 1948. He was thirty-two years old, and I was just twenty-four.

On January 29, 1949, we were married. In spite of the fact that my father was not at the time a member of the Church, he arranged the wedding for me and my dear husband and invited members of the Church, including the district president Brother Fritz Lehnig and the Relief Society president from Cottbus, Sister Voigt. The only thing that made it possible to hold a wedding celebration in those days was the welfare goods we had received from the Church—wheat, canned fruit, milk, and foods containing fat. At the time, my father and my second mother raised a rabbit on the balcony so that we could have some meat. I will never forget it. It was a wonderful blessing from God. The only sad thing about the wedding was that my dear mother, who had died on February 14, 1945, could not be there. She was such a dear and faithful mother. Before her death she had written in my autograph book:

Nicht der ist reich, wer vieles hat,
Und immer trachtet mehr zu kriegen.
Du bist ein Reicher in der Tat,
Wenn Du Dir lässt an Gott genügen.

[He is not rich, who filled with greed,
Is always striving to get more.
You are rich, and rich indeed,
If you are satisfied with God.]

It was especially sad for me that our children had to grow up without knowing a wonderful grandmother.

A dear old sister, Sister Simon, who had had ten children who were all married except for one daughter, took my husband and me into her apartment and gave us one and a half rooms so that we could live alone together. At the time, my husband was the president of the Sunday School. Later he worked in the MIA, and then he taught the lessons for the elders quorum, which he enjoyed very much.

Our first daughter, Christine, was born on November 11, 1949, and my husband and I were happy people. She was healthy, strong, and lively, and could never get enough to eat. Everything turned out well. I had to go looking for work because my husband was often ill from his experiences in the war and in a POW camp. So I looked for a job so that we would not go into debt. But I was often sick myself, and a companion at work told me, "You are getting a stomach ulcer." She was right. Then I had to quit work because my daughter Christine had to be taken care of. In those days, there were no kindergartens.

On September 17, 1951, we had our second daughter, Edith. Since food supplies were so meager, she didn't get enough calcium, and a double hip inflammation was discovered. I had to do something right away so that she would not be injured permanently and have to limp or something. I had the good fortune to get a diet for her from a doctor that consisted of grains of rye crushed and mixed together, with a broth of calf bones and vegetables (no butter). By following this diet for one year, everything turned out well. Of course she had to lie bandaged for a year, and it was not easy for her nor for me. But with time she became stronger and healthy. My aunt had put her name in the temple for me. We bought a used tricycle for her to strengthen her legs because she was so frail. But in spite of all that, we were happy that we had two sweet little girls.

And now my great desire was to have a son who would run up and down the stairs and up and down the street and who would sing. We saw a movie about the famous singer Caruso, and that's the kind of son I wanted to have. My desire was fulfilled, but then in my eighth month, I suddenly developed a heart problem. I had to be sent to a treatment center for mothers up in Mecklenburg. While I was up there, my husband had to move. My father-in-law and my father had both married again and helped with the move. Actually, I didn't want to go way up there, but the doctor insisted. However, I had a wonderful time there and brought a healthy, husky little boy into the world. My dear Heinz was overjoyed when I finally returned home. Our son was the very image of his father. He was so cute and very good. We were very happy. Even though these were difficult times, I would not have done without them.

But after my third child, I had to have an operation on my legs because of poor blood circulation, and my convalescence took nearly two years. During that time, my husband, Heinz, often went alone with the children walking in the woods or on other excursions until I was able to go with them. Walks in the woods were some of the most beautiful times we had together. My husband was such a good naturalist, and the children would ask, "Daddy, what kind of a tree is this?" or "Daddy, what is that?" They were always so proud that their father knew. And when they had a class on nature at school, the teacher would always say, "Where did you learn that?" "My Daddy taught me." They were very proud of their father.

We were very poor, but my husband did not want me to go to work because it would have been at the expense of the children's health. So for breakfast he ate oatmeal cooked in water with pieces of dry bread, and I stayed home with the children. Finally, when my son was ten years old (1964), I couldn't stand it anymore and went looking for work. It was not easy, but we needed the money, so I had to do it. I worked in an office. I had had some part-time work before to earn a little money. Once I had worked for six months in a post office so that I could buy the children some clothes. At that time, I couldn't always go to church because I didn't have the strength. Today I realize that I didn't always do everything just right in those days. Nevertheless, I wanted to help my family.

Little by little, things got better. Whenever I did anything wrong, Father in Heaven sent me a trial, and when we tried our best to obey the commandments, we were blessed.

In 1971 my husband had a sudden stroke and was taken to the section of the hospital for the seriously ill in Kreischa. I could see that it was not the best place for him to get well, so I asked to see the head doctor, and he listened to me. After some struggle, I was able to get my huband declared an invalid so I could take him home with me. From that time on until I received a pension at age sixty, I had to work so that we could get along. For many years, my husband stayed at home and helped me with the housework and shopping because he could not work. Unfortunately, his health did not get any better.

My husband comes from Meerane. Later, his parents moved to Grüna, then to Chemnitz, and finally to Dresden. For several years, he had bleeding on his brain. That was caused in part because of the fact that he almost drowned when he was four years old. But in spite of that, he attended elementary school and graduated from a trade school. He then had an apprenticeship for salespeople in the animal feed business in which he worked. But then came the war, and he was with an antiaircraft unit, which was not good for his head injury. After that he ended up in a POW camp in Yugoslavia and with very little nourishment was put on a crew building roads. He had a lot of health problems there, including problems with the sciatic nerve, dysentery, fever, and many other things. In September 1947, he returned home totally destroyed. Many of his problems became evident only years later after we were married. Once he passed a kidney stone. Those were difficult times.

In November 1985, I quit working and had so looked forward to a time when we could go walking together and take trips together. From my work with the railroad, I had a free pass on the trains. Unfortunately nothing could be done after my retirement [because of her husband's health], which I regret very much. I had wanted to show my husband so many things, but it was too late.

G. Davis: But you were able to go to the temple, weren't you?

Käthe: Yes, on the first day the temple was opened, in 1985. That was the most wonderful thing. The temple was open, and we had to go there on the train, but with the trains, well, you can never tell. The train came into the Freiberg station at the very last minute, so what did I do? I ran up to a man who was unloading some bottles from a truck and asked him if he could take us to the temple. It was urgent. I told him I would pay him. Would he please do that for me? And he said, "Yes, I'll do that, as soon as I unload these bottles." And he drove my husband and me to the temple. Oh, what a blessing it was that we made it on time. I gave him some money, but he didn't want to take it. "No, no, no. I appreciate the offer, but I just did this for you." He was a total stranger. After the temple session, we went home on the train.

During the open house, I took eight days vacation and spent those eight days helping at the temple. I must say that was like a fairy tale come true when I think back on it. I stood there watching the visitors to see that everything went well, that nothing happened. One day two hikers came, husband and wife. They had on their hiking shoes and carried hiking sticks. I will never forget them. They had a little baby in a basket. They put the basket with the little baby down beside the door, put their walking sticks there, took off their hats, and went in. They looked over everything and were very astounded. Then they came back. The baby hadn't cried a bit. It was very small. No one had said anything; we just all stood there. But the little baby must have been comfortable in its basket. They came back, picked up the baby and went on their way.

It was a little hard on me; that was my last year of working, 1984–85. I remember a brother came up and said, "Sister Wöhe, can you stand here any longer, or are you going to fall down?" I said, "Well, I am getting pretty exhausted." "As soon as that brother gets back from lunch, you go eat something yourself," he said. Everything was so wonderful there. And it went on for eight days.

One day a scholar came; I guess he was anyway; he wanted to know this and that. And our job was to instruct them that they couldn't talk inside. We told them to look at everything, and then when they had questions, if they would please turn to the missionaries who were waiting outside, they would explain everything to them. But inside everyone had to be still. And they were.

The most beautiful thing was when my colleague from work came. I had to tell her where I was going, but I never in all my life expected to see her there. Suddenly there she was. That was something that she came, that she saw and heard everything.

G. Davis: Had she known before that you were a Mormon?

Käthe: Yes, she knew. But we could not take someone by the hand and lead them to church. That was out of the question. You could say this or that. You could invite them to a concert, but you could not invite them to church. We couldn't do that. We never did it. We could tell them that our church was putting on a concert.

We had beautiful concerts, there in the old meeting place on the Dr.-Kurt-Fischer Allee. Of course, it is nice here in the new building on Tiergarten Street, but I think we were more spiritual out there because we grew up in that building. We had to clean it ourselves. We had dramas there, and dramas with our Primary children. Those were beautiful times. Well, we were tied to the old building.

Now we have had to move over here. Oh, it is very beautiful here, but that was a big change. It was like it was when we had to move out of our house in Frankenberg Street, where we had lived for thirty years, two-thirds of our life, and where our children had grown up. But my husband didn't want to move. He didn't want to leave, and I told him, "Hans, you are not getting any better. We will have a smaller apartment there. I can't take care of this place anymore, but I can manage over there. You will have a balcony and can sit outside. You will like it." That's the way it is with many things; you just have to get used to them.

G. Davis: So, in those days did you have a feeling of isolation from the Church here in the GDR?

Käthe: Yes. Well, I would like to say, one always had this longing to be able to travel somewhere, to see how conditions were with other people. But that wasn't possible. That was not permitted. Because I worked for the railroad, I did have a chance once to travel to Hungary, but then I couldn't do it because Papa was not well anymore. He couldn't travel then. I was sixty and he was sixty-eight and we couldn't do anything like that. You know how it was. It was sad.

During the last few years, it was hard. I had to lock the door when I went out, or he would have got out. That happened once when I was out for a visit, and I couldn't let that happen. The doctor had told me that I had to lock the door when I went out. I had to be careful.

One time something happened. It wasn't a laughing matter, but now I can smile about it. Some mornings he would get up early in his nightshirt, or whatever he had on, go out into the living room, put on his shoes, put on his suit, and comb his hair. "I have to go to work," he would say. You know, then I had to bring him back in and tell him that he was retired now, that he didn't have to go to work anymore, and that I would like to go back to sleep. It would be about four or five in the morning. It was not easy.

G. Davis: And what were you able to do in the Church during all this time?

Käthe: Well, the same thing as all the others, Relief Society work or whatever. To be honest, I couldn't do much because I had my hands full taking care of my husband. There was always something. I could never be totally at ease. I was always thinking, "Now I hope nothing happens; now I hope everything is all right." I always had this worrying feeling. I will say that I am very thankful that my husband lived to be seventy-six, but if I had not been very attentive, I don't believe he would have lived so long.

I wanted to bring him to church as long as he could walk. But even then I had to bathe him, shave him, comb his hair, everything. He couldn't do anything for himself anymore. I always said that as long as he could walk a little I would bring him. And that's what we did. When he couldn't walk anymore, I said it was no use. Then it was too hard.

We went to the temple for several years; I don't know how many now. One of the workers said, "Sister Wöhe, we can't do this anymore. We can't keep everyone waiting because we have to dress him and do everything for him and that holds everyone up." But President Burkhardt said, "Sister Wöhe, it doesn't matter that we all have to wait. As long as your husband can come to the temple, we will gladly work with him." I always liked him, Brother Burkhardt. He is really a fine man. He sent Heinz a letter to congratulate him on being a member of the Church fifty years. I still have it.

I didn't think badly of anyone. No one can understand who hasn't been through such a thing as this, and I didn't always tell everyone. That would have just made it harder if I had to tell everyone. I just couldn't do it. I just had to help myself the best I could.

On July 15, 1989, our son did a wonderful thing for his father. He took him around to all the places where he had grown up—Meerane, Grüna, and Chemnitz. He was overjoyed and could hardly contain himself. At the end of the day, we went to the zoo in Chemnitz, which he enjoyed very much.

In September 1989, our daughter Edith and her family went West, which was very sad for us, but we understood. Twice our son made it possible for us to visit our daughter and her husband and family. The first time it was in Obernkirchen, and then we visited them in Stadthagen near Hannover, where the family is very active in the Church. My husband was able to enjoy this with me, but it was really too much for him, and unfortunately we couldn't do that anymore. So our daughter Edith came over to see us for a few days on his birthday. She loved her father very much.

My husband had many intellectual interests. My daughter Edith is the same, and that is why she always had so much in common with her father. My husband loved music, and it moved him very much. We celebrated his seventy-sixth birthday on April 18, 1993, in our home, but it was such a strain on him that he had to lie down several times. A week later, our son took us and our little Paul on an excursion to the Oak Forest, which was hard for him.

But he so enjoyed going to the forest by car. We walked for two hours. We used to do it on the streetcar—there, two hours walking, and then back on the streetcar, but we hadn't been able to do that for a long time. Walking was getting harder and harder. We took some nice pictures to remember it by.

From the beginning of May 1993 until December 1993, my husband was bedridden. I took care of him as well as I could with help from the social welfare people. During that time, I could not attend church. Everyone understood, supported me, and told me that my husband was now my most important assignment. I did this gladly. I cared for him up to the last moment, and I am happy to have done that.

But I was so pleased last Christmas, Christmas 1993. Brother Ortlieb came to see him and talked with him and asked him if he would like him to sing to him. He loved music. He had two missionaries with him, and they sang and prepared the sacrament for him. Heinz put out his hand and said, "Thank you, Brother Ortlieb." He was so happy. I was happy, too. Then Brother Spengemann came and said, "Brother Wöhe, can I read something to you?" He understood everything. I was right there, and he asked him if he understood, and he said, "Yes." He sang for him too, and Heinz shook his hand. He could always feel it when there was someone here who was spiritually close to him. He could feel it. It made me so happy that a few brothers would come over and lighten the time for him.

But it was hard because he was going downhill. After I had bathed him for the weekend and spruced him up, I would say, "Come on, Heinz, things will get better." But he would just shake his head. He knew.

Just before Christmas, I had to go out to buy a little wrapping paper because I didn't have enough for the grandchildren's presents, so I went down to the Stritzelmarkt. When I returned, I said to my husband, "Heinz, I found something pretty." He looked at me, and I said to him, "Look at this little Christmas tree with the pretty colored lights and with the gold hangings. We can plug it in and put it by your bed. Would you like that?" "Yes," he said. So I put a chair by his bed, made it a little higher, and lit the little Christmas tree every night.

About a week before it got very bad, my son Michael carried him out. He ate his supper in a chair, looked around, and talked a little. I said, "Maybe you can do this again, when we put up the Christmas tree." But that day never came. He couldn't get out of bed again. He was too weak.

G. Davis: But you never lost your faith.

Käthe: No, never. That would have been worst thing of all. No. We have had many wonderful blessings, and I know for sure—this is my testimony—that I will see my husband and be with him again.

Because of my work during the open house at the temple and because of the poor health of my husband, we were able to go through the temple right away, on July 27, 1985, and be sealed for time and for all eternity.

On January 2, 1994, my dear husband died as a consequence of his fifth lung infection. I worked as hard as I could for him and hope that my Father in Heaven will count it to my credit. I did whatever was possible to relieve his suffering. He wanted to die at home and was able to do that. I washed his body for the last time, and the bishop and my son dressed him in his temple clothing. He looked so handsome. The men at the funeral parlor said they had not seen a more handsome man for some time. That was a consolation to me.

We had a wonderful funeral. One could feel the good spirit. Because my husband liked music so much, I had "Ave Maria" played. Everything was so harmonious. So I am so thankful for everything and thankful that my Father in Heaven gave me the strength to overcome it all.

Now on Sunday I am at church and rejoice at the good spirit and the lessons which sustain me. I thank my Heavenly Father for all of his help during these last difficult times. My doctor confessed to me that if I had not expended so much energy for my husband over the years he would never have lived so long—from April 18, 1971, to January 2, 1994.

There are many things yet I could say, but now I want to close and express my thanks for everything that was so beautiful in our life together. The important thing is that we stay together as husband and wife and that we give our children a beautiful home with love and security.

26

The Gospel and the Government

Erich Dzierzon, Gisela Dzierzon Heller, and Manfred Heller

Erich Dzierzon and his wife live in Freiberg. We interviewed Erich at the home of his daughter, Gisela. She and her husband, Manfred Heller, live in Freital, a small town outside Dresden. Both the Heller family and the Dzierzon family have a long history of service in the Church. They feel great joy that one of the first young men permitted to leave the country to serve a mission was Brother Dzierzon's grandson. Among many other responsibilities, Manfred Heller served as bishop of the Dresden Ward at the time the first missionaries returned to Dresden. At the same time, he was director of the Church district office in Dresden. He now works in the geneaological offices at the temple in Freiberg.

Erich: I was born in Grossschirma near Freiberg in Saxony. My grandmother was taught by missionaries from America. She was converted and accepted the gospel, so I was born into the Church. I was baptized in Freiberg when I was eight years old. Freiberg was our branch, and we had to walk or ride our bicycles seven kilometers each Sunday to attend church. I spent my childhood in the Church and learned a profession. Then came the war. I served in the German army for seven war years, in Poland, in France, and in Russia, and came home without a scratch, which was a miracle.

During the war, I became acquainted with my wife through some relatives, and I was able to bring her into the Church. It was a case of love at first sight, and I told her that if we were going to be together then it would be best if we had one religion. She had been raised in the Evangelical-Lutheran Church and accepted the gospel as soon as I told her about it. We were married during

Manfred Heller in the district office, Dresden chapel. At this time, Brother Heller shouldered much of the responsibility for the Church's day-to-day operations behind the iron curtain in addition to his duties as bishop of the Dresden Ward.

the war, and our daughter Gisela was born during the war. All the other children were born after the war.

During the war, I had neglected my church duties, and now that the war was over I had to repent and make up for what I had lost. What callings did I have? I have been everything except president of the Relief Society. I guess I have spent more time in the Sunday School than in any other auxiliary. Over the years, I have been the Sunday School president several times. I was also the leader of the MIA and conducted many evenings of entertainment. I guess that comes from my personality. I have a humorous nature, and we had many fun evenings. I was in the district leadership of the elders quorum, and then I was in the branch presidency. As I said, I have been in every organization but the Relief Society. It was a wonderful time. We have six children, and they have all been raised in the Church and are all active members.

Jumping ahead, after the war was over and we had this so-called communist regime, we tried to do our duty with joy, and I had many interesting experiences. I would like to say that during these times when we were so hemmed in, restricted in our activities, the members of the Church really stuck together—not only our members but the other citizens of the country as well. The entire population followed the principle that in trial the people must stick together. We had this togetherness.

There were many problems in this country. We, ourselves, started with a typewriter store that soon developed into a printing shop. Everything that we printed had to be approved, and this was a very exhausting experience because the state authorities were always afraid that we might print something directed against the regime. We never did. We tried to conduct our lives according to the principles of the Church. My experience was always this, and this was reflected in the lives of many other members: if you conduct your life according to the principles of the Church, you will not be in conflict with the regulations of the State. We tried to do our duty in the Church.

The brethren who were involved in the various businesses kept the Word of Wisdom. I have heard directly from many communist bosses that our brothers and sisters who lived the gospel earned a great deal of respect. I'll give you one example. At the dedication of the temple in Freiberg in 1985, the press held an interview with President Hinckley and with the state minister for ecclesiastical affairs. We did not see the interview on television here because of the fortunate circumstance that immediately after the dedication of the temple we traveled to Salt Lake City to visit our children there. But they had all made a recording of this interview, and it was interesting for me to be in America and hear the state minister for ecclesiastical affairs in the GDR say to President Hinckley, "We know your five thousand members in our GDR to be reliable and conscientious citizens." That was quite moving for me. It taught me that we had been watched and that it was beneficial for the Church when the members tried to live according to the principles of the gospel. That was a testimony to me.

Perhaps I could say a few words about the present state of affairs, if you would like.

G. Davis: Yes, please do.

Erich: Following the reunification [of the two Germanys] which we have just gone through, it became clear that in the past, forty or fifty years ago, things were much worse. My grandparents told me some stories of how things were. If they were having a little Bible study group, they would always put out coffee cups. If the police came, they could hide the bibles and say they were just getting together for a little coffee because it was forbidden to meet together to study the Bible. I remember those stories from my own grandmother and from my mother.

But then, to our joy, things began to stabilize somewhat. There were no difficulties when I was a student or with my colleagues at work. No one picked on us anymore. I can remember when I was a child people pointing fingers at us because we were going to church. But over the course of the years everything changed, even the Communists. People began to recognize that the Dzierzons, even though they went to church, were good and reliable people. And it was the same for the other members who attended church. That has been my experience anyway and my testimony. And it made me think when I heard our state secretary Gysi tell President Hinckley how important it is for people to transform their religious beliefs into actions wherever they live and whether there are difficulties or not.

G. Davis: When were you first able to go to the temple?

Erich: I would like to say something about this, because those who have not lived under the kind of regime we have lived under will not be able to understand without some explanation. After it was announced that the regime had given the Church permission to build chapels and to build a temple, the Church became known to many, many visitors at the open houses. That was for us a new period of self dignity, and we began to recognize that the Lord's Church could truly be expanded here, that it would be recognized by many, many thousands of people.

It was exactly as had been spoken by President Monson when he dedicated this country. He prayed that the people of this country would become curious about the Church and that this curiosity would develop into an interest for many people. That is exactly what we have experienced. During the time of the Communists, the people became curious, they came to Freiberg to see what was going on, to see the temple and the new chapel, and their curiosity turned into an interest. We had many baptisms in the late eighties, 1986 to 1989, just in Freiberg. To experience these things moved us very much because without this curiosity we would never have experienced these things during the communist period.

G. Davis: That is very interesting. I have heard it said that the Church ought not to have made these agreements with the communist government in 1988, that the Church had thereby lost its independence, so to speak. But I gather that you would not agree, that you see only advantages for the Church in the agreements, which made it possible to have missionaries come into the country again and have young people here go on missions outside the country.

Erich: I know that the head of state, Erich Honecker, at the time he met with President Monson, Brother Burkhardt, and others, spoke the words, "We have observed you for twenty years. Your application is approved." From that day on, missionaries were able to come here, and our young people, if they had completed their military service, were permitted to go on missions to other countries. We saw that as a miracle, and I must say that this contact with the government officials was a good thing in and of itself, and a positive thing for the development of the Church. That was important.

The people here recognized that the communist government was cooperating with the Mormons, and this gave our members a feeling of confidence. They recognized that our Father in Heaven was directing these events and that they would enjoy much more security in fulfilling their duties and obligations in the Church. The relationship was good. We were no longer isolated. We had lived according to the principles of our belief and had honored and taught the basic principles of the Church. We never compromised or changed these principles, so far as I know, and the State accepted us.

It may be important to understand that in a communist regime, the regime thinks of itself first. And they knew that a brother in the Church who worked in a company or firm was reliable, that he would neither smoke nor drink, that he would not loaf on the job or show up for work drunk, because the Mormons do not do these things. Mormons have their own principles. The State recognized this even though they were of a different political opinion. We were not restricted, and those who applied the principles of the Church in their own personal lives were recognized.

This was true of other Christian friends with whom we worked politically. I am thinking in particular of the Christian Democratic Union, the CDU Party. I was active in this party myself because there all Christians worked together for the political good and we were not restricted.

G. Davis: Perhaps Manfred and Gisela will tell us something of their family and how they came into the Church.

Manfred: Well, I was a war child. I was born March 21, 1942, right in the middle of the war. My father had been in the war since 1939 and finally returned home from a POW camp in 1948. During these difficult war years and then in the very difficult years right after the war, I was alone with my mother or she with me. My mother had been a member of the Church since 1924. At that time, there was a small group of members of the Church in Freital, near Dresden, maybe fifteen or twenty people. They had been baptized by a missionary by the name of Erich Berndt, who was the father of Elder Dieter Berndt from Berlin, who later became our Regional Representative. I have my first memories of the Church from when I was four, five, and six years old, in the years 1946–47.

My mother had lost all contact with the Church, but the visiting teachers of the Dresden Branch Relief Society had rummaged about and found her address. They came out here to Freital after the war to visit her, and that's how we came back into contact with the Church. There was no longer a group in Freital, and any members here belonged to the Dresden Branch. So my mother was visited by the members from the Dresden Branch and, of course, I took part in these visits also.

As a five- or six-year-old lad, I would put on my rucksack on Saturday evening and march from Freital-Poisental over to Freital-Zauckerode where I would spend the night with my mother's stepmother, Sister Grosche, and then I would go to church with her the next morning. We had very little to eat in those days. We used to eat thistle soup and beet greens, and I was so excited to find out that Sister Grosche had cracked wheat and apricots. This was part of the welfare plan in action that helped the members so much here in East Germany.

I can still remember events from my life in the Dresden Branch. I used to go to Primary in the middle of the week. That meant a long ride on the streetcar with several changes, all the way out to the branch house on Dr.-Kurt-Fischer Allee. That was like a trip around the world for me. That is where I learned about the principles of the gospel and learned to love the gospel. On August 12, 1950, I was baptized in the Briesnitz Lake out on the Dresden Heide [heath or moor]. At that time, we did not have a baptismal font in the branch house, so we held all of our baptisms in the open. It was a beautiful day; I remember it well. There was a whole group of young people my age who were baptized at the same time.

In the following years, most of them went over to the West, to West Germany or to America or to Canada. Only a few of them stayed here in the country to help build up the Church and make it strong so that the conditions could be such that the Church could continue to develop and realize the blessings we enjoy today. I must say that all of these blessings—the temple, the missionaries, the entire development of the Church—have come about because of the faithfulness, the strength, and the willingness of the members in this country to sacrifice. Those were the conditions. Without these things, none of this would have been possible. And those were beautiful times.

Once a week, we had MIA for the entire branch including the Primary children, and once a week, we had priesthood meeting and Relief Society for the older brothers and sisters. Sunday morning and Sunday evening we had regular church meetings.

Of course, that was a big financial sacrifice for us as a family, as well as a sacrifice of time, because we had to add a few hours just to travel to and from the branch house. We started out early Sunday morning. Church was out at noon. We came home, had a bite to eat and rested for a few minutes and then started out for the branch house again to get there by six. We got home again about nine o'clock. That means that the entire Sunday was taken up by church meetings. No one in those days had a car, so all of our traveling had to be by public transportation. The members in those days were very, very active. Everything they did was for the Church. We put on plays and had many other activities. Here in Dresden we put on some wonderful plays and had so much fun.

I was eventually ordained a deacon, then a teacher, then a priest, and then I had to get my military service out of the way—two years, 1960 to 1962. This was right at the time of the Cuban crisis and when the Berlin Wall was built. But I must say that I never experienced any difficulty because of my membership in the Church. When you follow the path of the gospel consistently, when you try to live according to the principles of the gospel, you will be accepted by others because they recognize that your word means something. They understand that when you say yes, it means yes, and when you say no, it means no.

We married in 1963, my wife Gisela and I. She is a Dzierzon, and we knew each other for many years here in Freiberg. We have had six children, each one prettier than the other.

Our testimony of the gospel and the Church is that when one obeys the commandments and the laws of the Lord then one will be blessed abundantly. We have always tried to pay an honest tithing, and the Lord has always helped us. We have been able to get along even though there were times when it appeared that we had come to the end, financially and otherwise. Trying to raise six children in the former GDR did not allow much leeway. But our Father in Heaven always blessed us so that we got clothing from here and other things from there and never had to suffer actual hunger or deprivation. The Lord was always there to help. It is also our testimony that the Lord does not hold back. He always keeps his part of the covenant and blesses those who try to serve him with all their heart.

I was called to be the first counselor in the branch presidency when I was relatively young: that was in 1967; I was twenty-four years old. The branch president at the time was Wilhelm Schlüter. In 1977, Brother Schlüter died, and I was then called to be the branch president, from 1977 until 1982. Then when the Freiberg Stake was formed, I served on the high council until 1986, when I was called to be the bishop of the Dresden Ward, where I served for four years. During this time, we built and moved into the new chapel on Tiergarten Street.

I remember the years we were in the old branch house on Dr.-Kurt-Fischer Allee very well. Many beautiful experiences bind us to that building. Practically all of the larger events held in the Dresden mission were held there because there was no other place to hold them, no space large enough. That's where we held all of the youth conferences, all of the mission conferences, all of our genealogy weeks, and everyone who participated in these events will remember them with great fondness. And through certain connections, ways were always found to provide food on these occasions; ways were found that were not possible for normal mortals, unless they got them under the table. Connections were found.

There was Sister Kaden, who worked in a butcher shop, and she could always get meat for us one way or another. Brother Burkhardt and Brother Schulze were always able to get fruit from the small grocers, from Mr. Schmalz, for example, who as a greengrocer had things that were really hard to come by.

We youngsters sat up in the balcony in the old branch house and could look down on everything. Of course, we were into a lot of mischief such as sailing paper airplanes off the balcony and nonsense like that. But I would like to say—and this is something that we have always taught our children again and again and something that we as a family or as parents advise over and over—that we should gratefully participate in all of the activities of the Church. We should not hold back, but we should join in with all of these activities where the youth of the Church or where all of the members get together. It is by this coming together that we strengthen our testimony, that we remain firm in the gospel of Jesus Christ. It is such a great blessing to us that our three older children, who are now married and have their own children and families, are firm in the Church and in the gospel. I hope that our other three children, who are still at home, will follow the same path.

I was speaking about the meetings we had in the old chapel, the missionary conferences and such. I believe someone counted that twenty-seven General Authorities have spoken in that old branch house or in Dresden.

It began with a visit from President Heber J. Grant, who visited Dresden in 1932, and continued until the visit of the Prophet Spencer W. Kimball, who was in Dresden, in 1977, I believe. Then there were other Apostles and members of the Seventy and the Presiding Bishopric. These conferences were always the high point in our lives and gave us strength to carry on.

G. Davis: I gather you didn't feel yourselves isolated from the Church in Salt Lake City?

Manfred: What does it mean to feel isolated? We had everything we needed. We had the standard works of the Church, we had the basic principles, and there were always possibilities for visitors. Everything else was taken care of in the GDR by President Burkhardt himself. He was the person who had the complete confidence of the General Authorities and the First Presidency of the Church. He was one of the few who was permitted to travel to the general conferences; he had received this permission from the government. Later this permission was extended to his counselors in the mission presidency and then later even to the district presidency.

Also, the leaders of the Church were always watching for opportunities to make contact with us. An important possibility for contact was, for example, the Leipzig Fair, which was held twice each year, in the spring and in the fall. Foreigners were permitted to enter the GDR to attend the fair without going through too much red tape. So at the time of the fair, a conference was always held in the old Leipzig branch house, and there were often General Authorities present who then instructed us.

In addition, President Burkhardt received information and instructions that were necessary for us from the First Presidency when he attended general conference. And, of course, there were always written instructions, which were then passed on to the individual branches through the regular priesthood lines. I mean, we didn't have direct contact with the leadership of the Church here all the time, but as far as the basic principles of the gospel were concerned, we had what we needed to progress in the gospel.

G. Davis: Perhaps in that sense, neither do we have "direct contact" with the leadership of the Church.

Manfred: Yes, that was assumed. But I mean also that we had no Church literature except for the standard works. The older members had some books they had had from before the war—*Principles of the Gospel* or *The Articles of Faith* or something on the programs of the Church. Those things were still here. Several had a copy of *The History of the Church,* and some of the members had old copies of the *Stern,* and these were also available in some of the branch libraries. As far as teaching manuals go, that was a big problem. These had to be smuggled into the GDR by someone who came over to visit or by someone who through some circumstance or other was allowed to go out. In some cases some things could even get through the mail. Then the sisters had the wearisome task of producing fifty or sixty copies on the typewriter, eight carbon copies at a time. These were then distributed to the individual members or to the branches.

Erich: Printing was officially forbidden.

Manfred: Yes, printing was forbidden. Everything was forbidden: all written material that had anything to do with an ideaology, that could influence the people's thinking, anything that the State found unpleasant, that did not support their materialistic philosophy of life. That was hard. We had to be very, very careful. We had to find ways. Nothing could be printed, but we could write with our hands, couldn't we? That's the way it was with all of our Church literature.

And the tithing that the members in the GDR paid had to be collected by the mission office, which later became the regional office, and kept here. It could not be sent out of the country. It could not be exchanged for foreign currency, so the business of the Church in the GDR was carried on with our own tithing. Part of the money was kept in a bank, and part of it was distributed for the maintenance of the branch houses.

That was extremely difficult in the GDR because all building material was controlled—every brick, every sack of cement, every board had to be allocated. You could not go to a lumber store and buy what you want as you can now. You had to have permission to buy anything. You couldn't just go out and build something; you had to have permission to build *[Baugenehmigung].* In spite of everything, the members tried to keep the buildings up as best they could, sometimes at their own personal expense. Brother Krause from Prenzlau was our great leader in this area. He knew all the building skills, and he traveled from branch to branch, building, remodeling, expanding wherever it was possible.

G. Davis: You could buy material as a private person, but not as a church?

Manfred: Yes, as a private person, but in small quantities.

Gisela: In very small quantities. For example, we might have to have several members apply for one sack of cement each.

Manfred: The branches were kept in pretty good condition, at least the interiors. The exterior was often pretty shabby because they were for the most part rented facilities. The Church did not own any property, and the State was not interested in keeping up our buildings. If we had not done it ourselves, nothing would have been done. So we paid particular attention to the interiors of our buildings so that the members would feel comfortable.

Well, that's the way things were. In this area, we tried to live according to the principles of the gospel, and I believe the older members look back on these times with fondness. I work now in the Genealogical Department of the temple in Freiberg, and we placed in the archives there many of the records from the old regional office. When you look through these records of the branches from the 1950s, say, or a little earlier or later, it is very interesting to see what sacrifices the members of the Church made in those days.

There is a story, for example, of a member who had to ride his motorcycle from Annaberg in the Erz Mountains to Blauental in the winter when it was ten degrees below zero, and he was so frozen they had to help him off his motorcycle. When you read these stories about the branches up in the Erz Mountains, or from anywhere, they illustrate what strong testimonies these members had in those days. Those brothers and sisters were the real leaders of the Church here in the GDR.

G. Davis: Do you know of other examples of the difficulties the members of the Church had to overcome?

Manfred: Well, things began changing a lot in the eighties, but earlier, before they could hold any church meeting or have any activity, it had to be reported to the police.

Gisela: At first that had to be reported each week. Then later they said that it could be reported monthly.

Manfred: Strictly speaking, only ecclesiastical meetings could be held in a church building, that is, religious meetings or worship services. Social activities like dances and other entertainments did not come under approved church activities and were not allowed.

Gisela: But you made special application.

Manfred: These activities were carried out more or less illegally, or we would just say "Church activity," even though it would be a social activity. But we always proceeded with the assumption that every activity of the Church has a spiritual or a religious component and we could represent these activities as such.

G. Davis: So that included dramas as well as dances?

Manfred: Yes, yes. Dramas and such could not officially be held in a church building. That was the social domain of the Young Pioneers and the Free German Youth. Such things did not belong in a church.

G. Davis: But when you had a dance . . .

Manfred: Then the doors were locked, you see.

G. Davis: So that was a religious meeting.

Manfred: That was, yes, that was a religious meeting.

Gisela: The members knew that if they came too late it might be too bad. The doors had to be locked.

Manfred: I've told you about some of the difficulties we had getting permission to import Church literature. A good example is how long it took us to get two thousand songbooks. President Burkhardt had to make four applications, and one of the applications went all the way up to Walter Ulbricht, the head of state. Can you imagine? The head of state has to concern himself with whether or not a church can have two thousand songbooks! There was a lot of back and forth that lasted for over a year before we received permission to have the books.

I suppose the difficulties and problems are what strengthen one's faith. When everything comes smoothly and easily, our testimony does not grow. If an organization or a religion does not demand sacrifice, that religion will not be successful. That has been proven here time and again.

But I should also say that I do not like to designate those times for us as a time of sacrifice. I think of them now as beautiful times, which only goes to show that one forgets the bad and the unpleasant times and remembers only the beautiful. Isn't that always the case?

When we held a youth camp up on the Baltic or on Schwerin Lake, all the young people from the entire region were there. But it was not possible to reserve an area for a large group, so each individual had to make application to put his or her tent in the same area, and that way we could have a youth camp.

Gisela: The Church owned the tents, but each individual had to apply for permission to go camping and to bring his or her tent permission form along *[Zeltgenehmigung]*. But the Church set up the tents, and then we had our camp. It was all set up when we arrived. But it was so much fun to be together; it was always very, very lovely. We had so much fun. We played games. One time someone almost drowned; that was sad. But, that's the way it was.

Manfred: As I said, the district conferences, the activities in the branches and in the districts—these things really held us together, and I can only see these times in a very positive light. I would not like to even suggest that I regretted any of it.

Gisela: No, not at all. On the contrary. We stuck together.

Manfred: Of course, we didn't have a chance to go to the temple until the temple in Freiberg was built and dedicated in 1985. That blessing was for only a very few who had the possibility to travel to West Germany, people who were retired. There were a few exceptional cases where someone got into Switzerland to receive his or her endowments, but those were very, very few. I mean, of course that is a terrible restriction.

But we know that our Father in Heaven is a just God, and our Church leaders told us that whoever keeps the commandments of the Lord and is worthy to go to the temple and is not permitted to go through no fault of his or her own, that person will be accepted by the Lord. I mean, we couldn't go, but those who died and couldn't experience the temple during their lifetime can still receive these blessings through our doing this work for them. It will not be counted against them. That was the only really serious problem—that we couldn't have the temple and that we were not free to travel where we wanted.

Gisela: We were not free to preach the gospel.

Manfred: Yes, that is part of the story. Until the Wall was built in 1961, we had our own missionaries here in the GDR. There are a large number of brothers and sisters in the branches who served missions, who went tracting door to door, and who held the branches together by serving as branch presidents and priesthood leaders during those times.

Gisela: Sister Ortlieb, Brother Ortlieb, Brother Zwirner, and Bishop Schulze were missionaries. Our stake president, President Frank Apel, was the last missionary permitted to serve in the GDR.

Manfred: There were certainly some who took advantage of the opportunity. But I mean that was also certainly a sacrifice because it wasn't like it is now, go away for two years and then come back to your old profession. They were more or less held up to ridicule in public. The education system in the country was totally communistic so that there were frequent conflicts of conscience between those who were trained, so to speak, in the school system and those who were trained in the Church. On the other hand, the Church was always oriented toward obedience to the laws of the land—those who obey the laws of God will have no reason to disobey the laws of the land. That was always a basic principle of the Church to which we clung.

Take for example the events of 1988, when President Monson and the priesthood leaders met with Erich Honecker. One has to have faith in the leaders of the Church, faith that they are acting under the influence of the Spirit of the Lord and that they have made the right decisions. After all is said and done, the attacks of the devil are always turned to an advantage to promote the work of the Lord.

The Communists did not make these concessions out of pure humanitarian love and just for the sake of the Mormons. They were looking to their own advantages, financial advantages, for example. They knew that the Church would be building new buildings and that thereby Western currency would be coming into the country because all of the buildings would be paid for in hard currency. And they could also show that they were open to others and were trying to ease tensions according to the Helsinki agreements that were made, when was it, 1975, I believe. You have to see all of these things in context.

My belief is that we should see the entire history of the world in harmony with the history of the house of Israel and the development of the Church. Consequently, you can understand these things only in their context. You can't separate one event from another.

It was by means of this very intelligent Church leadership, working under the influence of the Spirit of God, that made it possible for us to have missionaries in our country again, for us to have a temple, for us to enjoy an easing of tensions so that we could import printed material, Church magazines, teaching manuals, etc. All of this has come about under this influence. And a mission has been opened, and we can have a patriarch. The first patriarch appeared suddenly overnight. Do you remember that?

Gisela: That was a real shock for us.

Manfred: That was the father of president Hans B. Ringger, Karl Ringger. He was the patriarch for Switzerland, and he got permission to come in for some occasion, probably a mission conference—it couldn't have been anything else. But suddenly, there he was, and the word went out that a few members of the branches now had the possibility of receiving their patriarchal blessing. Suddenly. Overnight.

Gisela: We were really surprised.

Manfred: Yes, of course. We were totally unprepared for such a thing. We didn't know how to go about it because we had never had such a thing before. It was such a surprise that here, in this country, we suddenly had the possibility of having this blessing. Later on, Brother Fetzer was called to be the patriarch for the Dresden mission, and he served until the stakes were organized. Then we had our own stake patriarchs.

I remember as a boy, as a twelve-year-old deacon, I gave my first talk in Semmelsberg. Semmelsberg is near Meissen, maybe thirty or thirty-five kilometers from Dresden. There was a little group there who were supported by members from the Dresden Branch, and every Sunday elders and sisters went out to visit them. We had to travel by public transportation. I went from Freital to Semmelsberg on a narrow-gauge railroad. It's gone now. It was torn up twenty years ago. Anyway, we met in the house of Brother and Sister Rudolf. We had our sacrament meetings in their house. We passed the sacrament and preached our sermons, did everything that belongs to a Church service, but all right in their living room.

G. Davis: And you gave your first talk there. What did you talk about?

Manfred: I don't remember anymore. I would have to look and see what's in the archives. But I'm sure it was something from the New Testament, some parable or event from the life of Christ.

G. Davis: You were bishop of the Dresden Ward when the first foreign missionaries arrived. What was that like?

Manfred: Yes, I was bishop at the time. On the day they arrived, we were having a wedding celebration at the chapel for our daughter Dörte. They immediately began with their new missionary methods that were totally foreign to us. They had such enthusiasm and, I must say, much more courage than we. They were so aggressive. They spoke to everyone without the slightest hesitation.

I mean, it was not that way with us here in the GDR. You couldn't just go up and speak to anyone; there were ears everywhere. You could never know when you were speaking to your neighbor whether or not he worked for the secret police. We were always very cautious; we talked around every subject and spoke only to very close friends and then behind closed doors.

But the missionaries who came in knew nothing about our habits. They were totally unburdened and talked with anyone and everyone, and I must say they had immediate success. Of course, that was the right time, when people were approachable about new things, when they were seeking, when they were curious to hear some new thing, a different ideology, a different religion, such things. That's one reason why they were so successful and got so many people to listen to them.

Gisela: And also one reason why so many of them no longer come.

Manfred: Yes, that's true, but you must admit, there are some who are still active.

Gisela: A very small percentage of them.

Manfred: Anyway, that was a totally new experience for us, the new missionaries.

27

We Couldn't Have Church Literature

Peter Menzel and Doris Menzel

We interviewed Peter Menzel and Doris Menzel on the balcony of their apartment in Leutewitz, not far from Sister Wöhe's home (see chapter 25). The Menzels are a quiet, unassuming couple with many talents. Brother Menzel is currently serving as bishop of the Dresden Ward.

Doris: My grandmother joined the Church in Breslau, and in 1945 we were evacuated from Breslau to Halle. My grandmother was the first one in our family to come into the Church.

G. Davis: And your mother?

Doris: She came to see a play my older sister was in. She just wanted to see what was going on, and she stayed. The thing my grandmother liked best about the Church was that she could do work for the dead and that she could live with her husband again. I think that was the major point, that she would see him again. So, I grew up in Halle, and that is where I met my dear husband, at a Church program in Halle. But that was a long time ago.

Peter: That was in 1960.

Doris: Then in 1965 we moved here to Dresden.

G. Davis: Were your parents already members of the Church, Peter?

Peter: No, none of my family were members. When I was eight years old, my mother took me for some medical treatment. The man who was treating me asked me what I had done the preceding Sunday, and I told him that I was chopping wood. He said that there were better things to do than chop wood on a Sunday and invited us to come to church. That was in Bischofswerda, and that is what brought my mother and me into the Church. The following Sunday, we attended church, and it wasn't long before we were both baptized.

G. Davis: Where did you learn to play the piano and the organ?

Peter: I started learning at home when I was twelve years old. I took lessons for about six months, and then there came a time in the branch when there was no one to play for them anymore, so I had to play.

Doris: Halle was a very small branch; there were about forty-five members on the records, and there were usually about fifteen or twenty in attendance.

G. Davis: Why did you come to Dresden?

Peter: I grew up in a small town, and my wife grew up in a large city. She said she wanted to live in a large town, so we came to an agreement that the first one to get an apartment, that's where we would live. I had just started my studies here in Dresden and got an apartment. That was the deciding factor. We moved to Dresden, and here's where we have stayed, much to the distress of my wife, who at first wanted to go back to Halle. Now she doesn't want to go back there anymore.

Doris: No, that's not entirely true.

N. Davis: So what was the Church like when you first moved to Dresden, in the former GDR?

Doris: To be honest, I have to say that I liked it better then than I do today. We were all so close to one another. I am not trying to say that I have anything against the new converts, quite the contrary. I think it is marvelous that the ward is growing. But in those days, everyone knew one another, there were not so many of us, everyone watched out for one another, and we all knew one another's problems. I find that with so many new members things are a little helter skelter.

Peter: There were many who came to the Church because they had problems, and when they saw that the kind of problems they had would not be solved by the Church, they stopped coming. Only a small percentage of the new converts are still active.

Doris: That's the way it is when things are not going so well, when we don't know what is coming next. There were many like that who were very receptive to the gospel but who now that things are going better would rather relax at home on Sunday. We used to have two hundred visitors when we had an open house; now very few show up.

Peter: When we have an activity, ten investigators may be there, not more. Last Saturday we had a concert. It was very nice, but the attendance was not good. That's the way it is now with all of our activities. People's interest has really dropped off.

Doris: They are oversaturated. Everyone is trying to work two or three jobs just to get along. I think it is too much. They have to really work hard nowadays, and they say that when the weekend comes they have to rest or do the housework.

G. Davis: It seems somewhat paradoxical to me that at the time when atheism was officially taught in the schools there was an interest in religion, but now that the people have freedom to think as they will, there is less interest in religion. Is that correct?

Doris: No, I don't think so. There was not much interest in religion in the GDR times. That came only during the transition period, when the people were so anxious about everything. They didn't know where to turn or what was going to happen. Some of them looked for an anchor in the Church.

Peter: Toward the end of the GDR, anything that was new attracted a lot of interest. There was an enormous number of visitors at the open house for the temple in Freiberg and also here in Dresden when we opened our new chapel. That was still during the GDR time, September 1988. There were a lot of people who came through the building. We had an activity every month. That was before the missionaries came, but there was a lot of curiosity and interest.

Doris: There were many people who stood in long lines at the temple up to four hours in order to get in and also at our new chapel. We had tours through all the rooms.

Peter: I remember one day we had an open house on a Saturday afternoon and had over five hundred visitors. That was back in the GDR time. We took people through the building, answered their questions, and told them about the basic doctrines of the Church and things like that. And we had a lot of visual material out. We had different rooms decorated to represent the various organizations—the Primary, Young Women, priesthood. We also showed some videos that attracted a lot of interest.

G. Davis: Was there any problem with the government because of the large crowds?

Peter: At the end of the GDR time, there was no problem. Of course, in the earlier years, this would have been out of the question.

Doris: There were hard times until the temple was built, and they allowed the temple to be built because that brought in hard currency. They could do nothing else.

Peter: The temple was built in 1985.

Doris: Then they became more generous.

Peter: The temple came first, and then approval was given for several new chapels.

G. Davis: Now young people are able to go into foreign countries on a mission.

Doris: Yes, the first missionaries that were called went to America; that was during the GDR time. Now that we can travel wherever we want, there is not so much interest in going abroad. Many are happy to stay here in Germany on their missions.

Peter: Well, that decision is made by the First Presidency. No one knows where he or she will be called.

G. Davis: What other interesting experiences have you had in the Church?

Peter: I remember a very interesting experience we had. One day we were in the branch house cleaning up . . . .

Doris: We were cleaning up in the coatroom.

Peter: We had just finished cleaning up, and suddenly the mission president came up to us and asked us if we would like to have a patriarchal blessing. We put away our brooms and rags and went into the office with the mission president for an interview and then directly into a room with the patriarch, where we received our patriarchal blessings. It was in 1971, and the patriarch was Brother Karl Ringger. He had just come to Dresden for a short visit and wanted to give some patriarchal blessings. It was our good fortune that we happened to be in the branch house doing some cleaning.

Doris: No one ever dreamed that a patriarch would come to visit our country.

Peter: That was unheard of at the time.

Doris: Unheard of. They wouldn't let anyone come in.

N. Davis: When did Brother Krause become a patriarch?

Peter: That was several years later. First Brother Ringger came in; then there was Brother Percy Fetzer. He came now and then, and a few had a chance to receive a patriarchal blessing. Then later Brother Krause was called to be a patriarch.

G. Davis: Had you ever been to the temple before 1985?

Peter: No.

Doris: But I had saved some money because my patriarchal blessing said that I would go to the temple one day and that I should prepare myself. I had saved two thousand marks. Two thousand marks was a lot of money for me at the time, and I saved it just to go to the temple. It would never have been enough, but I thought that with two thousand marks I was almost a millionaire.

G. Davis: You were saving your money to go to Switzerland.

Doris: That's right, but they wouldn't let us go.

G. Davis: What did you think when you heard that you would have a temple here in the GDR?

Doris: You could have knocked me over with a feather!

Peter: But that told us a lot. It drew attention to the fact that the GDR was so desperate, and since the temple would be built with dollars, they saw their chance. I mean, our Father in Heaven was directing things, that's understood, but hearts softened when they saw the hard currency; that smoothed the way.

N. Davis: Perhaps we could say that our Father in Heaven makes use of what is available.

Doris: Yes, that's clear. That was the only way we could ever have had a temple. The saddest thing about those days was that we couldn't have Church literature. I was at home in those days because I had three children, and I spent a lot of time copying teaching manuals with a typewriter and carbon paper. We didn't have copy machines or computers then. I tried to make eight copies at once.

N. Davis: And if you made a mistake, you had to correct eight copies?

Doris: No way, we left the mistakes alone. There weren't so many mistakes, and if there were a few typos, that wasn't so bad.

N. Davis: That must have been a lot of work.

Doris: A *lot* of work! It was permitted to make copies of things for your own use, and, no one ever went looking for the originals.

Peter: We had so few Church books, just the triple combination and a songbook.

Doris: There was a time when they told us we had to destroy our old copies of the *Stern,* copies we had from our grandparents that were thirty or thirty-five years old.

Peter: Everything we had from right after the war that had been brought in up until about 1950 or so had to be destroyed.

Doris: It was so wonderful when someone with permission to travel to the West would bring something back with them.

Peter: Everyone was so happy back then to get a magazine or a book, and now that you can get anything, there are plenty of people who have no interest in such things. When you don't have it, you try to get it, and when you have it, you don't use it.

28

In the Valley of the Naive

Manfred Schwabe and Elke Schwabe

When guests sit down to a meal at the home of Manfred Schwabe and Elke Schwabe, they are asked to join hands around the table as the blessing is asked. This practice illustrates the unity and love that permeates the lives of this couple and that is evident in the following interview.

Manfred: I came into the Church through two neighbors who first took my sister with them to the branch.

G. Davis: Your parents were not members?

Manfred: No, my parents were not members; my parents were divorced. There were five children in the family; my mother raised us alone. At first we made fun of my sister for going to church because we didn't know anything about it. I was maybe fourteen years old at the time. Then we decided that it might be interesting for us, because in those days the Church took a great interest in the youth, and by and by we began to attend MIA. I ought to add that we had to walk about half an hour to get to the branch house. In those days, MIA was held during the week, and on Sunday we had Sunday School in the morning and sacrament meeting in the afternoon. So we had to do a lot of walking when we walked half an hour to church in the morning and half an hour home again and repeated this in the afternoon.

   I wasn't baptized for quite a long time. I was seventeen years old when I was finally baptized, but I had been active in the branch activities all that time. We had a fairly large branch for those days. In 1956, I moved to Leest and continued to be active in the Church.

G. Davis: What positions did you have in the Church?

Manfred: That's hard to say now. I don't really remember. You see, in a small branch everyone has to do something, so I must have also done something, but that was all too long ago. I don't remember all the things I did in the Church. The history of the Leest Branch is an interesting one. When I arrived, there was this Sister Kolbin. Her maiden name was Bade. Her mother was very instrumental in building up that branch. She had the missionaries come.

Elke Schwabe and Manfred Schwabe. On their wedding day, July 3, 1982. Courtesy Elke and Manfred Schwabe.

Elke: Two missionaries came, and they taught this Sister Bade. She became a member of the Church and made her home available for meetings. Things were rather primitive in those days. There was no running warm water. She did have electricity but not much room.

Manfred: She just turned over the main floor of her house.

Elke: She tore out a wall of the house, and out of the two rooms—a bedroom and a living room—she made one large room, which was then used for the Church meetings.

Manfred: This was the meeting place of the Church until the new ward building was completed.

Elke: By then both of the parents had died, and the only one left living in the house was a daughter-in-law.

Manfred: She remodeled the barn and lived in the barn.

Elke: We continued renting this house until the new chapel was completed.

Manfred: Old Brother Kolbin was a Russian POW who had been captured during World War I and was working here in Germany as a POW when he met this Sister Bade.

G. Davis: So Kolbin is a Russian name.

Manfred: Yes. His son was the branch president; that was about 1960. His counselor, Brother Richter, was then branch president for a long time until his son took over the branch.

    That was a nice life in such a small branch. There were thirty members, maybe thirty-five, and we all worked together. In a small branch, everyone helps one another more than in a large branch. It took us a long time to get used to living here in the Dresden Ward with 150 to 200 members.

    But this Sister Kolbin, she was the sister who brought our family into the Church in Naumburg. She was born in Naumburg and lived just a few houses down from us. Through her family, my sister came into the Church. She married one of the Kolbin sons, and they moved to Leest.

    From the very beginning, my mother thought our joining the Church was fine. She had only asked us that we first all be confirmed into the Evangelical Lutheran Church. In my case, I did this but then left the Evangelical Church and was baptized in the LDS Church. I was baptized in the Saale River. It was in October, and the water was plenty cold, but I was so full of enthusiasm.

    Nowadays it is no big thing to step down into the baptismal font with the warm water. Back then they used to baptize in a lake. It didn't matter how cold the water was. We were just talking about that recently. There are some members who want to baptize their children where they were baptized here in Dresden, in the Briesnitz Lake. Now they can baptize them in the font at the ward house, but the children say, "No, Papa. We want to be baptized where you were baptized." So they go out to Briesnitz Lake and baptize their children.

Elke: Would you like to hear my story?

G. Davis: Yes, let's hear about your family and how you came into the Church.

Elke: Well, my grandmother, Martha Gebauer, and my mother, Hedwig Gorczychowski, were taught by the member missionaries in the Leest Branch. I think it was Sister Anna Meier. I don't remember who her companion was, but they taught Grandma and Mom about the gospel. They taught them for a long time until they understood everything about the gospel, and then they were baptized. Dad was never baptized during his lifetime. He was Evangelical Lutheran and was determined to remain Evangelical. Of course, it was often pretty hard for Mom to maintain the proper balance. When both husband and wife are not in the same church together, it can be rather difficult.

I was baptized in the summer when I was eight years old. I was afraid of the water. I had always had trouble with my ears and I was afraid I would get an ear infection. Nothing happened, fortunately. I grew up as one of the young people in the Leest Branch. I had a lot of friends. We put on a lot of productions, and the young people from Berlin often joined us. Because Leest is such a small place, just a little village, there were a lot of woods in the area, and we played there a lot, the kind of games little kids play. I was a Beehive girl and worked on my beehive. I remember my teacher, Ursel Zobel. Later when she got married she was Sister Brünning. She spent a lot of time with us.

In 1954 we had a big youth conference here in Dresden. We camped out in tents. That's where I met Manfred. We began writing to one another, and then he started coming to visit me on weekends. He often rode his bicycle all the way from Naumburg to Leest, 250 kilometers. He would start out after work on Friday, ride all night, and get to Leest early on Saturday morning. I could never understand it in those days—so much energy, so much courage, and, well, probably a little portion of love. But I was probably too young, too much of a child to really understand it. We were together this way for three years, including our common activities in the Church at the youth conferences.

In 1957 we split up. We somehow thought we didn't belong together, or maybe we were still too young. I thought, "I'm too young to get married at seventeen." But then I married out of the Church! There were not very many young men in the Church, and I married out of the Church, and I sorely regretted it.

I realized then what kind of a life my mother had had. Maybe it was even a little harder for me because I couldn't attend church. I couldn't take the children to church, and I couldn't teach them at home. But as long as I lived in Potsdam and Bonnstadt, the members visited me. Then my marriage reached a crisis. There was a divorce, and I could finally become active in the Church again with my daughter. Of our three children, she was really the only one I could teach, and we had wonderful experiences together. The young people in the Church in Leest helped her a lot. She had friends in the Church, and they became her example. She learned a lot from them and decided to be baptized.

It was a very rainy day. I remember thinking, "If it doesn't let up, how are we going to get from the bus down to the lake?" It was bad. The baptism was to be outside in a lake. But we had a meeting first, and then we drove to the lake, and while we were driving, it cleared up. That was really a testimony for me. The sun came out, and we had a beautiful baptism. It was so lovely. My daughter was so excited. We were just a small group. Many of the members had little children and couldn't get away, but it was so lovely. There was a wonderful spirit there.

Manfred came to the baptism, and that was a new beginning for us. He had been divorced for some time, and I had just gotten a divorce. My husband really wanted me to come back to him. He made me an offer. I had just gotten my driver's license, and he said he would buy me a Trabi [a small, East-German automobile] if I would come back, but I had other ideas. Manfred and I married, and from that day on, we have both been active in the Church. We were married in 1982, and we moved to Dresden in 1983. I was the Sunday School secretary; then I went on a stake mission; then I taught Primary. Then we both went on a stake mission, my second mission. That's my story.

Manfred: Mine is quite different. My first job in the ward here was as president of the Sunday School. That's an interesting story. Brother Erich Ortlieb had been a missionary in Leest back in 1959 or 1960. The missionaries often came to eat dinner with us. That was quite common then; we always invited them over for dinner. When I showed up in the Dresden Ward, he was the first one to recognize me although to be honest I didn't recognize him anymore. He was the bishop of the ward, and he asked me what I could do in the Church.

I had very little self-confidence. I had been active again for only a short time, but he said: "How would you like to be the president of the Sunday School?" I said, "No! I could never do that. I'm not qualified. I'm just new in the ward." "You can do it. You can do it. I'll support you. You just need a couple of counselors, and you'll be on your way." So I was on my way, and I must say I was quite surprised how well things went.

I was president of the Sunday School for a few years, and then we were called on a stake mission. It was just at the time when we had the open house at the temple in Freiberg. There had been so many visitors to the temple, and we helped with the open house. And then suddenly we had thousands of names of people who wanted to know more about the Church, long lists of names. They all wanted to know about the Book of Mormon. We started going through this list of names and giving out copies of the Book of Mormon. After our stake mission was over, Elke became secretary in the Relief Society, and I became the ward financial clerk.

Elke: Then came another stake mission.

Manfred: That's right. They needed more stake missionaries, so now we are missionaries again.

Elke: We were called just three weeks ago.

Manfred: When we first came to Dresden, we were back and forth between Dresden and Potsdam before we got this apartment. It's not always been so easy to get an apartment here. In Pilnitz, I had a little apartment which was damp and smelly because the drain system was not working properly. Because of that, we thought we could count on getting an apartment here from the AWG Collective.

G. Davis: AWG?

Manfred: It is called the *"Arbeiterwohnungsbaugenossenschaft"* [Workers Housing Construction Collective].

Elke: Was called.

Manfred: Yes, now it is called the *"Eisenbahnerwohnungsbaugenossenschaft"* [Railroad Housing Construction Collective] or just "the Collective." All of the apartment buildings in this whole area and where Sister Wöhe lives are buildings built by the Collective. The group here, which forms the middle axis, are the so-called communal houses. They belong to the city or to the Communal Housing Authority. There are altogether about fifteen thousand apartments here.

Anyway, the way it was back then, if you wanted to get an apartment, you had to pay a certain amount as a down payment, and then you had to put in a bunch of hours in labor. You had the choice of putting in your labor hours with your business or for the AWG. If you put in your hours with the AWG, you had to do landscaping, etc. We put in our hours at the business. We had to clean out all the old files from an entire archive in the place where I was working at the time.

Elke: The entire floor was covered with all the old files from the old bureaucracy.

Manfred: Clear back to 1910. We spent several weekends on this old dirty floor.

Elke: Yes, covered with dust. I about ruined my elbows. Lots of pain. I had to have X-rays.

Manfred: But that is how we actually got this apartment so quickly.

Elke: We had to put in 780 hours of labor and pay 2,300 marks down. Then we had to pay an additional 1,300 marks to have a kitchen installed, which we never got to see before we moved in. They said: "When you have paid for the kitchen, you can have a key to the apartment." So we bought the apartment without ever seeing the kitchen. But the most important thing in the whole matter—and this was a real testimony to me—was the way we fasted and prayed that we would get the apartment. I wanted to get out of where I was living. My divorced husband was still living in my apartment in Potsdam, and there was often a lot of friction.

[Marriage and divorce had little to do with housing in the GDR. Because housing was controlled by a state or city housing authority and apartments were assigned solely on the number of occupants, divorced couples were commonly forced to continue occupying the same apartment after their divorce. This does not imply that they were "living together." Obtaining another apartment was often quite impossible.

Also, newly married couples frequently had to continue living with their own parents, sometimes for a year or more, because they were normally not allowed to apply for a joint apartment until after they were married. It was common for a couple to have one or two children before they could begin occupying the same apartment.]

Manfred had a damp place which was actually just a room and a half. Very small, no water. Not even a washbasin, nothing. So we prayed hard that it would work out.

A co-worker in Manfred's business who was in charge of apartments told us, "You'll never get an apartment in less than three years. I've put through so many applications and have chased around between so many offices. You can just forget it."

Manfred: Listen to this. I was allowed to apply for only a two-room apartment. I decided I wanted to apply for a three-room apartment instead of a two-room apartment. My co-worker, the one who worked with the Housing Commission (every business had its own housing commission), the one who oversaw the distribution of apartments in cooperation with our business, said, "You'll never get it. You'll never get a three-room apartment. I've been all the way up to the city commissioner, argued about this and that. It doesn't work." I said, "You know what? I'm going to try it anyway." "Forget it. No use even turning in the application."

But we prayed about it and said it had to work. We made an appointment with the head of the collective. We both went. I laid out my problem to him. He took up his pen, crossed out "two-room" and wrote in "three-room." Did she stare at that, my co-worker! She said, "That can't be!" As we were going out, she said, "You know what? Either you are very lucky or something. . . . Something's not going to work out. That *can't* be. I could never have pulled that off. And you go in, tell him what you want, and you get it."

There was another thing. We were supposed to have waited at least three years. But actually, from the moment we were accepted into this collective, the waiting period—with all its red tape—was just exactly eleven months until we moved in. There were three men ahead of me who were supposed to get an apartment. One of them said he didn't need it at the time. The other one said, "I'm not moving out to Grobitz in that dirt pile." It was really terrible out here while they were building. We had to wear rubber boots when we went to work in the morning. Then the other one said, "No, I'm not moving out to Grobitz," and suddenly I was at the top of the list. I couldn't believe it. Can you imagine that?

Well, that was a testimony to me that prayer helps. My co-worker had said, "It can't be done. It can't be done. If I hadn't seen that with my own eyes. . . . You come in, tell your story, and he takes his pen and changes the two-room into a three-room." She said, "And I've fought and fought and fought a dozen times with that same guy. He never changes a policy. Never!" Well, he did!

N. Davis: Did I hear you say that your former husband was still living in your apartment in Potsdam with your family after you were divorced?

Elke: Yes, I was living in Potsdam, and my former husband was still living in the apartment. He had one room to himself, but we had to share the kitchen.

Manfred: Kitchen and bath.

Elke: He always had to come through my room to get into the kitchen. It was a little difficult. Besides, the apartment had been tacked on to make it larger, for a doctor's family I believe. There were actually five or six rooms. Two families lived on that floor. The back part was divided off. We had the back part, and another family lived in the front. There was only one bath for both families, and it was just divided off by a curtain. It was a little complicated.

We had divided the bath off so that we could have a kitchen. At first there was no kitchen in our apartment. The kitchen was then about two square meters, I think.

Manfred: About like this one.

Elke: Well, I think this one is a little larger. You see, my daughter Petra wanted to come with us, and the boys stayed in Potsdam. The older boy was about finished with his schooling, and the younger one wanted to stay with his father. But Petra wanted to come with us, and a two-room apartment would have been too small. That's why we tried to change the two-room apartment into a three-room one. I have a few pictures here of the muddy swamp we lived in at first. It was interesting.

G. Davis: What were your happiest times in the Church?

Manfred: When I was growing up.

Elke: I would say so, too.

Manfred: We had very little money, so there were not many possibilities. But we traveled. We traveled by bicycle. On Saturdays we worked until noon, and then we jumped on our bicycles. We rode out to see the Fuchs family. They had seven boys. They belonged to the Naumburg Branch. They lived about twenty kilometers away. If there was someone there, we took them along. We went on to Jena. Sister Kolbin's sister, Anna Rose Bock, lived there. After visiting her, we went on to Weimar. That was another twenty kilometers. That makes forty, sixty kilometers on a Saturday afternoon. Oh boy, the members in Weimar were happy to see us. "Man, we were just going for a bike ride, over to Badberger. Come with us. We'll make a picnic out of it." Of course, we went along.

We had a good relationship with the members in Weimar, and they always invited us over to the National Theater. They got good tickets for us, and the Naumburgers and the Weimarers went to the theater together. I can still remember as well as if it were yesterday, seeing my first great opera performance, *Tannhäuser.* It was organized by the Church. Well, there was always something going on. We were always going somewhere. There was no TV. We didn't have that problem, yet, of sitting in front of the TV. And we put on plays or did a little scene or just spent the evening talking. At MIA there was always something, but we had to do it ourselves. Oh, that was a lot of fun. Everyone brought out whatever talent he or she had. Everyone did what he or she could. One person set up the stage and decorated it a little. The others put on the play. There were many, many, many beautiful hours that we spent together.

Elke: And my childhood and growing up in the Church was the most beautiful time of my life, too. I learned many, many wonderful lessons during those postwar days—mostly from the older members, as I think back. I would go out with my mother and grandmother into the fields to glean some wheat or some leftover potatoes. Or after we had eaten the evening meal, our neighbors, members, came over to visit with us, and we sat around the kitchen table by candlelight and listened to them tell stories about their lives. Those were the most impressive times for me.

Or there were the youth conferences we held when the Berliners came out to visit us. Our mothers in the Leest Branch got together and donated what little they had and made a potato salad, and one donated some sausages and another something from their kitchen. The parents prepared this for us, and we had a wonderful afternoon. We did that at least twice a year, in the spring and in the fall. The Berliners lived in the big city, and they liked to come out to see us. Those were beautiful times.

But like I said, with the older members, that was also beautiful, out in the fields and then together in the evenings. We had a lot more time for one another than we do today. We don't have so much contact with one another today, and maybe even less here in the large ward in Dresden. Of course, the members here in Dresden are all very nice and dear brothers and sisters, and there is no one I don't like. But still, the togetherness was much more evident in our small branches. There were only a few men and maybe only thirty or thirty-five members all together.

Right after the war, significantly more people came out because the Church took care of them. We had food packages and used clothing, and things went better for us. But there were many who later left, who had come to us just because they were hungry. But this togetherness has given me so much, where there were so few of us, and we had so little, and we had to help one another with what little we had.

I remember that Mom used to make "spinach" out of other leafy garden plants, and sometimes we ate it with a few potatoes. We didn't have meat very often. We had a garden, and Dad used to try to grow grain, and we had rabbits and small animals, chickens, and a few ducks. Once we had a goat for milk.

Manfred: And a sheep.

Elke: Yes, later we had a buck sheep. Anything, so that we could have a little meat. After the war, we had to have ration cards for food.

You could have a certain amount of sugar and a certain amount of flour. And you got your meat and milk according to your card. Those who had children got considerably more. But you had to watch how you went through your food supply. The rich people who had a lot of material things—they could say, well, I'll just trade my jewelry with a farmer for some food. Lots of people came out of the cities to trade with the farmers.

Manfred: People traded rugs. Yes. The farmers were all rich. They could have carpeted their cow barns.

Elke: Those were hard times. Many people were starving.

G. Davis: But I have heard others say that in spite of the hard times, those were also the happiest times in the Church; everyone supported one another and stuck together.

Manfred: Yes, that's right. In 1954, when we had the youth conference here in Dresden, when we got acquainted, we slept on straw. You couldn't imagine such a thing nowadays. Brother Bory, who is dead now, worked for the racetrack here in Dresden, took care of the horses. He arranged it so that we could sleep on straw. The girls slept somewhere else.

Elke: We slept in the chapel. A few had air mattresses, but we slept on straw, too, for the most part, with just a blanket over us. Usually upstairs, above the large hall—that's where we slept.

Manfred: Once we joined with the West Berliners and took a bus over to Webitzburg near Paderborn.

Elke: That was in 1957.

Manfred: We went to West Berlin and went across the border with them.

N. Davis: That was before the Wall.

Manfred: Yes. We went to the Teutoburger Forest in Westphalia, near Paderborn. There is a small youth hostel there, and that's where we had our youth conference. I can still remember when we crossed the border: the West Berliners just sat in the bus, but we East Germans had to get out of the bus and go through a passport control. We were traveling in a West Berlin bus, and they wanted to know what we thought we were doing. We had official authorization to go out of the country, but they had to check everything over. Back then if anyone had permission to travel to the West, they looked you over very suspiciously.

G. Davis: Were there other difficulties with the government?

Manfred: After the political change [*"Wende,"* i.e., the reunification of East and West Germany], I was able to look at my personal files, including letters of recommendation, which I had not been permitted to see up to that time. In the files was a report on my "civic reliability" from 1959. It stated that I had been a good worker but that I had been dedicated member of a religious sect in Leest. That was in my files.

Elke: And that is the reason you were not allowed to go to the university.

Manfred: Yes, I think that's right. Back then I had made an application for a program in what they called "Socialistic Industry." That was a program different from the program for craftsman, which wouldn't have helped me anyway because I could not have gotten a job with a craftsman degree in a government-owned firm *[Volkseigener Betrieb]*. Anyway, I was turned down. That was in 1959.

I was forced to continue in the craftsman department where I was. I could not advance because I could not get the technical training I needed. That cost me a lot of money over the years. If you owned your own shop, a craftsman degree would be fine, but that was impossible for me. So, I could learn the theoretical things, but I could not get a degree because I was not permitted to do the practical side. I ran up against the same problem later when I wanted to study engineering. There was no way in. And they really needed trained engineers who could take over important positions in industry.

As it turned out, I was often given assignments in our firm for which I should have had an engineering degree, but, as I said, I had not been allowed to get one. Some time later, when I was older, I gave it another try and was accepted! But then I developed some health problems and couldn't finish. I just couldn't do it. I was over forty then. Trying to do it on the side while working full time—that was the problem. I had to take at least one day a week away from my job and let my own work go. Then, of course, when I came back the next day, I had twice as much to do. And then I had my homework on top of that. My health just wouldn't take it. I had to give it up after two years. I just couldn't do it. If I had had a job without a lot of responsibility, I might have been able to do it, but when one has a responsible position, doing an engineering degree on the side is impossible.

G. Davis: So, you had these difficulties in your profession. Were there other troubles because of the Church?

Manfred: No. No. No. When one makes a firm decision for the Church, when one makes it clear where one stands, they watch you pretty closely. You are not looked up to like those who join the party. That much is clear. The party comrades had their own circle, and I was not a part of it. And whatever was decided by the party leadership became the law in our firm. Consequently, there was not much of an opportunity to influence what was done. But, all in all, when you did your work, there were no major problems.

There were disadvantages, however. Your "social contributions" were also evaluated, and when it came to bonuses, you would have to figure that you would earn considerably less money in comparison to those who belonged to the party or who went along with the party. That was normal procedure. I might have done just as much work as the person next to me, who was a member of the party, but we both knew that when our "social contributions" were evaluated, we who did not belong to the party would be rated lower and consequently would be left out when the bonuses were distributed. It made no difference how hard you worked. The other guy could be a terrible worker, but if he belonged to the party, he would get just as much as you. That's the way it was.

G. Davis: Did you participate in the demonstrations?

Manfred: Basically there were two demonstrations. There was one on the first of May. You had to participate in that whether you wanted to or not.

Elke: That was obligatory. If it came on a weekday, we had to make up the work on Sunday. On this day, everybody marches, and so we had to march. That's the way it was arranged.

Manfred: In the last few years, it was sometimes possible to say, "I can't come to work on Sunday." If I had a particular assignment in one of the meetings, for example, I might just say I couldn't come. "I'm very sorry, but I have an assignment at church." They grumbled but accepted it.

G. Davis: That is interesting. So these demonstrations were organized by your firm.

Manfred: No. The firm was told what to do. They were told how many of their workers had to participate. It was all organized from higher up.

G. Davis: Did you participate in any of the political demonstrations against the government at the time of the big political upheaval [in 1989]?

Manfred: The Monday demonstrations. Yes, I participated just to see what was going on. But for those officially orchestrated demonstrations, you had no choice. When we were still in Potsdam and an official government delegation came into Berlin, we had to stand at the Potsdam train station and wave and wave and clap and clap. Each firm had to produce so many wavers and clappers, but we got off work to do it.

Elke: They just came to where we were working and pulled us off. Sometimes we were taken into Berlin in a bus.

Manfred: In those cases, there wasn't much you could do about it. But, as I said, more recently (at least it worked for me once) I just said, "Today is Sunday, and I have something to do at Church. I'm sorry, but I can't join you. Normally, I go along, so please don't take it the wrong way, but this time I can't go to the demonstration with you." So!

N. Davis: But you did participate in the demonstrations of 1989?

Manfred: Yes, I went a few times, yes.

Elke: You went by yourself.

Manfred: Yes, but we followed the development of events for sure. When we were in Potsdam, we had the possibility of receiving West German TV. Here in Dresden, it was at first a little hard. Dresden was known as the Valley of the Naive and Out-of-Reach Dresden. That was just a little joke because Dresden was beyond the reach of the ARD—the West German television transmitters. Everyone in East Germany could pick it up except Dresden. But what happened was that the whole housing project was connected to a cable system and fitted up with a satellite dish. That was in 1987 or 1988.

Elke: The cable was already installed.

Manfred: Yes, the cable was there, but then it was fitted up to the satellite dish so that we could pick up western TV in this entire housing area. Then it came into all the new housing areas because the people were so furious that everyone else could pick up western TV and they couldn't. So, eventually we here in Dresden also got a look at western TV. But there were still problems. There are two systems in Europe and a third in America. The GDR had the French SECAM system. We were lucky. We brought our TV from Potsdam that had both European systems built into it.

I was in Leest for two weeks without an antenna and didn't know it. I only noticed that one evening when I was switching the

GDR channels to pick up an old movie. They always showed an old movie on Monday evenings—one from the 1950s, or even earlier. I liked to watch them. Then I noticed that I didn't need an antenna. I could see the West Berlin TV tower when I looked out the window—right in front of my nose. It couldn't have been more than fifteen kilometers away. So I could pick it up.

Well, getting back to the political developments; they began coming to a head in 1989. You could see from the economy how things were developing. There were a lot of people who were saying openly that we were returning to a "natural" economy, that is, an economy based on the barter system: you give me that, and I will give you this in exchange. Money had become useless, you see.

The system was I need this and that for my firm, and if you can get that for me, I can provide you with this in return. One firm needed heaters, and the other firm needed heating elements. One firm had the elements, and the other had the heaters, or he knew where he could get them—from a guy who needed something else. The whole economy was being run by this method. You needed something for your work and you had to get it one way or another and that was usually by knowing someone who needed something you could supply. The whole thing was very official, no deception, no smuggling. We called it "mutual socialistic assistance" *[gegenseitige sozialistische Hilfe]*.

Here's how it worked. I go to a firm from which I need something, and he gets from me a piece of paper which says, "We request in the form of mutual socialistic assistance the following," and then we declare that we are prepared to exchange this thing or the other. In that way, each firm had a bill, and the bill was marked "paid in full." The value of the goods was immaterial; it was just a formality. It was just our goods for your goods.

Elke: Well, that's not the whole story. There were plenty of times when the goods you needed were simply not available. I would also like to add that there were a lot of things that were available only to certain firms but not to the people. Many things were very hard to get.

Manfred: That's right. Basically the economy had come to a dead-end, and everyone was saying it couldn't go on like this. It was an economy based on central planning, and everything ran according to the plan. But there are plenty of things you simply can't plan. You see, if I know that I have to plan two years in advance what material I am going to need to produce something—makes no difference what—but I don't yet know what I'm going to be producing two years from now, then what's to plan? It doesn't make sense. And when you see the whole picture, you can see that very often we had to operate right on the border between what was legal and what was illegal in order to keep the plant going.

Officially, maybe it was forbidden. So, they made a deal with the plant. They would say: "Now look. You put your people on vacation, see. Then you make us this or that machine. We will pay you, not officially through the firm, but we will pay the workers individually, on the side." They called it the New European Way. That was going on. It was legal, but you could never do it officially! At that moment, the whole production of the plant broke down. Something had to be done.

Elke: I would like to say that there was a positive side to all of this political business and that was the social side. Everyone had a job, and it was guaranteed. No one had to worry that he or she would have to go looking for work, unless they had really messed up. Otherwise they had a job, and mothers, too, and pregnant women.

Manfred: And women with little children.

Elke: They had their jobs. And they knew very well that if I am going to have a baby then I will have a certain amount of time in which to recuperate, and I know that my job is secure. I know I am not going to be thrown out in the meantime. I will get my job back, and I can keep working. That's not the case anymore. I think some things have gotten worse, especially for us older people.

Manfred: But sometimes they took this too far. If a man in your company was an alcoholic, for example, the collective in your department would have to worry about him and would have to try some way, well, to keep things going, to help out. Actually, there were many, many things at the plant that were just pushed aside. The State should have taken some action.

Elke: But there was no unemployment, was there? And there were no homeless, not one. We didn't have that. The State saw to it that people in jail had a place to live when they got out, that they had a roof over their heads. The State provided at least a minimum of furniture and took care of them, so to speak. They worked them back into some business or firm so that they had a place to live, and they had work so that they could pay their own way. That wouldn't be possible today.

Manfred: Yes, and there are plenty of people today in the GDR who are ending up in jail because they can't make it out there. But that's another matter.

G. Davis: Have you had much success as stake missionaries?

Manfred: Some, some.

Elke: Well, convert baptisms? In that sense, we haven't had too much success, but we have taught a lot of lessons.

Manfred: You know what I really like, what's really beautiful about our second stake mission, is giving the fellowshipping discussions after the baptism. You can do a good work by helping the new converts take their first steps in the ward. I find this really helps the new members. You know from your own experience where the little cliffs are, where the little problems lie. If you build a trusting relationship with the people you are teaching, it stays. They come back to you again and again because they know they can rely on you, that what you tell them is right.

You know what? As a stake missionary, you learn more than the people you teach. We learned this on our first stake mission. You suddenly know things that you didn't know you knew. The influence of the Holy Ghost—even if you can't describe it, you can feel it the moment you start talking with investigators or with other people. On our first stake mission we worked with the lists of temple visitors. We were often invited to speak to groups: Catholic groups, Evangelical groups, and so on. Then came the questions. I can honestly say that in such a situation you know things, things you get directly from the Spirit, because you really didn't know them before that moment.

Elke: There were a lot of people who wanted information, but we didn't actually bring any of them into the Church. We gave the discussions. We had many very interesting discussions with people who were, I would say, quite open-minded. But the last step was somehow lacking. Maybe I should say we lacked the courage to help the investigators overcome that last hurdle.

G. Davis: But what Manfred was just telling us is when you learn something yourselves that is also a form of success.

Manfred: You know, Garold, we have invited colleagues or neighbors in and have invited the missionaries to meet them, but usually they liked to listen and then that was all. Or we have made appointments, and sometimes the missionaries didn't keep them.

Elke: Yes, and then the missionaries changed off with one another. And then they were transferred somewhere else, and the whole thing fell through. That was certainly the case with us once. We had an appointment with a colleague of mine. We spoke to her later, and she was still interested. She wanted to learn, but the children were . . .

Manfred: Were against it. That was back before the big political change. But it is true. When you are active in the Church and work hard, I have learned that no matter what, the end result is that you benefit the most. It doesn't matter what calling you have. We are just talking about missionary work because that is what we have done the most of. I say this in spite of the many disappointments, and we have had some disappointments.

Elke: Many times I went out the door crying.

Manfred: You know, when you have been with some investigators and you are going back one evening and you are thinking to yourself, "I hope, I hope . . ." And then they open the door, and say, "Na. We're not interested anymore." So, you turn around. What else can you do. But all in all, you experience tremendous spiritual growth—you really feel the workings of the Holy Ghost. I have to say that. Many a time when we came home from doing missionary work, we just looked at one another and said, "How were we able to discuss this or that with the investigator?" Sometimes it was so strange.

We had an investigator once who lived out here in Grobitz, and we had a program at the ward building, the old one. We didn't have a car at the time, so he brought us home in his car. We parked on the corner, and then came one question after another. After an hour, we were still sitting in the car. There were things that came up that, I must admit, that I had never known before. I would have said to myself, "You can't answer that question." But I did, because in that moment I felt the guidance of the Spirit.

Elke: I would like to say that that is part of missionary work as such, whether you are a stake missionary or not. When we have been on vacation, we have run into people who wonder why we don't drink coffee or alcohol.

Manfred: That is usually the opening. Why don't you drink alcohol?

Elke: We give them a direct answer. There was someone in our tour group who came to the church and brought us some information about his club. But he was interested. He wanted to see the building, and after the meeting, we gave him a tour. We answered his questions and invited him to come back, you see. There are some members who will misconstrue this. I don't always go up to the front at testimony meeting and bear my testimony before all the congregation, but when I am asked in this way, an answer is always there. To be honest, I've always been that way, whether I am a missionary or not. Every member is a missionary.

Manfred: You know, this is how it is. I can say so from my own experience. There was a time after my divorce when I did not come to church. Everything was in a turmoil. But then there comes a time when you say to yourself that life can not go on like that, because you have been used to something else, because you have known something better. You realize how things are going, but God is always guiding you. When you have turned away from the Church and from the members and don't attend anymore, you have to notice that something is missing from your life.

I had come to this point when everything was coming together. But as soon as I made my decision to go back to church, I had the feeling that stones were being thrown in my path to hinder me. I really had the feeling that Satan was trying to hold me back with force. It was just exactly at this same time that Elke and I met one another again. When I was beginning to feel a little better about myself, suddenly there was Erich Ortlieb to bring me into full activity. And there I was. You just can't imagine what it was like. For years I was inactive, and suddenly I was the president of the Sunday School.

Well, I have to repeat it; when you work in the Church and always try to do what there is to do and what they ask you to do, you grow. You grow, and you don't notice it, and then suddenly you see that you have come a little further, a little further. You have gained a little more understanding.

But you have to maintain your relationship with the members so that you feel good about yourself. We had a few problems in the large ward at the beginning, as I said. But now I find I can't stay away. You really miss it when you can't be at church on Sunday. That's why when we are on vacation somewhere and have the opportunity to go to church, we always take it.

Elke: To sum it all up, when we met the second time, I said to myself, "If I ever marry again, then only in the Church. Only in the Church."

PART IV

A BRIGHTER DAY

In 1979, President Thomas S. Monson assembled a small group of Church leaders on a hill between Meissen and Dresden. Looking down into the Elbe Valley, he offered a prayer in behalf of the members of the Church in the German Democratic Republic. [See *Ensign,* May 1989.] In 1982 the first stake was formed. In 1984 the second stake was formed. In 1985 a temple was dedicated. In 1989 the Dresden Mission was opened, and ten missionaries were permitted to leave the country—the first in fifty years—and were assigned to missions in South America, the United States, Canada, and England. The following spring, a second group of ten missionaries were called; this group included five sister missionaries. Now "all of the promised blessings have been fulfilled."

In the three short chapters that follow, Elke Schulze writes about her reaction to the building of a temple. Then follow six short testimonies by some of the first converts to the Church after the opening of the Dresden Mission. These convert testimonies were written at our request shortly after their respective baptisms. Finally, we conclude these "recollections" with a short interview with two of the sister missionaries called from the Dresden Ward in the spring of 1990.

Reception for LDS missionaries given by the minister of ecclesiastical affairs of the GDR. The reception was just one important sign of the official acceptance of the Church's missionary program. East Berlin, June 1989. *First row, left to right:* Elder Roger Muir, President Henry Burkhardt, Stake Secretary for Ecclesiastical Affairs Kurt Loeffler, Martha Müller, Frank Apel (president of Freiberg Stake), Norma Davis, Garold Davis, President Hans B. Ringger (First Council of the Seventy, one of the several brethren who worked diligently to reestablish the missionary program), Manfred Schütze (president of Leipzig Stake), and Wolfgang Paul (president of Germany Dresden Mission). *Second row:* Elder Jörg von Allmen, Elder Thorsten Ludwig, Elder Clarke Hilbig, Elder Dale Moss, Elder Robbie Dean, Elder Steven Smith, Elder Craig Miles, Elder Mark Smith, Elder Jeffrey Engleke. *Third row:* Elder Dale Tingey, Elder Christopher Karpowitz, Elder William Powley, Elder Stephen Anderson, Elder Christian Yost, Elder Mont Diderickson (head down), Elder Fred Grimmer, Günter Schulze (head down). Courtesy Norma and Garold Davis.

29

A Temple in Our Country

Elke Schulze

Elke Schulze is the daughter of Günter and Hannelore Schulze (see chapter 17). Elke was one of the first sister missionaries to be called from the GDR and served in the California San Bernardino Mission, 1990–92 (see chapter 31). Before her mission, she was a dental assistant. In May 1995, she married Richard L. Walker in the Freiberg Germany Temple. She has been invaluable to us in preparing the material for this book.

On Sunday, October 10, 1982, our entire family was together—my parents [Günter and Hannelore Schulze]; my brothers, Olaf and Bernd, with their wives, Heidrun and Maja [Ortlieb]; and myself—and our papa invited us to go with him on a drive, an outing, on the following Saturday. Of course, the questions began then: "Where?" "Will we need to pack a lunch?" "What should we wear?" "How far are we going?" But we got no answer out of him to any of these questions. He just sat there silently, smiling. We tried our questions out on Mom, but she said, "I'm sorry, don't ask me. I've just heard about this for the first time myself." That seemed somewhat strange to us since our parents nearly always did things together. Suddenly we were all talking about a "pilgrimage," but no one knew where we were going, how far, or when we were coming back.

In the course of the week, my brothers called Papa to find out when we would be leaving. The week went by much too slowly to satisfy my curiosity. Finally, it was Saturday, October 16, 1982. Our pilgrimage began at 9:30 A.M. When we were all seated in the car trying to guess which direction we would be going, we soon found ourselves on the little highway leading over to Freiberg. At a special conference held on August 29 that year, the Freiberg Stake had been organized. The

Schulze family. *Left to right:* Günter Schulze, Hannelore Schulze, Norma Davis with her granddaughter Annika Davis, and Elke Schulze. The Schulze family were visiting in Provo at the conclusion of Elke's mission. October 1991. Courtesy Norma and Garold Davis.

stake president [Frank Apel] lived in Freiberg, but why were we going to see him, or would we be going further? No. Papa stopped the car outside the city overlooking a small rising piece of ground surrounded by a hedge and bordered by a small sports field. We all got out. We crossed the deserted street and walked out onto a large field. At the far end of the field, we could see a small housing development.

Papa became very serious, and with tears in his eyes, he put his arm around Mama's shoulder and said to us, "On this piece of ground a new chapel will be built for the Freiberg Ward—and—a temple of the Lord." It was unbelievable. A temple in our country! He then explained to us when the construction would begin and where the buildings would stand. We were speechless, and then the words from my patriarchal blessing came to mind: "You will experience the covenants, the holy covenants in the house of the Lord, which are necessary." Now this promise was going to be fulfilled so soon? I had often thought of these words. What possibility would I ever have of going to a temple—unless it would be after I was old enough to retire. This promise, which had always seemed something far, far off in the future, would now be fulfilled before any of the others. It was all so wonderful!

Then Papa said to me, "Elke, now you can understand why I could not satisfy your curiosity but had to be silent. I was not even allowed to tell Mama. Since 1978 negotiations have been going on between the Church and representatives of our government and we—the mission presidency of the Dresden Mission (Papa was second counselor at that time and Henry Burkhardt was president)—gave President Monson our word that we would not discuss this with anyone until the prophet made an official announcement about the building of the Freiberg Temple. And that is what he did at the fall general conference."

I was so proud of Papa. Mama didn't even know, and she had never asked him about it in spite of the many rumors that were going around. I had often thought to myself, Papa must know, he works for the Church. And after he told me, I was ashamed of myself because of my curiosity. And then Papa answered all of the many questions that were buzzing around in our heads. In the true sense of the word, this had been a wonderful and beautiful pilgrimage for us. We were very happy.

The ground breaking took place in the spring of 1984, and the construction on these beautiful buildings began.

In the summer of 1984, the institute program of the Church was inaugurated under the general theme, "What can I do to prepare myself for eternal marriage?" Sister Eva-Maria Bartsch [sister of Hans-Jürgen and Reiner Schlüter; see chapters 22 and 23] was the institute teacher in Dresden for the single adults, and her lessons were wonderful and spiritual. When our first year of institute came to an end, our temple was about to be completed, and we spoke frequently about sealing for eternity in the temple. We had so many questions and so many problems. There were many young sisters over twenty-one who could not be sealed to their parents until they had received their endowment. But we were all obsessed with the idea that it would be much more beautiful to receive the endowment for the first time with a partner to whom we would then be sealed for time and all eternity. I struggled with this problem. I did not want to go to the temple "alone." But I often heard the still, small voice telling me, "Do you know how long you may have to wait? The temple will soon be dedicated. The promises you have been given should be fulfilled, and you are not ready."

I fasted and prayed a lot during this time. I knew that it would not be right if I didn't go to the temple with my family, but I didn't like to feel this compulsion. I wanted to go because of an inner desire and to experience this joy myself. While I was studying and trying to prepare myself, I found my answer in my institute manual under the topic, "We Can Receive Personal Revelation in the Temple."

> When you have a problem think about it on your own, come to a conclusion, and then turn to the Lord with your problem and He will then give you an answer. However, if you do not receive an answer then I will tell you where you must go. Go to the house of the Lord. Go there with the righteous desire to do your duty. Then when you are within the holy walls of that building, where you are entitled to the Spirit of the Lord, then in a moment of stillness the answer will come. (Melvin J. Ballard)

This was my answer. I now had the desire to go to the temple even if I had to go as a single person. After making this decision, I felt so happy and so grateful. I copied out this quotation and sent it to another young sister thinking that it might help her also.

The beautiful time of the open house was from June 1 through 16, 1985, and I had the privilege of doing "temple duty." I helped people get their overshoes on and off in front of the temple, or I helped maintain silence in the temple, or I helped do missionary work in the chapel and on the temple grounds. It was a beautiful time of service and sacrifice. On a single day, there were seven thousand visitors, and in all ninety thousand people stood as long as five hours in the rain and storm in terrible weather in order to see our temple. The earlier prayer of Elder Thomas S. Monson as he dedicated this country—that the people would come and ask about the gospel—was now being fulfilled.

The laying of the cornerstone of the temple was held on June 28, and dedicatory sessions were held on June 29 and 30, 1985. It was so wonderful to see the General Authorities and to hear everything and to be permitted to participate!

Thursday, July 4, 1985, was a beautiful, sunny day. This was the day on which the members of the Dresden Ward were permitted to go to the temple for the first time. My mother had a responsibility in the nursery, so I went through the temple alone. I needed a lot of strength, and I received it as it beamed forth from the brothers and sisters in the temple. It was so beautiful to see all of the members of our ward united there together.

It is beautiful to receive the blessings of the temple. Since that day, I have been to the temple often to do work for the dead, and it is also beautiful to do something for others. But the thing that has brought me the greatest happiness has been that I have been able to feel a peace, a calmness, and a security about my own future. Now I know that if we are true to our Heavenly Father then all of the promises he has given us will be fulfilled.

Open house for the Freiberg Germany Temple. June 1–16, 1985, long lines of people waited their turn to tour the temple, sometimes in rainy weather. Elke Schulze was one of the Saints who helped host the visitors. Courtesy Elke and Manfred Schwabe.

30

Conversion Stories

Annett Kaiser, Leipzig Ward
Baptized May 7, 1989, Age 17

On April 29, I visited the church house in Leipzig for the first time to watch the baptism of a good friend. He had already told me a lot about the missionaries and also about the discussions. I was very interested and also very impressed with the baptism and with the members. It was my first time there, but they accepted me as if I had been coming for years.

After the baptism, a missionary approached me. He introduced himself, told me where he was from and why he was here. Elder [Johannes] Grimmer invited me to hear the six discussions. On May 2, I heard the first discussion. Elder [Roger] Muir and Elder Grimmer introduced the Book of Mormon to me and told me many other things.

They frequently asked me how I felt about certain things or how I felt about prayer. I answered them truthfully. I told them that I felt an inner warmth and peace, and they told me that this was the Holy Ghost. With his help, I would be able to find out if what they were telling me was true or not. We read together Moroni 10:3–5. These verses helped me a great deal when I was alone at home. I prayed before I began reading. I asked the Lord to show me if the scriptures were true. I had the most wonderful feeling while I was praying and also while I was reading. I suddenly knew that it had to be true. I knew I would have to be baptized in order to be able to return to my Father in Heaven.

When I was asked if I would like to be baptized, I answered that I was ready to take this step. I knew I would have to totally change my life, but I wanted to do it. I knew full well that I would experience some difficulties, but I also knew that with the help of God, I would be able to overcome my problems. I was certain my Father in Heaven would give me the means and show me the way.

I had never imagined, for example, that I would be able to do without my daily coffee, but I was able to overcome my desires. My parents were a much greater problem than the coffee. They simply could not understand why I would want to be baptized. They found a thousand arguments to keep me from taking this step that was so important for me. But as time went by, they saw that it was of no use, and they agreed with my decision. That was truly an answer to my prayers. I had prayed that my parents would understand me and that we would not be driven apart. Now my parents support me, and this is a clear answer to my fasting and prayers.

As I have mentioned, the Church has totally transformed my life in keeping the commandments, the Word of Wisdom, and the law of chastity. Also I now have entirely different goals. I want to go on a mission and want to be married in the temple. My philosophy of life has changed since I have learned about the plan of salvation.

I know the path I have chosen is the only correct one, and I am thankful to the missionaries from the bottom of my heart that they helped me find this path.

[Annett Kaiser married Kai Berthold, who served a mission in California. They were married in the Freiberg Temple. As of 1995, Annett is a teacher in the Sunday School in the Leipzig Ward.]

Anita Jander, Dresden Ward
Baptized June 11, 1989, Age 41

At the outset, I must say that, before I became acquainted with the Church, I was without faith and was just existing. I am so full of joy and happiness that I have found the way to God, I would like to describe it.

My name is Anita Jander. I am forty-one years old and have three sons, ages nineteen, twelve, and six. I have been divorced for one year.

One Saturday evening, I was out for a little drive with my two sons, something we did frequently. On the way home, I passed by the church, and it seemed to me as if an inner voice was calling out to me that I had to stop the car and go in. I followed the instructions of this voice and went into the building with my two sons. We received a very friendly greeting at the door from Brother [Steffan] Gabber, and he offered to show us the building and explain it to us. I was overwhelmed with the love and friendliness that surrounded us. I had a feeling of happiness in my heart that I had never known before. I wanted to learn more about faith, about the gospel, and about the Mormons. We were all so impressed that we talked and thought about it all the way home and into the evening. We were invited to receive the lessons from Elder [Thorsten] Ludwig and Elder [Jörg] von Allmen, and we gladly accepted the offer.

So my faith grew, and I realized I had chosen the right path. On June 11, I was baptized along with my son Danilo Kenneth. I cannot express in words what I felt on that occasion. I was so happy. My heart was full of joy and humility. It was indescribably beautiful. I am so thankful that I have found the right direction for my life and that I now have a goal in life. At my blessing after the holy baptism, I felt the Holy Ghost so distinctly in my heart that I became a totally new person. My life and that of my family has changed.

I am so thankful that I am no longer alone, that I can turn to God with all of my sorrows and problems and he will help me through them. Before, I was in such despair with my problems, but now I know that if I approach God in prayer he will not deny me his help. This knowledge has made me strong. I simply could not live anymore without my faith, and I am so full of joy that I would like to shout it out to the whole world—to share it with everyone. I have a strong, a firm, testimony.

I have faith that God lives, that the gospel is true. I have faith that the Book of Mormon is true, that God loves all people equally. We are all children of God and can turn to him at any time. God sent his son Jesus Christ to the earth so that all mankind could be saved, so that our sins could be forgiven if we will come to him in prayer. Knowing this gives me such joy. I love to live the commandments that have been given to us, and I hope someday to be worthy to enter the temple. I want to prepare myself for that event.

My desire is also for many more people to realize that this is the true way. I want them to be as happy as I am.

I say all of this as my testimony, and I say it in the name of Jesus Christ, Amen.

[Anita Jander has served as a stake missionary and as a teacher in the Relief Society. As of 1995, she is a teacher in the Sunday School in the Dresden Ward.]

Birga Weber, Freiberg Ward
Baptized June 11, 1989, Age 22

I have been a member of The Church of Jesus Christ of Latter-day Saints since June 11. I would like to tell you how I came to this church.

I was certainly not burdened with a predilection toward any church. In my family there was no one who had the slightest belief in God, to say nothing of a desire to visit a church. So I pushed all thoughts and feelings about God far from me, although in the depths of my heart I always hoped that there might be a God.

Since I am a great lover of American Indian culture (I am a member of an Indian Studies group), I was, of course, present for the performance of the Lamanite Generation in Freiberg. It far exceeded my expectations. After the performance, I got into a conversation with Elder [Mont] Didericksen and Elder [Robbie] Dean. I already knew that the members of the Lamanite Generation were Mormons, but I had only the most superficial knowledge of the gospel. The missionaries asked me if I was interested in the Mormons, and they told me a few things about Jesus Christ, the Book of Mormon, and the gospel. In that moment, I knew immediately: this is it. And I was absolutely certain that I would become a Mormon. Nothing in the world could prevent me, and I felt an irresistible longing for more knowledge. This all took place in a matter of seconds, one thought after another. I gave the two missionaries my address. They promised to visit me and tell me more about the gospel.

For a week, I could hardly wait, but they finally came. I felt such a wonderful feeling in their presence, and it became stronger and stronger. It is hard to describe. They radiated such warmth, goodness, and friendliness. My entire life changed, inwardly as well as outwardly. I have become much calmer, more even tempered, and more satisfied. I now see life from a different perspective.

Within a week, I received the six discussions and was baptized on the following Sunday, just one week after the missionaries first visited me. The baptism was the most beautiful experience of my life. I know I will never regret this step. I have never in all my life felt such genuine friendliness, goodness, and security as I feel here in the one true church of God. This is what I had always been seeking but had never found. I am happy again, and I know that there is someone who loves me and my son (two and one-half years old), someone to whom I can turn and who will help me always if I live according to his commandments and continue to study the gospel.

I know that God lives and that his son Jesus Christ is in charge of this world. They require nothing that is impossible for us. I know they will continually test me because only in this way can I become more like God and return to him when I have found and fulfilled my assignment on this earth.

It was not accidental that the missionaries found me just at this time. God had prepared me, and I am so thankful to him for this and love him with all my heart. This is my testimony in the name of Jesus Christ, Amen.

[As of 1995, Birga Weber is the music leader in the Freiberg Ward.]

Uta Schmidt, Annaberg Ward
Baptized June 25, 1989, Age 29

I have known about the Church for several years because of my sister, who has been a member for fourteen years. She is the wife of the current bishop. They have both attempted numerous times to tell me about the gospel. I did not want to listen, and I refused to accept any religion. I continued to smoke, drink my coffee, and even drink alcohol occasionally.

About two years ago, my life took a dramatic change. In my apartment, I had an accident that injured my spinal column, and since that time, I have been severely crippled. Six months ago, the doctors informed me that within two years I would be confined to a wheelchair, but my health has deteriorated much more rapidly than they anticipated.

From that time, I began to think more seriously about the meaning and purpose of life. I constantly asked, "Why?" My marriage of seven years ended in divorce five years ago. I was plagued by one sickness after another. My son, who is now eight years old, had to learn very early to be self-sufficient. About the end of June, I reached the lowest point in my life. I could simply no longer deal with the fact that I was a cripple. Did God really intend that at age twenty-nine I would no longer be able to walk? I had so many plans, so many things to do, and I still had a child to raise. In any case, I was filled with despair and bitterness! I no longer wanted to live, not even for my child.

Just at this time, the missionaries arrived in our city. I asked my brother-in-law (the bishop) if he could send them by to see me. Some time earlier, he had asked me if I would like to receive the missionaries. I had many questions, which no one had ever been able to answer for me, such as Why are there so many churches? I knew there was a God. But which was the true church? If I had not been filled with such despair, I would probably never have asked my brother-in-law this favor.

The missionaries were there within the hour. Their presence was a comfort to me. I had a very good feeling. They immediately noticed that I needed help. We got into a conversation, and they gave me the first discussion without my realizing it. I was inspired by their presence, their confidence, their manner of presentation, their friendliness, and the love that flowed from them!

Elder [Dale] Moss and Elder [David] Tingey asked me to read 3 Nephi 11. I read this chapter several times, and it moved me so much that I wept each time I read it. I prayed to God to ask him if the things I was reading were true, if this book was true, and if I was doing the right thing. I wept with each prayer. I had such an unusual feeling in my heart, something I had never before experienced.

At the second visit of the missionaries, Elder Moss explained that my tears were an answer to my questions, that I had learned that the Church was true! But still I had many, many questions.

After the second discussion, the missionaries asked me when I would like to be baptized, on June 26? I indeed knew that the Church was true, but I declined to be baptized. My desire for baptism had to come from my own heart. The missionaries were somewhat disappointed at my answer, but nevertheless they continued to visit me and share with me their love.

On the following Sunday, my sister and her husband took me to church with them. I was looking forward to this occasion because on this Sunday there was to be a baptism. I had never seen a baptism, and I was rather anxious to see one. Today I realize that I had within me the desire to be baptized at that time.

It was an unforgettable experience for me. I was so touched by it all. When the new converts were being given the gift of the Holy Ghost, I was overcome once again by an amazing feeling, but this time much stronger than before. I was brought to tears, my heart was pounding, and something within me said, "Now!"

As the converts were being congratulated, I went over to the missionaries and shared with them my decision. They were rather amazed, and my sister stood there with an open mouth. They were all very happy about my decision, but my joy was too great. Not two minutes later I lost my strength completely. For the rest of the day, I was unable to walk, but I was indifferent to that; I had made a decision that would change the course of my entire life.

On the following Sunday (June 25), my son and I were baptized. I am so grateful to my Heavenly Father that he has accepted me and my child. I have finally discovered a meaning and purpose to life! Our Heavenly Father has accepted me, he leads me and guides me. I have faith; I have hope—my support for life.

My physical condition is no longer of such importance to me, even though I must use a wheelchair from time to time. I have a duty; I have a calling, which I am attempting to fulfill as well as I possibly can. I have friends and a feeling of fulfillment. I can share my joy with others. I can tell them that God loves even me, that I am so thankful for the knowledge I have received. I am so thankful I can have a testimony. My faith has helped me so much to keep the Word of Wisdom. I have not had the slightest difficulty giving up smoking, coffee, and alcohol. I knew I was damaging my body with these things, and to this day, I have not had the least desire for them. I also realize that I would never have had the strength to give up my smoking without my faith.

The Church brings fulfillment to my life! I am happy and so thankful that I can be a member of The Church of Jesus Christ of Latter-day Saints. Every Sunday I receive what I need for my life from the Church and from the members. It is such a powerful feeling. I once heard a saying, "Yes, my body is weak, but in exchange my soul has been healed." That is the way I feel, and this saying helps me at times, such as when I must lie down and when I feel such pain. I have lost many "friends" because of the Church, but I have gained many more. I feel strong, and that is very important to me. I have a testimony that God lives, that he hears my prayers, that he helps me when it is necessary.

Our Heavenly Father knows that I am so thankful for his laws and commandments, for his Son Jesus Christ, for his eternal gospel, for the missionaries that have been able to come into our country to bring the gospel to so many people.

I pray for all of those people who are seeking the truth, who are ready to accept the gospel and take upon them the name of Jesus Christ. May they, with God's help, find their way. Amen.

[As of 1995, Uta Schmidt is a teacher in the Relief Society of the Annaberg Ward.]

Katrin Richter, Annaberg Ward
Baptized July 13, 1989, Age 23

I became acquainted with the Church through my present husband, who invited me to attend with him in April 1988. Gradually, I came to understand better the true principles and teachings of the gospel. I had already lived according to the Word of Wisdom before I knew the Church, but everything else was new to me. We were married in July 1988. My husband and I visited the temple grounds in Freiberg and attended the spring conference of the Church, which was held in Dresden. We regularly attended Church services in Annaberg. I read the scriptures and received the discussions from the stake missionaries. I intended to be baptized someday; we just didn't know when we would do it.

On July 1, 1989, I had been at the maternity clinic for about a week as we were expecting a baby at any time. I had had a difficult day. I felt separated from my husband and lonely. Above all, I felt a dark and evil influence. On other the hand, I had received a priesthood blessing. At the same time, I was pondering the talk of a newly baptized sister. I felt I understood for the first time what it was to be so down and then to feel the influence of the Holy Ghost. I wanted to have this spirit with me continually. Because of these feelings, I was, on July 13, driven to leave the clinic—at my own risk.

As I was walking along, I saw the two American missionaries. I had not yet met them, but they were speaking English and were carrying the scriptures. I am normally very shy, but on this day, I spoke to them and asked them if they were missionaries. I told them of my desire to be baptized. I invited them to our home for that evening.

We talked about the Church, about our Heavenly Father, and about baptism. Since we could not find another day, the missionaries suddenly asked me if I wanted to be baptized that day. And so it was that at 9:30 that evening we held an open-air baptismal service. It was an unforgettable experience for me, for my husband, and for the members who had assembled on short notice. I had finally found someone who understood me and had made it possible for me to feel the Holy Ghost fully and completely. The Lord was with me. And so not only was my baptism held without complication, but three days later our daughter Mandy was born without complications.

Because of the Church, I have become an entirely different person. I have grown in faith and confidence in God. The birth was much easier than expected, in spite of its being a breech birth. I have learned so many things. We have become a better family, we understand one another better, and we have more in common. I also have an inner peace and calmness because I have learned to pray again, as I used to do when I was a child. Through the Church, I have learned to enjoy contact with other people. Many members are friendly to me and have become my good friends.

[As of 1995, Katrin Richter is a teacher in the Primary in the Annaberg Ward.]

31

We Hope They Call Us on a Mission

Cornelia Ortlieb and Elke Schulze

Cornelia (Coni) Ortlieb is the daughter of Erich and Marianne Ortlieb (see chapters 19 and 20). She is an accomplished violinist and, had political circumstances permitted, would have studied music. Before her mission to South Carolina, she was working in a hospital. (For more of Elke Schulze's story, see chapter 29.)

Cornelia Ortlieb and Elke Schulze were among the first group of sister missionaries to be called from the former German Democratic Republic (East Germany). While a missionary in Dresden, Sister Davis had offered an English class once a week in the Dresden chapel. One Tuesday during class in the fall of 1989, before there was any thought that sister missionaries would ever be allowed to leave East Germany, Sister Davis gave an examination to her English class. She announced that she would give a special prize to the top two students. Before taking the test, the class asked what the prize would be. Sister Davis jokingly said, "A trip to the United States." The class laughed. Cornelia Ortlieb and Elke Schulze were the two highest and won the prize. In November 1989, the Berlin Wall fell, and the border to the West was opened. In the spring of 1990, Cornelia Ortlieb was called to serve in the South Carolina Columbia mission; Elke Schulze was called to serve in the California San Bernardino mission. This interview was made shortly before they left for the Missionary Training Center in Provo, Utah—their prize for being the top students.

Cornelia: I am twenty-two years old, and I was born in Dresden.

N. Davis: What had you heard about missionary work when you were a child?

Cornelia: Missionary work for me was something that was sort of unreachable. I mean, we had no missionaries here, and it was more like a fairy tale when we had a lesson about some missionary. For me personally, it was simply something I thought about, but somehow I never believed it would be possible.

Preparing for a mission. Norma Davis is teaching English to Cornelia (Coni) Ortlieb and Elke Shulze in the spring of 1990, Dresden. Courtesy Norma and Garold Davis.

Elke: I am twenty-eight years old and was born in Bischofswerda. I have heard about missionary work from my childhood because my father had been on a mission and had always told me about it with great love. He had also told me how my grandparents had supported him with money and in other ways so he could make the best of his missionary time. He talked about the members in the cities where he had served with such love. Then I spent a lot of time at the grave of the first missionary in Dresden, Brother Ott. There was always a feeling of respect and love for missionaries there. But the idea that I would ever have the opportunity to serve seemed pretty unlikely.

Cornelia: In school I talked a lot about the Church, and a few of my friends came with me to activities at the church. I was often approached by friends to tell them about the Church, and I often had to stick up for the things I believed in because, until recently, things were a little more difficult here than they are now. In those days, if you were religious in this country some people would look at you as if you were weird. But that was something of a challenge, and if you met the challenge, especially in your school class, then everyone knew who you were and it was OK.

Elke: We were taught at home to be honest and open everywhere about our membership in the Church. Even as a small child, I let people know at school. Whenever there was any kind of a school program on a Thursday evening (the day we held Primary), we didn't go but went to the churchhouse. On Sundays when there was some kind of school activity, we went to church. So I learned to talk about it everywhere, openly and honestly, and to stick to it. It was not hard.

N. Davis: What were your feelings when the missionaries first entered the country?

Cornelia: It was such a surprise, at least for me. We had heard that missionaries were coming, even to our ward, but we didn't know when they would arrive. There happened to be a wedding celebration on this particular day, and we saw two nicely dressed young men in the meeting. I thought, "Aha! That must be the missionaries." A lot of things have changed in our ward since they arrived, or so it seems to me. I feel an entirely new spirit here. I am more directly involved in missionary work. The missionaries approach you and ask you to invite your friends, to have the courage to bring them to church, and to introduce them to the missionaries. Since they arrived, things have changed drastically for me in relation to missionary work.

Elke: Yes! It has brought us so much real joy. I have also been much more active in missionary work than I was before. The missionaries give you the task of looking for investigators, of engaging them in more serious conversations, of inviting colleagues from work, and of spending your time with the missionaries helping in discussions with investigators.

Cornelia: So often you really feel the Spirit. I can remember when the first missionaries were here, and I could participate in the lessons. That was somehow like attending a wonderful conference. There was always such a spirit present. Even when the missionaries were in our home, our entire family felt it—not that there was ever a bad spirit at home—but somehow we were strengthened again, and we went about things in a different way. We prayed together for someone we wanted to bring into contact with the missionaries, or we fasted together. Somehow, those are experiences that we owe principally to the missionaries.

Elke: It was also the joy one felt when one was together with them and with the other people. I really experienced this joy for the first time when we had the open house in Dresden. Before that I was always afraid to do missionary work in public. But I felt so happy working at the open house. One truly has an unusual feeling of joy in this work.

N. Davis: What were your thoughts when the first missionaries went out from this country?

Cornelia: Well, my brother was among them, so it was felt somehow much more intensely at our house. I have to admit that I cried because no women were allowed to go. I thought to myself, "Oh, I am almost twenty-two. If much time goes by before they let women go, I will be too old, and I will never be able to go on a mission." I was very sad at the time. But I was of course very, very happy for the missionaries.

My brother has changed a great deal because of this mission. Even before, when he learned that he would go on a mission, there was something special about him. It is a great blessing that missionaries are now permitted to go out and that we can have missionaries here. It is like the dawning of a new day for us here in the German Democratic Republic.

And there are so many new members in the branch. It's a completely new time from what it was before. Back then we were one big family, and everyone knew one another. Now it is very different. At first I just had to get used to the new atmosphere in the branch, get used to the fact that there were so many new people there, and that there was somewhat more of a disturbance than in the past because of all the coming and going. But in spite of all that, it is a beautiful time. Now, in any case, I feel much more at ease. During the transition, the members would think, "Oh, no one pays any attention to me anymore; all the attention is centered on the new members." But now we feel more at ease, at least I do.

Elke: At the time when the young missionaries went out, you could check off one promise after another that was being fulfilled according to the blessing of President Monson. And you can see it unfolding further. It is amazing. Our family has prayed repeatedly for the protection and security of the missionaries because it is all so new for them, the things they will learn and the things they will have to learn to cope with. They simply need additional strength because everything is so different.

N. Davis: What kind of church activities do you like best? What was it like before? What did you like to do in the Primary or in the Young Women? What are your pleasant memories?

Elke: My most pleasant memories actually have to do with the weekly activities *[gemeinsamen Themenzeiten]*. All of us got together to put something on, a drama or a fairy tale, just for our own pleasure, or something at Christmas for the children, when we were in the Young Women. Somehow we learned things together as a group, how to make others happy. Like when we went as a group to the retirement homes to visit the older sisters who were there, to sing something for them or read to them or bring them presents. When we did something for others.

Cornelia: Oh, I remember how I loved being with the other children at Primary. That was something special for me because I am actually a person who can get very homesick. When I went on an excursion with my schoolclass, I was homesick after the first day. But when I went on excursions with the Church—that is with the young people or with the children when I was little—I could have stayed away for months. It didn't bother me at all because everything we did drew us together.

I gained so much strength from the youth conferences that for the next two months I thought of nothing but improving myself. I wanted to become better, and I went at my work with a renewed strength. The youth conferences always had that effect on me, that somehow I approached everything with firm resolutions.

The activities where we did things for other people have left beautiful memories, especially at Christmas. It has become a tradition with us that we in the Young Women visit the older members from the branch or that we go to the rest homes and sing or put on a little program. That always gave me the most inner joy.

Elke: I would like to add that it was a beautiful thing when the seminary program was introduced. It didn't affect me directly, but I was there at the time. A bishop from Frankfurt was responsible for getting it started. He directed the seminary at that time, and three years later, he started the institute program for us older members. Now I have finished six years of institute. That was a time for us young people to have a goal of organized study during the week and not just on Sunday. That really helped us.

N. Davis: Do you remember any particular teachers? Or what particular problems did you have as members of the Church?

Elke: There were problems. Especially when it came time to choose a career. My brother wanted to be a teacher, but he was turned down because of his religious beliefs, and a few years ago, I wanted to study medical pedagogy, and I was talked out of it because of my religious beliefs. I was told that I would run into trouble with the Marxist-Leninist philosophy. So I forgot that and applied for something else and was accepted and am still there.

I have a friend who had to work for four or five years as a nurse at a station in the hospital. He wanted to become a doctor, but his application was rejected because he had spent only one and a half years in the army. He was supposed to have stayed three years. He didn't want to stay in that long. It was too hard. So then they made him wait a long time, but he was patient and applied again and again until they finally let him in. That's the way it was in many situations. They tried to put barriers in your way.

Now it seems so normal that we can order the *Stern* [Church magazine in German] and that we can have other Church books. It wasn't always that way. We had the Bible and the Book of Mormon, and maybe, if Grandma could get a permit to travel, she could smuggle in a Church book or a copy of the *Stern*. All of the lesson manuals were smuggled in secretly and then typed off on typewriters by the members so that we could have any kind of teaching material. Things were not so normal as they are now.

Cornelia: A girlfriend of mine always typed an article off for me so that I could have at least something from the *Stern*. We were not supposed to take the *Stern* to church to read something from it. That was not allowed.

Elke: It was not allowed because the *Stern* was forbidden. We were not supposed to have it. That was a very unpleasant affair. And if someone had a teaching manual, we were not allowed to bring it to church either because it had been smuggled in. We could have gotten the Church into difficulties because we were being dishonest by bringing these things in.

But you asked about our teachers and pleasant memories. We were taught with so much love in the Church. I once had two teachers in Sunday School, Sister Ziegler and Sister Schlüter, who took us on an excursion just to reward us for a successful year. They taught us with so much patience and skill.

I had my grandmother for my teacher for a short while. I will never forget that. She had received a gift, a book that had a lot of information about Salt Lake City and about the Salt Lake temple. It had a picture of the baptismal font with the twelve oxen. I could never forget this picture and the way the baptismal font represented the twelve tribes. And when I then later stood in front of a similar baptismal font in the temple in Friedrichsdorf, I was reminded of all these times and the things I had been taught. Those are pleasant memories.

N. Davis: Why do you want to go on a mission now?

Elke: As I mentioned before, I have had this joy in missionary work only since 1988 [at the open house of the Dresden chapel] when I found the courage and strength to stand in front of people and talk about the gospel. I was so happy during the week. I would go to work, and after work I would come to the chapel and work until very late in the evening. I was never physically tired. I was simply filled with joy. Now I want to share this with others because there are so many people who are seeking for this joy and it is such a wonderful work.

Cornelia: With me it is simply that by doing missionary work I will have an opportunity to thank my Father in Heaven. In principle I want to thank him for what he has always done for me by dedicating one and a half years of my life to intensive work for him and for other people. I was not always the best girl. I mean, I have not always done everything just right, and somehow I feel that I want to do something on my own in order to make up for my weaknesses or just show my Father in Heaven that I truly love him and that I really want to participate in his plan.

I want to help more people find the truth so that they can have the true joy that I have discovered and know that there is nothing better. I mean, one can try a different path or try to deviate somehow just a little from the path, but there is no happiness in that. You remember that you were once much happier and that you just have to come back because you don't feel right about yourself. Because I have experienced this myself, I really want to give what I have learned to others so that they can know why they are here. They can truly be happy and feel the love that their Father in Heaven has for them.

Elke: I think we have received so much here on the earth, whether it is joy or not, all the things we have, and for me this is just a little way of saying thank you, by doing this for my Father in Heaven.

Cornelia: It may be that I will never again have the opportunity of doing something with such intensity. I mean, later maybe we will have a family, and then we will have other duties. Now is my chance. I am so happy that it has come to me now and not much later. I mean, I would have been so mad. Of course, even then I would have said, "Sure, OK, that's the way it is," but I am so thankful that it is possible for me to fill this mission now.

N. Davis: Do you think that you will have some personal gain from this mission?

Cornelia: I think that a mission is probably the greatest personal blessing for every missionary that he or she can receive in this life. It is really a school; on a mission you learn everything you need for your future life so that you can then stay on the right path and have sufficient strength to continue on this path and above all, you can have a relationship with God that is much closer and more intimate than before. I mean, now one really struggles, in one's personal prayers, for example, to feel that Father in Heaven hears you or that you really know with all your heart that the gospel is true. But I believe that you can feel the Spirit more intensely on a mission and that you can really get closer to your Father in Heaven. We know our Father in Heaven is always close to us, but we are often a little ways away from him. And I believe that through the work on a mission that if you are really serious and give your all that you will be blessed and you will really be able to feel his presence everyday.

Elke: I also think that you will surely have the strength then order your life according to the commandments of God. You will learn somehow to pay closer attention to the inner voice, I think. Personally, I surely hope to learn during this time something that I have not learned up to now: to become independent, to take care of my own money, to be respectful of others, to fit in with others. I believe we will experience some growth since, from the time we were born, we have always had to live and think inside little guarded borders.

At the Freiberg Germany Temple prior to leaving for the Missionary Training Center. *Left to right:* Elke Schulze, Norma Davis, Cornelia Ortlieb. Freiberg, 1990. Courtesy Norma and Garold Davis.

INDEX

*References to illustrations are printed in **boldface** type.*

Albrecht, Joachim, 131, 150–72
Allen, Wendel G., 104
Allmen, Jörg von, **330,** 338
Annaberg, 84
Anti-Communist uprising, 161–65, 212
Apel, Frank, xiii, 183, 299, **330,** 332
Ballard, Melvin J., 334
Bartsch, Eva-Maria Schlüter, 333
Bautzen, 155–56, 164
Bautzen Branch, 153–56, 165, 170
Benson, Ezra Taft, 14, **41,** 45, 185
Berndt, Dieter, 291
Berndt, Erich, 291
Berthold, Annett Kaiser, 336–37
Berthold, Kai, 337
Bischofswerda Branch, 143, 156–59, 170–71
Bock, Anna Rose, 317
Böhme, Ingrid, 257
Böhme, Walter, 63
Bötscher, Hans M., 181–82
Böttcher, Ilse, 98
Brünning, Ursel Zobel, 312
Burkhardt, Henry, xii, xiii, **53,** 67, 72, 84, 93–95, 125, 128, 131, 134, 136, 145, 147–49, 159, 160, 172, 179, **182,** 200, 203, 211, 228, 235, 284, 290, 294–95, 298, **330,** 333
Burton, Theodore M., 102
Church literature, 131–33, 159–60, 200, 227–28, 236, 295–96, 298, 307–8, 349
Church of Jesus Christ of Latter-day Saints. *See* names of specific branches; Conversion account; Missionary work; Temple; Welfare shipments; Youth activities; Youth conference
Condie, Dorothea Speth, 26, 32–37, **34, 208**
Condie, Spencer J., 32
Conversion account, 30–31, 38, 71, 150, 152, 174–75, 209, 263, 278
Davis, Annika, **332**
Davis, Garold, **330**
Davis, Norma, **330,** 332, 345, 351
Dean, Robbie, **330,** 339
Didericksen, Mont, **330,** 339
Döbeln Branch, 122–23
Dräger, Georg, 80
Dresden
 bombing aftermath in, 5–9, **6, 10,** 19–24, **21, 25, 28,** 35–37

 bombing of, 1–4, 9, 18–19, 32–35, 264, 271, 273, 277
 first conference in, 55, 58–61
 missionaries arrive in, 13
 missionary conference in, 61, 264–65
 Russian occupation of, 12, 21–23, 36–37
Dresden Branch (Ward)
 centennial celebration of, 43, 125
 chapels, 13–14, 55–58, **58, 208,** 245–46
 Freiberg Temple trip, 193, 334
 new members of, 148–49
 open house, 243–44
 plays performed by, 126–28
 welfare supplies arrive in, 14, 37, 41–42, 45
Düennebeil, Dieter, 35
Dzierzon, Erich, 287–91, 296
Dzierzon, Gisela. *See* Heller, Gisela Dzierzon
Ebisch, Lothar, 146
Education, 197–98, 202–3, 212–15, 223–33, 235–36, 261–62, 268–70, 276–77, 320
Emigration, 168–69, 240–41, 249
Fetzer, Percy K., **53,** 75, 93, 255, 306
Franke, Alexander, 98
Freiberg Germany Temple
 brings hard currency, 306–7,
 callings to serve in, 96, 100, 136–37
 dedication of, xiii, 289
 member preparation for, 192–93, 333–34
 missionary work and, 172–73, 290, 313
 open house, 282, 305, 334, **335**
 personal experiences and, 281, 284, 286, 332
 unofficial news of, 43, 135, 147, 333
Fürll, Franziska, 223
Gabber, Steffan, 337
Gäbler, Eberhard, 79–81, **81**
Gebauer, Martha, 311
Genealogy work, **76,** 107, 157
Gera Branch, 110–11
German Democratic Republic. *See* East Germany
Germany, East. *See also* specific cities
 emigration from, 168–69, 240–41, 249
 rededicated for missionary work, xiii, 54, 141
 temple to be built in, 43, 54, 148, 172–73, 243, 335

352

Glaus, Arthur, 85–86, 93
Gorczychowski, Hedwig, 311
Graf, Liesel, 108
Grant, Heber J., 105, 294
Gregory, Herold L., 86, 93, 125, 176
Grimmer, Johannes, 336
Groitzsch chapel, 107
Grosshartmannsdorf, 116, 118–19
Grosshartmannsdorf Branch, 115
Haas, Moroni, 142
Hales, Robert D., **148**
Hauptmann, Gerhart, 127
Heller, Dörte, 301
Heller, Gisela Dzierzon, 287, 293, 297–302
Heller, Manfred, 129, 248, 287–88, **288,** 291–302
Herbert, Werner, 68
Hermann, Erika, 16–31, **17**
Hiller, Elisabeth. *See* Singer, Elisabeth Hiller
Hinckley, Gordon B., 100, 288–89, 290
Hitler, Adolf, 141–42
Höhle, Annelies, 127, **244,** 263–75
Höhle, Ingrid, 257
Höhle, Robert, 127, **265**
Höhle, Ursula. *See* Schlüter, Ursula Höhle
Höhle, Winfried, **244,** 265–67, 271
Honecker, Erich, 290, 299
Jander, Anita, 337–38
Jander, Danilo Kenneth, 338
Jelitto, Erhard, 80
June 17 uprising, 161–65, 212
Kaden, Berndt, 118
Kaden, Elke. *See* Schlüter, Elke Kaden
Kaden, Herbert, 80, 115–40, **117**
Kaden, Ilse, 115–40, **117**
Kaden, Rainer, 118, 120, 123
Kaiser, Annett. *See* Berthold, Annett Kaiser
Kiessling, Karla. *See* Liebscher, Karla Kiessling
Kiessling, Wilfriede, 38–45, **39**
Kimball, Spencer W., xiii, 14, 45, 53–54, 165, 173, 243, 260, 294
Kindt, Walter, ix, 55–62
Kirchert, Alfred, 50
Korth, Ida, 71
Kowitz, Christel, 63
Krakow, Otto, 101–4, **102**
Krause, Edith Schade, ix, 3–15, **14, 53,** 55, 57, **76,** 77, 93
Krause, Harald, 11, 13
Krause, Hella, 11
Krause, Helmut, 9–12
Krause, Lottel Schäfer, 11–12
Krause, Walter, ix, 3, 49–62, **50, 53,** 64, 67, 69, 75, **76,** 77–78, 94, 101, 114, 129, 138, 145, 149, 178, **186,** 235, 253, 296, 306–7
Lamanite Generation, 339

Lehmann, Rudi, 146
Lehnig, Fritz, 143, 178, 270, 278
Lehrig, Joachim, 145
Leipzig
  chapel, 99
  conference in, 85, 205, 295
  missionary conference in, 98–99
  welfare supplies arrive in, 177–78
Leipzig Fair, 85, 165, 185, 200, 295
Liebscher, Karla Kiessling, 40
Loscher, Peter, 93
Ludwig, Thorsten, **330,** 338
Lund, Maja, ix
Maeser, Karl G., xi
McKay, David O., 92, **92**
Meier, Anna, 311
Menzel, Doris, 228, 303–8
Menzel, Peter, 303–8
Meyer, Franz, 71
Missionary work
  in Bautzen, 155–58, 164
  belief in, 344–47, 349–51
  in Eastern Europe, 173
  Freiberg Temple and, 172–73
  in the GDR, xi–xiii, 43, 182, 299, 301–2
  government and, 164, 184, 199, 209, 290–91, **330**
Monson, Thomas S., xiii, **53,** 54, 100, 139, 147, **148,** 193, 290, 299, 329, 333–34, 347
Moskva, Herta, 127–28
Moss, Dale, **330,** 341
Moyle, Henry D., 165
Muir, Roger T., **330,** 336
Neubrandenburg chapel, 102–3
Nikol, Frank, 153, 172
Nikol, Kurt, 153–73
Nikol, Marianne, 153–73
Noack, Neinhold, 80
Oaks, Dallin H., 244
Ortlieb, Agathe, 93
Ortlieb, Cornelia, 177, 344–51, **345, 351**
Ortlieb, Erich, 174–206, **197,** 299, 313, 327, 344
Ortlieb, Luka, 177
Ortlieb, Maja. *See* Schulze, Maja Ortlieb
Ortlieb, Marianne Zwirner, 174–205, **197,** 209, 299, 344
Ortlieb, Olaf, 144, 146, 198–99
Patriarchal blessings, 300–301
Paul, Wolfgang, **194,** 244, 261, **330**
Pawlowski, Elfriede, 67– 70, **72,** 71–78, **76**
Polish army, 142–43
Polzin, Elli, 63–70
Polzin, Hans, 64, **65,** 67, 70, 73
Ranglack, Richard, 49, 79, 98, 101
Reading, Renate, ix

Richter, Katrin, 342–43
Ringger, Hans B., 147, 188, 300, **330**
Ringger, Karl, 300, 306
Ritter, Lothar, 106
Ritter, Renate, 105–9, 107
Ritter, Roland, 106
Ritter, Wolfgang, 106
Robbins, Burtis F., 93, 180
Russian occupation
   of Dresden, 12, 21–23, 36–37
   of Grosshartmannsdorf, 116, 118–19
Schade, Edith. *See* Krause, Edith Schade
Schäfer, Lottel. *See* Krause, Lottel Schäfer
Scharschuh, Martha, 143
Scherzer, Fritz, 80
Schiebold, Johannes, 209
Schiele, Walter, 180
Schlüter, Elke Kaden, 123, **235**
Schlüter, Hans-Jürgen, 243–61, **244**, 333
Schlüter, Reiner, 234–42, **235**, 333
Schlüter, Ursula Höhle, 243–44, **244**, 251, 255–62, 263–75
Schlüter, Wilhelm Heinrich, 248, 261, 293
Schmeichel, Walter, 63, 71
Schmidt, Paul, 110–12, **111**
Schmidt, Uta, 340–42
School. *See* Education
Schreiter, Dorle, 96
Schreiter, Herbert, 96–100, **99**
Schreiter, Irene, 99
Schreiter, Lisbeth, 98–99
Schulze, Berndt, 144
Schulze, Elke, ix, x, 144, 329, 331–35, **332**, 344–51, **345**, **351**
Schulze, Günter, 141–49, **148**, 294, 299–300, **330**, **332**
Schulze, Hannelore, 300, **332**
Schulze, Heidrun, 300
Schulze, Maja Ortlieb, 202, 300
Schulze, Olaf, 144, 146, 254, 300
Schumann, Hans, 98
Schütze, Inga, **48**
Schütze, Manfred, ix, xiii, 47–49, **48**, 54, 63, 96, 99, 101, 105, 110, **194**, **330**
Schwabe, Elke, 309–27, **310**
Schwabe, Manfred, 309–27, **310**
Schwabe, Petra, 317
Schwerin Branch, 63–70, **67**, 73, **126**
Selbongen Branch, 145
Sellner, Erich, 146
Sheffield, Scott, ix
Singer, Elisabeth Hiller, 276
Singer, Käthe. *See* Wöhe, Käthe Singer
Singer, Walter, 276

Skibbe, Gerd, 68
Smith, Joseph, 71, 76, 94, 239
Smith, Lucy Mack, 94
Spafford, Belle, 86
Speth, Dorothea. *See* Condie, Dorothea Speth
Speth, Helga, 257
Stalin, Joseph, 142
Stern, 132, 159–60, 200, 228, 296, 308, 349
Stover, Walter, 43, 79, 252, 256
Swiss Temple, 88–89, 166, 133, 135, 203–4
Tabernacle Choir, 88, 165
Tate, Joel, 93–95, 185, **186**
Television, 322–23
Temple. *See* Freiberg Germany Temple; Swiss Temple
Tingey, David, 341
Tithing, 146, 161, 296
Ulbricht, Walter, 298
Walker, Richard L., 329
Walter, Stover, 14
Warnemünde, supplies arrive in, 249
Weber, Birga, 338–40
Wechsteter, Rudolf, 152
Welfare program, 15, 80, 125, 177, 265, 292
Welfare shipments
   in Bautzen, 156
   in Bischofswerda, 143
   distribution of, 80
   in Döbeln, 123
   in Dresden, 14–15, 37, 41–42, 278
   in Gera, 111
   in Leipzig, 177–78
   in Warnemünde, 249
Winter, Heinz, 248, 250
Wirthlin, Joseph B., 145
Wöhe, Christine, 279
Wöhe, Edith, 279, 284
Wöhe, Heinz, **208**, 258, **277**, 278–81, 283–86
Wöhe, Karl, 141–42, 270
Wöhe, Käthe Singer, 276–86, **277**
Wöhe, Michael, 285
Wolgast Branch, **66**, **114**
Würscher, Käthe, ix, 47, 82, **84**, 84–95
Youth activities, 241–42, 298
Youth conference, 138–39, 188–89, 204–5, 231, 254–55, 318–19
Zobel, Ursel. *See* Brünning, Ursel Zobel
Zwirner, Grit, 223, 226
Zwirner, Karin, 30, 207, 220–33
Zwirner, Marianne. *See* Ortlieb, Marianne Zwirner
Zwirner, Uta, 222–23, 226
Zwirner, Wolfgang, 207–33, **208**, 299